The Dynamics of
Latin American Foreign Policies

Also of Interest

Politics and Public Policy in Latin America, Steven W. Hughes and Kenneth J. Mijeski

Latin American Nations in World Politics, edited by Heraldo Muñoz and Joseph S. Tulchin

Politics and Economics of External Debt Crisis: The Latin American Experience, edited by Miguel S. Wionczek

Mexico's Dilemma: The Political Origins of Economic Crisis, Roberto Newell G. and Luis Rubio F.

Latin America and the U.S. National Interest: A Basis for U.S. Foreign Policy, Margaret Daly Hayes

Latin America, Its Problems and Its Promise: A Multidisciplinary Introduction, edited by Jan Knippers Black

The State and Underdevelopment in Spanish America: The Political Roots of Dependency in Peru and Argentina, Douglas Friedman

Latin American Foreign Policies: Global and Regional Dimensions, edited by Elizabeth G. Ferris and Jennie K. Lincoln

*Available in hardcover and paperback.

Westview Special Studies on Latin America and the Caribbean

The Dynamics of Latin American Foreign Policies:
Challenges for the 1980s
edited by Jennie K. Lincoln
and Elizabeth G. Ferris

A sequel to *Latin American Foreign Policies: Global and Regional Dimensions* (Westview, 1981), this collection of original essays presents a comprehensive view of the principal foreign policy issues of the nations of Latin America and lays the foundation for understanding the challenges facing those nations in the 1980s. The book begins with an introduction to the major themes of conflict and cooperation in Latin American foreign policies, an overview of U.S.-Latin American relations, and an assessment of contemporary research in the field. The authors then analyze the economic challenges, regional conflicts, and security concerns of the nations of South and Central America, with case studies of the foreign policies of Argentina, Brazil, Chile, Peru, Venezuela, Colombia, Mexico, Nicaragua, and Cuba. A concluding section suggests future directions for research on Latin American foreign policies in the 1980s and offers a theoretical framework for the analysis of foreign policy behavior in the region.

Jennie K. Lincoln is an associate professor in the Department of Political Science at Miami University, Ohio. Elizabeth G. Ferris is a professor in the Department of Government at Lafayette College.

The Dynamics of
Latin American Foreign Policies:
Challenges for the 1980s

edited by Jennie K. Lincoln
and Elizabeth G. Ferris

Westview Press / Boulder and London

Westview Special Studies on Latin America and the Caribbean

Copyright © 1984 by Westview Press, Inc.

Published in 1984 in the United States of America by Westview Press, Inc., 5500 Central Avenue, Boulder, Colorado 80301; Frederick A. Praeger, Publisher

Library of Congress Cataloging in Publication Data
Main entry under title:
The Dynamics of Latin American foreign policies.
   (Westview special studies on Latin America and the Caribbean)
   Bibliography: p.
   Includes index.
   1. Latin America--Foreign relations--1948-   --Addresses, essays, lectures.   I. Lincoln, Jennie K.   II. Ferris, Elizabeth G.   III. Series.
F1414.D93   1984   327'.098   84-15213
ISBN 0-86531-782-8
ISBN 0-86531-783-6 (pbk.)

Composition for this book was provided by the editors
Printed and bound in the United States of America

10 9 8 7 6 5 4 3 2 1

To Frank, Ben, and Doug

To Barry, Jon, and Sara

Contents

Tables and Figures

xi

Acknowledgments

We wish to express our appreciation to the many people who assisted us in the preparation of this volume. We are very grateful to our contributors for their diligent efforts and helpful suggestions throughout the process.

We also wish to express our gratitude to several people who helped to put the manuscript together: Linda Giesecki and Michael Curtis for their assistance with the bibliography, the index, and proofreading; Dotti Pierson for typing several drafts; and Elayne Bleill, who typed the final manuscript.

Last, but not least, we thank our families, whose steadfast support was vital to the completion of the book.

Jennie K. Lincoln
Elizabeth G. Ferris

The Contributors

JENNIE K. LINCOLN is a Fulbright Professor in the Escuela de Relationes Exteriores de la Universidad Nacional de Costa Rica (Heredia) where she is also conducting research on regional security issues in Central America. She will return in 1985 to be a Faculty Research Associate with the Mershon Center of Ohio State University. She has conducted field research in Costa Rica, Mexico, and Peru and is the co-editor with Elizabeth G. Ferris of Latin American Foreign Policies: Global and Regional Dimensions (1981).

ELIZABETH G. FERRIS is Assistant Professor of Government and Law at Lafayette College. From 1981-1982 she was a Fulbright Professor at the Universidad Nacional Autonoma de Mexico. She has written on Latin American foreign policy issues and her work has appeared in journals such as International Organization, Latin American Research Review, Journal of Inter-American Studies and World Affairs, and Journal of Developing Areas. She is presently completing a book on Central American refugees.

MAX AZICRI is Professor of Political Science at Edinboro University of Pennsylvania. He has written extensively on the domestic and foreign policies of Cuba and is presently completing a major project on the Cuban socialist legal system. He has also conducted field research in Nicaragua and contributed "A Cuban Perspective on the Nicaraguan Revolution" in Nicaragua in Revolution, edited by Thomas W. Walker (1982).

JACK CHILD is Associate Professor of Spanish and Latin American Studies at the American University, Washington, D.C. He has conducted field research in Colombia and in various institutions of the inter-American military system on U.S.-Latin American security relations, geopolitical thinking, and conflict in Latin America. He is the author of Unequal Alliance: The Inter-American Military System, 1938-1978 (1980).

JUAN M. DEL AGUILA is Assistant Professor of Political Science and Associate Director of the Center for International Studies at Emory University in Atlanta, Georgia. He has conducted field research in Venezuela and Costa Rica and is the author of Cuba: Dilemmas of a Revolution from Westview Press (1984).

YALE FERGUSON is Professor of Political Science at Rutgers University-Newark and is the co-author of The Web of World Politics: Nonstate Actors in the Global System, the co-editor of Continuing Issues in International Politics, and the editor of Contemporary Inter-American Relations. He is also the author of numerous articles and essays on U.S.-Latin American relations and a Contributing Editor of the Handbook of Latin American Studies. Currently, he is beginning a major project on the historical evolution of the international system.

DENNIS R. GORDON is Assistant Professor of Political Science at the University of Santa Clara. His recent publications include "The External Dimension of Civil Insurrection — International Organizations and the Nicaraguan Revolution" and a study of the role of various international organizations in the Falkland/Malvinas war.

WILLIAM HAZLETON is Associate Professor of Political Science at Miami University, Oxford, Ohio. He has written on U.S. human rights policy with regard to Latin America and his research interests include Latin American international relations.

WALTRAUD QUEISER MORALES is Assistant Professor of Political Science at the University of Central Florida in Orlando. She has conducted field research in Bolivia, Nicaragua, Paraguay, and Peru and is contributing author to Violence and Repression in Latin America (1976). Other publications include Social Revolution (1974) and articles in Current History, International Philosophical Quarterly, Journalism Quarterly, Revista/Review Interamericana, Encyclopedia of Political Systems, and Television Coverage of International Affairs. Her research in progress includes a country profile on Bolivia for Westview Press, forthcoming in 1985.

HOWARD T. PITTMAN, a retired Colonel in the U.S. Marine Corps, holds a PhD from American University and is an independent lecturer and researcher on geopolitics in the Southern Cone. His chapter, "Geopolitics and Foreign Policy in Argentina, Brazil, and Chile," in Ferris and Lincoln, eds., Latin American Foreign Policies: Global and Regional Dimensions,was published in Spanish in GEOSUR. He is also the author of "Algunas Tendencias Geopoliticas Especificas en los Paises del ABC, Nuevas Applicaciones de la Ley de las Areas Valiosas," Revista de Ciencia Politicia (Universidad Catolica de Chile), No. 1-2 (1981).

WAYNE SELCHER is Professor of International Studies at Elizabethtown College (Pennsylvania), with research interests in Brazilian politics and foreign policy. In addition to many articles and studies, he has authored The Afro-Asian Dimension of Brazilian Foreign Policy, 1956-1972 (1974) and Brazil's Multilateral Relations: Between First and Third Worlds (1978), as well as edited Brazil in the International System: The Rise of a Middle Power (1981).

PAUL SIGMUND is Professor of Politics and Director of the Latin American Studies Program at Princeton University. His most recent books are The Overthrow of Allende and the Politics of Chile, 1964-1976 and Multinationals in Latin America: The Politics of Nationalization.

The Dynamics of
Latin American Foreign Policies

Part 1

The Dynamics of
Latin American Foreign Policies

1

Introduction to Latin American Foreign Policy: Latin American Governments as Actors in the International System

Elizabeth G. Ferris
and Jennie K. Lincoln

INTRODUCTION

Latin American governments play many roles in the international system. Having been politically and economically tied to the U.S. throughout much of their history, they are struggling to define a new relationship with the U.S. government and to develop more egalitarian institutions within the "inter-American system." As Latin American governments, they have developed a complex set of relationships with one another where traditional rivalries and border conflicts frequently inhibit cooperation in other spheres. As Third World governments they are seeking to develop closer ties and increased solidarity with Third World movements, yet find avenues of cooperation limited by their economic dependence on the U.S. and by their lack of interaction with African and Asian nations. Finally, Latin American governments are seeking expanded relations with other developed nations--both capitalist and socialist--to reduce their reliance on the U.S. and to expand their international capabilities.

In spite of the evolving complexity of Latin American participation in the international system, scholars have generally focused on Latin American nations as the targets of the foreign policies of other nations--principally the U.S. From the perspective of the U.S. government, Latin America's importance has depended on its role in U.S.-USSR competition. But the subject of Latin American governments as actors in the international system--pursuing foreign policies to protect and enhance their own national interests--has received scant attention. This book, like the one which precedes it, seeks to remedy this imbalance by focusing on Latin American foreign policies from the perspective of the Latin American governments themselves. Foreign policy in this context is understood as those actions taken by governments to influence the behavior of other governments. In contrast to the dominant approach of viewing Latin America primarily in terms of its importance to the U.S., the essays in this volume address the determinants and consequences of Latin American foreign policies in regional, hemispheric, and global contexts.

The study of Latin American foreign policies is important for several important reasons. For North Americans concerned with issues of war and peace, understanding Latin American perspectives on world affairs is crucial. The revolutions occurring in Central America and the political changes taking place in the Southern Cone affect the security and the well-being of the region and of the U.S. As the part of the Third World with the strongest economic and political ties with the U.S. government, Latin America plays a

3

central role in Third World negotiations concerning foreign debts and demands for a restructuring of the global economic system. The pressures faced by Latin American governments are similar to those encountered in other parts of the Third World. But the Latin American response to those pressures is conditioned by its historic dependence on the U.S., by its social and cultural heritage, and by its political systems. Latin American foreign policies in the 1980s are not created in a vacuum but rather are formulated within a political and economic context which structures national responses to contemporary issues. This chapter seeks to provide an overview of that context, to survey the principal theoretical approaches used in understanding Latin American foreign policies, and to assess contemporary challenges to Latin American policy makers.

THE CONTEXT OF LATIN AMERICAN FOREIGN POLICIES

Contemporary Latin American international relations are shaped by the region's historical experiences--experiences which date back hundreds of years. Political instability and economic underdevelopment coupled with the overwhelming dominance of the U.S. limited the region's ability to formulate independent policies. Instead, Latin American governments devoted their energies to intra-regional wars and to defining a political relationship with the United States. By World War II, national borders had become stabilized (with a few festering exceptions) and the region appeared ready to work with the U.S. in the creation of an inter-American system. Pressures to contain U.S. intervention through regional organizations and legal instruments coupled with the strong legalistic tradition of Latin American diplomats led to a series of hemispheric organizations. Disillusionment with the inter-American system in the 1970s along with changes in the international environment contributed to nationalistic policies with respect to the U.S., efforts to increase intra-regional unity, and intensified commitment to Third World solidarity. But the roots of Latin American foreign policies in the 1970s and 1980s are to be found in the political events of the last century.

Ever since independence, Latin American governments have vacillated between fighting with their neighbors over territory and seeking expanded cooperation with them through regional organizations. The Congress of Panama was formed in 1826, at the initiative of Simón Bolivar, to form a treaty of union creating a defensive alliance against foreign aggressors. Although the treaty was never ratified, it served as a symbol of unity for the next century. Throughout the nineteenth century, representatives of Latin American governments met to discuss ways to defend their sovereignty and territorial integrity against foreign incursions. These efforts responded to U.S. military interventionism and foreign economic penetration at a time when Latin American governments were weak. Other regional conferences sought to formulate common legal principals and to draw up international treaties.

It was not until 1889, however, that the Pan American movement achieved continental participation. At that time, the first international conference of American states was held in Washington, D.C., at the initiative of the U.S. This conference created the Pan American Union in 1890 (initially designated as the International Union of American Republics), which studied issues of common concern, including uniformity of sanitary regulations and documents, transportation, and freedom of navigation of rivers. For the next fifty years, representatives of Latin American nations met with U.S. officials in international conferences with the effect of moving toward mutual codification of international law as well as developing defense alliances.

Although Latin American governments had been meeting for years, it was the U.S. initiative in 1889 that led to the creation of an inter-American organization and the U.S. has dominated inter-American organizations ever since. This dominance has its roots in U.S. political and military intervention in Latin American affairs based on a tradition of U.S. superiority and expansionism (à la Manifest Destiny), economic needs of an expanding U.S. industrial base, and weaknesses in Latin American governments themselves. Latin American governments often perceived that they could benefit more from their relations with the U.S. than from their ties with each other. U.S. dominance of the region was resented by Latin American governments who sought means of limiting military intervention by the U.S. and European governments. In 1868, the Calvo doctrine stated that intervention by a foreign government to resolve problems of its citizens (or corporations) was unjust, illegal, and violated the sovereignty of Latin American countries. The Drago doctrine of 1902 maintained that it was illegal for foreign governments to intervene militarily to try to collect public debts. Those Latin American nations most directly threatened by U.S. interventionism were particularly concerned with developing international legal instruments and formulating national foreign policies to combat such a threat. Mexico, for example, suffered most at the hands of the U.S. government, losing half of its national territory in the Treaty of Guadalupe Hidalgo in 1848. In response, Mexico sought and continues to seek legal restraints on U.S. action by supporting international organizations and by a virtual unswerving commitment to nonintervention in its own foreign policies (Ojeda, 1974, 1976, 1980; Poitras, 1981; Pelicer, 1972a, 1972b, 1974, 1980).

During the nineteenth century, when U.S. dominance of the region was being constructed and while Latin American foreign policies were concerned with the creation of an inter-American system, Latin America's intraregional relations were characterized by constant conflicts. Bolivar's dream of continental unity was shattered in the first half of the nineteenth century as the fledgling Latin American republics carved out national boundaries based on colonial administrative and religious jurisdictions. Central American nations broke away from Mexico and then dissolved their own union. Border conflicts between Brazil and its neighbors usually ended with Brazil acquiring increased territory. The War of the Pacific, in 1889, culminated in a humiliating defeat for Bolivia and Peru at the hands of Chile. The disastrous Chaco War, the Peruvian seizure of one-third of Ecuador's national territory, and dozens of minor border conflicts erupted in this century. The U.S. was able to achieve its hemispheric dominance in part because of fragmented and conflictual intra-regional relations. While the U.S. government maintained a commitment to hemispheric unity, many observers have noted that the U.S. was the prime beneficiary of Latin American disarray. In fact, many Latin American scholars directly attribute Latin America's disunity to U.S. actions (Stavenhagen, 1974; Bodenheimer, 1971). The U.S. wanted (and wants) to keep Latin America disunited and weak, the argument goes, because by doing so, the U.S. is able to maintain its hegemony in the hemisphere. Regardless of one's ideological convictions, it seems clear that the relationship between regional and hemispheric relations is a reciprocal one: the U.S. was able to dominate the region because of its disunity while, at the same time, Latin American governments' concern for healthy relations with the U.S. inhibited moves toward Latin American unity.

The nature of the inter-American system which developed between 1928 and the present was shaped by U.S. foreign policy needs. As Atkins (1977) notes, the development of the inter-American system may be analyzed in three stages. Before 1928, the U.S. was not interested in mutual security arrangements within the hemisphere, preferring to arrange its security unilaterally. Latin American governments, however, desperately wanted assurances that the U.S. would not intervene in their internal affairs. In the second stage between 1928 and 1945, Latin America and the U.S. had mutual goals for the inter-American system and were able to work together in relative harmony. For example between 1930 and 1936 the U.S. accepted the principle of noninterventionism. This change may have reflected the fact that the U.S. government needed Latin American support in light of the developing European war. Latin America supported the allied war effort and U.S. intervention in the region seemed to decline as evidenced by the fact that the U.S. government did not send troops when Mexico nationalized the oil industry. The third phase, according to Atkins, in effect since the end of World War II, has been characterized once again by diverging goals. In the postwar era, particularly with the development of the Cold War, the United States sought allies in its foreign policy goals and looked to the inter-American system to provide such support. Latin American governments, on the other hand, sought to use inter-American institutions to control U.S. interventionism and to foster their own economic development. The system which developed was the result of compromise between those conflicting priorities. In 1947, the Inter-American Treaty of Reciprocal Assistance (TIAR or the Rio Treaty) was signed. Described as the "first military treaty of the Cold War" (Ojeda, 1974b:514), the Rio Treaty secured hemispheric cooperation in the interests of the United States. In addition, Lowenthal writes that a network of inter-American military schools, training programs, and defense councils were developed which "provided a means to ensure continuing U.S. influence in that sphere through devices ranging from standardized weapons and procedures to personal influence" (1976:204). Although the Rio Treaty has been applied in sixteen cases, all were in response to reported aggressions in this hemisphere. Instead of being used to ward off expansionist powers from outside the hemisphere, the Rio Treaty has been used by nations seeking regional support in their border disputes (Child, 1980).

Meeting in Bogota in May 1948, the Ninth International Conference of American states drew up the charter of the Organization of American States, which created the region's principal mechanism for economic and political cooperation. The OAS provided for the peaceful settlement of disputes and was based on an absolute commitment to the doctrine of nonintervention--a commitment which the U.S. government regularly flouted. Tension over different priorities surfaced in the 1950s. In 1954, the Tenth Inter-American Conference meeting in Caracas debated the issue of the organization's response to communism in the region--and particularly to the Arbenz government then in power in Guatemala. After long debate, the so-called Caracas resolution was passed, which condemned international communism as incompatible with inter-American principles. The vote on the resolution was 17-1 with Guatemala opposing, and Mexico and Argentina abstaining. This resolution was used by the U.S. government to justify the overthrow of the Arbenz government by U.S.-supported forces in 1954. Clearly in this case--as in many others--Latin American concerns were overshadowed by U.S. foreign policy interest and the OAS provided a degree of legitimacy to U.S. intervention. Latin American interest in social and economic development of the region finally led to U.S. support for international financial institutions to aid in this endeavor. In 1959, the Inter-American Development Bank was established to provide financial assistance to Latin American nations to pursue developmental priorities.

Changes in the international system in the early 1960s--particularly the rise to power of Fidel Castro in Cuba and the subsequent Cuban missile crisis--led to changes in the inter-American system. From the U.S. perspective, the concept of hemispheric defense shifted from external to internal security in which "the main effort was devoted to countering internal subversion through a program of military aid and military technical assistance in counter-insurgency techniques" (Ojeda, 1974b:516). The counter-insurgency doctrine which evolved was another development in U.S. hegemony over Latin American nations which furthered penetration of U.S. interests into the national affairs of those nations. Overt military intervention occurred in Cuba (Bay of Pigs) where U.S.-trained Cubans unsuccessfully tried to overthrow the Castro regime and in the Dominican Republic in 1965 where U.S. Marines intervened to forestall a possible communist takeover. Once again, in the case of the Dominican Republic, the OAS was used to legitimate U.S. military action. The OAS gave its seal of approval to the occupying forces under the aegis of protecting the region from foreign penetration. Regional efforts to prevent the spread of communism were of interest to Latin American governments for several reasons. By supporting what was clearly a U.S. priority in the hemisphere, Latin American governments could win favor in Washington. In fact, Latin American governments learned that an appeal for U.S. assistance to combat the forces of international communism was much more effective than appeals for economic assistance. Furthermore, many of the Latin American governments were genuinely fearful of a Cuban-style revolution in their own countries. Fidel Castro's dissolution of the Cuban military struck fear in the hearts of Latin American generals everywhere.

As the Cold War intensified throughout the decades of the 1950s and 1960s, the U.S. expanded its military assistance to Latin America. Concurrent with the increase in military assistance from the United States to Latin America under the Kennedy administration was the development in the early 1960s of an extensive social and economic aid program, the Alliance for Progress. U.S. governmental interest in the region was paralleled by an increase in multinational corporate penetration in Latin America. As Cotler and Fagen discuss (1974:10-11), there is little consensus among scholars about whether the Alliance for Progress was intended for the economic development of Latin America, the economic subjugation of Latin America, or some combination of the two. The timing of the extensive aid program, however, clearly coincided with U.S. efforts to rally political support against Cuban influence in the area. U.S. interest in securing the loyalty of the region through economic assistance is further exemplified by the quintupling of the OAS budget after 1961 and by a similar expansion of the programs of the Inter-American Development Bank (Lowenthal, 1976:205).

But as the U.S. presence in the region intensified, Latin American reactions to U.S. influence increased. By the late 1960s, national movements and governments throughout the region came to power. Growing awareness of the activities of the multinational corporations led to nationalization of U.S. companies in Peru, Bolivia, Chile, and Venezuela. Nationalism in Latin America has a long history. Every Latin American country has both its heroes who resisted Yankee domination and its intellectuals who criticized the hegemonic power of the U.S. government. It is important that North

Americans understand that the works of José Martí, Mariateguí, and Emiliano
Zapata and the actions of Sandino, Castro, and Túpac Ámaru (to cite but a
few examples) provided an important Latin American heritage of independence. While nationalism has existed as part of Latin American culture for
generations, during the past twenty years, this nationalism has increasingly
been expressed in governmental policies. Latin American góvernments have
moved to assert greater control over their own economic development and
over the foreign companies active in their lands. In doing so, they have
aroused the concern and frequently the active opposition of the U.S. government. But the influence of nationalism in Latin American foreign policy has
had other consequences as well.

At the same time that U.S. interests were penetrating the domestic
political activities of Latin American nations, many Latin American governments turned toward economic integration or an alternative, developmental
nationalism, as vehicles to accelerate their economic development. Given that
(1) the United States appeared to have had greater interest in mutual defense
of the region than in its economic development; and (2) that economic growth
in Latin America had slowed from the post-World War II era causing foreign
trade difficulties (Teubal, 1968:124), Wionczek notes that some Latin American
nations found proposals for regional cooperation "attractive" (1972:509).

The concept of regional economic integration in Latin America was
proposed by the United Nations Economic Commission for Latin America
(ECLA) based on a Western European model of free trade. ECLA proposed
that regional economic cooperation would "stimulate the Latin American
framework of an expanded and protracted regional market" (Wionczek, 1972:
509). A series of integration measures including liberalization of intra-
regional trade, an adoption of a common tariff for members of a regional
trade organization, and the coordination of investment policies theoretically
would make the regionalization of import substitution policies more viable"
(Teubal, 1968:128). Two vehicles for regional cooperation eventually evolved
from the ECLA proposals: (1) The Latin American Free Trade Association
(LAFTA) created in February 1960 by the Treaty of Montevideo signed by
Argentina, Brazil, Chile, Paraguay, Peru, and Uruguay (later joined by Colombia, Ecuador, Venezuela, and Bolivia by 1968); and (2) the Central American
Common Market (CACM) established by the Treaty of Managua in December
1969 by Costa Rica, El Salvador, Guatemala, Honduras, and Nicaragua
(Cochrane and Sloan, 1973; Milenky, 1973). These efforts at regional economic
integration are important in that they signified Latin American efforts to deal
with economic problems through purely regional organizations. The U.S. was
not included in these organizations although it sought to use them for its own
benefit. Ianni (1974:29-31) suggests that the penetration of Latin America by
multinational corporations was facilitated by inter-American organizations
such as LAFTA and the CACM which promoted policies favorable to U.S.
corporations.

In spite of their importance as symbols of regional resolve, the integration schemes were ultimately unable to overcome the pressures resulting from
the region's economic dependence on the U.S. Historic patterns in which each
Latin American country perceived that it had more to gain from dealing
bilaterally with the U.S. than with directing its energies to purely Latin
American efforts made regional cooperation difficult. There have been many
attempts to explain the reasons for integration's lack of success in Latin
America. The disparate size and levels of economic development of the
various Latin American nations were significant obstacles to economic

integration. As Agor and Suarez explained (1972:22):

> ... the largest and most developed countries--Argentina, Brazil, and Mexico--appear to have benefitted disproportionately from intrazonal trade, and they have been reluctant to grant concessions to countries classified as with "insufficient markets" (Chile, Colombia, Peru, Uruguay, and Venezuela) or "least developed" (Bolivia, Ecuador, Paraguay).

Changes in governments of the member countries and in the economic development choices those regimes favored made regional cooperation more difficult. As Milenky (1977:75) notes, both LAFTA and the CACM were unsuccessful in promoting economic integration primarily due to shifting ideologies toward development through central or state planning "rather than reliance on private enterprise or a more open economic setting, and complete structures of industry over a share in a regional market." Traditional rivalries and hostilities between members prevented integration efforts from realizing their full potential. Certainly the outbreak of war between El Salvador and Honduras illustrated the lack of the existence of even minimum levels of trust and shared values which are the basic conditions posited by integration theorists as requisites for the success of economic integration (Deutsch, 1957; Haas, 1975).

As a result of Latin America's discouraging experiences with integration as a means of accelerating the economic development of its members, Latin American governments increasingly turned to an emphasis on developmental nationalism. As explained by Milenky (1971:75), this strategy is based on sharing (but not "pooling") natural resources and on industrializing individual national economies through "balanced and controlled interdependence" (Milenky, 1971:78). While "nationalism" and "integration" may be competing concepts, Drier (1968:490) suggests:

> ... nationalism actually contributes, however illogically, to the movement for regional integration. For although it is true that nationalism often erects barriers to regional economic agreements, it is also true that nationalist enthusiasm for economic development leads to the positive support of integration as an essential goal.

In addition to efforts to use regional organizations as a tool of economic development, Latin American nations have also, on occasion, used regional groupings as a way of increasing their negotiating power on the international scene. In 1969, CECLA (The Special Commission for Latin American Coordination) met to formulate a list of specific demands for dealing with the U.S. on economic issues. Two years later, CECLA again met, this time to condemn the Nixon administration's decision to impose a 10 percent surcharge on all imported goods. But CECLA, like other ad hoc groups which emerged to deal with specific issues, was unable to transform itself into a permanent mechanism for addressing Latin American concerns in international forums.

By the mid-1970s, changes in the international system had created a different set of foreign policy pressures on Latin American governments. In seeking to decrease their economic dependence on the U.S., Latin America looked outside the hemisphere for alternative economic and political relationships. As the nations of Latin America extended diplomatic and economic interactions within and beyond the region, the result was not only a "diversification of dependence" (Cochrane, 1978:457), which lessened the dependence on a single nation (the U.S.), but also a symbolic declaration of independence. The underlying principle in Latin America foreign policies which has evolved is a quest for independent recognition in the international system. Atkins notes that the pursuit of this independent status is not only difficult but paradoxical in that achievement of independent status requires an increase in strength in relation to the outside world.

> ... [T]o become strong they must obtain some sort of assistance from the outside world toward which they wish to be independent, thus increasing the chances for a dependent relationship. Latin America's continuing dilemma, then, is this: how are nations to improve their capability position and modernize their societies while preventing inordinate influence in their economies and political systems? (Atkins, 1977:49).

Changes in the international system coupled with changes in the domestic policies of many Latin American nations led to the emergence of foreign policy strategies of regional and global interdependence. A decline in the bipolarity of the international system and the evolution of a multipolar system with an increase in the weight of the Third World as a political actor increased the significance of Latin America in the international configuration. Efforts by Latin America to work with other Third World governments in pursuit of common goals intensified throughout the 1970s. Latin America's long tradition of concern for international norms and treaties has been useful in Third World efforts to formulate new international structures such as the UN's Special Session on a New International Economic Order and the Law of the Sea. Latin American diplomats found that they had much in common with their Asian and African counterparts. Not only could Third World cooperation increase Latin America's bargaining power in the international arena but it could also strengthen the position of governments at home. Declarations of Third World solidarity went hand in hand with nationalist and anti-Yankee slogans throughout the Third World. However, the movement for Third World solidarity has been hard-pressed to deliver concrete political and economic achievements to Latin American governments. Policies which move beyond symbolic support toward increased trade and technical cooperation and the creation of commodity cartels have been difficult to implement. While Latin American governments--like those of other Third World nations--want to increase their exports to other Third World countries, they still seek imports from the U.S. and other developed countries.

Moreover, there are fundamental splits within the Third World. Differences between OPEC members (Ecuador and Venezuela) and non-OPEC members divide Latin American governments within the Third World just as they separate Third World governments in general. A more fundamental Third World division for Latin American governments is the emergence of the so-called NIC's (Newly Industrialized Countries)--those Third World governments with significant manufacturing capabilities who have the potential to exercise economic power on a global level. Governments of countries such as Argentina, Brazil, Mexico, Venezuela, and Chile are not committed to a fundamental restructuring of the international system (though they may well extend symbolic support for such efforts) but rather to increasing their share of the rewards within the present international system. These nations have a vested interest in maintaining the present system albeit with a more equitable distribution of resources within that system. The fact is that not only are their economies growing as a result of their participation in the current system, but their political systems have developed in support of such economic goals. Thus, at the meeting of Latin American governments to discuss joint strategies for dealing with foreign debt in Quito in 1983, Brazil and Mexico effectively prevented radical alternatives from being approved. Latin American participation in the Third World movement is frequently characterized by a fundamental split between the rapidly industrializing nations and the rest. In general terms, however, Latin American nations are much wealthier--even leaving aside the NICs--than the bulk of Third World countries. While Latin Americans played leadership roles in the early years of the Third World movement sheer growth in the number of Third World states has diluted Latin American influence within the global movement. But in spite of the very real difficulties in Latin American participation in Third World organizations, identification with other Third World governments is very important to most Latin American nations.

In the 1970s, U.S. political involvement in Latin America seemed to lessen with the decline in the perceived threat of the Castro regime and the exposure of the CIA involvement in the overthrow of Chilean President Salvador Allende in 1973. Events in other parts of the world--particularly the rise of OPEC and continued crises in the Middle East--signaled a decline in U.S. interest in Latin American issues. In the wake of the military and civilian reform governments which had emerged from the political and social movements in Latin America during the late 1960s and early 1970s, the nationalist leaders (both civilian and military) rejected the hegemonic presumption of the United States in the region. The intensification of nationalistic ideologies and an increase in the capabilities of many Latin American governments brought about foreign policies which imposed tight restrictions and controls on foreign investment; increased multilateral diplomacy in the region; and increased diplomatic and economic relations beyond the hemisphere.

In an effort to pursue the quest for independent recognition in the international system and to counter past U.S. influence in the region, Latin American foreign policy strategies turned to increased interaction on both regional and global levels. However, with the arrival of the Reagan administration, the corresponding revival of the Cold War mentality, and increased difficulties for Third World unity, Latin American governments are once again being challenged to develop policies which will exert national and regional independence. The challenges currently facing Latin American governments include: (1) defining their relationship with the U.S. in light of the Falklands/Malvinas war and the U.S. invasion of Grenada; (2) responding to current economic crises, particularly the limitations imposed by foreign debts; and (3) responding to the Central American revolutions. The ways in which Latin American governments respond to these challenges are shaped by a long tradition of U.S. dominance, efforts to develop meaningful regional cooperation schemes, and by support for Third World unity. Just as the Latin American governments are challenged by contemporary political developments, so too the dominant paradigms for studying Latin American foreign policies are being called into question. We turn now to an examination of the principal theoretical approaches useful for understanding Latin American foreign policy behavior.

LATIN AMERICAN FOREIGN POLICIES: THE SEARCH FOR
EXPLANATIONS

Reflecting the political and economic dominance of the U.S. in the
region, most theoretical approaches used in studying Latin American international relations were developed for analyzing U.S.-Latin American relations. However, as might be expected, there are significant differences in
the approaches taken by U.S. and Latin American scholars studying those
relations. Initially North American academic approaches to the subject
paralleled the development of U.S. policies toward Latin America. In the
years immediately following World War II, the creation of inter-American
institutions was paralleled by U.S. scholars' emphases on the development of
Latin American political institutions and on U.S.-Latin American relations.
During the 1960s, when democratic reform and economic progress were
heralded by the Alliance for Progress, scholars provided the theoretical
foundation for such U.S. aid programs by hypothesizing a causal relationship
between economic growth and the emergence of democratic political institutions. By the end of the 1960s, however, when leftist movements had surged
forward and nationalists had become an accepted reality, Latin American
formulation of dependency theories focused attention on the U.S. from a
different perspective (e.g. Frank, 1977; Cardoso, 1973, 1977; O'Donnell,
1973; Cardoso and Faletto, 1969). Changes in the nature of U.S.-Latin
American relations along with the growing dominance of dependency theories
had made the traditional approaches obsolete. Latin American policies which
evolved prescribed a new set of nationalistic foreign and domestic policies as
a means for changing the unacceptable Latin American dependence on the
United States. As Latin American governments sought to overcome economic
and political dependence on the U.S., analysts of Latin American foreign
policies began to realize that there were more aspects to Latin American
foreign policies than just U.S.-Latin American relations. The initiatives taken
by Latin American governments to form integration schemes were accompanied by a host of studies applying integration theories (largely developed in
an European context) to Latin America. These theories sought not only to
explain what was happening with Latin American regional behavior, but also
to guide the process by serving as a rationale for specific policy initiatives.
The problems experienced by regional integration schemes in the late 1960s
and early 1970s reflected the failure of the theories buttressing the system as
well as the policies themselves (Haas, 1975; Schmitter, 1972, 1974; Nye, 1968;
and Pentland, 1973). The developmental approaches and the tendency to study
specific Latin American cases through analysis of unique country-specific
variables gave way to the widespread application of dependency theories.
Latin American dependency theories had their roots in the region's
nationalist tradition, in the doctrines formulated by ECLA in the 1950s and
1960s, and in Marxist approaches to the international system. The emergence of dependency theories for studying Latin American development roughly
coincided with the rise of general systems theories in the U.S. In applying
systems theories to international politics, only a few authors specifically
addressed the situation of Latin American nations (e.g., Lagos, 1963) although
in recent years there has been more attention given to systemic approaches to
Latin American international relations (e.g., Jaguaribe, 1973, 1979; Drekonja,
1981; Tomassini, 1975). Both dependency and systems theories underscore the
structural determinants of politics.
Dependency theories were formulated to explain the lack of economic

development in Latin America--not Latin American foreign policy. But their emphasis on economic factors and on the structural underpinning of policies directed scholarly attention away from specific contemporary political events and toward more historical, structural dimensions of international relations. The dependency theories emphasized the constraining role of the international system in policy formation and made it impossible for subsequent analysts to ignore the region's asymmetrical economic relationship with the U.S. Dependency theories have called into question the traditional concepts of national sovereignty and national interests as tools for understanding foreign policy behavior of dependent states. Furthermore, dependency theories have served as a guide for policy makers in their assessment of structural reform as essential for expanding Latin American policy choices (Muñoz, 1981). Strategies for overcoming the region's dependency--including both national and collective self-reliance--have been addressed as a consequence of dependency theorists' concerns.

But dependency theories are unable to explain all variations in foreign policy behavior. As Van Klaveren points out (1982:16), "These [Latin American] societies continue to be characterized by a general situation of structural dependency, but the new realities of the international system and, also, the relative autonomy of the state and its bureaucracy vis-à-vis the dominant classes, allow, nevertheless, for considerable independence in the field of foreign policy." In fact, as Van Klaveren also points out, some of the Latin American nations which are economically the most dependent on the U.S.-- such as Mexico--have displayed remarkable independence in their foreign policies. Nevertheless, studying the ways in which a nation's economic dependence has structured its foreign policy choices is a promising area of inquiry. By looking beyond the words and actions of current foreign policy makers, dependency theorists are able to underscore the vital importance of historical and economic determinants of policy.

The efforts by North American scholars to apply dependency theory in studying Latin American foreign policies have had mixed results. Latin American critiques of U.S. efforts to quantify dependency reflect the conviction that North Americans are "missing the point" by quantifying and de-historicizing a condition which is historical and qualitative in nature. Although U.S. scholars continue cross-national empirical studies of the relationship between foreign policy behavior and economic dependency, a more promising approach has been the in-depth single nation study, such as those by Evans (1979), Hewlett (1980), and Gereffi (1983) in which foreign policy is analyzed in the broader context of other policies.

In the U.S., the study of Latin American foreign policy has been approached from various perspectives, determined in part by developments within the field as a whole. The study of Latin American foreign policy from a comparative perspective has traditionally been more firmly rooted in the area-specific concerns of comparative politics than in the discipline of international relations. While international relations scholars seek to explain action of Latin American nations in relation to global configurations of power or to discern behavioral uniformities in the interactions of nation-states, Latinamericanists focus on unique national behavior and on the region's specific attributes and traditions. If anything, the gap between international relations specialists and Latinamericanists has been growing larger. A major dilemma confronting those seeking to understand Latin American foreign policies has been whether to adopt a theoretical focus emphasizing the unique characteristics of Latin American nations or one which places Latin American international concerns in a broader theoretical context. Most of the selections in this volume have adopted the former approach; however, the broader issue is addressed once again in the final chapter of this collection.

Problems in the study of Latin American foreign policy also parallel problems in the discipline of political science as a whole. In general, the problems and traumas of self-examination that characterized the field of political science (and later international relations) in the period following the 1960s behavioral revolution have just arrived on the Latin American political scene. The bitter debate between Latin American proponents of dependency theories and U.S. international relations specialists seeking to quantify and to determine causal relationships between dependency and behavior are reminiscent of those 1960s debates which generally questioned the validity of empirical analysis of political phenomena. The question of methodological approaches is, of course, not just a question of methodology but of theoretical orientation as well.

The literature of Latin American foreign policies is further characterized by unequal coverage by nation and by region. United States scholars have tended to study the international and domestic policies of Latin America as a region in those times when the region has been of particular concern to U.S. governmental and economic interests. Furthermore, U.S. scholars have tended to study primarily those countries of particular importance to U.S. foreign policy makers. Specifically, the pre-1970 literature on Latin American foreign policy concentrated heavily on those nations which had significant trade patterns with the U.S. (Mexico, Brazil, and Argentina); military penetration by the U.S. (Guatemala, Cuba, and the Dominican Republic); or significant U.S. multinational corporation presence (Chile, Peru, Bolivia, and Venezuela). With the exception of Cuba and the Dominican Republic there was a marked absence of foreign policy analysis of the Caribbean as well as most of Central America in the pre-1970 literature. The position of the United States was so predominant that the concept of "Latin American foreign policy" usually referred to U.S. foreign policy toward Latin America rather than to foreign policies of Latin American nations individually or collectively toward any other nation.

As we noted in our earlier work, studies of Latin American foreign policies for the most part have been based on case studies of the foreign policy behavior of individual nations. Any cross-national attempts usually have been based on grouping countries in terms of a specific national attribute such as location (the Andean nations, the Plata Basin nations, Central American nations, or Caribbean nations); or size (large nations such as Brazil, Argentina, Mexico as well as the small nations such as the Central American republics and the Caribbean nations). These studies have included the following components: (1) analyses of external and internal determinants of foreign policy behavior; (2) analyses of the decision-making structures and processes involved in foreign policy behavior; (3) analyses of the substantive contents of individual foreign policies; and (4) analyses of the subsequent consequences of foreign policy behavior.

In order to analyze the determinants, processes, and consequences of foreign policy behavior, most Latin American foreign policy studies have included historical descriptions of specific policy decisions and actions taken by the government. These foreign policy decisions have been explained in terms of governmental actions in response to one or more external or internal determinants of foreign policy behavior. The external variables most frequently explored in the Latin American foreign policy literature include:

(1) changes in the international system which affect a nation's foreign relations; and (2) penetration by an external actor in a nation's domestic politics. Internal variables most frequently explored include: (1) national attributes--such as capabilities, size, or level of economic development; (2) regime orientation--political ideology and goals of the government; (3) social forces within a nation; and (4) specific national experiences--such as catastrophies or extraconstitutional changes in government.

In analyzing external and internal determinants of foreign policy behavior it is often difficult to separate the overlap between the two sets of variables. It is indeed the overlap, or the "linkage" (Rosenau, 1969) between these variables, that provides the most powerful explanation of determinants of foreign policy behavior in Latin America. Linkages between domestic and foreign policies allow foreign policies to be instruments through which policy makers may accomplish their principal domestic goals: national development and national security.

Scholars analyzing the foreign policy in Latin America have looked more often at the particular historical and contemporary pressures on national governments. The nature of government's preferred developmental model and the mobilization of domestic political forces are the principal factors used in explaining foreign policy decisions (e.g., Muñoz, 1981; Wilhelmy, 1979; Ojeda, 1976; Schneider, 1976; Milenky, 1978; Wilson, 1975; Paz and Perrari, 1966). Decision-making approaches which focus on governmental actors and roles and bureaucratic politics perspectives which expose bureaucratic in-fighting have been used to examine the foreign policy process in some cases (Ameringer, 1977; Cooke, 1968; Courtier, 1975; Gomez, 1964; Goodsell, 1974; Lincoln, 1981; M. Martz, 1975; Moran, 1975; Pinelo, 1973; Schneider, 1970; Tugwell, 1975; Tyson, 1975; Van Klaveren, 1982). Further studies of the process by which policies are formulated offer a great potential for understanding Latin American foreign policy. Also, given the relatively high concentration of power and governmental centralization in Latin America, studies on leadership would provide additional insight to the foreign policy-making process.

The differences in approach used by Latin American and North American researchers are troublesome. While the North American analyst typically focuses on one country at one particular point in time, or to a much lesser extent, systematically employs cross-national data to arrive at empirically verifiable findings, the Latin American approach is generally much more theoretical in nature and more historical in its treatment of foreign policy issues. For example, while the essays included in Relaciones Internacionales, the publication of the Universidad Nacional Autónoma de México, show a concern for the historical manifestations of dependency and imperialism, the occasional articles providing case studies or cross-national research are almost invariably written by North Americans.

Latin American foreign policies do not occur in a vacuum separate from the centuries of interactions which determine their contemporary form. One area in which there seems to be considerable convergence between Latin American and U.S. analysts is in the field of geopolitics. Geopolitics has a long tradition in both Latin American military circles and among U.S. academics. In Latin America, geopolitical thinking has been used as a principal tool for understanding regional conflicts and border disputes. Its development in Latin American military journals and training institutions (Child, 1979) has given it a key role for understanding military behavior. In the U.S., geopolitics builds on the realist approaches and their emphases on geographical components of power. The application of geopolitical thinking to explaining Latin American foreign policy behavior is becoming increasingly evident in the works of both U.S. and Latin American scholars.

Both North American and Latin American scholars tend to oversimplify foreign policy actors. Thus North American writers typically treat Latin American nations as single, monolithic entities (e.g., "Brazil moved closer to the U.S." "Peru adopted a more nationalist stand"), ignoring the diverse political interests within the nations. Latin Americans in turn (with a few exceptions, such as the Centro de Investigación y Docencia Económica, CIDE), tend to treat the U.S. as a monolithic actor with little analysis of the multiple political roles within the system. It is common, for example, for differences in regime (e.g., between Carter and Reagan) to be brushed aside and for the policies of the U.S. government to be identified exclusively with the multinational corporations. While there is a great deal of support for these assertions, the reality is much more complex. North Americans need to learn from their Latin American colleagues that the structural components of foreign policies are crucial for understanding Latin America's role in the international system. Similarly, given the crucial role that the U.S. plays in Latin America, it would be beneficial for Latin American scholars to understand the various components of the U.S. political system--e.g., the role of interest groups or realities of partisan presidential elections. CIDE, for example, has been able to incorporate some of the aspects of decision-making approaches into its analysis of U.S.-Latin American relations.

As Latin American governments face new challenges to develop appropriate foreign policies, so too the theoretical approaches for studying Latin America's role in the international system must be re-examined. There is a need both for more case studies describing Latin American foreign policy behavior and for studies addressing significant theoretical issues. The challenge to those writing about Latin American foreign policies is to integrate specific cases and policies into a broader theoretical context which will be useful in explaining other foreign policy situations.

The complexity of the policy-making process must be recognized and theories which take into account the interactions between a variety of cases and consequences must be formulated. The relationship between the structural constraints posed by a nation's economic dependence on the U.S. and the perceptions of national decision-makers as to the nature of these limits is an exciting area of inquiry. The ways in which developmental choices affect regional foreign policy behavior are important for Latin American policy makers as well as observers interested in the theoretical interrelationships.

LATIN AMERICAN FOREIGN POLICIES: CHALLENGES FOR THE FUTURE

Latin American governments today face challenges in defining their role in the international system on at least three fronts: (1) the need to respond to the region's mammoth foreign debts; (2) the re-assessment of the inter-American system (and the concept of nonintervention) in light of the Falklands/Malvinas war and the Grenada invasion; and (3) the phenomenon of the Central American revolutions. This collection of essays addresses the dynamics of Latin American foreign policies in light of challenges which question the fundamental nature of Latin America's role in the international system. The way in which Latin American governments adapt to changing international and regional situations will establish a new context for the region's foreign relations in the future.

The debt situation of Latin American countries reflects the region's past developmental choices. Today Latin American nations owe an estimated $300 billion to international financial institutions and commercial banks (LARR, October 28, 1983:1). This accumulation of foreign debt has affected Latin American foreign policies in several ways. The International Monetary Fund (IMF) has obviously increased its power in the national affairs of those nations seeking to reschedule their debts or to acquire new foreign loans. In country after country, the imposition of IMF-mandated austerity measures has weakened governmental popularity, limited developmental options and reduced regime capabilities. In spite of speculation about the formation of a Third World debtors' cartel, the debt crisis appears to have had opposite effects in Latin America, where governments perceive their best hope in negotiations lies in presenting themselves as unique and individual cases. The rise of Latin America's debt is, of course, accompanied by the growing power of commercial banks in national politics and by a relative decline in the power of multinational manufacturing enterprises. The terms of the relationship between international banks and Latin American governments differ from that between multinational corporations and the governments. The banks are a much less visible presence in Latin American affairs than are U.S. manufacturing and extractive industries. The indebtedness means that the governments bear the direct political costs of imposing unpopular austerity measures rather than the corporations themselves. It is the Latin American governments who must drastically cut public expenditures in order to comply with IMF demands. However, the governments have a certain degree of leverage vis-a-vis the banks in that the banks are financially dependent on Latin American repayment of the debts and thus have an incentive to keep rolling over the debts and to make new loans to protect their investments. Moreover, the banks fear a default by a Third World government (as several regimes have threatened to do) might trigger defaults in other hard-pressed Third World countries.

The phenomenon of Latin America's debt brings economic issues to the fore throughout most of the region. The energies required to renegotiate debt arrangements inevitably mean that less attention will be paid to other foreign policy issues. While the debt burdens have the potential of inspiring increased cooperation among other debtor nations, so far the debtor nations have shown a reluctance to engage in collective pressure on the international financial institutions: the costs of losing credit are simply too great. The debt has also meant a shift in U.S.-Latin American relationships with U.S. influence increasingly exerted through multilateral financial institutions and with the increasing power of commercial banks whose interests and goals do not always coincide with those of the U.S. government.

The need to reassess U.S.-Latin American relations has been further highlighted by U.S. support of Britain in the 1982 Falklands/Malvinas war and by the 1983 U.S. invasion of Grenada. In the immediate aftermath of the Falklands/Malvinas war, Latin American governments expressed dismay at U.S. actions and there was considerable speculation that inter-American relations would deteriorate. This deterioration did not occur although undoubtedly many Latin American governments became even more skeptical about the region's collective defense agreements. While many governments did not support Argentina's use of force in attempting to reclaim the islands, most nations supported Argentina's claims vis-à-vis Great Britain. The reluctance of the Reagan administration to consider those claims caused a temporary rift in regional relationships.

The U.S. invasion of Grenada marked an even greater break in relations between Latin American nations and the U.S. The invasion, in clear violation of inter-American agreements and the OAS charter, was roundly condemned throughout Latin America. Even nations which have close ties with the U.S. felt threatened by the invasion; if the U.S. could intervene in Grenada, future interventions in other Latin American nations became more likely. The need to contain U.S. intervention in the national affairs of the region has become more obvious in light of U.S. support for Britain and the Grenada invasion. This need is given urgency by the Reagan administration's bellicose posture in Central America. Latin American reactions to U.S. action in Grenada and in Central America have been affected by the region's debt. Thus, governments such as Brazil, while opposing U.S. intervention, have been hesitant to be too critical because of the need for U.S. support in debt refinancing negotiations.

The Central American revolutions pose a third challenge to Latin American governments seeking to define their roles in the international system of the 1980s. U.S. opposition to the revolutionary Nicaraguan regime and support for the Salvadoran and Guatemalan governments in their struggles to maintain power have once again demonstrated the U.S. intentions to prevent revolutionary change in the region. These actions have also inspired some governments, particularly Mexico and those in the circum-Caribbean, to seek alternative political solutions to the conflict. The efforts of the Contadora Group are most notable in this respect. As Latin American governments struggle to assert their right to intervene in the violence-plagued region, they are constantly confronted by U.S. intervention on a massive scale. The Central American revolutions offer Latin American governments the challenge of both controlling U.S. intervention in the region and of developing coherent, positive policies toward the region. The dangers are also manifest. Central American revolutions threaten established governments who, to varying degrees, are seeking to control revolutionary movements in their own coun-tries. The possibility of failing to achieve a lasting political solution is a real one as are the dangers inherent in opposing U.S. policies in the region and in backing a losing side.

The essays in this volume present an extensive analysis of the foreign policy challenges facing Latin America in the international arena in the 1980s from varying perspectives. In the chapters which follow in Part 1, Child examines changes in the nature of inter-state conflict in Latin America from a time of relative tranquility prior to 1960 to a time of national security threats in the post-1960 era. Ferguson, on the other hand, looks at the attempts at cooperation in the region, principally through efforts toward economic integration. Sigmund analyzes the change and continuity in U.S.-Latin American relations from the Carter administration to the Reagan administration and confirms the traditional focus of the U.S. as a dominant force in Latin American foreign policy.

Analyses of the major economic challenges and regional conflicts in South America are presented in Part 2. Gordon looks at the impact of both the Falklands/Malvinas war and the ensuing economic crises in Argentina on its foreign policy. Selcher examines the foreign policy decision structure in Brazil and its response to debt pressures and regional security issues. Pittman details Chile's pursuit of geopolitical goals in the Southern Cone which domi-nate its foreign policy. Lincoln analyzes Peru's foreign policy since the return of democratic rule in view of severe economic pressures due to foreign debt and IMF-imposed austerity measures and strong military pressures to provide for an adequate defense against the growing internal threat from Sendero Luminoso and possible external threats from Ecuador and Chile. Hazleton reviews the foreign policy capabilities and interests of Venezuela and Colombia as they face economic and security issues in the region. Morales analyzes the impact of domestic politics on Bolivia's foreign policy, especially with regard to its search for an outlet to the sea.

Part 3 focuses upon the conflict in Central America which overwhelmingly influences intra-regional foreign policies as well as relations of these nations with the U.S. Lincoln presents an overview of the security issues in Central America which reflect the concern of all the nations in the region for the civil war in El Salvador and the contras' war against Nicaragua. Ferris examines Mexico's contradictory foreign policies in the region which reflect its national interests in supporting progressive, revolutionary movements in El Salvador and Nicaragua on one hand, but oppose Guatemalan guerrilla movements (closer to home) on the other hand. Azicri evaluates the Sandinistas' attempt to forge a nonaligned foreign policy for Nicaragua in the face of U.S.-supported contra opposition in Honduras and Eden Pastora's contras in Costa Rica who are attempting to overthrow the Sandinstan regime. From another point of view del Aguila discusses support of and constraints upon Cuba's foreign policy in Central America and the Caribbean.

In Part 4 Ferris proposes a theoretical framework for future exploration of Latin American foreign policy behavior, suggesting that progress in the development of theories of foreign policy behavior can best be achieved through developing theoretically rigorous and empirically testable hypotheses. This volume represents the efforts of many to focus attention once again on the study of Latin American foreign policy from the perspective of the Latin American nations themselves.

2
Inter-State Conflict in Latin America in the 1980s

Jack Child

THE NATURE OF INTER-STATE CONFLICT IN THE 1980S

Recent Changes in the Conflict Panorama

The nature of inter-state conflict in Latin America has undergone drastic changes in the last quarter century. Prior to 1960 Latin America was considered a relatively tranquil region in which significant inter-state conflicts erupted only at infrequent intervals. Thus, the twentieth century marked an extended period of peace interrupted only by wars such as the Chaco conflict between Bolivia and Paraguay (1932-1935) and the fighting between Peru and Ecuador (1942). Other inter-state strains in this period rarely reached the shooting stage, and if they did, that stage lasted for only a very short period of time before it was snuffed out by outside parties, the limited logistics of the contending armies, or the general reluctance of the nations in conflict to actually go to war. This period up to 1960 can now be seen as one of "traditional" border and territorial conflicts in Latin America which were limited in nature, relatively simple to resolve, and well within the ameliorating and peace-making capabilities of the inter-American system.

This panorama began to change in the 1960s with the emergence of the ideological conflict associated with the Cuban revolution, Cuba's links to the Soviet Union, attempts to export the Cuban revolution using the "foco" concept of guerrilla warfare, and the responses of the United States and the inter-American system. Although the guerrilla warfare which Latin America experienced in the post-1960 period did not involve nation states as such, the support for insurgent groups across national borders set the stage for the polarized inter-state conflict which characterizes parts of Central America and the Caribbean Basin in the 1980s. In southern South America this same period since the 1960s witnessed a very different phenomenon: urban and rural guerrilla groups were eliminated with brutal efficiency by powerful military establishments, which then turned their attention to ruling their nations through direct and authoritarian military rule. They did so equipped in many cases with a coherent set of ideas and plans which became known as the "national security state." One element of this set of ideas was geopolitical thinking, which became increasingly important in South America in the 1970s and has left a legacy of tension and power politics which will affect the inter-state conflict panorama of the Southern Cone well into the 1980s.

Reasons for the Changing Nature of Inter-State Conflict

The new elements of ideology and geopolitical thinking which characterized the nature of inter-state conflict in Latin America in the 1980s made these conflicts much harder to resolve than the old traditional conflicts involving relatively minor territorial disputes. Other factors also contributed to the increasing danger of conflict in the 1980s.

One of these was the gradual but significant decline in the effectiveness of traditional mechanisms to reduce and ameliorate conflict. The relative power of the United States to influence events in the hemisphere, especially the southern part, declined in recent decades as the larger Latin American nations grew more independent. Although in many respects this is a healthy and positive development, it has had the unfortunate effect of reducing the ability of the United States to persuade Latin American nations to avoid direct military confrontations. At the same time, the Organization of American States and its instruments for peaceful settlement, which had played an active role in many conflict situations in the past, has been ignored, bypassed, or discredited in many of the new conflict situations. This process was especially evident in a series of crises in the early 1980s, starting with the Falklands/Malvinas war, which for many Latins proved the irrelevancy of the Rio Treaty to their security needs (Connell-Smith, 1982). A year later the invasion of Grenada by the United States and a group of English-speaking Caribbean nations ignored the OAS and established the unsettling precedent of a selective multilateral approach to security problems. Perhaps more disturbing, the growing crisis in Central America in this period and the real possibility of a regional conflict seemed outside the power of the OAS or other existing instruments to influence or settle (International Peace Academy, 1983, 1984).

The traditional twentieth century inter-state conflicts in Latin America generally involved remote frontier areas of little economic significance. This reflected the fact that since colonial times Latin America had tended to develop national core areas separated by considerable stretches of relatively empty space. The old Spanish colonial frontiers cut through these empty areas, and most of the resulting national frontiers followed the colonial ones. However, in the second half of this century much of Latin America has developed beyond these original national core areas, and has begun to fill many of the previously empty spaces. Under the pressures of demographic growth and modernization, what was once seen as relatively worthless frontier areas are increasingly perceived as important resource regions awaiting development. Geopolitical theories in vogue in many of the South American nations stress this concept, along with a sense of competition with neighboring states and a concern that these same neighbors will develop the areas unless one gets there first. Compounding this situation is the fact that a number of border areas which are the scene of inter-state tension are now perceived to contain the energy resources which so many of the Latin American nations lack. The increasing importance now being given to the sea has also exacerbated a number of conflict situations as nations extend their economic and sovereign maritime areas far beyond the original three mile limits (Pittman, 1981a).

One final reason for the changing conflict scenario in Latin America has been a military and technological one: the Latin American military establishments have in recent years grown in size and power to the point where many of them are significant regional forces. Cuba now represents a military threat to Caribbean sea lanes, and the unprecedented buildup of the Nicaraguan military has been paralleled by the increasing military capabilities of other Central American states and an equally unprecedented U.S. military presence on the Isthmus (Atlantic Council of the U.S., 1983). In South America the larger military establishments have achieved greater independence from the United States by diversifying their arms sources and by stimulating their own arms industries. In many cases they now possess the manpower and weapons to be taken seriously by major military powers. As demonstrated in the Falklands/Malvinas conflict, relatively inexpensive modern missiles can serve as significant "equalizers" for regional military establishments. Further, at least two Latin American nations (Brazil and Argentina) are threshold nuclear powers which have the means to construct an explosive nuclear device with military applications if they should choose to do so (Cardier, 1982).

The Caribbean and the Southern Cone

These considerations suggest not only that the conflict panorama in Latin America in the 1980s has undergone significant changes, but also that actual or possible inter-state conflict in the Caribbean Basin is fundamentally different from that in the Southern Cone of South America. This reality is reflected in the organization of this chapter, which deals with these two areas separately. In the Caribbean Basin (defined as the United States, Mexico, Central America, the Caribbean islands, and the northern states of South America) there is a strong ideological element in conflicts, as well as major superpower interests; this, in turn, results in a tendency toward polarization and making superpower confrontations out of relatively low level inter-state conflicts.

In the Southern Cone the ideological and superpower elements are much less significant (except for the South Atlantic-Antarctic conflict). The predominant characteristics are the emerging role of subregional military powers, the impact of geopolitical thinking, and the national security state. As will be argued below, this combination produces a heavy emphasis on power politics and competitive international relations and suggests the possible emergence of a balance of power system not unlike the one that existed in South America in the late nineteenth and early twentieth centuries. Any consideration of South American inter-state conflicts must also include an interlinked series of quarrels which could involve not only the nations of the area but also a significant group of outside countries, including the superpowers. This includes the Anglo-Argentine dispute over the Falklands/Malvinas and also the much broader issues of influence in the South Atlantic and the ultimate control of Antarctica. This latter issue is potentially the most dangerous of all, since it involves the United States, the Soviet Union, and a number of other countries. This conflict will probably become increasingly tense as the 1991 date for possible revision of the existing Antarctic Treaty nears.

Classification of Latin American Conflict Situations in the 1980s

A number of authors have attempted to classify the range of conflict situations in Latin America (Grabendorff, 1982; Child, 1980a). The typology presented here is based on the more important categories of conflict behavior and forms the basis for the summary of the conflicts listed in

Table 2.1 and the map in Figure 2.1. It should be noted that Table 2.1 shows that most of the conflicts are a mix of several of these categories, and that a characteristic of conflict in the 1980s is that old border and territorial conflicts tend to become more acute and dangerous when exacerbated by ideological or resource factors.

The oldest and most traditional types of conflicts are border and territorial conflicts, many of which have roots in the inadequate definition or demarcation of colonial and early national frontiers. Territorial conflicts have traditionally involved land, but are increasingly involving maritime areas as Latin American nations extend their exclusive economic zones and their law of the sea sovereign claims. Border conflicts frequently also involve territory, but fundamentally stem from the tensions that arise when two national sovereignties meet at a frontier. Differences over political systems, smuggling, refugees, and other factors all contribute to this type of conflict.

Influence conflicts are also deeply rooted in that they involve competitive efforts to enhance and project national prestige and power. Power is a central concern of the national security state, and as a result this type of conflict has shown up in a number of Southern Cone situations.

A frequent byproduct of other types of tensions, whether internal or external, is the migration of large numbers of refugees to the point where it is possible and necessary to speak of migratory conflicts as a separate category stemming from large-scale movements of persons across frontiers.

As suggested above, ideological and resource conflicts are now increasingly significant because of their tendency to polarize participants and to involve the superpowers or their surrogates; consequently they are much less tractable to the traditional conflict-resolution mechanisms.

THE CARIBBEAN BASIN: IDEOLOGICAL CONFLICT AND POLARIZATION

The Significance of the Ideological Component

The principal significance of the ideological component in Caribbean Basin conflict situations is that it raises the dangerous possibilities of a superpower confrontation and tends to exacerbate and exaggerate the significance and impact of conflicts which could otherwise be kept at a lower level. The ideological component and superpower interest thus give an East-West dimension to situations which are fundamentally internal or subregional in nature.

In the case of the current crisis in Central America the roots of several inter-state conflict situations are found in a long history of exploitation and social injustice under a traditional and conservative oligarchic order whose disappearance is creating fertile ground for ideological, political and military struggles (U.S., National Bipartisan Commission on Central America, 1984). This form of change is especially unsettling for the United States, which has long regarded the area as one of special strategic and economic interest under its strong influence. Historically, the U.S. influence was so overwhelming that it was common to speak of the Caribbean as a "U.S. Lake " and to see the region as an economy of force area which permitted the United States to maintain order with a minimum of effort and few resources.

This situation lasted from the Spanish-American War of 1898 until the coming to power of Fidel Castro in Cuba in 1959. Castro's links to the Soviet Union and Eastern Europe broke the United States strategic monopoly in the area and led to the presence of an ideological element in a number of

TABLE 2.1
Latin American Conflict Situations in the 1980s

Map reference	Conflict	Parties involved	Type of conflict
1	Mexico–United States	Mexico, United States	Migratory, resource
2	Caribbean	Caribbean states, U.S., U.S.S.R.	Ideological, resource, migratory
3	Island of Hispaniola	Dominican Republic, Haiti	Border, migratory
4	Central American	Central America, U.S., Cuba	Ideological, influence, migratory
5	Honduras–El Salvador	Honduras, El Salvador	Territorial, migratory
6	Belize	Belize, Guatemala, Great Britain, U.S.	Territorial
7	Panama Canal	Panama, U.S.	Territorial, resource
8	San Andres and other islands	Nicaragua, Colombia	Territorial
9	Gulf of Venezuela and border	Colombia, Venezuela	Territorial, resource, migratory
10	Essequibo (Western Guyana)	Venezuela, Guyana	Territorial, resource
11	New River Triangle	Guyana, Suriname	Territorial, resource
12	Argentine–Brazilian rivalry	Argentina–Brazil	Influence, resource
13	Bolivia–Paraguay	Bolivia, Paraguay	Territorial, resource
14	Northern Andean	Ecuador, Peru	Territorial, resource
15	Central Andean	Peru, Bolivia, Chile	Territorial, resource (Bolivia)
16	Southern Andean	Argentina, Chile	Territorial, resource, border, migratory
17	Law of the sea, maritime zones	Coastal states	Territorial, resource
18	Falklands/Malvinas Islands	Great Britain, Argentina	Territorial, resource
19	South Atlantic	Argentina, Brazil, outside powers	Resource, influence
20	Antarctica	Treaty signatories, others	Territorial, resource

26

Figure 2.1

Map of Latin American Conflict Situations in the 1980s

See Table 2.1 for list and type.

Not shown: #2. Caribbean; #4. Central American; #17. Law of the Sea and
Maritime Zones; #20. Antarctica

Caribbean Basin conflict situations. Although the early attempts to imitate and export the Cuban Revolution through the "foco" model failed, much was learned from this experience, most notably the reality that while insurgent movements require external support to succeed, they cannot be exported to countries where the conditions for insurgency do not exist. As a result, Castro's most significant contribution to the Nicaraguan insurgency of 1978-1979 was not so much direct support as the advice and assistance involved in forging a single Sandinista Front out of the various factions.

The ideological element in Caribbean Basin inter-state conflicts shows up at present in links between left-wing insurgents in several countries and Cuba and Nicaragua; it is also present in the overt and covert United States support for contra insurgent movements which oppose the Sandinista regime in Managua. The ideological element is also potentially involved in a number of other historic inter-state conflict situations which, given the appropriate circumstances, could raise traditional territorial and border issues to a much higher level of conflict potential. For example, the Guatemalan-Belizean territorial conflict could rapidly escalate if a threatened government in Belmopan were to request Cuban assistance for its defense, as Guatemalan military authorities have insisted that it would (LAWR, January 11, 1980:1). In a similar vein, the Venezuelan-Guyanese territorial conflict could take the same path if an insecure regime in Georgetown were to seek protection through a link to Cuba (U.S. FBIS, March 18, 1980).

Because it was an economy of force area, the Caribbean rarely demanded a high U.S. military presence (with the exception of bases in the Panama Canal region). Thus, the large and extended United States military maneuvers in Honduras in 1983 and 1984 represent a significant change and, when linked to Honduran-Nicaraguan tensions and the U.S. covert support for contra guerrillas inside Nicaragua, increase the possibility and scope of a regional war (International Peace Academy, 1984).

The Tendency Toward Polarization

The presence of an ideological component and the possible involvement of superpowers or their surrogates appear to be leading the Caribbean Basin toward an increasingly polarized conflict situation. The basic polarization involves the United States and its Central American and insular Caribbean allies on one side and Cuba and Nicaragua on the other (until October 1983 the revolutionary regime in Grenada would also have been included in this equation). Both poles have links to insurgencies in various Central American countries and provide varying degrees of support to them. The Cuba-Nicaraguan pole of this axis also has important economic and security links to the Soviet Union and various Eastern European nations. For the Soviet Union, Cuba provides an invaluable logistical and intelligence base which in time of a NATO-Warsaw Pact crisis could require the diversion of substantial United States military forces from the European theater (Atlantic Council of the United States, 1983).

The October 1983 invasion of Grenada, while unique in many respects, serves to illustrate some of the dimensions and implications of this polarization. Apparently dismissing the multilateral instruments of the Organization of American States, the U.S. opted for a more selective form of multilateral action to provide a legal justification (albeit a somewhat shaky one) for the invasion. The specific instrument was an obscure paragraph in the 1981 Charter of the Organization of Eastern Caribbean States which served as a basis for the OECS to request assistance from the U.S., Barbados and Jamaica. This precedent of selective multilateralism used in the Grenadan case has applicability to the Central American conflict environment, where there is a somewhat analogous legal arrangement dating back to the early 1960s. Known as the Central American Defense Council (Consejo de Defensa Centr-americano--CONDECA), it involves the United States, El Salvador, Guatemala, and Honduras (the membership status of Costa Rica and Panama is somewhat clouded, and Nicaragua withdrew after the fall of Somoza in 1979). The relationship between the OECS selective multilateral precedent and CONDECA could become significant in a possible scenario in which a collapsing regime in El Salvador invokes CONDECA to request support from Honduras, Guatemala, and the United States.

The tendency toward polarization of Caribbean Basin conflict situations is viewed with much concern by many of the states of the region. Some, like Costa Rica, have attempted to remain outside the polarization by opting for neutrality (La Nación, June 16, 1983; September 23, 1983). Others, such as the Contadora Group made up of Mexico, Colombia, Venezuela, and Panama, have taken a more active diplomatic role in hopes of defusing the polarization and resolving the region's conflicts (International Peace Academy, 1983, 1984).

Despite these efforts, the predominant and potentially most dangerous inter-state conflict situation in the Caribbean Basin in the 1980s is the polarization in Central America and its tendency to involve peripheral conflicts which might otherwise remain at a lower and simpler level.

The Caribbean Basin Conflicts (see Table 2.1 and Figure 2.1)

Apart from the polarized Caribbean and Central American conflicts described above, the region contains a number of other potential conflict situations. Two involve the United States and special relationships with Mexico and Panama.

The potential United States-Mexico conflict has some unique aspects stemming from Mexico's oil and its position as the only Latin American nation bordering the United States (Fagen, 1979). The geographic contiguity has been a major factor in the relationship between the two countries and has led to both positive and negative aspects of the relationship. In terms of conflict potential, the most salient of these in the 1980s is the pressure of migration stemming from continued violence in Central America or unrest within Mexico. Should refugees from these situations attempt to cross the border in massive numbers, the United States might consider sealing the Mexican border by military means, thus exacerbating relations with Mexico as well as tying down considerable U.S. defense resources.

Currently, the potential for conflict with Panama over the Canal is overshadowed by the generally healthy spirit of cooperation which has dominated the relations between the U.S. and Panama since the signing of the treaties in 1977. However, the potential for misunderstanding between the two nations over the provisions of the Treaties is significant, and the complicated details of the transition process provide many opportunities for this misunderstanding. As the end of the transition period draws near there will be an understandable temptation on the part of Panamanian nationalists to insist on an acceleration of the process; at the same time there will be a strong tendency on the part of the United States to conserve the strategic and economic advantages gained from a U.S. presence in Panama for as long as possible.

The Honduras-El Salvador and Guatemala-Belize territorial disputes are

examples of situations which the old conflict resolution system would have
been able to handle with relative efficiency, but which are today made much
more complicated by their potential involvement in Caribbean Basin polarization. The El Salvador-Honduras dispute primarily stems from historic migration patterns in which Salvadorans move from their densely populated nation
to relatively empty Honduras (Martz, 1978; Durham, 1979). In recent years
the dispute has been complicated by refugees fleeing the fighting in El Salvador and the fact that the territories in dispute are ones in which the leftist
guerrillas in El Salvador have exercised considerable control. The Guatemalan
claim on Belize's territory also involves Great Britain as the former colonial
power. The British government is under economic pressure to withdraw its
garrison from Belize, but to do so would leave Belize at the mercy of the
Guatemalan military and create a situation where the government in Belize
might be forced in desperation to seek help from any source to counter the
Guatemalan threat.

The northern tier of South American nations present a string of potential conflict situations, some of which have links to the polarized Caribbean
Basin conflict. Colombia, for example, has a dispute with Nicaragua over the
islands of San Andres and Providencia as well as a number of smaller islands
and keys. These all lie much closer to Nicaragua than Colombia, but have
been under Colombia's sovereignty and control since independence. In this
respect the situation is reminiscent of the Falklands/Malvinas conflict and is
one element accounting for Nicaragua's strong support for Argentina in that
crisis; it also explains Colombia's neutrality. The conflict was dormant until
the new Sandinista regime denounced the 1928 Treaty which confirmed
Colombian sovereignty, arguing that it was signed under duress while U.S.
Marines occupied Nicaragua (Drekonja, 1982). In the face of Nicaragua's far
more serious domestic and insurgency problems in the mid-1980s this dispute
has been downplayed, but it remains a potential source of conflict with links
to other strains involving Nicaragua.

The Colombian-Venezuelan dispute over the waters and some islands in
the Gulf of Venezuela is more of the traditional non-ideological type, but also
includes a very important contemporary resource element in that valuable oil
deposits may exist in the shallow waters of the Gulf, which lie close to
Venezuela's major oil-producing area of Maracaibo (Holguin Pelaez, 1971;
Monagas, 1975). This dispute, like the more serious one Venezuela has with
its eastern neighbor Guyana, reflects the greater international and power projection role which Venezuela has sought since its oil revenues increased its
economic clout in the mid and late 1970s. Venezuela's two disputes are' somewhat similar to the geopolitically based conflicts prevalent in the Southern
Cone in that such geopolitical thinking is influential in Venezuela (Ewell,
1982; Carpio Castillo, 1981). Venezuela, like several Southern Cone nations,
feels it has been "geopolitically victimized" by aggressive neighbors who have
taken away important portions of its territory in the past. In Venezuelan eyes
the dispute with Guyana is really with a colonial and imperialistic Great
Britain, which in the nineteenth century expanded its colony of British Guyana
at Venezuela's expense. This perception in turn explains the fervent Venezuelan support for the Argentines during the Falklands/Malvinas conflict and
has been an element of strain in Venezuelan-United States relations.

The two remaining Caribbean conflict situations are isolated from the
polarized Central American conflicts and appear to be dormant. The conflict
between Haiti and the Dominican Republic has deep roots in racial differences and in migratory patterns that go back to the colonial and early

independence period, with frequent charges of abuse and exploitation of Haitian migrants who cross the border in search of work in the Dominican Republic. The last dispute concerns the so-called New River Triangle, an inaccessible area along the frontier between Guyana and Suriname which could have economic significance in terms of bauxite.

THE SOUTHERN CONE: GEOPOLITICS, CONFLICT, AND THE NATIONAL SECURITY STATE

The Significance of Geopolitical Thinking and the National Security State

The presence of strong currents of geopolitical thinking in the Southern Cone states, coupled with authoritarian military regimes based on the national security state model, give inter-state conflict and international relations in the Southern Cone a markedly different tone than in the Caribbean Basin. Further, the military establishments in this region are considerably larger, more powerful, and more sophisticated than in Central America and the Caribbean. As a result of these factors and the distance from the United States and other centers of world power, the Southern Cone conflicts have much less to do with outside ideological and superpower influence. The exception to this generalization concerns the possibility of strains and even conflict in the South Atlantic and Antarctica, which would probably involve the superpowers, the other members of the "Antarctic Club," and a number of other states.

Geopolitical theories originated in Western Europe in the nineteenth century as a blend of geographic, political, and biological ideas which were employed to explain how states evolved, grew, projected their influence, and eventually declined. The starting point for these geopoliticians was the organic theory of the state, a vision that presented the nation-state as a living organism which had to struggle to gain resources and space (lebensraum) in a hostile world populated by other states in competition for the same resources. European and U.S. geopolitical writers put forth a number of worldviews which served to explain the relationship between the environment, nations, and power projection: the maritime view of Admiral Alfred Thayer Mahan, the continental view of the British geographer Sir Halford Mackinder, and the aerospace view of Alexander de Seversky. Geopolitics as an academic discipline received a severe setback during World War II when the German school under Karl Haushofer provided Adolf Hitler with a number of ideas which were twisted and shaped to provide justifications for Nazi theories of conquest and ethnic superiority. As a consequence, the whole discipline of geopolitics fell into disrepute in Western Europe and the United States for a generation after the war (Collins, 1973).

However, in the Southern Cone a small group of military officers and their civilian counterparts picked up and preserved the original ideas of the European geopoliticians and used them as the basis for several Southern Cone "schools" of geopolitical thinking, most notably in Argentina, Brazil, and Chile (Child, 1979). These schools remained somewhat isolated and had relatively little influence outside of military circles in the 1950s and 1960s, in large part because United States strategic thinking and doctrine exerted an overwhelming weight in the hemisphere. Thus, little was known of these currents of Latin American geopolitical thought outside of the region and almost none of their prolific output was translated into English or published in the United States. In the late 1960s and 1970s this situation began to change as U.S. strategic influence declined in South America and as the larger states of the region came under military rule (Brazil in 1964, Chile in 1973, Argentina in 1976). The ensuing regimes were quite different from previous military governments in that they came to power in response to a perceived serious threat from the left. Furthermore, they were committed to creating a permanent defense against such threats and to a long-term economic development program. As a result, the governments that emerged from this period placed a strong emphasis on authoritarianism, nationalism, corporatism, and security. This particular type of military regime became known as the "national security state," and geopolitical ideas provided much of the theoretical and practical foundation for its programs and policies (Comblin, 1978, 1980).

Many of these basic concepts of geopolitical thinking stem from the organic vision of the nation-state as a living organism struggling to survive in a hostile environment populated by an equally ruthless group of organisms. The geopoliticians warned that the fight for space and vital resources was becoming increasingly bitter as population pressures grew and as certain strategic resources, such as oil, became increasingly scarce and expensive. Because of this sense of struggle and projection of power, geopolitical thinkers have a very flexible concept of the frontier, which they view not as a fixed line on a map but rather as a movable boundary which could be pushed into a weaker state's territory if the stronger state so desired. This was especially true for regions that were perceived as critical for strategic or economic reasons, giving rise to the so-called "law of valuable areas" which argued that if a nation did not occupy and exploit its important resource regions, then another state would do so. This "law" was held to be especially valid for frontier areas or areas where sovereignty was not clearly defined, such as the sea and Antarctica. Another relevant geopolitical concept is the so-called "law of discontinuous borders," which maintains that nations with a contiguous frontier are destined to have strains and conflict, while those states which are fairly close together but are not contiguous will have much better relations and will tend to form alliances against the contiguous states (Pineiro, 1974).

Although there is much common ground in the geopolitical ideas held in Argentina, Brazil, and Chile, there are also some important national variants. In Brazil the geopoliticians provided much of the intellectual rationale for the Brazilian path to destino e grandeza (destiny and greatness) traced out by military governments since 1964. Brazilian geopolitical thinkers argued that this destiny was manifest and almost inevitable if the nation followed the geopolitical prescriptions of filling Brazil's empty interior spaces and then exercising a projection of power toward immediate neighbors, the Caribbean, Western Africa, the South Atlantic, and Antarctica (Meira Mattos, 1975). In Argentina and Chile geopolitical writers have started from the argument that they have been "geopolitically victimized" by other states in the past and that their internal development and international relations should be guided by the attempt to regain some of their past power (Guglialmelli, 1979a; Pinochet, 1974). These two countries have clashed over the years on border and territorial issues and the problem of defining the limits of their maritime territory in the Beagle Channel area as well as the Drake Passage between South America and Antarctica. Both Chile and Argentina have self-perceptions of their nation as a "tri-continental power" which includes territory on mainland South America, the strategic southern

islands, and an Antarctic claim. This sense of past losses and future greatness has strong geopolitical roots and accounts for much of the friction in
Southern Cone international relations (Pittman, 1981a).

The national security state operates in a cruel and ruthless world in
which a sort of political Darwinism justifies even the most extreme measures
to insure the state's survival. The supreme end of protecting the state's power
and existence thus justifies almost any means; this is particularly evident in
the actions of the defenders of the national security state when they are
faced with the threat of Marxist-Leninist subversion. An individual who is
"infected" with this disease loses his identity as a citizen of the state,
becomes a traitor, and may be exterminated if he cannot be persuaded to
change his dangerous views (Comblin, 1978, 1980; Chiavaneto, 1981).

In the mid-1980s there are strong indications that the political pendu-
lum may swing away from this national security state dominated by the military toward more democratic and open regimes in which these geopolitical
concepts would play a much less important role. Even in this case, however,
the influence of the national security state and the geopolitical thinkers is
far-reaching because of their legacy of ideas and programs, their patriotic
and nationalistic rhetoric, and their permeation of the educational systems
and the mass media in these three countries.

Should these mental frameworks prevail and continue to influence the
international relations of the Southern Cone, they may bring about the return
of a balance of power system similar to that which prevailed in southern
South America in the late nineteenth and early twentieth century (Burr,
1965). In the context of the 1980s this balance of power system would be
based on the geopolitical concepts of the organic state, the living frontier,
and the laws of valuable areas and discontinuous borders. The result would be
a series of tensions between the major states that have contiguous borders
and a series of understandings or even alliances between those which do not.
Leaving aside the smaller states of Uruguay, Paraguay, and Bolivia, which
play lesser roles as buffer states, the resulting pattern is one of strains
between Brazil and Argentina, Argentina and Chile, Chile and Peru, Peru and
Ecuador, and Peru and Brazil. The noncontiguous states which would tend to
form understandings or alliances would be Brazil and Chile, and Peru and
Argentina. The inherent weakness of this balance of power system is that a
conflict in any one of its critical regions might lead to conflicts in other
areas and a possible broader conflict throughout the system. Thus, an
Argentine-Chilean confrontation over the Beagle Channel Islands or their
competing Antarctic claims could draw Chilean forces to the south and thus
tempt Peru to recover the territories it lost to Chile in the 1879 War of the
Pacific; this distraction of Peru toward her Chilean border could in turn lead
Ecuador to occupy the Amazonian claim lost to Peru in the 1940s. It is the
geopolitical base and the linkages of conflicts through this possible balance
of power system that make the Southern Cone conflict scenario potentially
dangerous in the 1980s.

Conflicts Involving Only Southern Cone Nations

The Argentine-Brazilian Rivalry. Of all the Southern Cone conflicts,
the Argentine-Brazilian rivalry is the longest, most deeply rooted, and most
influenced by geopolitical concepts. And yet, it is also one of the least
likely to reach the stage of military confrontation; it will probably remain at
the level of political, diplomatic, and even cultural competition for influence,

especially in the buffer states of Uruguay, Paraguay, and Bolivia. Besides the competition for influence in the buffers, the Brazilian-Argentine rivalry also shows up in general competition for hemispheric leadership, as well as in more specific areas of tension such as the search for hydroelectric energy in the Upper Parana River, Brazilian penetration of Misiones Province, and Brazilian plans for extending its influence into the South Atlantic and Antarctica. The Argentine-Brazilian rivalry also has an ominous nuclear dimension in that these two countries have the means to develop a nuclear device in a fairly short period of time and have ensured that international restrictions against proliferation would not hinder their efforts to do so (Sanz, 1976). In recent years the rivalry between these two countries has been ameliorated by a series of cooperative agreements and by moves in both countries away from the national security state and its geopolitical tenets.

Bolivia-Paraguay. This conflict is essentially dormant, but will endure as long as the bitter memories of the 1932-1935 Chaco War remain. Small but influential geopolitical institutes in both nations focus on issues of the Chaco War legacy, and there are occasional incidents along the border. One cause of the Chaco War was the belief that there were important oil reserves in the area, and this belief has persisted, despite the lack of any significant commercial exploitation in the ensuing years.

Northern Andean (Ecuador-Peru). The dispute over Ecuador's Amazon claim dates back to colonial days, and resulted in the South American continent's last major war in 1941, when the Peruvians decisively defeated the Ecuadorans (Wood, 1978). The 1942 Rio Protocol was presumed to settle the matter, but Ecuador has maintained that its government signed under duress and therefore the matter is still open. Recovering the lost territories would satisfy a geopolitical ambition of Ecuador's to be an "Amazonian power," and would provide an access to the Atlantic Ocean via the major river systems which cross Brazil. Moreover, the territories in dispute may also contain oil, since they are fairly near the oil-producing areas of both Peru and Ecuador. Tensions between the two countries broke out into shooting incidents in both 1981 and 1984, and there is little prospect for settlement of the basic dispute in the near future.

Central Andean (Peru-Bolivia-Chile). This dispute is also based on territories lost in a past conflict, in this case the 1879-1883 War of the Pacific in which Chile defeated a Peruvian-Bolivian coalition and kept territory taken from both countries. This was especially significant for Bolivia, since the territory lost included its only ocean outlet, and Bolivians since that time have blamed many of their economic difficulties on their land-locked status. Chilean geopoliticians, including President Augusta Pinochet, explain their nineteenth century expansion northward as an example of classical and justified lebensraum (the struggle for living space) and argue that the matter is closed. Nationalists and geopolitical writers in Peru, and especially in Bolivia, will not let the matter rest, and it continues to be a possible area of conflict (Pinochet, 1974; Ponce Caballero, 1976).

Southern Andean (Argentina-Chile). Each of these countries sees the other as aggressive and expansionist, and each feels that it has given up too much territory in the past. Chile at one time exercised control over Patagonia, and Argentine geopoliticians today fret over the migration of Chilean workers into that region, calling it a "silent invasion" (Guglialmelli, 1979b). Border friction has further contributed to the conflict, as well as a sense of competition for influence in the southern passages from the Pacific to Atlantic Oceans. Although both nations subscribe to the "bio-oceanic principle" under which Chile has influence in the South Pacific and Argentina in the South Atlantic, there is disagreement over where the boundary between the two oceans lies (Carrasco, 1979; Villalobos, 1979). These differences found a specific focus in the dispute over three small islands at the Eastern mouth of the Beagle Channel, whose importance is related to the bio-oceanic principle and the possibility that if they were in Chilean hands Chile could project out into the South Atlantic and diminish Argentine control of this area. Argentine-Chilean tensions are further exacerbated by their over-lapping Antarctic claims on the Palmer Peninsula which juts out toward South America across the Drake Passage.

Conflicts Involving Outside Powers

Law of the Sea and Maritime Zone Conflicts. The Latin American nations have been in the forefront of Third World battles to extend maritime exclusive economic zones and even sovereignty well beyond the traditional three-mile limit. In so doing, they have become involved in conflicts with the United States and other nations with far-ranging fishing fleets and naval interests. Over the past two decades this issue has led to confrontations between the United States and a number of Latin American nations, including Peru, Ecuador, Mexico, and Brazil. In the Southern Cone nations this drive to consider the sea as a new and important type of "valuable area" is firmly grounded in geopolitical thought.

Falklands/Malvinas Islands (Great Britain, Argentina). The significance of this conflict, and the deep emotions involved in it, were evident during the fighting in April, May, and June 1982. Although for Great Britain the island colony was an anachronistic and almost forgotten remnant of Empire, for the Argentines it has always been a nagging symbol of humiliation and British aggression. The eventual recovery of the islands is a constant theme in Argentine geopolitical thinking and patriotic rhetoric, and provided a brief rallying point for the troubled Argentine military regime in 1982 (Gamba, 1982). In the minds of a great many Argentines, especially their geopoliti-cians, the Malvinas represent an essential element in their concept of a greater Argentina on three continents: South America, Antarctica, and the Southern Islands (Milia, 1978). These islands run in an arc from Tierra del Fuego to the Malvinas, South Georgia, South Sandwich, South Orkney, and South Shetland to the Palmer Peninsula and Argentina's Antarctic claim. Their loss, and their possession by Great Britain, severely weakens the tri-continental concept and correspondingly strengthens Great Britain's Antarctic claim. Argentine geopoliticians also suspect collusion between Great Britain and Chile on issues such as the Falklands/Malvinas and the Beagle Channel Islands, since they see a mutual interest on the part of these two countries in keeping Argentina weak in the region. The Falklands/Malvinas dispute also has a perceived resource dimension in terms of fish, krill, and possible oil deposits, although their exploitation by Great Britain would be difficult with-out a mainland South American base of operations.

South Atlantic. This influence and resource conflict involves the South American Atlantic nations (most notably Argentina and Brazil, but also Uruguay), as well as South Africa, Great Britain, the United States, and the Soviet Union. Naval geopoliticians in the Southern Cone have pointed out that the South Atlantic is a strategic vacuum in that there is no treaty or defense arrangement such as NATO to protect its sea lanes in time of con-flict; thus, their proposal of a SATO (South Atlantic Treaty Organization) to fill that gap (Quagliotti de Bellis, 1976; Moneta, 1983). The value of these sea lanes became more evident during the oil crises of the 1970s since most of the Persian Gulf's oil exports to Europe and the United States use sea lanes in the eastern part of the South Atlantic. The significance of the South Atlantic and the inter-oceanic passages is also related to the availability of the Panama Canal and to interests in the Antarctic.

Antarctica. The conflict for control of Antarctica is potentially the most serious of all the Southern Cone conflicts since it involves clashes of important interests of several South American nations as well as a host of outside countries, including the United States, the Soviet Union, and Great Britain (Auburn, 1982; Pinochet de la Barra, 1976; Moneta, 1981). In a broader sense the conflict involves all the nations of the world in that there is a strong Third World drive to ensure that Antarctica benefits humanity as a whole, and not just the nations that are closest or most able to exploit it. The most dangerous area of possible conflict is the Palmer Peninsula, where three states (Argentina, Chile, and Great Britain) have strong and competing sovereignty claims. These claims (along with a number of others) were frozen for a thirty-year moratorium period under the provisions of the 1961 Antarctic Treaty, which also provided for a number of cooperative scientific ventures on the continent. However, the Antarctic Treaty is open for major revision in 1991, and there will be increasing pressures among claimant states to improve their positions before that date. Argentine geopoliticians in particular (Moneta, 1983) have argued the need to consolidate Argentina's position in all its southern claims, and this may have been an important element in the decision to invade the Falklands/Malvinas. Brazil has recently shown an increased interest in the Antarctic and has mounted its first expedition. Several Brazilian geopoliticians have put forward a novel sector theory of Antarctic claims which would reduce Argentina's claim and award a substantial claim to Brazil, along with Uruguay, Chile, Peru, and Ecuador (de Castro, 1976; Meira Mattos, 1977). Oddly enough, in the Antarctic conflict the United States and the Soviet Union are generally in agreement: they have extensive experience in exploration and scientific activities, make no sovereign claims, recognize none, and oppose schemes for internationalizing Antarctica for the benefit of nonsignatory states. The number of nations involved in this dispute, the diversity of their positions, the overlapping sovereignty claims on the Palmer Peninsula, and the time pressure of 1991 all suggest that Antarctica may be a significant theater for inter-state conflict in the 1980s.

3
Cooperation in Latin America:
The Politics of
Regional Integration

Yale Ferguson

The idea of Pan-Latin American association harks back to Simón Bolivar, but it began to be realized only after World War II, indeed mainly since 1960 and to date only to a modest extent. The United Nations Economic Commission for Latin America (ECLA) provided most of the ideological inspiration for postwar regional and subregional cooperation. ECLA's Executive Secretary, Raul Prebisch, and his associates profoundly shaped Latin American thinking about development and eventually some of the policies of the United States under the Kennedy administration. After the Alliance for Progress incorporated many of ECLA's prescriptions, the organization ceased to be a leading regional actor. Prebisch himself went on to the post of Executive Secretary of UNCTAD. UNCTAD, dependency theory, OPEC, and proposals for a "New International Economic Order" (NIEO) have all provided an ideological foundation for aspects of post-ECLA regional organization. However, it was the decline of the "special relationship" with the United States, beginning in the mid-1960s, that had possibly the single most crucial impact. Additional intra-regional association appeared to be a precondition for dealing successfully both with a less-receptive United States and with extra-hemisphere developed and developing countries.

Over the years there has been a cyclic pattern of optimism-pessimism about the prospects for Latin American integration. (For an excellent overview of developments through the mid-1970s, see Milenky, 1977.) The outlook seemed bright for the first two major regional experiments in economic integration, launched in 1960, the Latin American Free Trade Association (LAFTA) and the Central American Common Market (CACM). Both started to bog down in the mid-1960s, however, and the CACM all but collapsed in the wake of the "Soccer War" in 1969. Meanwhile, an inter-American meeting of heads of state in 1967 (Punta del Este, Uruguay) attempted to put some momentum back into the process of integration. More concrete than the expression of support emanating from the 1967 summit were the creation in that year of an Agency for the Prohibition of Nuclear Weapons in Latin America (OPANAL); the establishment of a Caribbean Free Trade Association (CARIFTA) in 1968; and in 1969 the issuance of the Latin American "Consensus of Vina del Mar" (by CECLA, the Special Commission for Latin American Coordination), as well as the Formation of a La Plata Basin Group and an Andean Common Market (ANCOM). Nevertheless, each of these institutions soon ran into severe difficulties, including the most ambitious, ANCOM, which had to retrench and suffered the withdrawal of Chile in 1975. Offering some consolation to the proponents of integration were the establishment of two new organizations, a Latin American Energy Organization (OLADE) in 1973 and the Latin American Economic System (SELA) in 1975; the 1973 conversion of CARIFTA into the Caribbean Community (CARICOM); the conclusion of an Amazon Pact in 1978; and the 1980 revamping of LAFTA into the Latin American Integration Organization (ALADI).

Although the establishment of new organizations served to keep the concept of regional integration in Latin America alive, their accomplishments to date have been only modest and major advances do not appear likely for the foreseeable future. About all that can be hoped for is the preservation of existing levels of cooperation and perhaps some relatively minor advances. On the other hand, Latin America is currently in the grip of economic and political crises of monumental proportions, and in this climate, further disintegration is perhaps equally likely--or possibly even unanticipated progress.

Before making additional generalizations, at this juncture let us examine the evolution of specific regional and subregional institutions in greater detail.

LAFTA/ALADI

LAFTA and the CACM were the two economic integration efforts that derived directly from ECLA's vision of wider regional markets to support import-substitution industrialization. The 1960 Montevideo Treaty established the LAFTA organization, with a membership of Argentina, Brazil, Chile, Colombia, Ecuador, Mexico, Paraguay, Peru, Uruguay, and Venezuela. The original plan (see Milenky, 1973) was to achieve a free trade area by 1973 through periodic negotiated tariff reductions, but by the time of the 1967 meeting of heads of state it was clear that this deadline was not going to be met. Attempting to speed integration, LAFTA in 1967 authorized the formation of "subregions." The La Plata Basin Group and ANCOM both soon emerged under this provision, and especially ANCOM proved considerably more successful than its parent. It was then decided to aim for an all-Latin America common market by 1980.

This deadline, too, was not met. In fact, after twenty years, member-country imports from within the zone in 1980 accounted for a mere 12 percent of their total imports (up only .8 percent from the 11.2 percent level in 1970) (LAWR, September 24, 1982:10). About all that could be said was that there was an interesting diversification in the structure of regional trade, reflecting the increased industrialization of Latin America and a greater stress in Brazil and Mexico (and to a lesser extent, in several other countries) on industrialization for export rather than import-substitution alone. In 1961 raw materials represented 65 percent of intra-LAFTA trade; manufactures, 19 percent, and semi-manufactures, 16 percent. By 1980 raw materials had dropped to 43 percent; manufactures had increased to 30 percent, and semi-manufactures, to 27 percent (LAWR, September 24, 1982:10).

A sore issue over the years was one that has usually plagued integration experiments, the matter of an unequal sharing of benefits. Most actual and potential benefits plainly accrued to Argentina, Brazil, and Mexico, which in the 1970s together accounted for about 70 percent of Latin America's exports of manufactured and semi-manufactured goods. In 1979 these three countries were responsible for 56 percent of exports and 52.3 percent of imports within the LAFTA zone (Inter-American Development Bank, 1981:106). Nevertheless, from the outset none of the three giants evidenced much enthusiasm for

LAFTA because of their growing extra-regional trade and large home markets. Critics of LAFTA were also quick to point out that foreign multi-nationals were in the best position of all to profit from wider markets.

In 1980 LAFTA members decided to conclude a new Treaty of Monte-video that replaced the old organization with ALADI. The hallmark of ALADI was to be greater flexibility, including recognition of three levels of economic development among member countries and the potential for three different types of agreements. ALADI came into official existence only with the full ratification of the treaty in March 1981, so it is too early to assess its effectiveness.

The first type of agreement envisaged is a regional tariff preference that would initially be nominal and become more substantial over time. The preference would vary with different economic sectors, and member countries would be allowed to exclude a certain number of products. The most devel-oped countries (Argentina, Brazil, Mexico) would be allowed the fewest number of exceptions; intermediate countries (Chile, Colombia, Peru, Uru-guay), more exceptions; and the least developed (Bolivia, Ecuador, Paraguay), the most exceptions.

A second projected category is regional agreements, the most important of which thus far are two financial accords "inherited" (the so-called patri-mônio histórico) from LAFTA. The 1965 Accord on Reciprocal Payments and Credits, signed by the central banks of all member countries and the Domin-ican Republic, provides for reciprocal credit lines opened on a one-to-one basis between banks to finance trade flows. Other Latin American countries have been invited to join the accord, and some $U.S. 2.5 billion was trans-ferred in 1981. The other major agreement is a Multilateral Accord for the Attenuation of Transitory Deficiencies in Liquidity, signed in 1969, which created a common fund (now $U.S. 700 million) to help member countries overcome short-term difficulties in settling multilateral accounts.

A third ALADI category is partial agreements, starting with the rene-gotiation of the tariff reduction agreements reached during the two decades of LAFTA. All agreements between pairs or among groups of countries must be open to eventual multilateralization (through negotiation) and, meanwhile, are automatically open to the least-developed members on a most-favored-nation basis.

CACM

The other integration scheme directly fostered by ECLA was the CACM, which began to evolve with a series of agreements in the late 1950s and was officially inaugurated in 1960. Prior to 1960 there was considerable debate as to what the basic thrust of Central American integration should be, whether free trade or creating a regime of integration industries. ECLA, Costa Rica, Honduras, and Nicaragua favored the latter approach; while the most industrialized prospective members, Guatemala and El Salvador, with the backing of the United States, were dubious about the idea of creating subregional monopolies. This issue was resolved in 1960 when Guatemala, El Salvador, and Honduras created a tripartite free-trade arrangement among themselves, and Costa Rica and Nicaragua had little option but to follow suit. All five countries that same year subscribed to a General Treaty on Economic Integration, as well as to the creation of a Central American Bank for Economic Integration (CABEI). (On the CACM generally, see also

Karnes, 1976; Shaw, 1979; Kline and Delgado, 1978; Nugent, 1974; Schmitter, 1972; Cohen Orantes, 1972; and Cochrane, 1969.)

The General Treaty immediately freed most intra-regional trade, which soared from $U.S. 21.7 million in 1960 to $260 million in 1968, or from 6.4 percent to 17.2 percent of CACM member countries' imports respectively (Cohen Orantes, 1972:43). Currently, about one-fifth of all CACM exports stay in the zone, making the CACM the most inwardly focused trading unit in Latin America. In addition, member countries rapidly moved to create a wide-ranging common external tariff, which by 1966 embraced all but some 16 percent of total imports (main exclusions: wheat, petroleum, and assembly products) (Cohen Orantes, 1972:45).

With the CACM initially a tremendous success, new industries began to arise to take advantage of broader markets and member states also undertook joint road and communication projects. However, by the mid-1960s a number of serious problems started to surface. The lack of regional industrial planning engendered frantic competition for foreign investment and offered no guidance for the allocation of CABEI funds among member states; naturally, investment gravitated to the countries that were already more industrialized. Honduras and Nicaragua complained that they were not receiving their proper shares of CACM benefits. Honduras got some special concessions in 1967, and Nicaragua, in protest, temporarily reimposed tariffs against the other CACM members early in 1968. A second complaint, heard in nationalist political circles, was that, without a CACM code on the treatment of foreign investment, primary benefits were going--not even to the more industrialized members--but to foreign multinationals which were setting up a host of "finishing touch" industries in the subregion. Another difficulty, as Cohen Orantes has pointed out, was the sheer fragility of regional institutions, which forced CACM técnicos to be preoccupied with their own survival rather than acting as "supranational agents devoted to upgrading the common interest" (Cohen Orantes, 1972:85). Also, the fact that Central American governments often failed to fulfill their financial pledges meant that the CACM was all the more dependent upon aid from Washington.

In any event, the CACM virtually collapsed as a result of the disastrous 1969 war between El Salvador and Honduras. Late the next year Honduras withdrew from the CACM, negotiating bilateral agreements with the other governments (except El Salvador) to preserve some of the gains in intra-zonal trade. After a thirteen-year hiatus, trade has recently revived between El Salvador and Honduras.

Further hampering any revival of the CACM, of course, has been the political turmoil that swept the subregion, beginning with the fall of Somoza in 1978-1979. Guerrilla activities have disrupted normal communications and the growing of traditional agricultural exports in the countryside. Political differences foredoomed the Comunidad Democratica Centramericana (CDC) that was launched by El Salvador, Honduras, and Costa Rica in January 1982 to help pressure the Nicaraguan Sandinista regime toward greater pluralism (and away from the Eastern bloc). Guatemala was "prematurely" admitted to the CDC in July 1982, and the subsequent growing repression under the Rios Montt government deprived the group of what little legitimacy it had. The CDC's ties to Reagan administration policies were also something of an embarrassment, and in October 1982 it was effectively abandoned when representatives of nine countries met in San Jose upon a Costa Rican initiative to create a "forum for peace and democracy" (other participants were from the United States, Honduras, El Salvador, Colombia, Jamaica, Belize, the Dominican Republic, and Panama). This "forum" was itself upstaged after January 1983 by the peace initiatives of the Contadora Group (Colombia, Mexico, Panama, and Venezuela).

Interestingly enough, however, even as their governments were at political odds, the economy ministers and central bank presidents of the five Central American countries have continued to meet periodically to seek ways of increasing economic cooperation in the face of the severe recession and balance-of-payments difficulties confronting them all. Panama has on more than one occasion been invited to join the CACM, but to date has not indicated any real desire to do so. When the IDB and the Commission of the European Community jointly sponsored a meeting in Brussels in September 1983 to discuss Central America's need for additional development assistance from Europe, Panama almost did not attend and then came only as a member of the Contadora Group. At the meeting, a leadership role was assumed by none other than the delegation from Nicaragua, clearly illustrating at least the limited autonomy of economic and political issue-areas. While Honduras was providing contras a staging base for raids against the Sandinista regime, its delegation to the European conference was among those content to defer to Nicaraguan lobbying efforts (LAWR, September 30, 1983:9-10).

As the foregoing suggests, significant intervening variables in the Central American situation have been the impact of external powers and economic groupings. The current spotlight is upon the United States, Cuba, the Soviet Union, the EEC, and the Contadora Group. However, for over a decade Mexico and Venezuela have also engaged in a "friendly" rivalry for influence in Central America. Venezuela early-on bought CABEI bonds, and both countries have included Central America (with the Caribbean) in joint arrangements for concessionary oil sales. ANCOM governments (plus Panama, now an associate member of ANCOM) were leading moral and material supporters of the rebels in Nicaragua, and after Somoza's fall expressed their strong desire for democratic institutions in Nicaragua, El Salvador, Guatemala, and Honduras.

CECLA

CECLA was established on an informal basis to develop common positions among Latin American ministerial representatives on issues of international economic policy that were expected to arise at the first UNCTAD conference in 1964. Common positions were largely achieved and had considerable impact at UNCTAD. CECLA continued to meet sporadically and in 1969, its most important hour, presented the United States with a detailed list of Latin American demands (the Consensus of Vina del Mar). In 1971 CECLA roundly condemned the Nixon administration's temporary surcharge of 10 percent on all imports to the U.S.

The creation of CECLA was an exceedingly important milestone, not only because it excluded the United States but also because it represented an early attempt by countries of the developing world to present a common front in economic negotiations with the developed countries. However, the organization never established a permanent secretariat or headquarters, and it began to fade in the early 1970s. Chile (the Eduardo Frei and Allende administrations) and Peru (under Velasco) had been among CECLA's strongest supporters, and shifts to more conservative regimes in those two countries had a definite dampening effect. Nevertheless, some Latin American ministers did continue to gather on an ad hoc basis to prepare jointly for meetings of UNCTAD, the Group of 77, the Nonaligned, and the UN Law of the Sea Conference. CECLA also provided a precedent for the establishment of SELA in 1973.

OPANAL

The product of a Mexican initiative, the Treaty of Tlatelolco (the Treaty for the Prohibition of Nuclear Weapons in Latin America) was signed in 1967 and is now in full force for twenty-two Latin American countries. Parties to the treaty pledge not to develop, test, or import nuclear weapons. They are obliged to establish safeguards in conjunction with the International Atomic Energy Agency for nuclear development and are subject to "challenge inspections" by an organ of the Agency for the Prohibition of Nuclear Weapons in Latin America. Additional Protocol I pledges countries with territorial possessions in the Americas not to introduce nuclear weapons therein and has been ratified by all the relevant parties except France and the United States. The United States has thus far demurred because of its military bases in Puerto Rico, Guantanamo, and the Canal Zone and the fear of some key U.S. Senators that transit rights for nuclear weapons there or elsewhere in the region might be prejudiced (Redick, 1981:108). (The issue has been raised as to whether the United Kingdom violated its commitment during the Falklands/ Malvinas War.) Protocol II pledges countries which already possess nuclear weapons not to use or threaten to use them against parties to the treaty; and the United States, the Soviet Union, France, the United Kingdom, and China have all ratified.

Four leading Latin American countries (Argentina, Brazil, Chile, and Cuba) have neither ratified the world Nuclear Nonproliferation Treaty nor are as yet full parties to Tlatelolco. Brazil and Chile have ratified Tlatelolco but have elected to exercise a treaty option whereby it will not come into force for them until all relevant parties have ratified both the treaties and the protocols. Argentina has signed and announced its intention to ratify. Cuba is still entirely outside of the agreement, although a prominent student of the treaty, John R. Redick, believes the outlook for eventual Cuban ratification is good (Redick, 1981:109).

There is also a serious gap in the treaty in that it does not unambiguously forbid "peaceful nuclear explosions" (PNEs). Nevertheless, as Redick points out: "The Tlatelolco Treaty includes a method for managing and minimizing the political impact of an Argentine or Brazilian PNE. Article 18 restricts the means and methods whereby PNEs can be detonated in Latin America, establishing procedures which are public and calling for a distinct international presence at any such explosion by OPANAL and the IAEA" (Redick, 1981:133n).

Chile, Colombia, Cuba, Mexico, Peru, Uruguay, and Venezuela have nuclear programs in various stages of development, and there is an obvious potential linkage between nuclear energy development and weaponry. Moreover, there appears to be a growing interest among those countries in Latin America developing nuclear energy in incorporating the full fuel cycle, including enrichment, reprocessing facilities, and breeder reactors (see Luddemann, 1983). The Carter administration's main objection to West Germany's 1975 agreement with Brazil was that it involved enrichment and reprocessing without, in Washington's view, adequate safeguards that nuclear development would not ultimately be used for military purposes (see Gall, 1976; and Wonder, 1977). In late 1983, one of the first acts of the newly elected Alfonsín government was to announce that Argentina had finally developed its own enrichment technology.

In addition, as Redick suggests, there is a definite trend toward the horizontal transfer of nuclear technology, not only between developed and developing countries but also between one developing country and others. Within Latin America, Argentina "fully intends to become a regional supplier of heavy water, research (test) reactors, and other nuclear material" (Redick, 1981:127). Initial agreements between Argentina and Peru (1977 and 1979), to supply a reactor for experimentation and the production of radio-isotopes (plus auxiliary facilities), were fully covered by IAEA safeguards. Almost startling, because Argentina and Brazil have traditionally been bitter rivals, has been the "nuclear convergence" of these two countries since the signing of a pact on this subject in 1980. Brazil recognizes that its own nuclear program is exceedingly expensive and falling behind schedule, while Argentina would like to draw on Brazil's experience in exploring for uranium. Redick believes that Argentine-Brazilian bilateral cooperation will actually be of net benefit to the cause of nonproliferation, defusing dangerous competition and possibly leading to the construction of joint nuclear facilities in "buffer" countries like Paraguay or Uruguay. On the other hand, it could "lay the foundations for joint development and utilization of PNEs" (Redick, 1981: 32-33). Meanwhile, Brazil has also evidenced interest in possible nuclear cooperation with Venezuela and Chile.

CARIFTA/CARICOM

The Caribbean Free Trade Association was formed in 1968 and in 1973 was converted into a common market, the Caribbean Community. Members now include Antigua/Barbuda, the Bahamas, Barbados, Belize, Dominica, Grenada, Guyana, Jamaica, Montserrat, St. Christopher/Nevis, St. Lucia, St. Vincent, and Trinidad and Tobago. (General sources include Payne, 1981; Axline, 1979, 1977; Chernick, 1978; Millett and Will, 1979; and Paragg, 1980.) In July 1981 seven of the smaller islands--Antigua/Barbuda, Dominica, Grenada, St. Christopher/Nevis, St. Lucia, St. Vincent, and Montserrat-- formed their own Organization of Eastern Caribbean States with CARICOM to pool resources and services, as well as (on an optional basis) foreign affairs and defense arrangements. As it happened, the OECS soon was most noteworthy for its role, along with Jamaica and the Bahamas, in providing a fig-leaf for the U.S. armed invasion of Grenada in October 1983.

One of the more interesting aspects of CARICOM at the outset was its projected use of the public international corporation, involving the joint participation of two or more states in specific projects. Planned were a regional food corporation with subsidiaries engaged in marketing, processing, and production; and several joint aluminum smelters. However, these projects failed to materialize, and intra-zonal imports peaked at a range of 8-11 percent.

CARICOM stalled in the mid-1970s for a variety of reasons. The avowedly socialist, pro-Cuban course of Jamaica (under Manley), Guyana, and Grenada (later under Bishop) was a source of political tensions. Even more serious were the effects of the 1973-1974 drastic increase in oil prices and subsequent world recession. Oil-rich Trinidad and Tobago was the object of considerable resentment, and Jamaica and Guyana--as well as most of the smaller countries--suffered such severe balance-of-payments difficulties that they were forced drastically to curtail imports from the rest of CARICOM. Trinidad and Tobago responded to criticism and increased protectionism, as well as its own dislike of Jamaica's and other CARICOM countries' receptivity to increasing Venezuelan investment and influence in the subregion, by effectively boycotting CARICOM and erecting its own new controls on imports. The situation was further complicated by grave agricultural shortages throughout the subregion and by the fact that CARICOM's common external tariff made inadequate allowance for the different import requirements of divergent economies: e.g., tourism (Barbados), industry (Trinidad and Tobago), and agriculture (Guyana).

On the positive side, a Caribbean Group for Cooperation in Economic Development was formed in late 1977 under the World Bank, bringing together about thirty donors, Caribbean countries, and international financial institutions to mobilize and rationalize aid to the area. During the Carter administration, World Bank, IDB, and U.S. bilateral aid increased dramatically. The IDB also modified its regulations to allow it to lend to CARICOM's Caribbean Development Bank (CARIBANK), which could then extend credits to CARICOM members that were not IDB members. Moreover, in response to perceived Central American security threats and changes in governments in Jamaica (Seaga) and Grenada (from Gairy to Bishop), the Reagan administration produced a new Caribbean Basin Initiative. Reluctantly passed by Congress in stages through 1983, the CBI concept is aid primarily to private enterprise and increased incentives for trade.

CARICOM was again in the spotlight in 1982-1983. At the first summit meeting in seven years (November 1982, Ocho Rios, Jamaica), Barbados-- supported by Seaga's Jamaica and obviously aiming at Bishop's Grenada (and possibly Guyana)--attempted unsuccessfully to have the Community's treaty amended to allow as members only those governments giving adequate respect to the principles of democratic rule and human rights. In May 1983 Jamaica finally agreed to abandon a two-tier exchange system that had almost frozen trade among Jamaica, Barbados, Trinidad and Tobago, and the balance of CARICOM. The following July, a second summit (Port of Spain, Trinidad) admitted the Bahamas to membership but--because of Grenada's opposition-- withheld approval of an application from the Dominican Republic that had been put forward by Jamaica. The organization also declined to consider a long-standing (since 1971) application from Haiti, fearing that that country's government and ailing economy would be more of a liability than an asset to the system. Suriname, which earlier (like Haiti) had been granted observer status, was pointedly overlooked for membership because of the excesses of the Bouterse regime. Seaga's intention of raising the issue of possible Puerto Rican membership also went unfulfilled, at Governor Carlos Romero Barcelo's urging, whose judgment was that such an application would have to be initiated and approved by the United States. Otherwise, the 1983 summit went on record opposing the current exclusion of Grenada and Guyana from the CBI; supported the Contadora Group's Central American peace moves; deplored Guatemala's continued claim to Belizean territory; called for a negotiated settlement of the Essequibo boundary dispute between Guyana and Venezuela; moved to have Trinidad and Tobago's financially troubled British West Indian Airlines designated the regional air carrier; agreed to reactivate CARICOM's multilateral clearing facility which had been temporarily closed because of Guyana's mounting debts; looked to the creation of a regional energy program, made all the more urgent because of uncertainty as to whether concessionary terms for oil supplies from Venezuela and Mexico would be renewed; and requested the United States to lift restrictions on steel imports from Trinidad and Tobago.

So matters stood when the invasion of Grenada occurred. This crisis initially worsened relations among CARICOM members, as Trinidad and Tobago and Guyana were highly critical of the invasion. However, as the months passed, Washington appeared to be viewing Trinidad and Tobago's independence on this issue as being somewhat useful; indeed, there was speculation that Trinidad and Tobago might lend its political backing to a reconstituted regime in Grenada and might even go so far as to contribute military or police forces to help keep the peace after the initial occupation forces retired. Moreover, the fall of the leftist regime in Grenada at least temporarily diminished the ideological split with the CARICOM organization as a whole.

ANCOM

The idea of an Andean market originated with a 1965 report of several Latin American economists that was commissioned by President Frei of Chile. This was later endorsed by President Belaúnde of Peru, then by a subregional summit, and finally by the 1967 Punta del Este meeting of heads of state. The Cartegena Agreement that created ANCOM and an agreement establishing a companion subregional development bank, the Corporación Andina de Fomento (CAF) were signed and went into effect in 1969. Founding member states were Colombia, Ecuador, Peru, Bolivia, and Chile; Venezuela joined in 1973, and Chile withdrew in 1976. When it was founded, ANCOM was clearly the most ambitious and therefore intriguing Latin American regional integration scheme, and it remains so today despite major setbacks. (See Ferris, 1978, 1981; Hojman, 1981; Ffrench-Davis, 1978; Garcia-Amador, 1978; Fontaine, 1977; and Morawetz, 1974.)

ANCOM was originally designed to have two central institutions (apart from the related but autonomous CAF): a Commission composed of diplomatic representatives from each government and a three-person Junta or technocratic secretariat. In practice, the Junta and its small staff (somewhat analogous to the EEC's Commission) have become the principal initiators of proposals and administrators of Commission "Decisions." At critical junctures there have also been meetings of Andean foreign and economic ministers. In late 1979 ANCOM made the Council of Ministers an official organ and expressed an intention eventually to create yet another mechanism, an Andean Parliament. In 1980 an Andean Court of Justice was also established, with the task of helping to interpret and enforce the organization's complex rules. Over time the CAF has increased its capitalization and engaged in active lending in the subregion, although to date not mainly to strictly subregional infrastructure projects or sectoral industrial programs--because not all that much has as yet been produced in the way of infrastructure or sectoral plans.

ANCOM's claim to fame has never rested primarily on its trade measures. Its one genuine innovation in this regard was a rapid and almost complete elimination of non-tariff barriers to intra-zonal trade. Otherwise, only one quarter of the goods in intra-zonal trade (mostly food and raw materials) were subject to automatic tariff reductions, to a scheduled tariff demise on those items by 1980. It is those items that account for most of what little growth in intra-zonal trade has occurred, to a level of about 5 percent of the ANCOM total (that proportion holding steady since the early 1970s). A second trade list was made up of goods originally entitled to protection until 1985 (1990 for the two less-developed member countries, Bolivia and Ecuador); these are certain "national exceptions" granted to each country, ranging from 250 items for Colombia to 600 for Ecuador. This schedule was subsequently revised to finish in 1982 and 1987, respectively. Venezuela stayed out of ANCOM for several years because of its private sector's fears, expressed by the powerful national interest group, FEDECAMARAS, that trade liberalization would have a disastrous impact on infant industries. On the other hand, possessing a relatively competitive industry, Colombia did not take advantage of all the exceptions to which it was entitled and has remained a supporter of liberalization. Yet a third ANCOM list of goods included some 300 items to be involved in projected sectoral programs of industrial development, which will be discussed shortly.

In addition to lowering tariff and non-tariff barriers to some intra-zonal trade, ANCOM has been making only slow progress converting a minimum common external tariff into a full-fledged common external tariff. Currently, the common tariff covers just automobile components, petro-chemicals, and engineering products; and a commitment to extend it to all major product imports by 1981 was not met. A perennial problem has been the desire of Venezuela for more protection than especially Colombia, Bolivia, and Chile (before its withdrawal) have wanted to provide. Another problem has been the matter of member countries' integration into GATT. Colombia, for example, may have to raise its tariffs to conform to any new ANCOM common level, and this could complicate Colombia's position in GATT.

The most controversial aspect of ANCOM was Decision 24 of the Commission which established a common policy on foreign investment (in addition to works previously mentioned, see Cherol and Nuñez de Arco, 1983; Mytelka, 1979; and Moxon, 1977). The goal was to avoid the perceived error by LAFTA and the CACM of having foreign multinationals gain inordinately from a lowering of tariff barriers. Accordingly, certain economic sectors (e.g., banking, communications, insurance) were reserved for national and/or ANCOM development, with foreign enterprises already operating in those sectors given three years to give up 80 percent of their holdings. All new and existing foreign enterprises in the remaining non-reserved sectors were to "fade out" to majority local (state and/or private) ownership and management within a fifteen-year period. Complying foreign companies were not only to be assured stable rules of the game but also tariff-free access to the ANCOM market. Moreover, Decision 24 limited profit remittances of foreign firms to 14 percent of the capital originally invested. A major exception to all of these provisions was the extractive industries, which nevertheless experienced several subsequent takeovers in Chile (copper) and Venezuela (oil).

Decision 24 proved to be too confining for the new military government of Chile, which was anxious to re-attract foreign investment after the turmoil of the Allende years. Following attempts to adjust its national code in order to conform, Chile eventually insisted that Decision 24 should be completely abandoned. The other ANCOM members could not go that far, and Chile finally officially withdrew from the organization in 1976. Nevertheless, the remaining members did subsequently liberalize ANCOM policy, including an increase in the allowable profit remittance from 14-20 percent and an extension of three years in the fade-out period. Decision 24 was also waived for companies engaged in tourism and for those exporting 80 percent of production to third countries. Peru and Venezuela have been most restrictive in their attitudes toward foreign investment, both in their positions in ANCOM debates and in their own national codes. While Bolivia and Ecuador have technically complied with Decision 24, they have quietly subverted it, for example, by exempting foreign firms that do not expect to sell goods beyond the domestic market. Colombia has occupied a middle position on the foreign investment issue.

Has foreign investment in the ANCOM countries been unduly discouraged by Decision 24? It is difficult to know because there have been so many factors in the overall picture: Allende in Chile, Venezuela's oil nationalization, a worldwide recession, political instability in several countries, the broad ANCOM exception for extractive industries, chronic balance-of-payments crises, negotiations over debts, and the inherent appeal of extra-ANCOM giants Brazil and Mexico. Whatever the effect of ANCOM restrictions, in the 1970s Brazil and Mexico together accounted for 80 percent of the total net flow of direct foreign investment received by Latin America.

Another important ANCOM innovation was its plan to conclude a series of sectoral industrial development agreements, allocating new plants and production lines for specific products among the member countries. Decision 46 (later modified by Decision 169) also provided for the creation of ANCOM multinationals, which would have majority investment from one or more member states (perhaps some minority foreign investment as well) and enjoy special terms of access to the common market. The Junta in 1972 drafted a general plan for industrial development within the subregion. To date agreements have been concluded covering metal products (1972), petrochemicals (1975), and automobile (1977) industries. Because negotiations over the basic outline and implementation especially of the automobile agreement were so protracted, Commission consideration of additional proposed programs has fallen far behind expectations. Supposedly still on the agenda for the future are fertilizers, electronics and telecommunications, steel, pharmaceuticals, ship-building, glass, pulp and paper, and food processing. Of these, steel and pharmaceuticals have thus far received the most attention. Meanwhile, the existing metal products and automobile agreements have not been fully implemented and there is a consensus that the petrochemicals pact needs substantial adjustment.

Now that Chile has withdrawn, Bolivia is the most troublesome member of ANCOM from an economic standpoint (not to mention politics). In 1977 Bolivia protested officially, with some justification, that it was getting less out of ANCOM than the other four members. Because of the country's limited industrialization, tariff cuts are of little direct benefit, and Bolivia's claim was that it was neither receiving sufficient assignments under sectoral programs nor were the exclusive assignments which had been received being honored by all of the other members. ANCOM's response was a special aid program to Bolivia to promote existing industries and to explore new opportunities for the country in the sectoral programs. Subsequent political upheavals in Bolivia have so paralyzed its economy that these efforts have been of little avail. Recently, the Bolivian position has been that ANCOM should de-emphasize previous sectoral programs and, instead, foster a regional drive for self-sufficiency in food production.

Two interesting new trends characterized ANCOM's evolution in the late 1970s. The first was more overt "politicization" of the organization, of which the institutionalization of the Council of Ministers and plans for an Andean Parliament were concrete signs. Fellow ANCOM members also sided unequivocally with Bolivia in its dispute with Chile over an outlet to the sea. However, perhaps more significant was the fact that politicization took a generally pro-democracy, reformist direction.

Domestic political change was no stranger to the organization, including, in its formative stage, the rise and fall of Allende and the moderating of the radical-nationalist military "revolution" in Peru. Nevertheless, the accession to power of the civilian Jaime Roldos administration in Ecuador and the scheduled return to civilian rule of Bolivia and Peru had a different impact. Venezuela, traditional international campaigner for democracy-- together with a then slightly sheepish Colombia (whose democratic reputation had been tarnished by guerrilla violence and repeated government "states of siege"), Ecuador, and elements in Peru and Bolivia--joined in an active diplomatic effort to support constitutional government both within and without the subregion. This largely complemented, but occasionally clashed with, Carter administration policies. ANCOM countries gave their strong endorsement and some material aid to anti-Somoza forces and, along with Mexico, were instrumental in defeating Washington's proposal in the OAS to send an inter-American peace force to dampen conflict and assure a moderate political outcome in Nicaragua. In August 1979 the presidents of Ecuador, Colombia, Venezuela, and Costa Rica and the foreign ministers of Bolivia and Peru gathered in Quito to help celebrate Roldos' inauguration and there issued a "Quito Declaration," which stated that "only genuinely representative institutions can be an adequate instrument to guarantee the expression of liberty, respect for human rights and the satisfaction of people's real needs." The Andean countries were also in the coalition that assured the passage of several democracy and human rights resolutions at the 1979 OAS General Assembly in La Paz. They subsequently condemned the overthrow of the civilian government of Walter Guevera by a dissident military faction and later applauded the installation of yet another interim civilian regime.

A second and somewhat related trend in ANCOM has been the broadening and intensification of external relationships. Mexico made early overtures to ANCOM, including the extension of a $5 million credit to the CAF, but has neither asked nor been asked to join. Argentina did ask to become a member, but Colombia and Venezuela were adamantly opposed, on grounds of the difficulties involved in integrating Argentina's industrial economy and then-repressive military regime into the ANCOM mold. However, ANCOM's horizons did expand markedly in late 1979 and early 1980 with the addition of Panama as an associate member (in late 1983 the Panamanian government announced its intention to actively explore the possibility of becoming a full member) and an extension beyond the 1978 Amazon Pact (see below) of more cooperative links with Brazil.

Much of the initiative in the latter regard came from Brazil, a reversal in policy that requires some explanation. Brazil long held itself at arm's length from regional integration schemes. It joined organizations like LAFTA and SELA for whatever benefits might accrue, although it was never enthusiastic. Brazil, after all, was enjoying an "economic miracle"; its huge domestic market was booming; industrial exports were expanding; and there was every reason to expect that phenomenal economic growth would fulfill the country's ambition to achieve international "great power" status. Then the Arab oil boycott occurred and rising oil prices administered an "OPEC shock" to Brazil, which imported no less than 85 percent of its oil. Moreover, an energy crisis-induced recession spread around the world, demand slumped, protectionist barriers were to some extent re-erected in Europe and the United States, and Brazil's export drive began to flag. In 1979 the country began to experience a grave balance-of-payments problem. That same year inflation climbed to circa 75 percent and GDP stood at 6 percent, only half of the "miracle" rate. Brazil desperately needed to secure both dependable sources of energy and expanded markets for exports.

In the mid-1970s Brazil pragmatically began to shift its foreign policy to stances more consistent with Third World positions and actively started to woo Arabs and Africans. For example, Brazil startled some observers by its early recognition of the Soviet-and Cuban-backed Popular Movement for the Liberation of Angola (MPLA). In the late 1970s and into the 1980s, that same pragmatism dictated a renewed interest in Latin America. Brazil sought to calm fears of its expansionism experienced by neighboring countries; encourage the orderly exploration and exploitation of Amazon resources; advance stalled hydroelectric projects in the La Plata Basin; promote nuclear cooperation instead of rivalry; assure access to oil in Mexico and Venezuela; and find additional markets in Mexico, Colombia, Venezuela, and Latin America generally.

ANCOM's more moderate course on issues of foreign investment after Chile's withdrawal made ANCOM more attractive to Brazil, while Brazil's growing economic difficulties ironically made ANCOM more willing to extend to Brazil an "opening." Not only did Brazil seem less of a security threat, but also the end of the miracle contributed to a cautious liberalization in Brazilian domestic politics, which in turn made the country less of an international pariah. President Joao Baptista Figueiredo's policy of abertura made a distinct contribution to improved relations with ANCOM and other countries with political sensitivities like Mexico.

Closer ties with ANCOM were discussed when Peru's President Francisco Morales Bermudez, as the organization's representative, visited Brazil in October 1979. The ANCOM countries were apparently pleased by Brazil's "good neighbor" policy and its earlier suspension of relations with Somoza. President Figueiredo paid his first state visit, and the first ever to Venezuela by a Brazilian head of state, to Caracas in November 1979. The ANCOM Junta visited Brasilia that same month. In January 1980 a special meeting was arranged in Lima between the ANCOM Council of Ministers and the Brazilian foreign minister. Brazil was reportedly interested in such matters as the possible trade of ANCOM oil, minerals, and automobile parts for Brazilian manufactures. All the foreign ministers pledged to consult on a regular basis.

The two new trends in ANCOM that emerged in the late 1970s were definitely noteworthy. However, neither proved to be of monumental consequence as the domestic economic and political problems in member countries worsened dramatically in the 1980s. The emphasis, perhaps of necessity, shifted from exploring new international horizons to simple survival, with each country concentrating on meeting day-to-day challenges to political order and staving off a collapse of current accounts. The pro-democracy thrust of ANCOM at present finds its only echo in Colombia and Venezuela's (and Panama's) involvement in the Contadora Group. Moreover, Brazilian exports to every ANCOM country except Peru, where there was a large purchase of Brazilian buses, have been lagging badly.

LA PLATA BASIN

In 1969, the same year that ANCOM was established, another treaty formed Argentina, Bolivia, Brazil, Paraguay, and Uruguay into a La Plata Basin Group for the purpose of developing subregional hydroelectric power and water resources. Most of the subsequent negotiations involved Argentina, Brazil, and Paraguay. The Basin was to act in cooperation with a consortium of international organizations chaired by the IDB. However, cooperation gave way to mutual recriminations beginning in 1973, when Argentina raised serious objections to a Brazil-Paraguay agreement to construct the Itaipu Dam on the upper Parana River (the world's largest hydroelectric project). Argentina insisted that the project threatened an inadequate flow of water downstream for an Argentina-Paraguay dam at Corpus. Argentina and Paraguay were also deadlocked over relatively minor details in another project at Yacyreta.

Such was the situation until Brazil became convinced of the need to resolve outstanding disputes with its neighbors and to secure energy wherever it might be had. In late 1979 Brazil pressured Paraguayan dictator Alfredo Stroessner into moving ahead with the Yacyreta project and, as a gesture of Brazil's desire to revive tripartite talks, offered to reduce the number of turbines at Itaipu to a less-controversial eighteen (from twenty). These steps proved sufficient to reactivate negotiations, which resulted in the signature on October 19, 1979, of agreements to assure the essential compatability of all the Alto Parana projects. The next month Argentina and Brazil began serious discussions aimed at the construction of a hydroelectric complex at Garabi on the Uruguay River between the two countries.

OLADE

A Latin American Energy Organization (OLADE) was proposed in 1972 by Venezuela, primarily as a means of marshalling regional support for OPEC. The following year the Arab oil boycott and attendant price increases occasioned a meeting of Latin American energy ministers, where it became apparent that there were strong differences of opinion as to exactly what kind of organization OLADE should be. Many ministers argued for an organization that would control prices and supplies and facilitate negotiations between the region's oil-exporting and oil-importing countries. Peru and Ecuador wanted to see an even broader organization that would control prices and supplies of raw materials generally. Venezuela, by this time having second thoughts, only proved willing to offer financial assistance for an energy development fund. Moreover, Cuba's presence at the meeting was irksome to military regimes, especially Chile and Brazil.

Consequently, although OLADE was officially launched and given a substantial budget and secretariat, it was actually almost stillborn. The organization became mainly a rather ineffective pressure group for Latin American oil importers, while most of the real attention centered on the bilateral arrangements for concessionary sales to the Caribbean and Central America worked out independently by Venezuela and Mexico. More recently, given the profound economic problems suffered even by the oil giants, there has been some speculation that this practice might not continue.

The collapse of OPEC price levels also took much of the momentum out of a proposal by Venezuelan President Herrera Campins for the formation of a tri-national (Venezuela, Mexico, and Argentina) oil company to be called

PETROLATIN. The idea was for PETROLATIN initially to undertake only small projects in the region and later to expand cooperation with other continental state oil firms. PEMEX's new chief, Mario Ramón Beteta, has expressed his doubts as to whether market conditions justify setting up the tripartite company, but Venezuelan oil minister Huberto Calderón Berti insisted that Mexican President Miguel de la Madrid had encouraged him to move ahead to draft a financial plan. What view the new Luscinchi team in Venezuela and the Alfonsín government in Argentina will have on the project remains to be seen.

CARTELS

The spectacular success of OPEC led to Latin American efforts to form other cartels. One for bananas failed completely. Others for coffee and sugar have been slightly more significant.

La Compania Café Suaves Centrales was founded in 1975 with the financial support of Venezuela and the cooperation of Mexico, Costa Rica, Ecuador, El Salvador, Guatemala, Honduras, Nicaragua, and Panama. This was a marketing agency through which it was hoped to help stabilize prices for mild coffees by controlling exports. A more-inclusive organization, the Bogota Group--accounting for about 55 percent of world production--was established in late 1978 by Brazil, Colombia, Costa Rica, El Salvador, Guatemala, Honduras, Mexico, and Venezuela. The Group insisted that it was not seeking to function as a cartel per se but merely wanted to stabilize prices, preferably through a more effective International Coffee Agreement. Observers credited the Group with only limited success, as coffee prices fell well below the planned minimum.

As for sugar, an organization of some twenty-one exporting countries in Latin America and the Caribbean (GEPLACEA) was created in 1976. Its aims have been to coordinate policies at meetings of the International Sugar Organization (ISO), to negotiate price arrangements with consuming countries, and to ban sales below the daily market price. In late 1979 GEPLACEA also served the role of a pressure group, its members vowing to fulfill their obligations under the recently negotiated ISO agreement when it appeared for a while that the U.S. Congress might not ratify the agreement.

As the international debt crisis has worsened in recent years, there has been some speculation that a "cartel" of another sort was about to be formed: a "debtors cartel" or "club" that would advance Latin American demands for refinancing and rescheduling existing loans or, in some cases, defend a moratorium on payments or even outright repudiation of debts. The threat appeared to have diminished somewhat after a series of regional conferences through early 1984, partly because creditors of necessity were being more flexible, partly because regional leaders like Brazil and Mexico were going to extraordinary lengths to meet their (adjusted) obligations, and partly because an economic revival seemed to be underway in the United States. Nevertheless, at this writing, so many debtor countries continue to teeter on the brink of financial disaster that some defaults may yet occur, with possible severe consequences for creditor banks and even the international economy of the West generally.

SELA

By the mid-1970s the time seemed ripe for the establishment of a new institutional mechanism for regional consultation and action. For reasons previously mentioned, CECLA was no longer adequate. Although there was no strong support for the notion of abandoning the OAS, it was clear from such indications as the punitive exclusion of cartel members from benefits under the 1975 Trade Act and Washington's determined opposition to incorporating any principle of "collective economic security" into planned revisions of the OAS Charter that Kissinger's post-energy crisis interest in a "new dialogue" was not going to revive the old special relationship. Opportunities for cooperation with the Third World also appeared to be increasing. This, then, was the context out of which the Latin American Economic System (SELA) emerged. (See Bond, 1978b; Martz, 1979; Javier Alejo and Hurtado, 1976.)

The concept of SELA was initially advanced by President Luis Echeverria of Mexico in July 1974, and it attracted the almost immediate backing of President Carlos Andres Perez of Venezuela. The organization was established in August 1975 with a Council of Ministers and a Permanent Secretariat, and virtually all of the independent countries of the region--including the English-speaking Caribbean and Cuba--have joined. SELA's mission, couched in rather hazy terms, is essentially threefold: (1) to develop and advance common Latin American positions on issues of international economic relations; (2) to increase the production and supply of basic commodities, especially food; and (3) to promote the creation of Latin American multinational enterprises.

There is some background for the third function both in CARICOM and ANCOM and in the pre-SELA establishment of a major Caribbean shipping enterprise (NAMUCAR), a cooperative venture of Colombia, Venezuela, Costa Rica, Jamaica, Cuba, Nicaragua, Panama, and Mexico. SELA's initial contribution to the multinational category was an eleven-country fertilizer company (MULTIFER), and SELA action committees are continuing to examine the prospects for other Latin American multinationals in a variety of economic sectors. For example, the action committee on sea products has proposed a company to exploit the region's stocks of tuna fish and to protect them against overfishing by foreign fleets.

SELA may facilitate some useful joint enterprises and serve as a latter-day CECLA, as it did in August 1979 when member countries agreed to a united protest against U.S. plans to dispose of some strategic reserves of tin. The organization's experts have recently been preparing for a "renewed dialogue" with the European Economic Community, to combat increased protectionism in that quarter. Also, in January 1984 SELA co-sponsored with ECLA a major conference in Quito on the regional debt crisis. However, SELA is not likely to be of great importance in the near future, partly because current administrations in Mexico and Venezuela seem to be less enthusiastic about the organization than those which provided the impetus for its founding. Moreover, Argentina has never been a particularly keen supporter of SELA, and Brazil is hardly eager for too close cooperation with Cuba and other Marxist regimes.

AMAZON PACT

The first real manifestation of Brazil's good-neighbor policy was President Ernesto Geisel's initiation of an Amazon Pact. The pact was signed in

July 1978 by representatives of Bolivia, Brazil, Colombia, Ecuador, Guyana, Peru, Suriname, and Venezuela and is basically a mechanism for the loose coordination of the development by each sovereign unit of its own Amazon territory. An Amazon Cooperation Council meets annually and foreign ministers, bi-annually, to consider the implementation of various principles included in the accord. These principles concern such matters as free navigation of rivers, protection of flora and fauna, improvement of health conditions, and promotion of tourism and scientific research. (See Bond, 1978a; and Ferris, 1981.)

Most analysts interpreted Brazil's initiative as an attempt to reassure its uneasy neighbors that projects like the Trans-Amazon Highway were not intended to lay the groundwork for military adventures. Moreover, as Robert Bond has stressed, the agreement was additionally significant in that it signaled a warning in Brazil's relationship with Venezuela, which had been badly strained by Venezuela's resentment over Brazil's decision (in the early 1960s) to switch to lower-priced Middle Eastern oil, criticism of repression in Brazil, and abortive campaign (by President Rafael Caldera) to organize an alliance of Spanish-speaking countries to contain possible Brazilian imperialism (Bond, 1978a:635-650). However, in the last year or so, relations with Venezuela have again deteriorated because of Brazil's support of Guyanese development projects in the disputed Essequibo territory.

CONCLUSION

Looking backward over more than a decade of experience, one is struck by the fact that what the more sophisticated neo-functionalists have said about integration's not being a unilinear progression has been amply demonstrated in the Latin American setting. (For a review of much of the literature on integration, see Mansbach, Ferguson, and Lampert, 1976; see also especially Schmitter, 1977 and 1972.) There has been precious little in the way of (positive) "unintended consequences" or "spill-over" within the context of particular Latin American organizations. Indeed, the member states have been hard-pressed enough to fulfill effectively even the original intended consequences of cooperation, that is, the functions that individual organizations were expected to exercise. Substantial dis-integration (as in CACM), partial retreat (ANCOM on foreign investment), or encapsulation (LAFTA, unless one wishes to consider ALADI a redefinition thereof) have thus far been more common outcomes than major new advances within existing institutions.

However, a remarkable feature of the integration process in Latin America has been a form of "spill-around," an apparent impasse in one organization's leading to the creation of yet another institution. The integration ideal has often faltered, but never died--it has been reborn again and again in different guises. Twenty years of attempting both to avoid the mistakes of the past and to try new tasks have seen the establishment of a host of relatively functionally-specific institutions, lacking the comparatively unified direction and rational overall framework that has come to characterize the integration process in Europe. Perhaps this is not at all surprising, that subregional and/or issue-area (e.g., OPANAL, OLADE, Amazon Pact) integration has been more feasible than region-wide multifunctional organizations in any region as large and diverse as Latin America. Decentralization has thus been a necessity. It has also accorded with an often-observed Latin American tolerance for legal provisions and rhetoric that promise more than can be delivered and a regional "style" of problem-solving (identified years ago by Albert Hirschman) that emphasizes dramatic new departures rather than the hard task of making yesterday's policy or institution work more effectively (Hirschman, 1963:Chapter 4). Such an approach has at least fostered experimentation, and many of the Latin American institutions have consequently developed their own special strengths and ambitions: relatively high levels of intra-regional trade (for a time in the CACM), multinational enterprises (attempted in CARICOM and SELA and less directly in ANCOM), foreign investment policy and sectoral programs (ANCOM, with some attention to the latter in SELA), commodity price supports (Bogota Group), coordination of policies on general issues of international economic policy (CECLA and SELA), and so forth.

Generalizing about the effect of domestic political patterns and levels of economic development on integration is difficult from the Latin American record. Endemic terrorism, golpes, threats of civil and international wars, and grave ideological tensions--as in Central America today--are certainly not helpful. However, the fact that member countries are not of the same ideological persuasion--as they are not even now in CARICOM, were not even in the halcyon days of the CACM, and have not often been in ANCOM--has not proved to be an insuperable obstacle. It is instructive that ministers of economy and presidents of central banks in Central America have been able to continue at least a minimum level of cooperation while political tensions escalated to the point of armed conflict. Different levels of economic development tend to exacerbate the unequal sharing of benefits problem but can be compensated for if there is enough goodwill and imagination. On those rare occasions when member countries are on the same ideological track--as they were in the late 1970s in ANCOM--the stage would seem to be set for more overt "politicization," including efforts to export that ideology and joint diplomacy on "political" questions like Bolivia's outlet to the sea. Obviously, important domestic political or economic changes in a key country like Brazil are likely to have a greater impact on the prospects for integration than changes elsewhere. Even a shift in administrations, especially in countries that have been leaders in the integration process like Venezuela or Mexico, can have broad repercussions. Technocrats have made notable contributions to the design and day-to-day operation of organizations, but in the last analysis they have always depended on the support of presidents for most of the forward momentum.

A final variable that has been of extraordinary significance in Latin America has been the "external" one. Among the influential factors emanating from the external universe have been ECLA's initial inspiration, cautious support and occasional meddling from the Kennedy and Johnson administrations, the decline of the special relationship with the United States, the example of OPEC, general Third World activism, staggering increases in the price of oil, and protectionism in developed-country markets.

Looking toward the future of Latin American regional integration, one can only attempt to assess the likely impact of trends in the recent past and present: the Falklands/Malvinas War, world recession, the oil glut and its undermining of OPEC, the debt crisis, and ever-greater demands for protectionist measures in the developed countries. Some expected the Falklands episode to administer a final blow to the OAS and foster the birth of a pan-Latin substitute, but the inter-American organization once again appears to have weathered the storm--precisely because it does offer a useful forum for exerting pressure on the United States. The effects of the ongoing tumult in the international economy would seem to depend entirely upon whether recovery in the United States and the rest of the Western countries comes quickly enough to reinvigorate world trade, turn back the tide of protectionism, and alleviate developing-country balance-of-payments difficulties with an infusion of new capital. If current problems are prolonged, they will tend both to encourage and discourage Latin American integration. On the one hand, Latin American countries will have a strong incentive to compensate within the region for markets lost to protectionism abroad. On the other hand, as Brazil has discovered, regional countries in severe economic difficulties simply do not have the funds to be good customers. Furthermore, policy makers are so busy trying to head off imminent economic disaster that they have little time or energy to explore the full potential inherent in international cooperation.

About all that can be said with any degree of certainty is that we will continue to see a remarkable degree of Latin American consensus on many issues of international economic policy, a gradual growth in intra-regional trade, greater coordination of industry in certain economic sectors, and the creation of more Latin American multinationals. This outlook is far from the unified region that Bolivar envisioned, but it is sufficient to uphold Latin America's claim to being more advanced in terms of integration than any other area in the developing world.

4
U.S.–Latin American Relations from Carter to Reagan: Change or Continuity?

Paul E. Sigmund

The election of Ronald Reagan in November 1980 may not have actually led to victory parties in the capitals of the more conservative military regimes of Latin America, but it seemed clearly to indicate that there would be a significant change in U.S. policy toward that area. While Jimmy Carter's Latin American policy was not a central issue in the 1980 campaign, it appeared from statements by Reagan's advisers and from the conservative "think tanks" that prepared policy papers during the transition period, that there was likely to be a shift in Latin American policy as dramatic as the one that marked the early days of the Carter administration--in an exactly opposite direction. While the furtherance of human rights would not be completely abandoned as an objective of U.S. policy (Roger Fontaine, one of Reagan's Latin American advisers, had told a Chilean audience in September that "a concern for human rights did not begin with the Carter administration nor will it end with it"), it was to receive a much lower priority; and with friendly governments it was to be promoted through "quiet diplomacy" behind the scenes rather than through public denunciations and aid cutoffs.

A second shift that seemed likely to affect U.S.–Latin American relations was a renewed emphasis on the East-West conflict and a corresponding lessening of attention to so-called North-South questions such as development assistance and the demands for changes in the economic relations of developed and developing countries, summed up in the so-called New International Economic Order. The number one issue affecting contemporary international relations was considered to be the spread of Soviet expansionism, not the development needs of the Third World.

The shift on the part of a new Republican administration to a greater emphasis on "realism" in U.S.–Latin American relations, in contrast to the more idealistic programs of the Democrats, followed a long tradition. Franklin Roosevelt's Good Neighbor Policy and the development of the institutions of hemispheric collective security under the Truman administration had followed the "dollar diplomacy" and direct military interventions of earlier Republican administrations. John F. Kennedy's Alliance for Progress, even in its watered-down form under Lyndon Johnson, was abandoned by Richard Nixon in favor of a "low profile" in Latin America, and (with the exception of the Chilean covert interventions of 1970-1973 and a half-hearted attempt to develop a "New Dialogue" with Latin America in the mid-1970s) an almost total disregard of the area by Henry Kissinger during his tenure as Secretary of State under Presidents Nixon and Ford. Then in 1977 the Carter administration took up the banner of human rights, already being promoted as a result of congressional legislation, appointed an activist Assistant Secretary of State for Human Rights and Humanitarian Affairs, and used cutoffs of military aid and loan support to indicate U.S. disapproval of a number of the more repressive military and authoritarian governments of Latin America.

Perhaps the most important of the criticisms of the Carter policies was written by a former Democrat, Jeane Kirkpatrick, then associated with Georgetown University and the American Enterprise Institute. In a widely discussed article in Commentary (November 1979), "Dictatorships and Double Standards," Kirkpatrick distinguished between authoritarian and totalitarian regimes, and argued that friendly "non-democratic" autocrats in countries such as Iran and Nicaragua had been undermined by U.S. policy, which was "led by its own misunderstanding of the situation to assist actively in depositing an erstwhile friend and ally and installing a government hostile to American interests and policies in the world." The article is supposed to have brought her to the attention of Ronald Reagan and influenced her selection as his Ambassador to the United Nations. Before she took up her post, however, a second article was published in Commentary (January 1981) that focused the criticisms more specifically on the Carter policy toward Latin America. In "U.S. Security and Latin America" she argued that the Carter policies:

> not only proved incapable of dealing with the problems of Soviet/Cuban expansion in the area, they have positively contributed to them and to the alienation of major nations, the growth of neutralism, the destabilization of friendly governments, the spread of Cuban influence, and the decline of U.S. power in the region. Hence one of the first and most urgent tasks of the Reagan administration will be to review and revise the U.S. approach to Latin America and the Caribbean.

The supporting evidence for Mrs. Kirkpatrick's argument was drawn mainly from the Nicaraguan case where, it was asserted, the Carter administration "acted repeatedly and at critical junctures to weaken the government of Anastasio Somoza and to strengthen his opponents" in the service of a "globalist utopian" approach, promoted by a book written a decade earlier by Zbigniew Brzezinski under the auspices of the Council on Foreign Relations, the two reports of the Linowitz Commission on U.S.-Latin American Relations, and the conclusions of a study group of the Institute for Policy Studies-- the last demonstrating "how strong had become the affinity between the views of the foreign policy establishment and the New Left." The remedy, Kirkpatrick concluded, for the errors of the Carter administration was, like their cause, intellectual. It was necessary to abandon the ideological globalism of the previous administration, to build on the concrete circumstances of each foreign policy case, and to assess alternative policies in terms of their impact on "the security of the United States and on the safety and autonomy of the other nations of the hemisphere."

The Kirkpatrick approach was typical of the thinking of the new administration.[1] Reagan and his advisers came into office determined to alter significantly what they perceived to be the deleterious direction of the previous administration's policy toward Latin America (and the world) in two areas--the relation of human rights to security considerations and the priority given to the communist threat. Every new administration comes to office convinced that it will correct the mistakes of its predecessors. In this case, however, this involved more than a shift in emphasis back toward a more traditional balance-of-power diplomacy of the Kissinger variety.

National security was to be redefined as a militant anti-communism, and the U.S. stance in Latin America and the world was to be one of strength, rejecting the "gun-shy" attitudes of the previous policy. A military man--although one whose career had been as much political as military--was made Secretary of State and took office determined to "draw the line" against the Soviet Union and Cuba after the "losses" in Iran and Nicaragua.

Now, a year later, it may be possible to assess the impact of this determination. In what ways has U.S. policy toward Latin America changed, and in what ways have there been significant continuities in that policy despite the change in administrations?

U.S.-EL SALVADOR RELATIONS

El Salvador was the first area in Latin America where the new administration attempted to demonstrate that it was following a different policy from that of its predecessor. Long a backwater in an area of the world to which the United States paid little attention, Central America had been catapulted onto the front pages in 1978 and 1979 with the national uprising in Nicaragua against the 40-year reign of the Somoza family which culminated in the victory of the Sandinista-led revolutionaries on July 19, 1979. In neighboring El Salvador, a tiny overpopulated statelet the size of Massachusetts which had been ruled by the military and "the fourteen families," the shock waves of the Somoza overthrow had sparked a reformist coup in October 1979, led by army colonels in league with civilian politicians who established a junta to carry out long-overdue social and economic reforms. Several civilian members of the original junta resigned three months later, citing the lack of progress on reform and continuing repression by the armed forces and security services, but the military managed to strike a deal with the largest Salvadoran political party, the Christian Democrats, whose presidential candidate, José Napoleon Duarte, had been arrested, tortured, and exiled after an apparent victory in the 1972 presidential elections. The new regime called for continued implementation of a reform program, which included nationalization of banks and foreign trade, and an ambitious agrarian reform.

The Carter administration had maintained cool relations with the regime of General Carlos Romero before his overthrow in October 1979. Along with Guatemala and Brazil, Romero had rejected U.S. military aid in 1977 just before the United States itself cut off Salvadoran military assistance because of human rights violations. After the reformist coup, "non-lethal" military aid involving transportation and communications equipment was resumed in 1980, then in December it was cut off again, following the murder of three American nuns and a lay social worker. In early January 1981, two U.S. representatives of the American Institute for Free Labor Development and the head of the Salvadoran land reform program were murdered in the Sheraton Hotel of San Salvador, but as the Carter administration received increasing intelligence evidence of the shipment of U.S. weapons from communist sources through Cuba to the Salvadoran guerrilla movement, it authorized the renewal of military aid without the lethal vs. non-lethal distinction.

The presidential authorization of the aid renewal on January 16, 1981, four days before Ronald Reagan took office, came in the midst of a ten-day "final offensive" by the guerrilla opposition aimed at overthrowing the

Salvadoran government before Reagan took power. The offensive and the accompanying call for a general strike were unsuccessful in securing popular support, but the new administration decided to make El Salvador an example of its new approach to what it described as a "textbook case of indirect aggression by Communist powers through Cuba." That description was the conclusion of a collection of documents, Communist Interference in El Salvador (often referred to as the State Department White Paper on El Salvador), and an accompanying summary Special Report published on February 23, 1981. Three days earlier Secretary of State Alexander Haig conducted a briefing in which he referred to the flow of several hundred tons of military equipment to the Salvadoran guerrillas from "the Soviet bloc, Vietnam, Ethiopia, and radical Arabs," with "most of this equipment, not all but most," entering via Nicaragua (New York Times, February 21, 1981). Haig also referred in his briefing to the need "to deal with the source of the problem and that is Cuba," but did not specify what actions were to be taken in pursuit of that goal. The State Department documents, discovered in El Salvador in November 1980 and January 1981, included a detailed account of a trip in May and June by Shafik Handal, head of the Salvadoran Communist Party, to Eastern Europe, the Soviet Union, Vietnam, and Ethiopia in search of arms-- preferably those of Western make--as well as subsequent discussions in Havana and Managua to arrange the trans-shipment of the arms to El Salvador.[2]

The State Department publications and the announcement that U.S. economic and military aid would be increased and advisers sent to train the Salvadorans in the use of the helicopters and patrol boats provided set off an intense public debate in the media, with cover stories in Time and Newsweek on the background and nature of the Salvadoran conflict. Congress received a barrage of letters, many of them from church-affiliated groups, opposing U.S. military aid to El Salvador, and the press publicized the continuing killings of innocent civilians by both sides--with the majority of the killing being carried out by those associated with the government security forces. Church and human rights lobbyists pressured the congressional committees that were considering the administration's request for an increase in military and economic aid to El Salvador.[3] In El Salvador itself, the junta, now headed by Duarte as president, announced that it planned to hold elections for a constitutional assembly in March 1982, with presidential elections scheduled for 1983. When Colonel Roberto d'Aubuisson, a rightist military man who had been living in exile, returned with the announced intention of overthrowing the junta, the U.S. Embassy took an active role in discouraging him, and President Reagan surprised some of his conservative supporters by endorsing the Salvadoran agrarian reform program, including its successful effort to transform the 350 largest landholdings into agricultural cooperatives.

The public debate and heavy constituent mail on El Salvador had a direct impact on the actions of the two congressional committees considering the administration's request for $26 million in military aid and $87.7 million in economic assistance in the coming fiscal year. Over Secretary Haig's objections both committees voted to place conditions on U.S. aid requiring that the President certify every six months that the Salvadoran government was making "a concerted and significant" effort to control human rights violations, including those by its own armed forces, and was committed to holding free elections and agrarian reform and to negotiation with opposition groups for a peaceful settlement. The House version originally included an authorization of a congressional veto of further aid within 30 days of the presidential report, but that was later dropped, and the final version adopted by the full Senate in September also provided that the government was only required to be willing to negotiate with "groups which renounce and refrain from further military or paramilitary opposition activity."

The unanimity of the organized church groups in Washington in their opposition to military aid to El Salvador was something of a foreign policy first. Unlike Bishop Rivera y Damas who in his weekly homilies in San Salvador was careful to emphasize that both sides were guilty of human rights violations and impeding a peaceful solution, the U.S. churchmen, in calling for a cutoff of all U.S. military aid to El Salvador, emphasized only the well-reported abuses of the government security forces, giving little or no attention to the problems of the outside arms being supplied to the guerrillas and the murder and assassinations which they carried out.[4]

The opponents of U.S. military aid, including 35 members of the House of Representatives led by Gerry Studds of Massachusetts, argued that the level of violence by the regime's security forces and by paramilitary groups associated with them fell within section 502B of the Foreign Assistance Act, which provides for a cutoff of aid to any government engaged in "a consistent pattern of gross violations of internationally recognized human rights." They also claimed that an aid cutoff would force the junta to negotiate a cease-fire and coalition government with the Frente Democrático Revolucionario (FDR), the exile opposition alliance of Social Democrats, former Christian Democrats, and other groups, linked since mid-1980 to the Marxist guerrilla Farabundo Martí National Liberation Front (FMLN). (The credibility of FDR-FMLN offers to negotiate was somewhat undermined by the publication of a document, subsequently admitted to be authentic, entitled Proposal for International Mediation and dated February 3, which described the policy of support for negotiations as aimed at gaining "time to improve our internal military situation" following the defeat of the final offensive.)

West Europeans were divided in their reactions to the U.S. policy in El Salvador. Christian Democrats generally supported Duarte, while Social Democrats favored negotiations with the FDR, which was headed by a fellow party member, Guillermo Ungo. Concern about the European attitudes led to the dispatch of Lawrence Eagleburger, the new Assistant Secretary of State for European Affairs, on a mission to Europe to explain and defend the U.S. position.

In El Salvador, the Duarte proposal for constituent assembly elections was undercut by the continuing violence on both sides, and the likelihood that opposition leaders returning from exile would soon meet with assassination. Nevertheless the proposal for elections was endorsed by the United States, and when, following a lengthy behind-the-scenes ideological struggle, Thomas Enders, a career Foreign Service Officer, was appointed Assistant Secretary of State for Latin America, he made a public speech in July asserting that only a "political solution" could heal that divided country. That solution was elections, "open to all who are willing to renounce violence and abide by the procedures of democracy." Enders ruled out negotiations with the FDR-FMLN since "we should recognize that El Salvador's leaders will not and should not grant the insurgents through negotiations a share of power the rebels have not been able to win on the battlefield" (New York Times, July 17, 1981).

It was precisely a negotiated solution of the kind Enders opposed that the French and Mexican governments seemed to be aiming at, a month later, when they recognized the FDR-FMLN as "a representative political force"-- while not breaking their diplomatic relations with the Salvadoran junta. The

Mexican-French initiative did not seem to move the Salvadoran situation closer to a solution, although it received the editorial endorsement of The New York Times. Led by Venezuela's Christian Democratic government, nine Latin American countries denounced the statement as favoring those "who through violence are trying to twist the democratic destiny and the free self-determination of the people of El Salvador"; five others also indicated their opposition, leaving only Nicaragua aligned with Mexico, and Panama uncommitted.

By fall, the Salvadoran war seemed to have reached a stalemate. The rebels took over a small provincial town for a few days in late August, and were in control of the countryside in parts of the north and center of the country, but their principal efforts were now devoted to economic sabotage culminating in the dynamiting of one of the two major bridges linking the eastern third of El Salvador with the rest of the country. The test case of the new administration's resolve to "draw the line" and contain the spread of communism had simmered down to grudging and conditional support for continued economic and military aid by a reluctant Congress, occasional aggressive remarks by the Secretary of State about Cuban and Nicaraguan support for the guerrillas, and a general lack of enthusiasm for a civil war that seemed to have no solution. In September, when President Duarte came to argue his case on American television and in Congress, he received surprisingly little attention.

Later in the year the United States withdrew some of its 52 advisers but also announced that 1,500 Salvadorans would receive training in the United States or Panama. In December the Organization of American States voted 22 to 3, with Mexico, Nicaragua and Grenada voting in the negative, to support the March 1982 elections, and to send observers if requested to guarantee the "purity" of the vote. Yet critics like Mexico noted that without the participation of the Left opposition the elections were unlikely to resolve what appeared to be an interminable civil war.

The Reagan administration after nearly a year of deep involvement in El Salvador had not achieved the quick military victory it had sought. Indeed, its policy did not seem to differ much, except in its rhetorical emphasis on the external aspects of the problem, from that of the Carter administration. It too supported the political center, free elections, and social reform, as a way to prevent a takeover by the Left, and it seemed no more capable than was Carter of helping Duarte and the Christian Democrats to control the excesses of the security forces and paramilitary groups, whose continued indiscriminate killings undermined the U.S. argument that it was defending democracy against totalitarianism.[5]

The problem seemed intractable. As the leading presidential candidate in Costa Rica, Luis Alberto Monge told a U.S. congressional delegation in September that those who hold the real power on both sides are beyond the reach of the democratic forces on both sides. An international peacekeeping force was suggested to guarantee the security of the opposition in the March elections, but the Salvadoran armed forces rejected this as a violation of national sovereignty. A victory by the FDR-FMLN might produce the mixed economy and pluralistic democracy that the Social Democratic leader of the FDR, Guillermo Ungo, promised, but--in contrast to the Nicaraguan Sandinista guerrillas two years earlier--no one had a real understanding of the intentions of the leadership of the guerrilla FMLN except that they were Marxist-Leninists and that one of their representatives, Salvador Cayetano Carpio, had made statements that elicited invidious comparisons to Pol Pot in Kampuchea. Others, rejecting the Pol Pot analogy, talked of a "Zimbabwe solution," but there was neither leadership of the stature of Robert Mugabe, nor a neutral military like the British army.[6]

The March 1982 elections had mixed results from the point of view of U.S. policy. On the one hand, despite threats from some of the guerrilla groups, a record number of Salvadorans turned out to vote. On the other hand, the vote for the rightist parties enabled them to form a coalition to control the Constituent Assembly, despite the fact that the Christian Democrats received the largest percentage of votes (40%) and seats (24 out of 60). Roberto d'Aubuisson, the head of the extreme right ARENA party was elected president of the Assembly, but pressures from the armed forces and the U.S. Embassy resulted in the election of a respected moderate, Alvaro Magana, as president of the country. The cabinet included representation from all parties, but the ARENA controlled the Ministry of Agriculture and ISTA, the agrarian reform agency. This meant that the agrarian reform which had been a key element of the U.S. program for Salvador was seriously weakened, both in concept--the provisions in the constitution--and implementation.

Yet the U.S. continued to press for progress in the area of land reform, both because it was seen as an answer to the promises of the Left and because of the congressional requirement of presidential certification every six months that the program was being implemented. For the same reasons it continued to press for progress in the area of human rights, and the embassy began to keep a tally on the number of death squad assassinations reported in the press. The investigation of the murders of the U.S. trade unionists and religious women was painfully slow but in July and every six months thereafter, as required by law, President Reagan certified that there had been progress in all the areas listed by Congress.

The guerrillas were active mainly in the eastern third of the country and north of the capital. They were able to take towns temporarily but their main base was in the countryside, and their principal tactic involved sabotage, burning buses, and destroying the means of energy and communication such as major bridges and roads, electrical pylons, and oil storage facilities. In October 1982 the guerrilla diplomatic strategy shifted when they announced their readiness for negotiation "without preconditions," but the Salvadoran government did not respond to their offers. The readiness to negotiate of the guerrillas appeared more genuine in early 1983 when it was announced that Cayetano Carpio, known as the most intransigent of the rebel leaders, had committed suicide in Managua.

As the war dragged on without any visible indication that either side would win, the U.S. Congress continued to be skeptical about administration requests for military aid--in some cases substantially cutting the original budget figures. In April 1983, Reagan attempted to arouse public opinion to put pressure on the legislators by making a major speech on Central America in which he stated, "The national security of all the Americas is at stake in Central America. If we cannot defend ourselves there we cannot expect to prevail elsewhere. Our credibility would collapse, our alliances would crumble, and the safety of our homeland would be put in jeopardy." By 1983, the Reagan approach was being described as a "Two-Track Policy" both increasing military aid and training of the Salvadorans and keeping the lines open for negotiation (Sigmund, 1983). The latter policy seemed to be emphasized by the appointment of ex-Senator Richard Stone in April 1983 as a roving ambassador to Central America with a mandate to carry on discussions with all those concerned. (The word, "negotiations" which was anathema to the Salvadoran Right, was not used in describing his mission.) However this was followed in May by the sudden removal of Thomas Enders as Assistant Secretary of State for Latin America, allegedly for being too favorable to negotiations, as well as the firing of Deane Hinton, long-time ambassador to El Salvador, who had been speaking up more frequently in recent months on the need to control the death squads.

As it continued to be evident that the country and the Congress were not enthusiastic about a deeper involvement, the Senate passed a resolution introduced by Henry Jackson, a Democrat from Washington, and Charles Mathias, a Republican from Maryland, calling for the appointment of a bipartisan commission to make recommendations on Central American policy. The Commission, appointed on July 18, 1983, included six Republicans and six Democrats and was headed by ex-Secretary of State Henry Kissinger. While it held its hearings during the fall of 1983, the administration continued to pursue both a hard-line and a soft-line policy. In September Assistant Secretary of Defense Fred Ikle called for a military victory in El Salvador, and in November the president vetoed an aid bill that included a renewal of the certification requirement. Yet in December he also sent Vice President Bush to El Salvador with a list of military men who were implicated in atrocities, and several administration spokesmen spoke of the necessity of controlling the death squads. When the Kissinger Commission issued its report in January 1984, it was the same story. The Commission flatly rejected any concept of power-sharing by the guerrillas and called on them to accept participation in the elections scheduled for 1984 and 1985. At the same time, however, despite some reservations by Kissinger and two other members, the Commission recommended continuing to place conditions-- especially relating to human rights--upon military aid to the Salvadoran armed forces.

The basic lines of the Carter policy--elections, reform, and human rights--thus remained the cornerstones of U.S. policy toward El Salvador. The difference was that more emphasis was placed on military aid and on develop- ing and training a reformed officer corps which would be more effective and less brutal and corrupt than the older officers. The direct use of American combat troops was still excluded, as it had been since the outset of U.S. involvement. The policy did not seem to be any more likely to bring victory at the end of the Reagan administration than at the beginning, but neither did the rebels seem any nearer to overthrowing the Salvadoran government. At best a stalemate seemed likely for the foreseeable future.

U.S.-NICARAGUAN RELATIONS

Nicaragua was the second country where the administration was deter- mined to pursue a different policy. The 1980 Republican Party platform had deplored "the Marxist-Sandinista takeover in Nicaragua" and spoken of "support of the efforts of the Nicaraguan people to establish a free and independent government." Yet it was unclear what policy initiatives would be taken by the new administration to achieve that goal.

As in the case of El Salvador, the Carter administration had already toughened its policy toward Nicaragua before the inauguration of Ronald Reagan. In January 1981, faced with the evidence of a substantial increase in arms shipments through Nicaragua to El Salvador just before the final offensive there, the Carter administration delayed the projected disbursement of the remaining $15 million of the $75 million U.S. aid program voted by Congress in 1980, and cancelled authorization of negotiations for the renewal of Public Law 480 long-term low interest loans for the sale of wheat and cooking oil. In September 1980, President Carter had certified, as required by Congress, that Nicaragua was not "aiding or abetting or supporting acts of violence or terrorism in other countries," but in January, with new evidence of Nicaraguan government involvement in the supply of arms to the Salvadoran rebels, the new aid was not extended.

The Reagan administration continued the review of Nicaragua aid policy and despite a reported cutoff of arms flows by Nicaragua to El Salvador for three weeks in March a formal decision by the President to suspend the aid was announced on April 1. Yet Reagan did not demand repayment of the $60 million already expended (as authorized by the congressional legislation), previously contracted aid disbursements continued, and at the end of 1981 seven million dollars in unexpended but contracted aid still remained. The Nicaraguan government carried out a national and international propaganda campaign against the attempt to "starve Nicaragua into submission" (U.S. Agency for International Development, Nicaraguan Desk, 1981), and secured donations of wheat from Argentina, the Soviet Union, and Bulgaria as well as a long-term credit sale of $15 million for wheat and oil from Canada. It was reported that Nicaragua's campaign to secure foreign wheat was so successful that it sold surplus wheat to Costa Rica later in the year. In April, Libya announced a cash loan of $100 million and Mexico extended credit for all the petroleum it sold to Nicaragua during 1981, rather than providing a 30 percent loan as previously agreed upon. While the U.S. aid extended to Nicaragua during the first year of the Reagan administration dropped sharply from the $110 million spent during the last 18 months of the Carter administration, "pipeline" aid continued, assistance to the private sector amounted to $6.9 million between January and August, and aid from other countries more than offset the reductions in U.S. assistance. Nicaragua's economic prospects for 1982 were not bright, but the U.S. aid cutoff was not likely to be in itself decisive. However, as a symbolic act it communicated the continuing hostility of the American administration, while not achieving any effect on arms flow.

Press reports began to appear of a training camp outside Miami of Cuban, Panamanian, and Nicaraguan exiles as well as of raids into Nicaragua by exiles based in southern Honduras. The Sandinista government pointed to these groups to justify the expansion of its army to a projected 50,000 soldiers, plus a 200,000-man militia. The inflow of an estimated $28 million of Cuban and Soviet arms and an increase of 1,500 in the number of Cuban military and security advisers, along with renewed Nicaraguan government pressures on opposition party leaders, unions, radio stations and press (La Prensa, the respected newspaper that had spearheaded the opposition to Somoza, was closed on various pretexts five times between June and November),were cited by Secretary Haig to justify the need to take countermeasures against the military buildup. News leaked out about a Haig order to prepare papers on policy options that included a naval blockade against Nicaragua (New York Times, November 5, 1981). Reports were circulated-- quickly denied by Cuba--about the dispatch of 600 Cuban troops to the Salvadoran rebels--and the Secretary of State spoke ominously about the need to arrest the "drift toward totalitarianism" in Nicaragua. Yet Haig's statements were privately criticized in press leaks by other government officials (especially in the Defense Department, which feared the domestic and international impact of a "Bay of Pigs" in Nicaragua) or were publicly questioned by other governments with which the United States maintained good relations--such as Mexico and Venezuela. At a press conference in November, President Reagan declared that there were "no plans" for the use of American troops "anywhere in the world." Under the War Powers Act of 1973, such actions would require congressional authorization or a notification by the President to the Congress of an emergency involving a threat to American security. In the latter case the Congress by concurrent resolution can require the troops to be withdrawn. The troops must be withdrawn within 60 days unless Congress specifically authorizes their continuing presence.

The verbal escalation, it was later revealed (Washington Post, December 10, 1981), followed two months of secret negotiations between Assistant Secretary of State Enders and the Nicaraguan government. Enders apparently offered a joint reaffirmation of both countries' OAS obligations to refrain from aggression or interference, a renewal of economic and technical assistance, and U.S. action against anti-Sandinista exiles on its soil--in return for Nicaraguan termination of arms flows to the Salvadoran rebels and de-escalation of its military buildup. The exchanges ended with a note from Nicaragua on October 31 calling on the United States to enforce its own laws against the exile training camps and to cease generating military tension in Central America and the Caribbean. In November, U.S. influence seems to have been exercised to prevent a $30 million Nicaraguan loan from appearing on the agenda of the Executive Board of the Inter-American Development Bank. Yet the administration requested $33 million in new aid for Nicaragua for 1982 (over administration objections, the House restricted it to the private sector, with aid for the public sector permitted only if there is "progress" toward free elections), and the announcement in early January 1982 that France had agreed to a $17 million program of "nonoffensive" military aid to Nicaragua weakened the argument that it had become a military outpost of Cuba and the Soviet Union.

Vigorous criticism of the proposals for action against Nicaragua came from the opposition groups within Nicaragua, since they realized that such actions would destroy the very groups that the administration was purportedly attempting to save. While the imprisonment in October of three leaders of the Private Enterprise Council (COSEP) for accusing the government of engaging in "a Marxist-Leninist adventure that will only bring more bloodshed," and the apparently related resignation of the Nicaraguan Ambassador to Washington, seemed to confirm the Haig assertions, the Nicaraguan opposition continued to treat with the Sandinista government: after the government published a draft Political Parties Law, two opposition parties rejoined the quasi-legislative Council of State to discuss it. La Prensa was still being published (with a larger circulation than the two pro-government papers combined), there was no mass exodus by the middle and entrepreneurial classes, the church made public criticisms of the regime's policies in statements by the bishops' conference and the archbishop's Sunday homilies, and the Marxist-dominated Sandinista regime continued to permit a situation of "harassed pluralism" that contrasted with the administration talk of totalitarianism.

At the end of 1981 the administration gave the go-ahead to CIA plans to give military support to the Nicaraguan exiles. By November 1982 it was possible for Newsweek to publish an issue entitled "The Secret War in Nicaragua" providing a detailed account of U.S. support and training for

Honduran-based anti-Sandinistas--the so-called <u>contras</u> (for <u>contra-revolu-cionarios</u>, although many of them had been deeply involved in the revolution against Somoza) who conducted border raids and economic sabotage in northern Nicaragua, sometimes with considerable local support. Beginning with about 500 men, the force rapidly grew to 6,000-10,000 and it was later complemented by another group, led by Eden Pastora, "Commander Zero," the military hero of the Sandinista revolution--operating out of Costa Rica with less-direct CIA ties.

The arming of the <u>contras</u> was a clear departure from earlier policies, and the Democratic-controlled House repeatedly attempted to curb it, arguing that it violated international law and only reinforced Sandinista control. The Boland amendment in late 1982 forbade use of U.S. funds "for the purpose of overthrowing the Nicaraguan government"--but the administration claimed that it was only interested in preventing arms from going to the Salvadorans--despite the <u>contras</u>' own clearly announced intentions otherwise. By 1983 the cutoff of CIA aid had become a party issue, with a division in the House along straight party lines. However, the administration was able to use its Senate majority in conference committees to extend the support on a limited basis--both in amount and in time.

As in the case of El Salvador, the administration seemed to be following two different tracks. In April 1982 at the very time that military training of the exiles was being initiated, Secretary Enders was engaged in discussion with the Nicaraguans concerning an eight-point program which would exchange Nicaraguan termination of support for the Salvadorans for renewal of American aid. (The support for the exiles was not admitted by the U.S. so that it was not part of the bargaining.) No real progress was made in these negotiations, and American attention shifted to supporting the creation of a Central American Democratic Community centered in Costa Rica which would promote pluralism and democracy in Central America. As the Sandinistas clamped down on the opposition in Nicaragua, U.S. policy gave more and more emphasis to democracy as its response to the leftist challenge in Central America. Democracy was also emphasized by the Kissinger Commission when it called upon the Nicaraguans to be "responsive to serious negotiations" involving guarantees of pluralism and free elections and recommended that American aid to Central America be conditioned upon progress in the area of human rights and democratic self-rule.

Democracy also formed a part of the proposals worked out by the Contadora Group, made up of Mexico, Panama, Colombia, and Venezuela, which tried to mediate the Central American crisis, beginning in January 1983. More important, however, was a carefully negotiated list of 21 points involving the ending of foreign intervention, bases, and advisers, a reduction in arms inventories, and phased de-escalation of the military buildup. In July 1983, President Reagan endorsed the efforts of the Contadora Group, and the Kissinger Commission also described its efforts as "constructive." However, the Kissinger report emphasized that a successful regional settlement would have to involve cooperation between the U.S. and the Contadora powers and a recognition that the interests of those countries and of the U.S. might diverge. In addition, the Commission called for greater concreteness in the Contadora proposals, particularly in the area of free elections, and of permanent verification of any accords agreed upon.

Critics of the Commission Report argued that "democracy" was a code word for the overthrow of the Sandinista government. However, when the Sandinista government announced that elections would be held on November 4,

1984, it was difficult for its opponents to do more than criticize the lowering of the voting age to 16, argue that the opposition should have had increased access to the media (especially television), and attack government efforts to promote a war psychology (much of that due to the activities of the contras), since the Sandinistas seemed to be willing to permit a more open system--at least temporarily.

The other--or military--track was very much in evidence as well. While the Reagan administration supported the Honduran transition to civilian rule in January 1982 the U.S. military presence in Honduras was substantially increased. A base to train Salvadorans and other Central Americans was built at Puerto Castilla, maneuvers were carried out lasting many months and involving 6,000 American troops, and permanent naval patrols were carried out on both coasts. The military escalation was justified on the grounds that this would provide the Nicaraguans with incentives to negotiate--and this became a new rationale for the activities of the contras as well. Yet except for the Contadora efforts, no negotiation was taking place and the level of tension rose as the Nicaraguans feared an imminent American invasion. In an effort to appear more reasonable, the Nicaraguans even sent some of the Cuban advisers home and made concessions to the private sector and the church. In July 1983 they offered to join a regional accord prohibiting arms shipments to El Salvador, thus tacitly admitting their role as arms suppliers, but their proposals were criticized by the U.S. for not including provisions to reduce their own arms buildup.

How did Nicaraguan policy differ under Reagan? Clearly it was much more bellicose verbally. Military measures, especially the arming of the contras and the military buildup in Honduras, also received more emphasis, and negotiation was given less importance. Yet both because of public opinion and because of the possibility that it might actually produce some kind of regional settlement, the administration continued to support the Contadora efforts and to endorse dialogue with the Nicaraguans. This was not because the Reaganites were sanguine about the possibility of a change of heart by what they saw as a Marxist-Leninist, incipiently totalitarian regime, but because real constraints in Congress, in public opinion, and even in the Department of Defense prevented serious consideration of the elimination of Sandinismo by force, unless a direct threat to U.S. security such as the establishment of a Soviet base provided justification--something the Sandinistas were most unlikely to provide. This left pressure--it was never clear for what goal--and negotiations as the alternative--a policy which, except for the support of the contras, was very like that being followed by the Carter administration when it left power.

U.S. AND CUBAN RELATIONS IN THE CARIBBEAN

In September Belize, the former British Honduras, became independent, joining the many other mini-states of the Caribbean that had recently achieved that status. It was in the Caribbean that the new administration took its most significant step in its relationship with the rest of the hemisphere--the so-called Caribbean Basin Initiative. Like so many other administration policies in the area it was initially conceived as an explicitly anticommunist effort, but again like others it was considerably modified in application. (As in other cases it marked a further development of initiatives taken by the Carter administration, which had supported the establishment of the World Bank group on the Caribbean that resulted in a quadrupling of external aid to the region.)

Reagan administration attention was first focused on the Caribbean by the stunning victory in October 1980 of Edward Seaga's Jamaica Labor Party over Michael Manley's People's National Party. Seaga represented private enterprise, anti-communism, and a welcome to foreign investment, after years of rule by a Manley government which had been socialist in philosophy, friendly to Cuba in foreign policy, and critical of the leading foreign investors, particularly the U.S. and Canadian bauxite companies. After his election Seaga called for a "mini-Marshall Plan" for the Caribbean, and from the outset he echoed the militant anti-communism of the new U.S. administration. As a showcase for the Reagan philosophy of encouragement of private investment, Jamaica received support from the new administration for a $600 million loan from the International Monetary Fund with only mild conditions attached, Reagan appointed a U.S. Business Committee on Jamaica chaired by David Rockefeller to promote foreign investment in that country, and the administration's foreign aid request for Jamaica was nearly doubled to $90 million.

For Castro a very different set of policies was adopted. Legislation was introduced to establish Radio Martí, an exile propaganda station similar to Radio Free Europe; the administration began to enforce the legislative restrictions on trade with Cuba more strictly, even to the extent of requiring licenses for the import of Cuban publications; and in November Secretary Haig's earlier statements about getting at "the source" of Salvadoran guerrilla arms were given concrete focus with news reports that in June the Pentagon had been asked to prepare an option paper on Cuba which included such possible steps as an arms blockade and even an invasion.

In mid-December 1981 Assistant Secretary of State Enders testified to the Western Hemisphere Affairs Subcommittee of the Senate Foreign Relations Committee about what he called "a new Cuban strategy for uniting the Left" in the countries of the Caribbean Basin. Tracing a pattern of action beginning with Nicaragua in 1978 and continuing in El Salvador, Guatemala, Colombia, and currently in Honduras, Enders argued that the new Cuban approach was to bring together the various feuding leftist guerrilla groups and promise them arms and training if they agreed to unite and adopt a common strategy of armed struggle under Cuban guidance. The newly unified groups were instructed to attempt to form alliances with democratic movements on the Left, especially the social democrats, and to use them to get support from their counterparts in Europe. In addition, their guerrilla campaigns typically included economic sabotage aimed at undermining the deteriorating economies and tourist trade in order to exacerbate social unrest.

Enders' testimony was buttressed by a report submitted to the Committee on "Cuba's Renewed Support for Violence in Latin America" (U.S. Department of State, 1981b). Besides reviewing the evidence on Cuba's military aid to Nicaragua and the Salvadoran guerrillas, it detailed current Cuban efforts to subvert democratically elected governments in Colombia (an effort to unify the leftist opposition and the training of 100 to 200 "M-19" guerrillas whose capture in February had led to the suspension of relations between Colombia and Cuba), in Costa Rica (the use, documented by a Costa Rican congressional committee, of Costa Rican territory to smuggle arms to El Salvador and the training in the Soviet Union and Cuba of Costa Ricans involved in terrorism), in Jamaica (smuggling of arms used in attacks against the opposition during the 1980 elections as well as covert military training of

Jamaican students in Cuba), and in Honduras (attempts to unify the Left, Honduran attendance at training courses in Cuba, and the discovery of three "safehouses" in November with sizable arms caches). Enders concluded that "we must communicate to Cuba that the costs of escalating its intervention in the region will be very high." But the only specific measures he mentioned were the exile radio station and a tightening of the economic embargo and refugee controls.

The only real action against Cuba was through the tiny island of Grenada which had in effect become a Cuban satellite since the coup by Maurice Bishop in 1979. The Reagan administration attempted unsuccessfully to restrict its donation to the Caribbean Development Bank to prevent its use for Grenada; it terminated the existing U.S. aid program for Grenada; and it tried to persuade the Europeans not to finance a new airport, arguing that it would be used to transport and supply Cuban troops engaged in intervention abroad. The pressures may have had some results since Bishop came to Washington in mid-1983 seeking an improvement in relations. In October, however, Bishop was overthrown and later killed by a hard-line Marxist faction in his New Jewel Movement. Less than a week later U.S. troops landed on the island and captured it with relatively little loss of life.

This was the first use of gunboat diplomacy since President Johnson had landed the U.S. Marines in the Dominican Republic in 1965. Although fairly clearly a violation of U.S. treaty obligations--the nonintervention provisions of the Rio Treaty of 1974--it was justified by a number of arguments from the administration. First, it was said that 1,000 American medical students were in danger of being taken hostage by the new regime, although there was no evidence that this was about to occur. Second, the newly formed Organization of Eastern Caribbean States had requested the action--fearing the destabilizing character of the new regime. Third, somewhat belatedly it was discovered that the Governor General, Sir Paul Scoon, had requested the action, although this was not referred to at the outset of the invasion. Most important, however, in the eyes of the administration, the island was found to be bristling with Cuban and Soviet arms--in the words of President Reagan "a Soviet-Cuban colony being readied as a major military bastion."

The U.S. published a paper documenting the buildup of arms supplies and other materials which certainly seemed excessive for an army of 1,000 and a militia of 2,000 (U.S. Department of State, 1983a). Critics noted that there might have been other less transparently unilateral ways to deal with the problem, but there was no doubt that despite condemnations by both the United Nations and the Organization of American States, the action was generally popular both in the United States and in Grenada (where a Gallup Poll found 91 percent in favor of the U.S. action). The fighting only lasted two days, and all troops were withdrawn by December 15. The precedent, however, was worrisome, particularly to those who believed that the rules of international law should be promoted rather than violated by the United States. Along with the arming of the Nicaraguan contras, it was one of the two actions by the Reagan administration in Latin America that appears unlikely to have been initiated by a Democratic administration.

In February 1982 the President announced a variation on the Seaga proposal designed to strengthen the weak and dependent economies of the Caribbean states--and by extension to give multilateral support to the troubled Central American economies (thus El Salvador magically became a Caribbean and not a Pacific state). The Caribbean Basin Initiative, as it was called, was not a Marshall Plan at all. It was a program to promote trade, investment, and aid to the Caribbean and Central America by the United States, Canada, Mexico and Venezuela (and later possibly Europe and Japan) on a bilateral basis (thus bypassing the thorny issue of aid to Cuba and Grenada) and encouraging each of the four donor countries to increase their economic support for the area. The proposal tied in with existing programs such as the Mexican-Venezuelan 30 percent discount loans on petroleum for Central America, as well as Canada's already announced increased aid to the English-speaking Caribbean, while focusing attention on the weak economies of the Caribbean and Central American states with the hope that such steps as a regional investment insurance program and the lowering or elimination of tariff barriers could promote development and create jobs throughout the area.

The United States planned to make available to the countries in the area only a little more than a tenth of Seaga's original request--and this included the Central American countries as well as the Caribbean--so that it was not an ambitious program. However, it included some new elements, such as proposals for a temporary one-way elimination of tariffs for Caribbean exports (without the restrictions of the Generalized System of Preferences from which they already benefit) and the extension of special tax credits to investors. Whether the program could make much of an impact on the massive unemployment in the area, resolve the problem of declining export revenues from sugar and coffee or produce the takeoff in economic development outlined by its backers remained doubtful.

The Caribbean Basin Initiative faced some opposition in Congress, but it was finally adopted without the investment tax credit. In addition, a number of commodities were exempted from duty-free provision, including tuna, shoes, palm oil, and some leather products. Textiles and sugar also remained subject to special quota provisions. However, the adoption of the Initiative dramatized the U.S. concern, secured additional aid funds for the Caribbean and Central America, and probably will result in some genuine benefits in increased investment, employment, and development for the area.

U.S.-MEXICAN RELATIONS

The fact that countries with as different policies in the area as Mexico and the United States could cooperate in the program shows how flexible it was and how cordial the relationship between the United States and Mexico had become. Shortly after his election Reagan had taken the unusual step of meeting the Mexican President on Mexican territory, and during 1981 Presidents Reagan and López Portillo met four times. Those meetings indicated a dramatic turnaround in U.S.-Mexican relations, based more on the personal relationship which the two leaders developed than on any agreement on policy. On Cuba, El Salvador, and Nicaragua they remained far apart, and significant differences remained in the areas of Mexican undocumented workers in the United States, fishing rights, and Mexico's refusal to join the General Agreement on Tariffs and Trade, but the two countries seemed to be able to transcend their differences and maintain cordial relations even when their policy positions were far apart.

A striking example of this was the North-South meeting of eight developed and fourteen developing countries organized by Mexico at Cancun at the end of October 1981. The Mexicans respected U.S. insistence that

Cuba not be invited--despite Mexico's long-standing close relations with Castro. President Reagan agreed to participate despite U.S. opposition to the basic thrust of the Third World countries' demands, especially the attempt to give the one nation-one vote General Assembly the power to overrule the specialized economic agencies such as the International Monetary Fund and the World Bank where voting is weighted according to economic contributions. At the two-day meeting in Cancun the U.S. President again demonstrated his talent for disarming those who disagree with him with his personal charm, and the meeting concluded with an agreement that global negotiations to aid the poor nations should be held at the United Nations "on a basis to be mutually agreed and in circumstances offering the prospect of meaningful progress with a sense of urgency." The question of how decisions were to be made was simply sidestepped, and while President Reagan was correct in asserting on his return that "we did not waste time on unrealistic rhetoric or unattainable objectives" (New York Times, October 25, 1981), the meeting did not achieve any concrete results except to allow an informal exchange of views between North and South on such issues as agricultural development, energy, and international financial relations.

On the continuing problem of illegal Mexican migrants, some changes in U.S. policy were expected since Reagan as a candidate had spoken of the need for stricter controls coupled with an expanded "guest worker" program. In February a Commission appointed by President Carter and headed by Father Theodore Hesburgh issued a report recommending a one-time amnesty for illegal aliens already in the country, somewhat enlarged ceilings for legal immigrants from Mexico and the adoption of civil and criminal penalties for U.S. employers who knowingly hire illegal workers. President Reagan appointed his own Cabinet Task Force and in July the administration announced that it planned to introduce legislation providing for conditional amnesty for illegal immigrants living in the United States for ten years, an experimental "guest worker" program involving 50,000 Mexicans a year over the next two years, as well as employer penalties (Hewlett, 1981/1982:355-378). As in the case of earlier recommendations to deal with the problem, it seemed far from clear that the administration proposals would produce any concrete action on the part of Congress, but near the end of the year the death of sixteen members of a boatload of Haitians seeking to enter Florida illegally focused renewed attention on the problem.

In 1983 the Congress finally produced a legislative response to the problem. The Simpson-Mazzoli bill provided for the first time for employer sanctions for knowingly hiring illegal aliens. It also gave aliens already here opportunities to regularize their status and provided for a counterfeit-proof identity card. The bill passed the Senate in 1982 and 1983, but was not adopted by the House which was more responsive to pressure from Hispanic American groups that feared discrimination by employers against hiring persons of Hispanic appearance. The Mexicans too were not enthusiastic, preferring the present situation where Mexican indocumentados had little difficulty finding employment in the U.S. and remitted substantial sums to their families in Mexico.

Behind the public disagreements on international policy, immigration, and fisheries is the reality of the increasing economic integration of the Mexican and U.S. economies. Seventy percent of Mexico's exports and 60 percent of its imports are to and from the United States, and trade between the two countries has increased 50 percent a year in recent years. Despite a battery of Mexican regulatory legislation, U.S. investment in Mexico increased from $U.S. 4.4 billion to nearly $6 billion in 1980 (Survey of Current Business, August 1981), and 70 percent of Mexico's oil exports go to the United States. As a candidate Ronald Reagan had endorsed a further integration of the two economies along with that of Canada in a North American Common Market, but both Canada and Mexico publicly rejected the proposal in January. Mexico saw the proposal as the institutionalization of a dependent relationship, giving the United States preferential access to its energy supplies and cheap labor, while preventing Mexico from promoting its exports and regulating foreign investment in support of domestic industry. Existing Mexican regulatory measures and subsidies have created charges of unfair practices in international trade that have already led to the imposition by the United States of a countervailing duty on some leather goods, but for the present Mexico seems to have the best of both worlds, benefiting from special tariff arrangements for border assembly plants and from exemptions for many of its exports under the Generalized System of Preferences for Third World countries, while continuing to implement legislation that limits and discriminates against foreign--usually U.S.--trade and investment.

The most striking demonstration of the inter-relation between the two economies was the dramatically swift reaction of the U.S. to the sudden emergence in August 1982 of a foreign exchange crisis in Mexico. Within a few days, a rescue operation had been quietly mounted which included U.S. purchase of oil for its reserves, a Commodity Credit Corporation loan, a moratorium on the repayment of principal to private U.S. banks, and a large loan by the Bank of International Settlements. In return for the rescue program, Mexico was obliged to negotiate a new austerity program with the International Monetary Fund, but in the Mexican case this did not provoke the adverse domestic reaction that was caused by similar programs in Brazil and Argentina. Because of drastic devaluations Mexico was able to reduce imports and dramatically increase its exports--and even with the leveling off of the price of oil it had a steady source of foreign exchange. In addition, the new administration of President Miguel de la Madrid which took office in December 1982 was able to benefit from the initial honeymoon of a new president to carry out overdue belt-tightening.

U.S. HUMAN RIGHTS POLICY

The other major policy area where the new administration was determined to alter the Carter approach was the relative priority given to human rights in relation to security considerations. The previous administration had not been oblivious to security considerations or unwilling to allow them to override human rights concerns in its relations with such countries as the Philippines and South Korea. But in Latin America those considerations appeared to be less salient, and the repression by certain governments, notably in the Southern Cone (Chile, Argentina, and Uruguay), so serious that the Carter human rights policy had its most evident impact in relations with those countries. Already before Carter's election, the Congress had established a separate Human Rights Bureau in the Department of State and required annual reports from the State Department on the human rights situation of all recipients of U.S. aid. But at the beginning of the Carter administration the Executive took further initiatives, reducing or eliminating U.S. aid to several Latin American governments, voting against loans from international financial institutions on explicit human rights grounds, and supporting action by the Organization of American States and the United Nations condemning human rights violations.

Chile was the first and most frequent object of these sanctions. Congress adopted increasingly severe restrictions on military aid and sales between 1974 and 1976; loans to Chile by the World Bank and the Inter-American Development Bank were opposed by Carter appointees; and a series of sanctions including exclusion from joint naval maneuvers and prohibition of Export-Import Bank credits were adopted after Chile failed to extradite those involved in the 1976 murder in Washington of Orlando Letelier, Allende's former ambassador to the United States.

As for Argentina, as a result of human rights violations following the overthrow of Isabel Peron, Congress adopted the Humphrey-Hawkins amendment barring U.S. arms aid or sales, and Carter emissaries, including the Assistant Secretary of State for Human Rights and Secretary of State Cyrus Vance himself, raised the human rights issue directly during visits to that country. Most striking was the change in relations with Brazil, where the earlier Kissinger policy of promoting a special U.S.-Brazilian relationship was replaced by increasingly distant relations, both because of the human rights issue (Brazil rejected U.S. military aid in reaction to the 1977 human rights report) and because of Carter administration efforts to persuade the West German government not to supply Brazil with a nuclear reactor without full safeguards that it would be used only for peaceful purposes.

In the last two years of the Carter administration there was a significant reduction in repression in the countries of the Southern Cone. In Chile, DINA, the intelligence organization which had become almost a state within a state, was reorganized, its successor organization given more limited powers of detention, and confirmed cases of disappearance ceased--although torture, several killings, and short-term detentions and expulsions continued. In Argentina, where the number of missing persons between 1976 and 1979 was estimated at 5,600 by the Argentine Human Rights Assembly, the 1980 State Department human rights report estimated the number of disappearances at between 12 and 28--although 900 political prisoners remained "at the disposition of the executive power" under legislation enacted before the 1976 coup. In Brazil since the mid-1970s, but especially with the promulgation of an amnesty in 1979, the process of political opening (abertura) had meant that except for occasional confiscation of publications and legal action against strikers, the human rights violations of the early 1970s had ceased. In Uruguay, while there were still 1,219 political "detainees," no disappearances had taken place since 1978, and in 1980 the military had made an unsuccessful attempt to impose a constitution which would have permitted a transition to civilian rule while retaining wide powers for the military (U.S. Department of State, 1981a).

In these circumstances it was easy for the new administration to argue for a shift in priorities and to assert that public condemnations of governments with which the United States was allied militarily (through the Rio Treaty of Mutual Assistance) and politically (through the OAS) damaged the U.S. international position. Shortly after coming to power the administration lifted the ban on Chilean access to Export-Import Bank loans and participation in joint naval exercises and introduced legislation to remove the congressional prohibition on Argentine military aid. Similar legislation to lift the ban on Chilean military sales was proposed later in the year.

Despite denials by administration spokesmen--Secretary of State Haig at his confirmation hearings said that "other than in the most exceptional circumstances" the United States should not provide aid to regimes that "consistently and in the harshest manner" violate human rights--there were many who suspected that the new approach meant abandonment of a concern with human rights except when they were violated by communist regimes. Their fears seemed to be confirmed by the nomination of Ernest Lefever as Assistant Secretary of State for Human Rights. In July 1979, Lefever had testified to a congressional committee in opposition to human rights conditions on U.S. aid, and his Center for Ethics in Public Policy had been identified with a conservative position in international affairs. When his name was first mentioned in February, it elicited media criticism, but the debate over the new "tilt" in human rights was sharply intensified by the publication in April, both in book form and in a substantial excerpt published in The New Yorker, of a deeply moving account of the repression in Argentina, Prisoner without a Name, Cell without a Number, by the exiled Argentine publisher Jacobo Timerman. Along with horrifying details on torture and executions during his two years of detention on charges that were never substantiated by Argentine courts or the military themselves, Timerman's book denounced the Argentine military regime as anti-Semitic and totalitarian, comparing it to the early years of Nazism. Appearing on U.S. television in connection with the publication of the book, Timerman attributed his release in 1979 to the Carter human rights policy, which for the first time since the Marshall Plan had "captured the imagination of the world," and asserted that at one point the U.S. Embassy was the only source of legal advice for the families of those who had disappeared.

Conservative and neo-conservative writers attacked Timerman for not mentioning his financial connection with the late David Graiver, accused of acting as banker for the left-wing guerrillas, and for exaggerating the plight of Argentine Jews, but the debate focused attention on human rights in Argentina and the U.S. role there (Wall Street Journal, May 29, 1981; Falcoff, 1981). In May both the Senate Foreign Relations Committee and the House Foreign Affairs Committee conditioned the repeal of the ban on U.S. military sales or aid to Argentina on significant progress in the area of human rights as well as an accounting by the government for the "disappeared" persons--in spite of letters from the Secretary of State urging them not to do so. (The conditions were later softened to direct the President "to pay particular attention" to them.) When Lefever's nomination came before the Senate Foreign Relations Committee for approval in late May he was subjected to intense questioning about his earlier views on human rights issues as well as his Center's sources of financial support. Describing himself as a "compassionate realist," Lefever insisted that he had a long history of defense of human rights, although in a veiled reference to his predecessor's activism he did not see himself in a "Sir Galahad role going around the world on personal missions." Possibly the most damaging part of his testimony was his willingness to denounce the Soviet Union as "the gravest violator of human rights" in the contemporary world, while refusing to name any non-communist violators because that is "not my style" (New York Times, May 19, 1981). In early June, the Republican-controlled Committee voted 13-4 against his confirmation and he withdrew his name from consideration.

For a time it was reported that the administration was considering abolishing the Human Rights Bureau, but this would have required congressional action. After a lengthy interval, Elliott Abrams, then Assistant Secretary of State for International Organizations, was named to the post, and concurrently a State Department memorandum on human rights was published that called for application of the policy "evenhandedly" and on the basis of "a balancing of pertinent interests." It recognized that "A human rights policy means trouble, for it means hard choices which may adversely affect certain bilateral interests. At the very least we will have to speak honestly about our friends' human rights violations and justify any decision wherein other considerations (economic, military) are determinative" (New York Times, November 5, 1981). The memorandum proposed the appointment of three deputies to the Assistant Secretary and an expansion of the Bureau's coordinating role with other agencies, including defense attachés in U.S. embassies. Abrams, who described his obligations as Assistant Secretary as "to speak the truth" and "be effective," easily won confirmation and, if the memorandum is an indication of future policy, once again an attempt to carry out a substantial alteration in existing policy had been modified by the pressure of Congress and public opinion.

Despite the original intent of the change in human rights policy to remove what had become a persistent irritant to bilateral relations with the regimes of the Southern Cone, there was no immediate or striking improvement in relations with those regimes. In the case of Argentina there remained a difference in policy toward the Soviet Union; since the post-Afghanistan reduction of U.S. wheat sales, Argentina had become a principal supplier of wheat to the Soviet Union. In the case of Brazil as well, soybean sales to the USSR soared and the regime seemed much less willing than in the early 1970s to play the role of principal U.S. partner in South America--if only because its own problems with finding secure energy sources meant that friendly relations with Iraq, Libya, and Nigeria were more vital to its national interest as it conceived it. On the other principal subject of controversy between the United States and Brazil, nuclear proliferation, Vice President Bush announced on a visit to Brazil in October 1981, that Brazil would be given a special exemption to allow it to purchase enriched uranium for its U.S.-built reactor. There remained little prospect, however, of the re-establishment of the partnership between the United States and Brazil that Secretary Kissinger had begun to build in the last year of the Ford administration.

In the case of Chile, there were also continuing obstacles to improved relations--mostly of the making of the Pinochet regime. A new Chilean constitution, approved in a hastily called plebiscite in September 1980 and implemented in March 1981, not only gave Pinochet eight more years as president, but in its "transitional" provisions gave him power to censor all new publications, forbid public meetings, and expel or sentence to internal exile those who propagate subversive doctrines "or have the reputation of being activists for such doctrines and those who carry out acts contrary to the interests of Chile or constitute a danger for internal peace." Two days after a visit by Mrs. Kirkpatrick in August in which she announced the U.S. intention to "normalize completely its relations with Chile," Pinochet used his constitutional powers to order the immediate expulsion of Jaime Castillo, the chairman of the Chilean Human Rights Commission and Minister of Justice under former President Eduardo Frei, as well as three other prominent former political leaders who had signed a declaration criticizing the government's imprisonment of the leaders of a newly formed National Trade Union Coordinating Committee.

The expulsions, the continuing reports of the detention of regime opponents by police and the intelligence agency, and the refusal of Chilean courts to take action against those implicated in the Letelier case made it more difficult for the administration to move to lift the sanctions imposed by

Congress in 1976 against military aid to Chile. The House initially refused to do so, and in October when the Republican-controlled Senate voted to lift the ban, it accepted an amendment offered by Senator Percy, the chairman of the Foreign Relations Committee, providing that no military aid, credits or support assistance were to be provided until the President had supplied Congress with a report certifying that Chile had made "significant progress" in human rights, neither "aided nor abetted" international terrorism, and was taking steps to bring to justice those involved in the Letelier murder. Percy also agreed with Senator Edward Kennedy's request to hold full committee hearings on any such presidential certification. The objective of full normalization of relations with Chile still faced obstacles from the Congress and from the media (which published accounts of the importation of poison nerve gas from Chile by Letelier's murderers just as Congress was making final decisions on Chilean aid).

In 1982 the Chilean economy slid into deep recession, contracting by nearly 14 percent. Chilean reactions to the economic collapse included demands for a return to democracy and civilian rule. In 1983 a broad spectrum of parties from the Republican Right to the Socialists formed the opposition Democratic Alliance, and protests calling for the removal of Pinochet took place every month from May to November. The U.S. Embassy had already developed good relations with the opposition parties and trade unionists, and it now began to issue statements encouraging a return to civilian rule. Pinochet appointed a rightist civilian politician to conduct negotiations on holding congressional elections, but little progress was made because of Pinochet's insistence on remaining in power until 1989. Fearing that a radicalization of the opposition would benefit the Communists, the State Department sent various emissaries to encourage an accelerated transition, and in December 1983 Vice President Bush said to the press "We would like to see a greater adherence to democratic principles in Chile. If there were, you would see vastly improved relations between the United States and Chile." The prohibition of Chilean arms purchases remained in effect, since the human rights situations did not improve. As in Central America, although for different reasons, the administration had found that democracy and political freedom were important elements in U.S. policy toward Latin America.

The Bush statement was made on the occasion of the inauguration of Raul Alfonsin as elected President of Argentina in December 1983. The election of Alfonsin in October ended seven years of military rule, marked by massive violations of human rights, rising inflation, and a bungled attempt to take the Falklands/Malvinas Islands from Great Britain. During April 1982 Secretary of State Haig had attempted to mediate the Falklands conflict but finally announced at the end of the month that the U.S. would support its traditional ally, Great Britain. (It was later revealed that that support included material and satellite intelligence data.) When the British recaptured the Falklands in June, the military junta that had ordered the invasion was generally discredited, and the armed forces announced elections for 1983. When they were held Alfonsin's Radical Party won a surprising 52 percent majority. Alfonsin received from the military an economy with a 400 percent annual inflation, a debt of $40 billion, and pressing human rights problems involving an estimated 6,000-15,000 disappearances during "the dirty war" carried out by the armed forces against the Left in the late 1970s. The new president began trials (by military courts with appeals to civilian tribunals) of human rights abuses, postponed debt payments, and ended Argentine support for the CIA effort against Nicaragua. Relations with the U.S. remained cordial despite the memory of the Reagan administration's initial efforts to ingratiate itself with the military junta (which some critics argued had encouraged them to think that the U.S. would not oppose the Falklands invasion). The U.S. prohibition on military sales and credits was lifted-- although Alfonsín indicated the new government did not consider arms purchase a priority item.

Pressures for democratization were felt in other countries of the Southern Cone. In Uruguay 25,000 people demonstrated in September 1983 and a general strike was called in favor of democratization, leading the military to set November 1984 as the date for civilian elections. In Brazil municipal, state, and congressional elections were held in November 1982, leading to a victory of the opposition in the most economically developed areas of the country. Presidential elections were scheduled for 1985, and a debate raged over whether the system of indirect presidential elections which was subject to military control should be abandoned in favor of a direct vote. As in Argentina, the debt burden ($90 billion) was crushing, and the IMF adjustment program an easy target for the opposition. Food riots took place in São Paulo and Rio de Janeiro, and bankers worried about whether Brazil might default on debt payments if it returned to civilian rule.

The sturdy democracies of Venezuela and Colombia survived the economic pressures and carried out free elections in 1982 and 1983, while in Ecuador and Peru elected presidents battled economic setbacks and in the latter case, guerrilla opposition. U.S. support for democracy became formally institutionalized as the Congress authorized the creation of a National Endowment for Democracy in late 1983 to give financial and technical assistance to the promotion of democracy by U.S. political parties, trade unions, and business organizations. Given the recent continent-wide trend toward democracy, it seemed likely that a major portion of the Endowment's expenditures would be directed toward Latin America.

U.S.-LATIN AMERICAN RELATIONS: FROM CARTER TO REAGAN

Has U.S. policy toward Latin America changed under the Reagan administration? Yes, but not as much as those who articulated it at the outset indicated that it would. It began with the assertion of a dramatic turnaround of policy but found that domestic constraints in Congress and public opinion, as well as its international relationships, forced it to adopt policies that were in many cases not very different in substance from those of the previous administration.

In Central America, support for elections and reform and avoidance of identification with regimes that engage in systematic repression were prerequisites for the support of Congress and public opinion. Direct military intervention was exceedingly difficult because of the War Powers Act, and Congress still showed an assertiveness in foreign policy that limited presidential action. Human rights legislation remained on the books, including an Assistant Secretary of State with that special responsibility, as well as a congressional mandate for annual reports on the subject. Despite what looked like an ideological purge of some top career foreign service personnel, the permanent bureaucracy continued to exert an influence in favor of existing policies. Relationships with important Latin American allies such as Mexico and Venezuela required that policy be formulated in consultation with them, and their views taken into account. Before unilateral action could be undertaken, the impact of actions in Latin America upon U.S. worldwide responsibilities and relationships and on domestic opinion had to be considered.

Yet there were changes too. At the outset the Reagan administration continued to use aggressive rhetoric (often not matched by its subsequent actions) that emphasized the possibility of military solutions. Whether this was seen as a way to induce changes in the conduct of adversaries or was meant to justify its conduct to its conservative constituency at home, was not clear. Initially it seemed more interested in improving relations with Latin American military governments and despite the talk of using "quiet diplomacy" to promote human rights less willing to use any leverage the United States might have for the promotion of civil and personal liberties in friendly countries.

Yet in the course of the president's term it became increasingly evident that democracy and human rights had a continuing appeal and importance in the hemisphere. In Central America, it provided legitimation for military aid to El Salvador and Honduras and for economic aid to the region as a whole. In South America it was clearly the wave of the future as one military government after another returned to civilian rule.

What continued to worry its domestic and foreign critics was that in its determination to demonstrate that it did in fact represent a different approach, the administration might in a crisis situation take actions that might harm U.S. interests in the world and lead to the opposition of most of the hemisphere and the alienation of its European allies, who have become increasingly involved in Latin America over the past decade. Cuba remained an obsession, and from the time just before Ronald Reagan's inauguration when Castro attacked him as "fascist," "genocidal," and "covered with blood," it was clear that relations with that country were likely to deteriorate. In addition the flow of Cuban arms to Nicaragua meant that there was continuing pressure within the administration for forceful action against that country.

Yet this did not happen--both because of the arguments of the domestic and foreign opponents against a policy based exclusively on force and on "the hegemonic presumption" (Lowenthal, 1976:199-213), and because of the constraints built into the American system of government. And this is as the Founding Fathers, who called for "energy in the executive" especially in the area of foreign affairs, but also established a system of checks and balances, intended it to be.

The divergent approaches that the Carter and Reagan administrations have taken to Latin America suggest a number of continuing questions about U.S. policy in the Western hemisphere.

1. Should policy continue to be conducted as if it were a morality play-- with, in one case Soviet expansionism and, in the other, repressive governments, as the devils? Is it not possible to take a more pragmatic view of U.S. interests in the area?
2. As part of such a view, are not U.S. interests clearly greater in some parts of Latin America than in others? Crises or not, is it not time to recognize that in Mexico, the Caribbean and Central America, a special set of factors--notably geographic proximity and links of economics, energy and migration--argue for continuing U.S. concern for their defense from external subversion, and for the promotion of social justice, democracy and development?
3. What are the most appropriate means to achieve those goals--

particularly when they are in tension or conflict with one another? Are cutoffs in military aid an effective or useful way to achieve justice and freedom or simply a way of satisfying our consciences? Is a prohibition of military sales an appropriate way to influence the conduct of other nations when they can acquire what they need from other countries allied with us--notably France and Israel?

4. How can the United States best adjust to the development of divergent interests and relationships on the part of the countries of Latin America--in particular with Europe and Japan?

5. Why, except for a short period under the Alliance for Progress twenty years ago, have we not applied the policy recommendation made by Milton Eisenhower in the late 1950s--a handshake for the dictators, whether of the Right or Left, and an abrazo for the democratic governments?

Perhaps most important, the debate on Latin American policy reflects a large philosophical disagreement between those who regard force and national security as the central elements in international relations and those who believe that, at least in a democracy seeking to secure international and domestic support for its policies, the values and ideals of the United States must have an important role in the conduct of foreign policy. Is it not time to recognize that in practice neither view is sufficient in itself and that there are powerful constraints limiting any attempt to replace one conception with the other?

NOTES

1. For other examples of attacks on Carter administration policies by Reagan campaign advisers on Latin America, see the articles by Roger Fontaine et al. and by Pedro San Juan in The Washington Quarterly, Autumn 1980. These attacks also mention the Brzezinski book (Between Two Ages, New York: Viking, 1970), the Linowitz reports (published as The Americas in a Changing World, New York: Quadrangle, 1975, and The United States and Latin America: Next Steps, New York: Center for Inter-American Relations, 1976), and the study by the Institute for Policy Studies' Working Group on Latin America, The Southern Connection.

2. The White Paper seems to have been put together hastily, and it was subsequently subjected to critical scrutiny by The Wall Street Journal (June 8, 1981) and The Washington Post (June 9, 1981). They noted that the Spanish documents were sometimes inaccurately translated and summarized and that the figures as to the amounts of arms (800 tons committed, and 200 tons actually shipped to El Salvador) were exaggerated estimates not supported by the documentation. In addition, close scrutiny of the published documents showed an initial reluctance by the Soviet Union to support the guerrillas, as well as complaints in July 1980 on the Salvadorans' part of the lack of enthusiasm for their cause by the Nicaraguans, who were bent on protecting their own revolution. Nevertheless no one has denied that the trip was made, or that substantial arms of American manufacture traceable by serial number to Vietnam and Ethiopia did suddenly appear in, or en route to, El Salvador in late 1980. Nicaraguan and Cuban government officials have also admitted privately to third-country representatives that such arms shipments were made. See U.S. Department of State, Response to Stories about

Special Report No. 80, June 17, 1981. A follow-up State Department study, El Salvador: The Search for Peace, was published in September 1981. For evaluations of U.S. policy from a variety of points of view, see "Struggle in Central America," Foreign Policy, Summer 1981, and Richard E. Feinberg, "Central America: No Easy Answers," Foreign Affairs, Summer 1981.

3. For estimates by members of Congress on the strong constituent opposition to military aid to El Salvador, see The New York Times, March 26, 1981. The House subcommittee vote in March of shifting $5 million to Salvadoran military assistance was 8-7.

4. In the midst of the January final offensive, Bishop Rivera y Damas drew on Catholic moral teaching on the just war to set forth the four requirements for insurrection--serious abuse of political power, the exhaustion of peaceful alternatives, a positive balance between the evils of the insurrection and the good that could result, and the likelihood of success. Only the first condition, he said, was met in the current situation--thus imposing a moral obligation to continue to search for a peaceful solution. See Kerry Ptacek, The Catholic Church in El Salvador, Washington: The Institute on Religion and Democracy, 1981, p. 5.

5. Carter defenders argue that his administration was more willing to use aid as leverage to induce reform. See, for example, Richard E. Feinberg's essay on the Carter policy of "Creative Evolutionism" in Richard E. Feinberg (ed.), Central America: International Dimensions of the Crisis, New York: Holmes and Meier, 1982.

6. The Pol Pot comparison had been used by Jeane Kirkpatrick in the January 1981 article discussed above. On the Zimbabwe solution, see William LeoGrande, "A Splendid Little War," International Security, Summer 1981. For a discussion of the possibilities of international observer teams for the March election, see Robert Leiken, Prepared Statement, Subcommittee on Inter-American Affairs, House Foreign Affairs Committee, September 24, 1981, p. 13.

This chapter is a revised version of "Latin America: Change or Continuity," by Paul Sigmund which appeared in Foreign Affairs--America and the World 1981, Vol. 60, No. 3 (1982), pp. 629-657. Parts of the original version are reprinted by permission of the Publisher, Council on Foreign Relations, Inc.

Part 2

South America:
Economic Challenges
and Regional Conflicts

5
Argentina's Foreign Policies
in the Post-Malvinas Era

Dennis R. Gordon

> By virtue of its natural and industrial wealth, highly educated popula-
> tion, and agricultural potential in a hungry world Argentina is a middle
> power of some consequence. It is also a great trading nation, increas-
> ingly a source of industrial technology in its own right, and an active
> diplomatic presence in international organizations. . . .

Writing in the mid-1970s, Edward Milenky echoed the popular view
that Argentina was destined to emerge as a significant middle-range power in
global affairs (Milenky, 1978:7). Such optimistic views, though held by many,
were challenged by those who saw Argentina as having failed to utilize its
natural and human potential and was thus destined to be a comparatively
minor actor. In the aftermath of the costly defeat in the South Atlantic conflict of 1982, however, the debate over Argentina's potential as a regional and
global force seems less relevant. Paralyzed by serious economic problems
and with a civilian government attempting to repair the damage of eight
years of devisive military rule, Argentina's leaders face an international
environment where both their goals and policy instruments have been severely
curtailed. In this chapter we will consider the historical and contemporary
themes in Argentine foreign policy, with an emphasis on the combined impact
of defeat in the Falkland/Malvina Islands war and the continuing trade, debt,
and other economic difficulties. It will be argued here that although neither
territorial disputes nor sensitivity to the international economic environment
are new to Argentina, the structural nature of the current economic crisis
and the internal and external ramifications of defeat in war mark a new and
more limited international role.

TRADITIONAL GOALS AND POLICIES

With a strong resource base and a relatively homogeneous population
of European immigrants, Argentina has always possessed a definite view of
what its proper role in world affairs should be. Like other Latin American
states, historically Argentina's goals have included military-strategic,
economic-developmental, and status-diplomatic issue areas (see Chapter 15).
The goals of security and status were reflected in a desire for the formal
maintenance of national sovereignty and a legalistic emphasis on nonintervention. The concern with nonintervention frequently was aimed at the
United States. A desire for territorial integrity, reinforced by nationalism,

85

also produced specific geopolitical goals regarding Brazil, Chile, and the Falkland/Malvinas Islands. This emphasis on sovereignty was amplified by Juan Peron and more recently by General Leopoldo Galtieri who pursued what they saw as Argentina's rightful place in the global community.

The impact of Perón on the Argentine world view cannot be adequately assessed in this brief chapter. His nationalism and anti-imperialist rhetoric embodied in the so-called Third Position parallel many aspects of today's nonaligned movement. Perón's goal was to reap maximum benefit from both the United States and the Soviet Union while assuming a dominant place in regional affairs. The legacy of Peron's Third Position is seen today in Argentina's expansion of trade with the Soviet Union and Cuba and through efforts to directly influence events in Bolivia, Nicaragua, and El Salvador.

Hand in hand with a desire for sovereignty, security, and international recognition was the perennial need for economic development. With nearly 80 percent of its foreign exchange earned by agricultural exports, stable markets and prices were a continuing necessity. Historically Argentina looked to Europe and especially Great Britain for markets. After World War II Argentina, like most Latin American nations, sought to diversify its trade through import substitution, expanded foreign markets, and periodically, a nationalist-inspired effort to eliminate economic dependence on the more developed nations. In the search for greater independence, Argentina became a major Latin American industrial force. Following years of expansion, however, Argentina in the 1980s faced reduced markets for its industrial exports, a lack of local capital, and monumental debts. These economic problems, perhaps more than the somewhat symbolic issues of sovereignty and status, posed the most significant challenge to Argentina's decision makers.

FOREIGN POLICY DECISION MAKING

Guided by the general goals of political and economic sovereignty, Argentina's foreign policy has been shaped by its unique political culture and interaction with the international environment. Like all Latin American states, Argentina has been penetrated economically, politically, and culturally by North American and European influences. The agents of this penetration include a vast array of governmental, nongovernmental, transnational and supranational actors. Argentina's relationship with the more developed nations is characterized by what Keohane and Nye call "asymmetrical interdependence" (Keohane and Nye, 1977). According to this view Argentina possesses many resources to pursue its foreign policy goals. These resources include the nation's vast agricultural potential, its ability to offer markets and investment sites, its geopolitical importance, and its political support, particularly in the East-West competition. The elements of Argentina's power, however, lack the depth and dimension of other more developed nations and often can only be utilized at significant risk. The defeat by Great Britain in the South Atlantic is but one example of the limits of Argentina's power. The developed nations, in comparison, possess a varied arsenal of political, economic, and military instruments of power. While the United States, for instance, may be vulnerable on some fronts, the tremendous size and diversity of its economy and its relatively stable and homogeneous political institutions significantly expand its bargaining strength with the less developed nations.

In its dealings with other Latin American states, on the other hand,

Argentina's policy instruments are more useful due to its relative strength compared to most of its neighbors. Regional policies, nonetheless, are still limited by the bonds of interdependence as well as the legal and practical restrictions on military adventurism imposed by the Inter-American Treaty for Reciprocal Assistance (Rio Treaty) and the existent balance of power. It is within these global and regional power relationships that Argentina's internal formal and informal decision-making processes function.

Edward Milenky (1978:3-5) labels the two predominant tendencies among Argentina's foreign policy community as "classic liberal" and "statist-nationalist." Classical liberals generally stress free trade, export-led growth, openness to foreign investment, and a further integration into the global trade and monetary system. Politically, classic liberals tend to be conservative and aggressively anti-communist. They often promote strong ties with the United States and Europe. The military government of Jorge Videla and the short-lived regime of Leopoldo Galtieri with Roberto Alemann as Minister of Economics provide good examples of classic liberal regimes.

The statist-nationalist approach, as the name implies, is more overtly nationalistic and draws its economic policy from various formulations of the dependency perspective. The diverse group of statist-nationalist leaders questions Argentina's role in the international division of wealth and labor. As a supplement to agricultural exports, for example, statist-nationalists favor a diversification of trade patterns, expansion of state control over vital sectors of the economy, and management of foreign investment. Adherents to this approach may also stress stronger Latin American ties, regional integration, and a nonaligned foreign policy. Military leaders sympathetic to this point of view argue for more protectionism, local industrialization, and self-reliance as a method of insuring national autonomy. A strong industrial base, moreover, is seen as an essential component of national power.

Political factions emphasizing the statist-nationalist view have included first and foremost Juan Perón and his followers. Arturo Frondizi, president from 1958 to 1962, and his Movimiento de Integración Desorrollo (MID), also gave at least rhetorical support to statist-nationalist views. The election of Raul Alfonsín of the Unión Cívica Radical (Radicals) in 1983 inaugurated a leadership which promised to promote state intervention, protectionism, and a nonaligned foreign policy (LAWR, November 11, 1983:8-10).

A more extreme form of the statist-nationalist perspective is contained in the numerous socialist and communist parties as well as the more radical strains of Peronism. Drawing upon a variety of neo-Marxist concepts, this form of statist-nationalist thought is anti-imperialist, often overtly anti-U.S., and seeks basic structural changes in global trade and monetary relations. It also promotes a nonaligned foreign policy and as formulated by tercermun-distas emphasizes Argentina's natural identification with the Third World.

These ideological distinctions aside, the most influential groups in Argentine foreign policy tend to cluster in the middle. Except in extreme cases (such as the free trade policy of the Videla regime), most governments have employed aspects of both the classic liberal and statist-nationalist perspectives. During periods of constitutional rule, a strong executive, in combination with an inner circle of advisors, the Ministry of Foreign Affairs, and the military, generally establish and carry out the nation's foreign policy. A limited and select group of business leaders, intellectuals, and important foreign actors such as executives from transnational corporations, diplomats, military advisors, technocrats from developed nations and international organizations may also have input into the policy process. When the military was in power, especially the "institutional" regime from 1976 to 1983, the decision-making arena was further limited. The lack of civilian input allowed the military to dominate foreign policy as well as most other aspects of Argentine political life. Table 5.1 summarizes one dimension of this dominance, the growth of the military budget during the period 1975-1981.

TABLE 5.1
Military Spending: 1975-1981

	1975	1980	1981
Total, $U.S., millions	1,031	3,060	10,084
% of government spending	9.7	15.1	64.2
% of GNP	0.9	--	8.1

Source: Institute of Strategic Studies in Latin America Weekly Report, October 8, 1982:11.

The final component in Argentine foreign policy formulation is, of course, the general public. With a highly literate population and excellent coverage of international events in the press, the public is, by and large, well informed. The public is also highly nationalistic and civilian and military governments alike have utilized issues such as the Beagle Channel dispute, Falkland/Malvinas, and even the world futbol championship to build popular support and distract attention from internal difficulties. Still, the public's role in Argentine foreign policy is primarily a reactive one. Public input was virtually eliminated during the military government of 1976-1983. During periods of civilian rule, the strong presidency and other institutional factors have tended to limit direct public influence. The public's reactive power, nonetheless, cannot be totally discounted. Public outrage at the mishandling of the Falkland/Malvinas war (a situation exacerbated by government supplied misinformation), was a factor in the removal of President Galtieri. Still, with the government able to manipulate the flow of information and a military, either in power or waiting in the wings, the public's role must be considered limited.

In summary, decision makers attempt to make policy based on a minimum internal consensus which is also compatible with the external environment.[1] For most of its history, an internal consensus was difficult to achieve. Traditional rural-urban regionalism was complicated by the rise of Peronism and subsequent efforts to suppress the movement. The result was a lack of agreement not only on common goals, but on the basic ground rules of the political system. The lack of consensus, according to Frederick C. Turner, led to "political frustration, categorical reverses in economic strategies, military coups, terrorism and repression" (Turner, 1983:58). The inability to formulate and pursue a consistent and compatible foreign policy is seen in Argentina's dealings with its neighbors and the global community.

INTERACTION WITH REGIONAL ACTORS

Argentina's basic foreign policy issue areas, military-strategic, economic-developmental, and status-diplomatic, are evident in its regional policies. Historically, once the 1828 Treaty of Montevideo had created a Uruguayan buffer with Brazil, and the War of the Triple Alliance (1865-1870) ended Paraguay's efforts at empire building, regional concerns were not a top priority. Border disputes with Chile and general competition with Brazil aside, Argentina's economic and cultural ties with Europe defined national priorities. As late as 1929, only 6.4 percent of Argentine exports went to Latin America (Milenky, 1978:179). Following World War II, on the other hand, a variety of forces converged to direct Argentina's attention on regional matters. Factors affecting regional policies included:

1. the dramatic increase in Brazil's economic, technological, demographic, and military power;
2. the rise of Venezuela, Mexico, and other regional actors;
3. Cuba's revolution, offering an alternative model of development and support of insurrectionist movements;
4. rise of Soviet economic and political interest in the region;
5. rapid industrialization, fostering a need for regional export markets, and
6. the expanded penetration of the region by government and nongovernmental actors from the United States.

Argentina's expanded regional interest, to a large extent, focused upon Brazil, the awakening giant to the north.

Argentina's relations with Brazil are a curious mixture of geopolitical, economic, cultural, and,some would argue, psychological factors. Equally curious is the blend of competition and cooperation which characterize relations between the two states (Jaguaribe, 1975). Historically each nation has been suspicious of the territorial aspirations of the other, and both have vied for favor with the United States. Each has created formidable military establishments in the subtle competition for regional influence. Argentine fears are based in part on its indigenous school of geopolitical analysis developed at the well-respected Argentine Institute of Strategic Studies and International Relations. Clearly preoccupied with Brazil, this geopolitical perspective, according to John Child (1979:95), includes the following:

1. The fear of Brazilian expansion and hegemony.
2. A concern over a potential Brazilian-U.S. alliance.
3. A desire to promote Argentina's "natural" role as the leader of the Southern Cone.
4. Argentina's specific maritime emphasis, as opposed to Brazil's continental focus. This continental focus includes a desire to dominate the Amazon Basin and the buffer states of Bolivia, Uruguay, and Paraguay.
5. The goal of developing nuclear technology, especially if Brazil continues to advance in this area and appears capable of producing nuclear weapons.

Argentina's fear of Brazilian expansionism is not without justification. Possessing its own geopolitical goals, Brazil has pragmatically extended its penetration of neighboring states. One method of penetration, immigration and "colonization," is certainly not new to Latin America. In Paraguay, for example, approximately 80,000 Brazilians settled on unoccupied land, and in 1978 it was reported that 80 percent of the arable land in five frontier departments was occupied by Brazilians (Pittman, 1981:176). Brazilians are also reported to have settled in Uruguay, Argentina, and several areas bordering on the Amazon Basin. Such immigration, in conjunction with Brazil's many formal bilateral development projects, alarmed Argentina's leaders.

A concrete example of Argentine-Brazilian rivalry was the competing efforts to develop the hydroelectric potential of the Parana River (see Eliseo de Rosa, 1983). Each nation sought to exploit the Parana through a joint project with Paraguay, thus providing a reservoir of goodwill with an important neighbor while securing a vital energy source. Brazil's announcement in 1973 of an agreement with Paraguay to build the world's largest hydroelectric installation at Itaipu threatened Argentina's planned project downstream at Corpus. The Brazil-Paraguay project also challenged principles of international law long supported by Argentina. Argentina attempted to force Brazilian cooperation through various multilateral forums including the United Nations while courting Paraguay with its own proposal for a joint project at Yacryreta. Brazil, revealing its growing diplomatic prowess and power, offered Paraguay numerous inducements and stalled Argentina with a technical debate on international law while bringing construction at Itaipu to the point of no return. Argentina, preoccupied with internal matters (the return of Peron in 1973, the military coup of 1976, and the so-called dirty war against the Left), lacked a consistent diplomatic response to the Brazilian offensive.

Brazilian success with Itaipu, while revealing Argentina's diplomatic shortcomings, also shows the transitory nature of regional relations. Though Argentina lost its joint venture at Corpus, it continued plans to build the project at Yacyreta. After repeated postponements the final arrangements for the $U.S. 10 billion project were completed in October 1983, with construction scheduled to begin in 1984 and continue through the early 1990s. This timetable may actually enhance Argentine influence since the completion of Brazil's Itaipu project resulted in unemployment and other economic problems in Paraguay. A new infusion of capital, jobs, and consumer demand will be most welcome in Paraguay. Still, given Argentina's high foreign debt and other economic troubles, it remains problematic if it will ever be able to compete directly with Brazil for regional influence.

In spite of a history of competition, there are many areas of cooperation between Argentina and Brazil. In 1980, the two nations exchanged presidential visits and signed a variety of agreements on trade and technical cooperation, including the sale of 240 tons of fuel for Brazil's nuclear power program (LAWR, August 29, 1980:1). Brazilian exports to Argentina, encouraged by the military's free trade policies grew from $U.S. 331 million in 1976 to $U.S. 1,091 million in 1980. Brazil also provided correct, if not enthusiastic, support during the Falkland/Malvinas Islands war. This formal public support, nonetheless, concealed the true nature of relations between the two neighbors; while Brazil spoke of hemispheric solidarity, it also allowed "emergency" landing rights to the British during the war. Some have argued that this accommodation of the British by Brazil was granted in hopes of gaining a large sale of aircraft to the Royal Air Force (LAWR, June 10, 1983:3). In any event, cooperation between Argentina and Brazil may remain limited, due, in part, to mutual fears. Argentina will also continue to seek a military balance with a growing emphasis on nuclear research. "We don't know when it will happen," argues Argentine General Juan Enrique Guglialmelli, "but we are sure Brazil will build the atomic bomb. . . . If our neighbor gets the bomb, without a counterbalance, our own security will be affected" (LAWR, August 21, 1981:7).

Aside from its preoccupation with Brazil, Argentina's regional policy has been significantly colored by its western neighbor Chile. Possessing one of the world's longest common borders, relations between the two states have been a combination of territorial and ideological disputes mixed with important trade and economic interaction. Ideologically, Chile's pre-1973 history of constitutional government was quite distinct from Argentina's less stable civilian and military regimes. The relative ideological compatibility fostered by the pluralism of the Lanusse and Perón governments of the mid-1970s was shattered by the bloody Chilean coup of September 1973, a coup reportedly encouraged by Brazil. Though the establishment of a staunchly anti-communist regime of its own in 1976 restored a measure of ideological agreement, Argentina still feared a "Brazilianization" of Chile (Milenky, 1978:205). Underscoring these doubts were the more practical, long-standing geopolitical conflicts. Argentine-Chilean competition is best exemplified by the Beagle Channel dispute.

The Beagle Channel dispute focuses on three small islands, Picton, Nueva, and Lennox, which lie at the southern tip of the continent. Though the area has been occupied by Chile since the late 1800s, Argentina, citing international law and numerous treaties, claimed the territory as its own. After lengthy arbitration by a special British court, the area was awarded to Chile on January 25, 1978. That same day Argentina, noting the court's "errors, omissions, and overstepping of authority, declared the award null" (Embassy of Argentina, 1978:21). In spite of continued negotiations, both nations mobilized their forces. Amid border incidents, espionage, and a flurry of diplomatic activity, a temporary truce was achieved in December 1978 and the matter submitted to Papal mediation. Pope John Paul II, citing the desire for "brotherly coexistence" on the part of both peoples, called for the creation of a peace zone in the area (L'Osservatore, 1980:2).

Brotherly coexistence aside, Argentina has specific geopolitical concerns in the region. At the heart of the dispute is the "Oceanic Principle" which, according to Argentina's interpretation, consists of the following:

> The "Oceanic Principle," that is also called the Atlantic-Pacific Principle, establishes that Argentina has a right to the whole of the coasts, islands, and waters of the southern Atlantic, and Chile that same right to the coasts, islands, and waters of the southern Pacific (Embassy of Argentina, 1978:II).

Control of the Beagle Channel, along with the creation of a 200-mile maritime zone of sovereignty would make Chile an Atlantic nation, threaten communication with Argentina's Antarctic regions, and deny economic resources including potential petroleum reserves and fishing rights (Pittman, 1981:169). The three islands are essentially meaningless, but Chile as an Atlantic nation could cement bonds with Brazil, claim membership in any future South Atlantic collective security arrangement,[2] and deny Argentina passage to the Pacific in time of war.

Argentina's military leaders, though not rejecting the Pope's call for peace, remained noncommital on various proposed solutions, and turned their attention to the Falkland/Malvinas Islands and other more pressing problems. President Alfonsín, upon taking office, indicated that his government desired to settle the matter swiftly and would follow Vatican suggestions. The Vatican plan was reported to include granting Chile sovereignty over the islands while respecting the Ocean Principle through restricting Chile's maritime jurisdiction to three miles offshore. Free navigation, establishment of joint facilities, and the peaceful settlement of future disputes are also contained in the proposed agreement.

The settlement of the Beagle Channel dispute will be an important, but not a final, step in reconciling the two neighbors. Chile's all but overt support for Great Britain during the Falkland/Malvinas war, and continuing military cooperation is a major irritant to Argentina. Still, Chile and Argentina have strong economic ties. Argentine exports to Chile, for example, grew from $U.S. 91 million in 1970 to $U.S. 212 million in 1980. Thus as with Brazil, Argentina's relationship with its western neighbor continued to be marked by both cooperation and competition.

Argentina's concern about Chile and Brazil also influences its ties with other Latin states. Argentina's desire for positive relations with Peru, for instance, reflects geopolitical as well as economic priorities. Peru's traditional role as a balancer to Brazil, its access to the Amazon Basin, and its membership in the Andean Common Market, are all attractive qualities to Argentine policy makers. Although the radicalism of the "first phase" of Peru's military revolution (1968-1975) was occasionally troubling for Argentine leaders, the two states completed a variety of trade and other agreements, including a $U.S. 20 million Argentine credit to build a nuclear research institute in Peru. Argentina's subtle support for the Peruvian position during the renewal of the controversy with Chile and Bolivia over Bolivia's desire for an outlet to the Pacific reflected the goodwill between the two states. Support for Peru was also aimed at limiting Chilean expansion and preventing Brazil from obtaining easy commercial and other access to the Pacific by way of Bolivia (Gordon, 1979; Shumavon, 1981). Peru's clear support for Argentina during the Falkland/Malvinas war, including the provision of ten Mirage V aircraft, furthered good relations as did the even-handed peace efforts of Peruvian President Fernando Belaúnde Terry.

Another neighbor with which Argentina has maintained good relations is Bolivia. Argentina historically provided an important market for Bolivian natural gas and other exports. During the 1970s Argentina used economic and diplomatic means to expand ties with the conservative military dictatorship of Hugo Banzer. During the aforementioned renewal of the Question of the Pacific, Argentina successfully muted efforts by Brazil's President Ernesto Geisel to achieve a rapprochement between Bolivia and Chile. More recently, Argentine President Videla took an active interest in Bolivia by supporting the military coup led by General Luis García Meza which prevented President-elect Hernan Siles Suazo from taking office. Argentina was reported to have supplied intelligence officers who assisted with the coup and in suppressing internal popular opposition. Following the takeover, Argentina granted various forms of economic support including $U.S. 800 million in loans and credits during the period 1980-1982 (LAWR, February 19, 1982:2). Though Argentina's own economic and political difficulties during 1982 limited policy instruments, Bolivia remained an important and valued trading partner.

There are many other important aspects of Argentine regional policy, only a few of which can be mentioned here. One example of Argentina's independence in Latin American relations has been its policies toward Cuba since 1959. During the 1960s, Argentina adhered to OAS sanctions against Cuba. Following the staunchly anti-communist regime of General Ongania, however, President Lanusse's more pluralistic and pragmatic foreign policy recognized the potential economic and political benefits from an opening to Cuba. The Peronists who followed Lanusse in 1973 expanded his efforts to remove the U.S.-inspired boycott of Cuba and in the process increased trade and other contacts. Following the restoration of diplomatic relations in 1973, Argentina launched a massive trade campaign which produced over $U.S. 600 million in sales in less than one year (Milenky, 1978:218). Argentina not only built mutually beneficial ties with Cuba, but also set an example for its neighbors seeking independence in hemispheric affairs.

Since the mid-1970s relations with Cuba have waxed and waned somewhat. Still, in spite of vast ideological differences with the military regime of 1976-1983, Castro's government avoided direct criticism of Argentina and was a staunch supporter during the Falkland/Malvinas war. The growth of trade between Argentina and the Soviet Union has served to further Cuban interests and it is expected that relations will remain respectful and mutually beneficial.

The pragmatic if not contradictory nature of Argentine regional policy is seen in its treatment of civil insurrections in Central America. Due to splits within the military command, Argentina did not provide direct assistance in support of the faltering government of Anastasio Somoza in Nicaragua. Argentine representatives, in fact, voted in favor of the OAS resolution calling for Somoza's ouster (Gordon and Munro, 1983). Following the fall of Somoza, however, Argentina's military leaders became increasingly hostile to the Sandinista government in Nicaragua. As we shall see, some contend that President Galtieri's hostility towards Nicaragua in 1981 and 1982 was aimed at gaining support from the Reagan administration. Be that as it may, in February 1982 the Nicaraguan government claimed that Argentina had supplied $U.S. 50,000 to opposition groups. Argentina was also reported to have placed twenty to thirty military advisors in El Salvador and was considering sending a large contingent of troops to support government forces when events in the South Atlantic made such a move impossible (LAWR, February 12, 1982a:1-2). A curious aside to Argentine adventurism in Central America was the murder of former Nicarguan dictator Somoza in Paraguay reportedly committed by members of the radical People's Revolutionary Army (ERP).

In conclusion, recent history has seen a relative decline in Argentina's ability to pursue its security, status, and economic goals in the hemisphere. Once a regional actor of unquestioned importance, Argentina is undergoing a period of retrenchment and reevaluation of its goals and resources. In spite of economic and political setbacks following the South Atlantic war, Argentina still possesses the second largest military on the continent (approximately 185,000 regular forces), continues to acquire advanced weapons, and as we shall see below, has announced an acceleration of weapons-related nuclear research. The military is, nonetheless, seriously divided and a major change in the command structure has been undertaken by the Alfonsín administration. The economic cost of military adventurism as well as the Rio Treaty and other institutional aspects of the inter-American system all make direct conflict with neighbors unlikely. In order to solve immediate economic problems and confront what it considers negative structural aspects of the global trade and monetary system, the Alfonsín government will pursue greater regional cooperation.

Its current problems notwithstanding, Argentina has historically
enjoyed the respect of its neighbors. Its emphasis on international law and the
contribution made by OAS Secretary General Alejandro Orfila and other
representatives to international organizations, have boosted the national
image. The limits of Argentine power, made clear by the South Atlantic conflict, may actually enhance regional influence as the new leadership's interest
in the nonaligned movement produces more modest and hence realizable
foreign policy goals.

RELATIONS WITH THE DEVELOPED WORLD

Argentina's concern with sovereignty, security, economic development,
and international recognition is obviously tied to its relations with the
developed world. The developed world supplies arms, technology, and training
necessary for security and pursuit of geopolitical goals. The United States,
Soviet Union, Europe, and Japan provide major markets, vital imports, investment capital, and loans. The developed world also influences Argentina in a
number of overtly political ways including support for internal factions and
criticism of the human rights situation. Finally, the developed world also
provided the combatant for Argentina's only major military conflict in over
100 years.

Military-Strategic Issues

Historically Argentine global concerns have focused upon the United
States. Ironically, during the 1980 U.S. presidential campaign it was asserted
that Jimmy Carter's human rights policies had reduced American influence in
Argentina. In light of its growing trade with the Soviet Union, some charged
that Carter had actually "lost" Argentina. For the informed observer, the
notion of "losing" Argentina seemed somewhat humorous, for at most levels
of interaction, the U.S. never "had" Argentina. Indeed, relations between the
two states have been characterized by convergence and divergence. Historically Argentina's emphasis on respect for international law and nonintervention created friction with the "colossus of the north." During World War II,
for example, it required a major U.S. diplomatic effort to maintain Argentine
neutrality, let alone securing its active support against Germany. World War
II marked the low point in U.S.-Argentine relations. Since then relations
fluctuated around basic political and economic issues with agreement dependent upon the compatibility of various respective governments and the global
setting.

Like most other Latin American states, the Cold War provided Argentina with the opportunity to take advantage of many U.S. assistance programs. Between 1950 and 1979 Argentina received $U.S. 247 million in
grants, credits, and other forms of military aid. During the same period
4,017 military personnel were trained by the U.S. (Klare and Arnson, 1981:
48, 113). U.S. assistance was often rewarded. In the 1960s Argentina was for
the most part a supporter of U.S. regional and global policies. Argentina, for
example, originally backed U.S.-inspired sanctions against Cuba and the U.S.
invasion and occupation of the Dominican Republic.

Support for the U.S. was always tempered by the necessity to appear
independent. This was especially true for leaders from the statist-nationalist

perspective or those concerned with Argentina's regional image. With the rise of nationalistic governments in Latin America in the 1970s, Argentina was caught in a familiar bind. On the one hand it wished to become an independent force in the region. On the other hand, its leaders feared total isolation from the U.S., particularly when U.S.-Brazil ties appeared to be growing. In spite of this bind, both the Lanusse and Perón governments dropped ideological barriers and expanded contact with Cuba and other Third World states. Argentina was also increasingly at odds with the U.S. over a variety of economic and developmental issues. Although the military leaders which came to power in 1976 were anxious to improve relations with the U.S., their human rights abuses were a continuing roadblock. During the Carter years such disagreements led to a virtual halt in military aid. The election of Ronald Reagan and the rise to power of Leopoldo Galtieri in 1981 brought a renewed interest in the benefits available through strong ties with the U.S.

As we have seen, one aspect of Galtieri's courting of the United States was to offer military assistance in Central America. Galtieri also discussed granting the U.S. research facilities in Patagonia, providing troops for peacekeeping duty in the Sinai, and reducing trade with the Soviet Union. In return Galtieri hoped to secure assistance with debt and other economic problems. In keeping with his own political aspirations, Galtieri also sought U.S. support for Argentina's position in the Falkland/Malvinas dispute. The Reagan administration, in scheduling $U.S. 50,000 in military assistance for 1983, made a small but symbolic gesture toward closer cooperation. In choosing a military solution to the Falkland/Malvinas dispute, however, Galtieri's gross misinterpretation of U.S. priorities and of British values and national character (not to mention Margaret Thatcher's own political agenda), led to defeat and the end of his career. The South Atlantic conflict also ended any immediate illusions about the value of linking Argentina's foreign policy goals directly to the United States.

Following defeat in the South Atlantic, anti-U.S. feelings ran high in Argentina. A poll taken in June 1982 showed that while 30 percent of the residents of Buenos Aires considered Margaret Thatcher the "most hated" person in the world, 55 percent reserved that distinction for Ronald Reagan (LAWR, June 25, 1982:3). With the election of Raul Alfonsin it appeared that Argentina would become increasingly nonaligned, pragmatic, and oriented toward moderate Third World nations. Since the mid-1970s, Argentina had gradually expanded ties with several Arab nations and was reported to have received some minor assistance from Libya during the South Atlantic war. Like Brazil, Argentina sought to offer formal support for the Palestinian cause in the United Nations and other forums while not being overly critical of Israel. Though Argentina is essentially self-sufficient in oil, good Mideast trade relations are important to its economic recovery. Alfonsin also promised during the campaign to work for the withdrawal of Argentina from the Rio Treaty. Though the U.S. was somewhat tentative in embracing the new government, it promised increased military assistance and arms sales once the improved human rights climate could be verified. Alfonsin in turn made it clear that he expected debt concessions and other economic aid for Argentina's fragile new democracy.

The major turning point in Argentine political relations with the U.S. and Western Europe was the Falkland/Malvinas war. The territorial dispute has its origins in the late eighteenth century when England, France, and Spain almost went to war over the islands. Spain occupied the area in 1774, and the newly independent government of Argentina formally claimed sovereignty in 1820. Argentina maintained control of the islands until 1831 when a warship from the U.S. removed the Argentinians and set the stage for England to take control in 1833. Since 1833, the dispute has been a constant theme in Argentina foreign relations. In spite of long-standing but sporadic negotiations and various UN resolutions, a solution was not forthcoming. After months of fairly blatant preparations, Argentina invaded the islands on April 2, 1982. Though the causes of the conflict involve a variety of complex factors, Argentina's major motivations were clear.[3] Most agree that President Galtieri and his military colleagues viewed the conflict as an avenue to restore cohesion to a nation beset by political and economic cleavages. Victory in the South Atlantic, of course, would also serve Galtieri's own political ambitions. Behind these immediate concerns lay the geopolitical priorities discussed above and the hope that the region possessed valuable petroleum reserves. The leadership, of course, also seriously misjudged British resolve. "If Argentina had expected a muted and embarrassed British response," argued Lawrence Freedman (Freedman, 1982:200), "it was mistaken. Nothing could turn the Falkland Islands themselves into some great strategic and economic asset, but the circumstances of their loss turned their recapture into a popular cause." Lack of support from the U.S. combined with the inability of the United Nations and other organizations to forestall further violence put Argentina in a war for which it was ill prepared. The war itself revealed major disagreements among the military command and poorly trained troops. Only the sacrifices of the ground troops and pilots raised the costs for the British forces. Ultimately the war cost Argentina 1,366 casualties and millions of dollars in destroyed weapons, lost trade, and economic sanctions. The war also revealed Argentina's military flaws to its neighbors. With its president and general staff in disgrace, Argentina's claimed status as an important middle-range power was in serious doubt.

The question of the islands remains a major concern. Upon taking office, President Alfonsín stated that "we denounce as a grave threat to the security of our country . . . the installation of the military and nuclear fortress by the United Kingdom in the Malvinas . . ." (LAWR, November 11, 1983:11). Though shunning military solutions, Alfonsín promised that the recovery of the Malvinas will be one of the central aims of Argentina's foreign policy.

Economic-Developmental Policies

Though security and sovereignty are major foreign policy concerns, it is Argentina's economic relationship which is the most important aspect of its dealings with the developed world. Historically Argentina's trade was dominated by the developed world. Presently, 40 percent of exports go to the U.S., Western Europe, and Japan with Latin America taking 25 percent. The Soviets and Eastern Europeans receive approximately 25 to 30 percent of exports (LAWR, March 11, 1983:5). Argentina's major source of imports remains the developed capitalist nations which prior to the Falkland/Malvinas war provided nearly 70 percent of the total (LAWR, May 28, 1982:9). The U.S. alone supplies approximately 25 percent of all imports. The U.S. and Great Britain traditionally were also the major source of foreign investment, loans, and technology transfer.

Like other Latin American nations, Argentina relied on primary product exports (beef, wheat, corn), to earn foreign exchange. Also like other Latin Americans, Perón and other statist-nationalist leaders attempted to break dependence through import substitution industrialization. By the mid-1970s Argentina had reached near self-sufficiency in major industrial sectors such as autos and steel. The process of diversification, however, was by "industrialization by invitation,"--the importation of technology and the establishment of subsidiaries by transnational corporations. Thus ultimately the nature, but not the extent, of dependence was changed. Argentina became involved in a constant dialogue over technology transfer, profit remittances, and export restrictions imposed by the transnationals. Prior to 1976 Argentina's policy fell somewhere between the two extremes of an open door to foreign investment as characterized by the Chilean and Brazilian models at the time, and the "developmental nationalism" of Peru. During 1973-1976 the Peronists often found themselves involved in legal battles with various U.S. companies. The Peronists nationalized many foreign-owned firms including seven major banks and the Swift meatpacking plant. The resulting controversy, along with internal hostility towards foreign firms (a Ford executive was murdered in 1973), tended to reduce Argentina's attractiveness as an investment site.

The March 1976 coup brought a new look to Argentine economic policy. Faced with a balance of payments deficit of $U.S. 985 million in 1975 and inflation, labor unrest, and other problems, the military turned to rigid monetary controls and foreign borrowing (Frenkel and O'Donnell, 1979:191). A $U.S. 290 million loan from the IMF in September 1976 insured new public and private funds. Table 5.2 summarizes the evolution of Argentina's external debt.

TABLE 5.2
Argentine External Debt ($U.S. Millions)

1977	1978	1979	1980	1981	1982
8,210	11,193	18,299	24,543	30,794	32,100

Source: Economic Commission for Latin America (Iglesias, 1983).

In keeping with IMF conditionality, the classic-liberal policies of Videla's Minister of Finance José Martinez de Hoz produced a series of currency devaluations, wage controls, curbs on government spending, and the divestiture of many government-owned firms. Foreign investment was welcomed and protectionist measures reduced.

The successes and failures of the military's economic policies is a subject well beyond the scope of this study. Suffice it to say that a combination of internal factors, including speculation, capital flight, vast military expenditures, along with the external problems of global recession and rising energy costs plunged the nation into a crisis of major proportions. In 1981 consumer prices rose by 131 percent while gross national product fell by 6.1 percent (Iglesias, 1983:16, 11). Caught in the grip of stagflation, auto sales were off 30 percent and only 59 percent of the nation's industrial capacity was being utilized. Many local businesses failed due to competition from

Brazilian and other imports. The balance of payments suffered a $U.S. 3 billion deficit. President Galtieri's immediate response was more of the same. In early 1982 new denationalizations were announced and the once-sacred military industries were to be sold to the private sector. This further dose of the classic-liberal medicine was ended by a series of protectionist measures following the South Atlantic conflict.

The debt remains Argentina's most pressing economic issue. With public and private foreign debts of approximately $U.S. 40 billion at the end of 1983, 60 percent of annual export earnings were required simply to meet interest payments. Argentina is neither alone nor without international allies in the debt struggle. Indeed, more than one international banker has observed "if a country owes one billion, it's in trouble; if it owes 50 billion, the banks are in trouble." Alfonsin did not rule out collaboration with other debtor nations and made it clear that if democracy was to survive, some concessions must be forthcoming from banks and international agencies. Regardless of the terms, with foreign reserves standing at only $U.S. 300 million at the end of 1983, Argentina will continue to require loans and rescheduling arrangements for years to come.

One aspect of Argentine economics, its trade with the Soviet Union, has received significant international attention. Trade with the Soviets, of course, involves both a political and an economic dimension. Beginning in the mid-1970s, Argentina took a more active interest in the Soviet Union. Along with numerous trade agreements, various diplomatic and military exchanges took place. The Soviets avoided direct criticism of the military's human rights policies and occasionally supported them in international forums. Although Argentina voted to condemn the invasion of Afghanistan in the UN, its refusal to join the U.S.-sponsored grain embargo had major political and economic ramifications. Already Argentina's single largest market for corn, the Soviet Union imported $U.S. 3.4 billion in grain and beef in 1981. In the aftermath of the Falkland/Malvinas war, some estimate that the Soviet Union will provide 40 percent of Argentina's export market. This relationship is not without problems. The Soviets, for example, feel that the benefits of trade have been one-sided. Argentine exports to the USSR were $U.S. 3.95 billion between 1966 and 1980 while imports totaled only $U.S. 18 million (LAWR, November 20, 1981:4). Though the Soviets have pushed for a more balanced trade relationship, Argentine purchase of heavy equipment and other products have not been forthcoming. The relationship, nonetheless, is politically valuable for both states, particularly for Argentine leaders anxious to prove their commitment to a nonaligned foreign policy. Obviously the U.S. is not pleased with Argentina's newfound partner. Though claims of Soviet assistance during the South Atlantic war were exaggerated, the U.S. made its disapproval of Argentina's new friend clear. Be that as it may, Argentina and the USSR are, in many respects, natural trading partners, and the relationship has grown even during periods of extreme ideological incompatibility. It will take a concerted and costly effort to convince Argentina's leaders that trade with the Soviets is unwise.

CONCLUSION

In this brief study we have touched only upon the major themes in the formulation and execution of Argentine foreign policy. Although possessing a rich endowment of material and human resources, Argentina has witnessed its ability to fulfill foreign policy goals ebb away in recent years. In Latin America its influence and prestige have been directly challenged by Brazil's often subtle but powerfully effective economic and political expansion. Chile presents a direct challenge while Venezuela and Mexico enjoy prestige and influence once reserved for Argentina. Globally, Argentina's national image, already tarnished by human rights violations, suffered further by defeat in the South Atlantic. Although some nations sympathized with Argentina's territorial claim, few approved of the use of armed force. In light of these problems, it is difficult to assess the direction of future policy.

The revitalization of Argentine foreign policy is a difficult but not impossible task. The nation's agricultural resources, industrial base, and skilled workforce can provide the foundation for economic recovery. Economic recovery, of course, also depends on an end to the global recession and the availability of foreign loans on concessionary terms. President Alfonsín recognizes the potential strength in weakness and has made it clear that the restoration of democracy and protection of human rights depends, in part, on financial aid from the developed world.

One area which will have a definite impact on Argentine foreign policy is its nuclear research program. Argentina began independent research and production of reactors and fuel elements in the early 1950s. The Ongania government in the late 1960s opted for maximum independence through the establishment of its own research facilities and reactors. After a series of delays in the mid-1970s, the Videla government revitalized the industry and set a goal of establishing the complete fuel cycle (Luddemann, 1983:381). Argentina presently has several research reactors and two power plants (Atucha I and Embalse) in operation. In November 1983 the government announced that it had developed the uranium enrichment technology necessary for the development of nuclear weapons.

Argentina's goal of an independent nuclear industry and refusal to renounce the right to peaceful nuclear explosions has concerned the U.S. and many other states. Some critics feel that Argentina's decision not to sign the Nonproliferation Treaty raises serious doubts about the peaceful nature of the nuclear program. Argentina, for its part, has signed but not ratified the Tlateloco Treaty (Treaty for the Prohibition of Nuclear Weapons in Latin America) and accepted a variety of international safeguards on its research. Argentina has complained bitterly about restrictions on access to nuclear technology imposed by the developed nations. Following Britain's use of a nuclear-powered submarine to sink the cruiser General Belgrano, Argentina reserved the right to employ non-weapon nuclear technology in its own military applications (Luddemann, 1983:383).

There are many economic and technical impediments to the rapid development of Argentina's nuclear potential. Still an intense program could provide the ability to manufacture nuclear weapons in the near future. Such a development, though offering prestige, would provide little military advantage. Indeed, the decision to "go nuclear" would subject Argentina to enormous international pressure and could precipitate a regional arms race of unheard of proportions.

In a sense, the nuclear program is a reflection of the overall realities of Argentine foreign policy--lofty goals and some resources to pursue them, but a global environment where the major powers often frown on ambitious independent middle-range states. As Brazil has shown, it is possible to gain greater leverage through a carefully developed foreign policy. Given its serious internal and external problems, however, one can only speculate if Argentina can enjoy similar successes in the future.

NOTES

1. For a complete review of applications of the compatibility and consensus model see: Hanrieder (1967).

2. A South Atlantic version of NATO has been periodically discussed by the United States. Such an organization is usually seen to include Argentina, Brazil, Uruguay, and South Africa. See: Horowitz and Sklar (1982).

3. For a complete review of the legal aspects of the South Atlantic dispute see: Perl (1983). The military aspects of the conflict are discussed in Freedman (1982) and Laffin (1982).

6
Brazil's Foreign Policy: More Actors and Expanding Agendas

Wayne Selcher

Brazil's foreign policy decision process has recently become more complex and decentralized. The onset in 1982 of severe financial and trade problems, as well as the emergence of some unforeseen external political-security concerns, have drawn more governmental actors into participation in foreign policy decision and execution in political, economic, and military-security matters. Development of the governmental bureaucracy, greater direct foreign involvement of some private sector elements, and political liberalization had already been contributing for several years toward the institutionalization of a "foreign policy community" in the Western sense of the term. The heightened sense of urgency and national crisis starting in 1982 accelerated this trend and revealed diverse and competing points of view on national strategy and priorities which impinge on the full range of the country's foreign relations. These new interests resist channeling their activities through the Foreign Ministry and prefer to consolidate power by establishing their own direct relationships with foreign counterparts.

Although no clear manifestation of substantive change in the tone of Brazil's moderate international posture is yet apparent, different and more subtle considerations are increasingly affecting the decision process and the nuances of foreign policy. Different goals are being debated. Brazil traded the heady ambitions of imminent major power status of the early 1970s for the frustrations of coping as a dependent power with a 1980s environment which is more negative than positive for its growth. International economic recession hit Brazil at a high point of its international trade, finance, and capital needs exposure. The second petroleum price shock (1979) coincided with the highest cost period of its infrastructural investments, high international interest rates, and then a drop in world trade value. Thus ended the expansive global cycle on which the country had based its debt-led development. It became increasingly difficult to continue to stave off economic adjustment through massive foreign borrowing. Dreams of a "greater Brazil" gave way to the goal of a "viable Brazil."

Whereas formerly a technocratic separation between foreign policy and domestic politics was the rule, that distinction becomes less tenable as political liberalization progresses and international economic conditions require imaginative responses and domestic austerity. International affairs are negatively affecting Brazil's domestic life to an increasing degree, and more of those affected can be expected to demand policy consideration.

The balancing of short-run and long-run goals has become more problematic with the seriousness of immediate pressures and building uncertainty.

The government sees itself operating with reduced capabilities and less flexibility. At the same time, the country has developed a more sophisticated global policy and greater global significance by taking on a wider range of concerns and activities, including exports of manufactures, services, weapons, and military supplies. As the largest developing economy by far, Brazil looms increasingly large in international economic matters. This combination of more concrete stakes abroad and heightened international competition could well induce the government to take more assertive positions than in the past defending its national interests.

COMPETING AGENDAS IN THE FOREIGN POLICY COMMUNITY-- CONTROVERSY WITHIN CONSENSUS

The Fundamental Consensus

Brazil's foreign policy rests upon a broad consensus of values within the government, most of which have been developed and practiced by the Foreign Ministry as the long-term custodian and articulator of national diplomacy (Selcher, 1981:98-101). Sharp divisions within the government, over major issues, have been by far the exception rather than the rule. Controversies today are still more common over matters of priority and style than over divergent goals. The consensus of caution, gradualness, moderation, and an issue-by-issue approach is not in serious danger. Certain goals, however, are being questioned as other actors take on greater foreign policy roles and as policy divisions on more issues spread through the Figueiredo government. Most of the differences in foreign policy preferences are administrative turf battles traceable to varying bureaucratic priorities and prerequisites rather than to greatly divergent substantive orientations. Yet there is sufficient and growing diversity and nuance to make the foreign policy decision process more complicated leading to outcomes which are harder to predict.

Current Characteristics of the Foreign Policy Decision Structure

The Presidency-Central Authority in Disarray. Nominally, responsibility for foreign policy rests with the president. In practice, President Figueiredo has apparently delegated much authority, in spite of fairly frequent summit diplomacy. Deeply concerned about the economic situation and the threat it represents to political liberalization (abertura), his personal triumph, Figueiredo is largely absorbed in domestic affairs and the presidential succession process for the indirect elections of early 1985. Acknowledging his weakness in economic matters, he has left international economic affairs largely to Antonio Delfim Netto, Minister of Planning. Figueiredo, politically frustrated and suffering from heart problems requiring treatment in the United States, increasingly failed to provide firm leadership to resolve policy differences and coordination among his ministers. The result was an acceleration during 1983 of the diffusion of foreign policy power, with the various ministries seizing whatever opportunities presented themselves.

The president-centered foreign policy triad of ministers has been General Rubem Ludwig (Head of the Military Household), General Octavio Medeiros (Head of the National Intelligence Service), and General Danilo Venturini (Minister Extraordinaire for Land Matters). João Leitão de Abreu (Head of the Civilian Household) took on greater executive responsibilities during 1983 as President Figueiredo's effectiveness weakened with his health, but Leitão de Abreu's duties remained heavily directed toward domestic political matters. The chief executive decision body is the 9 AM group, which meets daily at that hour but deals largely with domestic matters. It is composed of Figueiredo, Medeiros, Venturini, Leitão de Abreu, and Delfim Netto. Foreign Minister Ramiro Saraiva Guerreiro is usually present when a foreign policy matter is on the agenda. Increasingly, foreign policy issues are also considered by the National Security Council (CSN), composed of the foremost military and civilian ministers. The National Intelligence Service (SNI) is also turning some attention toward foreign affairs. The staffs of both the CSN and the SNI prepare foreign policy studies and make recommendations to the president.

The Foreign Ministry--Overtaken by Events. The Foreign Ministry (Itamaraty) was until recently the single dominant bureaucratic actor (but not always the winner) in most foreign policy situations and enjoyed this position for decades. Its influence was probably the highest and least challenged under President Geisel (who had an above-average interest in foreign policy) and Foreign Minister Azeredo da Silveira (1974-1979). During this period, Brazil tilted deliberately toward Western Europe and the Third World and away from the United States on economic and political matters, with an ecumenical policy of ambiguous "responsible pragmatism." In many instances this stance took the form of opportunism and a sharp awareness of national vulnerabilities which avoided confining obligations and long-term commitments.

The Ministry attained leadership through an unusually successful schooling and socialization process which has established a degree of homogeneity, a high level of professional expertise, and relative continuity of policy. Even in the most repressive years of the post-1964 regime, the rest of the government tended to defer in foreign affairs questions to the Foreign Ministry, which in turn stayed carefully within the rather broad consensus parameters assigned to it. Although quite conscious of the ideological differences that separate them from typical diplomats, the military establishment as a whole has always shown considerable respect for the diplomatic service (in contrast to its view of other bureaucracies) because of its analogous career structure, professionalism, and nationalistic orientation (Barros, 1983b:5-6). Further, until recently the military command perceived insufficient foreign threats or opportunities to lead to military interest in international affairs to a degree which would give them the concrete stakes or incentives to challenge Itamaraty interpretations.

Since 1969, under three presidents, the Minister of Foreign Relations has been a professional diplomat, and very few nondiplomats have been named as ambassadors. To further enhance the ministry's power to coordinate foreign policy for the entire government, it assigns diplomats to the international affairs offices of other ministries with dealings abroad. In contrast to the experience of other ministries, Itamaraty has provided talent from its well-trained ranks for the other areas of government, but has suffered very little intervention itself.

Itamaraty, with its elitist recruitment patterns and emphasis upon merit, is the paragon of technocratism and has benefited greatly from the adoption of that mode of governance as it reached an activist zenith under Presidents Medici and Geisel (1969-1979). Ironically, even with the growing criticism of the technocratic process by the political element under abertura, Itamaraty with its success, capabilities, and reputation for competence and honesty is one of the few ministries in the Figueiredo government to enjoy significant prestige, consensus, and favorable public image. (In fact, its Third World stance has actually helped to limit to just a few cases opposition criticism of the government's foreign policy.) Yet the habit of that same closed, reserved style makes it difficult for the Ministry to adapt to the current conditions of greater competition and debate. Mounting an effective bureaucratic challenge would require new attitudes foreign to the institutional ethos and the personal style of the foreign minister.

In broader perspective, the gradual weakening of the Foreign Ministry's upper hand by competing forces has been a longer-term tendency, thrown into strong relief by the events of 1982-1983. Itamaraty retains in principle its function of providing overall coordination, philosophical orientation, conceptualization, and sense of coherence and direction in the framework for policy. In reality, it is being engaged on a broader domestic front and increasingly being overtaken in important functional areas in which vital decisions are being made and future political capital built. Sometimes the Foreign Minister has decided cautiously not to try to carve out a larger role, as in the case of the negotiations on the debt (which could go sour) and the information policy (which is a national security issue). The tendency is for the Foreign Ministry to be left with a core of judicial and formal representation functions and less with tasks of policy making and execution. This implies, of course, inability to coordinate overall policy and, in the absence of clear executive leadership, the rise of proliferating sectorial interests--what Barros (1983a) calls "irresponsible pragmatism."

The preference of upper-level economic and military officials to talk directly with their foreign counterparts and to travel abroad more extensively strengthens their agencies' powers of decision and further diminishes Itamaraty's opportunities for influence. In some cases, its diplomats on assignment to other ministries have taken on loyalty to the office where they are employed relative to the Foreign Ministry's position, as that office gains momentum of its own. Even the Foreign Ministry's role in presidential visits abroad has been diluted under Figueiredo, relative to the work of the president's own staff and the participation of other ministries.

During the expansive period of the economic boom and major power aspirations, the Ministry's penchant for a sense of history and the long-run view of Brazil's place in the world was more saleable and even somewhat intoxicating. With more somber immediacies on the current agenda, grand planning and major initiatives critical of momentary targets of opportunity are less viable, useful, or welcome. Generally speaking, the Foreign Ministry now has the freest rein in rhetorical pronouncements but finds that as harder assets or specialized competencies become involved, its role is progressively diminished by competing interests. The ministry's very success in fostering good political relations with all countries has ironically taken it from the center of current policy making. The governmental decision for Brazil to limit its political role abroad further restricts its expression beyond more traditional representational diplomacy.

The rise of economic, financial, and security issues (in which its competence is weaker) has further limited its bureaucratic position. The erosion in economic affairs is especially apparent as Foreign Ministry spokesmen defensively fight the idea that trade and debt matters in themselves constitute foreign policy or imply alignments which restrict the government's independence of political expression. To the contrary, they argue that the present international crises merely point up the accuracy of what Brazilian diplomats were proclaiming all along about the nature of international mechanisms and power relationships on the North-South dimension, and the need for structural readjustments. Yet, in practice, the ministry's political pronouncements during 1983 were subdued in order not to complicate solutions of economic problems.

The Economic Area--The Supremacy of Economics. The "economic area" is a term widely used to designate the Ministries of Planning, Finance, Industry and Commerce, and Mines and Energy, along with the Bank of Brazil and the Central Bank. Sometimes the term is extended to include state companies, as diverse as Petrobras (petroleum) and IMBEL (war materials). Of all these, Planning and Finance are the most important in foreign affairs, but Industry and Commerce, Agriculture, and Mines and Energy play significant roles in narrower spheres. Rivalry between the economic area and the Foreign Ministry dates to the early 1970s, when the aggressive and ambitious Antonio Delfim Netto, then Finance Minister, began to carve out an international role for his ministry. The consequent policy wrangles, in which Finance took positions more amenable to the First World and Itamaraty tilted toward the Third, continue along similar lines today.

The Foreign Ministry's current difficulties are multiplied by the greater breadth of the foreign affairs agenda, the overwhelming weight of economic issues, President Figueiredo's vacillation in settling disagreements, and the crucial ability of an even more powerful Delfim Netto as Planning Minister to field a well-located and cohesive interministerial monitoring and support team. While such functional specialization is common in developed countries, it is new enough in Brazil that the diplomats in the economic-commercial section still have difficulty becoming accustomed to being deliberately circumvented or more frequently overruled.

More than any other single factor, the drive to export manufactured products changed the task structure of Brazil's diplomacy. Prior to the early 1970s, Brazil's foreign sales were made up largely of agricultural commodities, whose commercialization was under the control of autonomous bodies (such as the Brazilian Coffee Institute) which still have a major role. In order to upgrade the relevance of their functions in the new Brazil evolving during the economic boom, the economically oriented diplomats started a Department of Commercial Promotion in the early 1970s. Led by the energetic Ambassador Paulo Tarso Flecha de Lima, it represented a revolution in the ministry's self-image. Eventually the promotion service was established in most of the diplomatic posts abroad. Yet, many observers feel, it lost out in sales aggressiveness to agencies from the economic area, which have more rapidly advanced their actions on a broader front. In addition, severe budget cuts for this department in 1983 badly hampered its activities relative to those of the economic agencies.

The Foreign Ministry assumes its most important trade role in the articulation of political positions on multilateral trade issues and in the skillful negotiation of bilateral trade agreements. Yet trade negotiations are increasingly carried out through coordination of all ministries involved which effectively dilutes the weight of any one. Industry and Commerce, for example, tends to disagree with Planning and Treasury on commodities policy. The Foreign Ministry is not central in setting general trade policy or in making allocations of resources supportive of export promotion, as in the politically sensitive area of export credits. This task is performed by the Foreign Trade Section of the Bank of Brazil (CACEX) under the Finance Minister and with the supervision of CONCEX, the Foreign Trade Council, an interministerial body which meets only infrequently. The Monetary Council also sets trade policy because of its infuence over credit and exchange rates. An across-the-board process is hard to define, because an issue is often decided by or channeled to the most interested official. A number of rivalries are based on workload priorities or personalities. At the sales level the Foreign Ministry is concerned chiefly with trade promotion, while the Finance Ministry establishes lines of commerce and offers direct credit support of specific cases through CACEX, the Bank of Brazil, and the Reinsurance Institute.

The substitution in February 1983 of Benedito Moreira, with fifteen years experience as head of CACEX, by Carlos Viacava, Secretary-general of the Finance Ministry, was widely interpreted as a consolidation of Delfim Netto's power in the trade area at the expense of Itamaraty. (The extent of the rivalry and of Delfim's power is shown by the fact that Moreira was not even informed beforehand about the 30 percent maxi-devaluation which occurred that month, ostensibly to promote exports.) The Foreign Ministry would find its commercial role completely eliminated should a Ministry of Foreign Trade be formed, but that idea is too controversial to be seriously considered, whatever its organizational merits. Meanwhile, coordination of foreign trade policy is made all the more difficult because seven ministries are now involved in international commercial activity, each within its own defined competence.

The rise of trading companies has also spread initiatives and power of decision at the implementation level. Whereas only 6.8 percent of Brazil's exports in 1976 were handled directly or indirectly by trading companies, in 1982 they accounted for 30.3 percent of all exports. In December 1982, 130 such companies were registered with subsidiaries in 42 countries (Trading Companies: 10 anos de exportacao, 1983). The largest is Interbras, the export arm of Petrobras which facilitates sales of Brazilian goods and engineering services, especially when oil is purchased, and accounted for 40 percent of the total sales of these companies in 1981. Interbras is often the Brazilian government's preferred bargaining/contracting instrument in government-to-government relations (including with Eastern Europe) and in negotiations with oil exporters. COBEC, the Bank of Brazil's trading company, specializes in agricultural commodities and maintains warehouses in key entrepôts. In 1981 it accounted for 13 percent of the total sales of the trading companies, giving these two official agencies over half the sales of the group.

During the last decade, the international operations of the state enterprises have been the leading edge of Brazil's expanding presence abroad. The most active is Braspetro, the international arm of Petrobras, which is prospecting, extracting oil, or lending technical assistance in over a dozen developing countries and represents Brazil in bilateral and multilateral relations with other Latin American state oil companies. Petrobras' success in procurement of supply contracts and investment opportunities has definitely benefited from the Foreign Ministry's establishment of good political relations with other developing countries. Its own record and self-confidence abroad with political support from the presidency, however, led it to pursue some independent courses of action. Its president, Shigeaki Ueki, has traveled widely for direct negotiations on petroleum supplies with foreign governments and companies.

One point of contention for several years was Petrobras' preference, during the height of OPEC's power, for purchasing somewhat cheaper petroleum from the more politically troubled Persian Gulf area, even though such key suppliers as Kuwait and Saudi Arabia showed no interest in making significant purchases from Brazil. With an eye to diversification and reducing the trade deficit with oil suppliers, which reached $6.08 billion in 1982, Itamaraty eventually prevailed with its decentralization plan to purchase more oil from those suppliers with significant internal markets open to Brazilian products, such as Nigeria, Mexico, Venezuela, and Angola.

Nuclear energy is another area in which the Foreign Ministry was once the front runner but then lost control to the economic sectors of government. Itamaraty was a major force behind the decision, about 1967, to acquire an independent national nuclear science and energy capability. Paulo Nogueira Batista, a career diplomat who worked on the political rationale for Brazil's rejection of the Nuclear Non-Proliferation Treaty, founded and became the first head of Nuclebras. The Foreign Ministry was central, with Batista, in the negotiation of the controversial 1975 nuclear technology transfer agreement with West Germany. Yet when the decision was made in early 1983 to decelerate the national nuclear energy program for economic reasons, as long urged by Delfim Netto, Itamaraty had no significant voice. That decision was made by the National Intelligence Service, the National Security Council, and the Ministry of Planning.

Contrary to the broad, political, principled, and long-run vision of the diplomats, the economic technocrats operate on narrower, tangible, ad hoc, immediate, and "bottom line" considerations and are less preoccupied with the idea of dependence and Brazil's developmental vulnerabilities. They are more content to compromise and work within the present international system than to demand a new order and are more amenable to consideration of a formalized Advanced Developing Country (ADC) or "graduation" status for Brazil in multilateral organizations. The economic technocrats, in search of ready dollars, are more prone to be critical of immediate costs inherent in longer-term ventures which may not produce to satisfaction, especially under current cost constraints. They are more likely to feel that foreign policy rhetoric concessions on issues of importance to the United States are an acceptable and really cosmetic price to encourage or repay what they see as crucial U.S. economic support in areas of Brazil's vital interests. Defenders of the more assertive Foreign Ministry outlook characterize this tendency to be purist, to rely on the U.S., and to do what the U.S. wants as a remnant of the simplistic old national complex fixed on imitation of U.S. patterns and styles.

In part, the rise in power of the economic area has been a function of the vigorous personal styles of Delfim Netto and his team, so a change in personnel could change its degree of aggressiveness and supposed First World orientation. That group of ministries is not and could not be as deeply socialized or homogeneous as Itamaraty. The "economic trio" of Antonio Delfim Netto, Ernane Galveas (Treasury Minister), and Carlos Langoni (Central Bank President, 1980-September 1983) suffered massive credibility gaps and lack of confidence at home. Yet even their substitution by a team operating under different premises would not cause a major institutional power shift, because the economization of foreign policy has proceeded too far.

The Military--Changing Concepts of National Security. Structurally, the military establishment or influential individual officers can find access to foreign policy most readily through the officers in the National Security Council and the National Intelligence Service, the two generals in the 9 AM group (Venturini and Medeiros), or personal acquaintances with President Figueiredo. These types of contacts have frequently entailed differences with policies contemplated or pursued by the Foreign Ministry, such as the concept of a "peaceful South Atlantic" appearing in joint communiques with African states. Cliques and networks occasionally adopt a foreign policy stance, but such dissatisfaction is no longer customarily expressed directly or openly in

spite of rare anonymous leaks to the press. Most officers are reticent to
comment publicly on foreign policy issues since Figueiredo's disciplinary
efforts, through Army Minister Walter Pires, to depoliticize the military and
weed out open dissenters for the sake of abertura. Even in cases such as the
Foreign Ministry's persistent courting of Marxist Mozambique, which rejected
many overtures, higher-level military officers swallowed their objections and
attended a 1981 state banquet for visiting Foreign Minister Chissano. To an
overwhelming extent and in strong contrast to the combative "ideological
frontiers" concept of the early 1970s, the Brazilian military has come to
accept the desirability of economic cooperation with a wide variety of
regimes, at least outside of South America.

It is likely, as the military disengages from internal politics, that it will
reassert its traditional role in international security concerns, which would be
seen as quite legitimate by civilian leaders, particularly after the Falklands
War. The air force and the navy have been more active than the army in
seeking such a role, partly as the result of the nature of that war and partly
because of a more outward-looking orientation. The rapidly expanding defense
industry, with strong government support and production directed to domestic
and Third World markets, is another logical outlet for increased attention. A
recent administrative reform of the ailing War Materials Industry (IMBEL),
while bringing in a civilian president, included an upgrading of army participation in administration of the state company. (Private companies such as
Engesa, on the other hand, are responsible for the bulk of national production
and operate under civilian control, with engineers predominant.) For the military, the arms industry has a strong national security dimension because it
provides a greater degree of economy of scale as well as production and maintenance autonomy for their own forces. Moreover, force modernization
implies international comparison and frames of reference.

The Congress--Search for a Role. Even in democratic periods, Brazil
has not developed a strong foreign policy role for the Congress, both because
congressional authority has been weak and because foreign policy power has
been concentrated for so long within the executive itself. The Senate has the
power to question (but not veto) newly appointed ambassadors and to approve
or veto treaties, but very seldom challenges the governmental position in such
matters. Frequently, governmental pretexts of inconvenience have been
sufficient to keep the Senate from exercising the right of examining the newly
designated ambassadors to foreign posts. Both houses have foreign relations
committees, which have been accustomed to debates with little consequence.

The more the government needs coalition politics to pass its programs
with an opposition majority in the Chamber of Deputies, and the greater the
domestic effect of foreign policy decisions, the greater is the opportunity for
a foreign policy role for Congress. Opposition victories in the November 1982
elections created an impetus for opposition parties to use Congress as a place
to register their differences with the government's Social Democratic Party
(PSD). At times, the domestic effects of foreign policy become the most
prominent national issue and Congress asserts itself. The most important
foreign policy role for the institution in 1983 was its assenting vote on Decree
2065, which cut wage and salary increases to levels under the cost of living
index as part of negotiated agreements with the International Monetary Fund
(IMF). Congressional ability to block passage of anti-inflation measures
central to official economic policy gives those critical of governmental
austerity programs a chance to strike a nationalistic blow against the unpopular IMF and pits abertura and congressional power against the executive

branch and the IMF. Even more appealing to the opposition are demands that Congress have the right to approve or veto any future agreements that the government concludes with the IMF.

A few senators, especially Marco Maciel (PDS, Pernambuco) are working toward a more vigorous foreign policy participation model closer to that of the U.S. Senate; however, these senators might well be content with considerably less. They have counterparts in the Chamber of Deputies in such as Jackson Barreto of the Foreign Relations Committee. The ambition for significance beyond rhetoric runs against a strong national tradition of executive dominance, as well as very weak legislative competence in foreign affairs. What is more likely is a more assertive oversight or investigatory congressional capacity, especially regarding issues of foreign debt, multinational corporations, foreign trade, and security. The government's Partido Democrático Social (PDS), however, would try to forestall or frustrate any congressional inquiry which would prove too embarrassing to the executive branch, even at the expense of undercutting Congress' institutional powers. In the informational and dialogue sense, in contrast to his predecessor, Foreign Minister Guerreiro has been cultivating relations with Congress, speaking to the body frequently by invitation and showing openness to their comments. Delfim Netto has spoken to both houses on international economic policy, but with favorable receptions and notably less openness.

Indicative of another type of effect, aimed at public opinion, was the petition to President Figueiredo of 196 congressmen of all five parties in May 1983 condemning "American imperialism" in Central America and requesting a clear Brazilian rejection of U.S. interventionism against the Nicaraguan revolution as well as asking for the designation of an ambassador (rather than the current charge d'affaires) to Managua. During July, a committee of 19 federal deputies from the Partido do Movimento Democratico Brasileiro (PMDB), Partido dos Trabalhadores (PT), Partido Democratico Trabalhista (PDT), and the Partido Democrático Social (PDS) visited the United States and Nicaragua to explore the matter further, and carried out the whole exercise with views critical of American policy. Whereas previously the government received sharpest criticism on foreign policy largely from the right (the conservative press and sectors of the military), this episode was a forerunner of more critical comments from the left.

The Press--Upsurge of Interest. Only a few metropolitan newspapers and national magazines consistently provide quality analytical coverage of foreign policy; furthermore this is the work of a small circle of journalists, about ten strong professionals at most. Even these are disadvantaged by the media's practice of assigning reporters to individual ministries rather than to functional topics, such as trade policy or international finance. Most of those covering foreign policy matters, then, are assigned to and enamored of the Foreign Ministry, accept its explanations largely at face value, defend its "prerogatives" against "encroachment" from other areas, and serve as sympathetic channels for "leaks" in bureaucratic battles. The relative scarcity of independent information, Itamaraty's mystique, and the suave ways of its diplomats hinder objective reporting. Weak training and ministerial loyalty, or the sense that foreign affairs "belong" to the Foreign Ministry, prepare most commentators poorly for taking a broad or evolving view of the diffusion of foreign policy power and of the limitations on considering Itamaraty as the definitive spokesman on all matters of foreign policy. Reporting on relations with the United States is rarely tendentious but tends to play up and overemphasize political differences between the two countries, miss the complete

picture, contain unreal expectations, and assume that Brazil bulks larger in
U.S. foreign policy than it really does.

The weight of foreign affairs in national life and the freer atmosphere
and euphoria of abertura are producing more frequent press comments and
editorials on foreign policy. The most consistent thread has been criticism
of Itamaraty's Third World policies by O Estado De São Paulo and Jornal do
Brasil, with editorial lines more sympathetic to the worldview of the economic
area. The impact of the press on foreign policy formulation has been at best
indirect and diffuse, serving as a conditioner of public opinion, a vehicle for
elite dialogue, and a source of ideas as alternatives are debated. The press is
becoming more investigative and critical than in earlier periods--a development which is spilling over into foreign policy when controversial events arise
and is creating cases to which the government feels a need to respond. This
new development is likely to continue.

During the 1982 Falklands War and the April-June 1983 episode of the
grounding of the four Libyan planes carrying weapons to Nicaragua, for
example, the quality press engaged itself seriously in investigative journalism
and publication of intragovernmental discrepancies and disagreements. Coverage of the latter affair in its earliest stages cast the issue in terms favorable
to the Air Force's hardline approach of retention, as against the Foreign
Ministry's inclination just to escort the Libyan planes out of national air space.
During the Falklands/Malvinas War, the press coverage, as with public opinion,
tended to be more critical of Argentina than was the official position. After
the war, the press created a diplomatic flap with Buenos Aires, to the chagrin
of Itamaraty, by revealing in June 1983 that dozens of British military planes
on the way to the Falklands were being granted refueling stops in southern
Brazil, with greetings from Brazilian Air Force officers. Press coverage this
time tended to bolster the Foreign Ministry against the Air Force.

In August 1983, the Estado de São Paulo, as part of a series on excesses
of the government and the state companies, published denunciations claiming
conflict of interests in the manner in which the Planning Ministry continued to
favor the trading company Comexport by extending large credits to Poland in
return for dubious promissory notes after the embassy in Warsaw's warnings
about that country's economic decline. (In so doing, Brazil became one of
Poland's major Western creditors at the level of $1.8 billion by mid-1983.)
These charges, part of a general attack on Delfim, cited the Secretary-
general of the Planning Ministry, a former director of Comexport, as a chief
benefactor in the case. Spreading accusations in the press of more irregulari-
ties in Planning Ministry trade procedures in other cases heightened the old
feud between the Planning and Foreign Ministries, and set off personal recriminations among several officials of the foreign policy community. So much
criticism was raised that Aureliano Chaves, acting president at the time, set
in motion an investigation and a congressional committee looked into the
affair.

Public Opinion--Expanded Need for Legitimacy. Because of habitually
low public interest in foreign affairs and the rather closed decision making
system which did not encourage such interest, the impact of public opinion on
foreign policy formation has been minimal. Domestic political liberalization
has not yet had a counterpart in foreign policy, and relatively few politicians
have demanded it. Foreign policy was not an issue in the campaign for the
November 1982 elections, largely because the opposition was in general agreement with the Foreign Ministry's views and identified those pronouncements as
representative of the entire government.

Over the last several years, some of Foreign Minister Guerreiro's speeches have contained general references to the domestic transition to democracy and diplomacy's obligations to the broadening of the political process. (This theme, at the very least, aided closer political relations with the democratic nations of Latin America.) President Figueiredo's September 1982 speech to the UN General Assembly, the first for a Brazilian head of state, was calculated in significant measure for the domestic audience during the election campaign period in pointing to the international causes of the nation's economic woes. However mild these cases may be, they represented a substantial departure from the customary post-1964 practice of largely ignoring public sentiments.

The educated urban segments, despite parochialism, are aware of international events and trends affecting Brazil. Various recent events sparked comments from the educated urban public to an unusual extent--the Falklands War, President Reagan's visit, the rapprochement with the U.S., the IMF agreement and its renegotiation, the first national expedition to Antarctica, and the Libyan planes incident. These episodes in a short space of time generated fundamental debate about nationalism, sovereignty, democracy, debt-led growth, regionalism, and the country's position relative to the United States, the West, and the Third World. The degree of sophistication among the recently aware may not be high, but nationalistic public pressure on foreign policy issues with an economic component will grow inevitably as the social impact of the austerity program takes hold and is linked to Brazil's international financial commitments. Such an impact could be felt in a diffuse way through the government's growing need for broad social and party support for its programs, through interest groups, or in a more specific way through a foreign policy-relevant role for Congress.

Judging from the results of the November 1982 elections, the opposition represents the most developed, best educated, and most affluent sectors of Brazilian society. It has no broadly enunciated foreign policy position, but does hold the attitudes to form one different from and more nationalistic than that of the Figueiredo government. Anti-IMF sentiments are especially prominent. These discontents spread during 1983 and now find wide currency among the political elite and the governmental bureaucracy. Yet, despite some ambivalence, insecurity, and distrust, most of the opposition is on balance favorable to the United States if Brazil is perceived as being treated "fairly." Most informed Brazilians see the United States as too vital to their country to antagonize it. There are presently quite a few skeptics regarding the rapprochement, some enthusiasts, but few outright opponents. Only the small Marxist-influenced Workers Party (PT) among the legal parties is hostile to American policies in a clear and systematic way.

There is a growing tendency in the educated public to associate the United States in a negative way with nationalist symbols--foreign bankers, the IMF, high international interest rates, multinational corporations, and commercial protectionism. There is some concern about supposed political conditions which are assumed to be the counterpart for U.S. help in the debt question. Brazil, on the other hand, is seen as a victim of circumstances beyond its control and as having few options. Accustomed to generations of nearly uninterrupted economic growth, starting in 1981 Brazilians had to adjust to what is widely perceived as an externally imposed period of negative growth or stagnation. Heavy U.S. participation in the current debt-led, foreign investment model which is increasingly discredited makes the U.S. a possible target of the radical opposition across several parties--a scapegoat for the economic crisis.

Public sentiment to repudiate the loans is still weak, but may well grow. In polls few Brazilians say they feel personal benefit from the foreign borrowing. The government could rely on a nationalistic streak should it choose in the name of sovereignty to resist the IMF more openly or to force a renegotiated stretchout of the debt profile. Its badly battered domestic image would certainly be partially restored by such a move, especially if tied to a partial rollback of austerity measures. In any case, should public consensus and the demands of the international bankers clash, the government can no longer be expected to conform to the bankers' demands and ignore or suppress public reaction.

The term "lobby" and the concepts behind it, in American practice, are still novel in Brazil. Few groups are yet organized as foreign affairs lobbies, beyond the existence of sectors pushing for advantages from government in foreign trade and sales of services, or broader segments speaking out on the debt. Some spokesmen of trade associations have approached American officials to explain their industries' point of view, and the National Confederation of Industry established a short-lived congressional liaison representation in Washington in late 1982. Given the weakness of internationalism in the Brazilian elite and middle class, nevertheless, it is not likely that abertura will produce a large number of specifically foreign affairs interest groups or greatly increase the serious foreign policy issue public. Sporadic injections of foreign affairs issues into the political process and pronouncements or actions on foreign relations issues by groups with a heavily domestic purpose (such as São Paulo businessmen) are more likely outcomes.

RECENT POLICY DYNAMICS IN ASCENDING ISSUE AREAS

Brazil's foreign policy process revolves increasingly around responses to finance, trade, and, to a lesser extent, political-security issues. Policy differences over these issues and separate or overlapping spheres of bureaucratic competence in these matters have recently been giving rise to more divergent views within the foreign policy community. The outcome of the debate led in 1982 to an upgrading of the value placed on the role of the United States as partner. This partnership is not yet fully established and is counterpoised in some sectors by lingering doubts about the ultimate compatibility of important national interests of the two countries. The policy dynamics of the contextual issues within which Brazil's future role and its relationship to the United States are being worked out are discussed below.

Finance

Management of the foreign debt of approximately $U.S. 94 billion (by the end of 1983) is the principal issue of the country's foreign relations, and the international financial community's chief problem. Faced with mounting inability to make all payments due in late 1982, Brazil reached an agreement with the International Monetary Fund (IMF) in December 1982 and with its principal creditors in February 1983. The IMF agreed to provide $4.9 billion over a period of time to strengthen reserves and cover anticipated balance-of-payments deficits. The creditors agreed to advance a $4.4 billion jumbo loan, refinanced the $4 billion in principal due in 1983, and continued trying to maintain $10 billion in inter-bank credit and $8.8 billion in short-term export credit. The United States provided $1.83 billion in bridge loans over a six-month period to help Brazil meet its external liquidity requirements, while the Bank for International Settlements (BIS) forwarded $1.2 billion in bridge loans.

Because of cash flow shortages, Brazil suspended payments on principal starting January 1, 1983, with creditor foreknowledge and acquiescence. Yet within several months it was obvious that the government continued to face liquidity problems as the IMF and interbank credit targets were not met. Incoming loans were being used to pay off loans coming due. Restoration of the inter-bank credit line was far below the amount requested. By early June 1983 Brazil was $1.2 billion in arrears in payments for the year and asking the BIS and other creditors for more time to pay. The IMF withheld for several months the payment of the second portion ($411 million) of its loan because of disapproval of parts of the government's austerity measures and its inability to meet agreed-upon goals. As a supporting action, private creditors withheld disbursement of the second portion of their jumbo loan. Brazil's official overoptimism, unwillingness to slash the federal deficit, opposition to reducing real wages, and frequent inability to balance the daily international financial ledger were increasingly contrasted with Mexico's progress in implementing adjustment measures.

In the face of minimal domestic economic progress in the first half of 1983, weak prospects for the remainder of the year, and the waning confidence of bankers, rumors of an impending moratorium to bring about a rescheduling of at least the short-term loan profile and perhaps a grace period of several years began to circulate in credible sectors in Brazil and abroad. Other authorities continued to defend a gradualist solution of continual adjustment and further lending through negotiations with the IMF and the creditors, hoping things would work out in the long run after the supposedly short-term current liquidity difficulties. Internally, the economy suffered a recession of several negative percentage points, inflation estimated at an annual rate of about 200 percent, and growing unemployment. Scattered disturbances and protests in São Paulo and Rio de Janeiro against two austerity packages in the first half of 1983 raised the possibility of political instability.

The decisions of debt matters in 1982 and most of 1983 were reached largely through a deepening conflict between Planning Minister Delfim Netto (and his network) and Central Bank President Carlos Langoni, his chief opponent in the economic area. (Treasury Minister Galveas had a much more limited policy role.) Delfim, of a somewhat Keynesian bent, tended to be casual or overly optimistic about setting economic targets and more concerned about opportunities for renewed growth and the internal political effects of the adjustment program. He characteristically defended compromises between IMF demands and growth policies, as well as a major negotiated extension of the repayment period through U.S. government rather than IMF auspices vis-à-vis the banks. Langoni, a Chicago-trained economist, was less tolerant of inflation and favored strict monetarist solutions with coherent effects and less gradualism. He was more intent than Delfim on setting realistic economic targets and then striving seriously to attain them. As a result, and partly because of a more forthcoming style, Langoni was preferred by foreign creditors and the IMF. But his image abroad also became tarnished by association with failing policies. Langoni's replacement by Affonso Celso Pastore in September 1983 marked a victory for Delfim Netto.

The Foreign Ministry has no effective impact on the decision process relating to debt negotiations (including the IMF agreement) and is sometimes only belatedly informed of major course changes. It is not a member of the important Monetary Council and has no line responsibility in financial affairs. The "economic trio" deals directly with banks, foreign ministries of finance, the U.S. Federal Reserve Board, and key foreign ambassadors in Brasilia. Itamaraty is one of the strongest centers of opposition in the government to Delfim, especially to his incrementalist solutions and his attempts to make the debt the only issue that matters. It is very critical of the way the negotiations have been handled and has led in defining debt repayment as a strategic political issue of solvency rather than a tactical or technical one of liquidity. The Foreign Ministry's consensus goes beyond the economic area's public position of continuing within the IMF agreement to defend a negotiated moratorium or, ideally, a new multilateral institutional arrangement to accommodate otherwise intractable Third World insolvency. Yet it does not support creation of an organization of Latin American debtor nations to pressure the creditors jointly.

President Figueiredo's September 1982 UN speech was drafted mostly by the Foreign Ministry, but the language was toned down at the insistence of the economic area, eager for U.S. help on the debt question. Even so, the tone of the speech made it clear that traditional IMF methods would be unacceptable and unworkable for Brazil. After this presidential attempt to open negotiating space, the economic team largely accepted the IMF formula in December. With events running against accomplishment of the IMF targets, the longer-term Foreign Ministry interpretation gained ground elsewhere in the government. Yet in renegotiation of the debt, a role is conceivable for the Foreign Ministry under current circumstances only as an advocate to foreign governments for a brief prepared by a body of economic specialists from around the government.

More officials are coming to see a vital role for the U.S. in stretching out the debt, which is a principal motive for fostering rapproachement. It is hoped that with U.S. government underwriting, more favorable terms can be obtained than if the Brazilian government had to deal directly with the banks by itself. Brazil depends upon what is termed the "moral debt" owed to it by the U.S. and the West, because of their own interests in Brazil's strategic position as the key country of South America, the largest developing economy, and the largest LDC debtor, suffering from negative economic trends emanating from the industrial world. The implicit threats of default or social upheaval serve as a bargaining tool in Brazilian efforts to secure easier terms.

Trade

Expansion of exports and restrictions on imports have been central to Brazil's debt management by providing a positive balance of trade. Despite a retraction of world commerce in 1981, Brazil managed to expand exports to $23.3 billion, with a record surplus of $1.2 billion, led by a surge in sales to the Third World (35.9% of its exports and 57.4% of its imports). However, in 1982 trade problems developed, with global recession, Third World debt, and the Falklands/Malvinas War cutting deeply into Third World sales. Protectionism in manufactured products threatened to restrict access to developed markets. Lower average prices per unit for most of Brazil's important products also contributed to reduction of total revenues to $20.2 billion. Even under these difficult conditions a surplus of $778 million was attained in 1982.

The $6.3 billion trade surplus target for 1983 under the IMF agreement put great pressure on trade promotion officials but was one of the few original goals of the IMF agreement which Brazil was capable of achieving. A number of factors brought circumstances favorable to a stronger trade balance in 1983, especially a 30 percent maxi-devaluation of the cruzeiro in late February, sharp curtailment of imports, a decline in petroleum prices, and American economic recovery. Trade promotion therefore continued close behind financial concerns as a chief foreign policy goal.

The main policy disagreement in foreign trade concerns the extent to which continued promotional priority should be given to newer Third World and East European partners as contrasted with increased attention to more reliable developed partners. Brazil's sales to developing country and East European markets during 1982 contracted much more rapidly than sales to developed ones. (See Table 6.1.) Payment problems with developing country and East European accounts by mid-1983 reached over $6 billion and $5 billion total in arrears, respectively, according to a former ambassador to Poland (O Estado de São Paulo, August 31, 1983:1). During 1983, the international trade of developing countries continued to decline. A number of the agreements the Foreign Ministry achieved to sell engineering services in developing countries, such as the Kapanda hydroelectric project in Angola, became unfeasible because of financing difficulties. Therefore the short- and medium-run economic payoff of Brazil's Third World economic initiatives came under greater scrutiny as the government pragmatically began to reconsider the more attractive and reliable First World alternatives, also the country's largest customers. Some Planning and Finance Ministry officials in particular have been critical of many developing countries' inabilities to pay in the hard currency Brazil needs to pay the debt, as well as the need to finance some of their purchases at promotional rates of interest which Brazil can ill afford.

TABLE 6.1
Variations in the Value of Brazil's Trade with Major Blocs, 1981-1982

Bloc	Exports (%) 1981	1982	% Variation in Absolute Value, 1981-1982	Imports (%) 1981	1982	% Variation in Absolute Value, 1981-1982
Developed Countries	51.1	56.5	- 4.0	40.0	37.3	-18.1
Developing Countries	27.1	24.8	-20.7	18.0	20.5	- 0.1
Oil Exporters	8.7	6.9	-31.5	39.4	38.5	-14.2
Eastern Europe	7.3	5.8	-31.5	1.1	2.4	+91.6
Total	94.2	94.1		98.5	98.7	

Source: Calculated from CACEX, Banco do Brasil, Brasil, 1982: Exportação e Importação--Balança Comercial, Mimeographed, 1983. (In these aggregate official statistics, Venezuela is classified in the developing countries category rather than the oil-exporter category.)

Brazil sells too many manufactures and purchases too many raw materials in the Third World to make an exclusive First World commercial option, however. In 1981, for example, 51.7 percent of Brazil's manufactured products and 36.8 percent of its semi-manufactured goods sold abroad went to developing countries. The Foreign Ministry, architect of the Third World emphasis, has suffered funding cuts which hinder its developing country economic initiatives, but it still defends the long-run complementarity Brazil shares with those economies. This view finds supporters in the government and in the military among those who believe that a Third World political identification is useful for commercial reasons because of the role of their governments in trade. On the other hand, trade and finance with the United States, Western Europe, and Japan are based more on market conditions.

A related policy problem is the damaging impact on the balance of payments of the chronically negative balance of trade with the oil suppliers, -$6.08 billion in 1982 and -$6.67 billion in 1981, contrasted with a surplus of +$6.9 billion in 1982 and +$7.9 billion in 1981 with all other partners combined. The solution to both difficulties has been a greater preference for oil and raw materials suppliers which are willing to pay in hard currency for Brazilian goods (especially manufactures) or services or, more commonly, to engage in what are essentially barter operations. Reciprocal credit accounts are then kept in dollars by the central banks to satisfy GATT requirements, keep foreign exchange outlays low, and make trade more balanced. Countries with which such bilateral agreements have been struck include Angola, Algeria, Mexico, Nigeria, and Venezuela, with others under negotiation.

In this way Brazil can still utilize its South-South complementarities and take advantage of bargaining power conferred by a weaker oil market. The system lacks the flexibility of hard currency operations and does not bring in dollars to build an actual trade surplus, but it can be used as part of a supply contingency plan for possible future credit squeezes and dollar shortages. Its role in securing petroleum is vital, especially if accompanied by a political understanding. The mechanism is a Foreign Ministry idea which has yet to prove its full efficacy, but its adoption by CACEX now has the ironic result of cutting the Foreign Ministry out of some major trade dealings. The dynamic Carlos Viacava, Director of CACEX, has been responsible for the negotiations and travels much more widely than did his predecessor. Under his tenure CACEX has emerged as foreign trade coordinator, in both exports and imports, as part of the Ministry of the Treasury. Most of the subsequent exchange of goods is carried out through Brazilian trading companies.

Economic area officials have been more content to work within GATT than have the professional diplomats, who feel more comfortable with global political solutions and with the Third World tone and support in UNCTAD. Treasury officials are most influential in setting overall trade policy and show more receptivity to U.S. interests. They have been more willing than the diplomats, for example, to use the export tax mechanism to avoid U.S. surcharges on Brazilian products benefiting from government subsidies.

Political Security

Traditionally Brazil has had few security concerns and has seldom been involved in the kind of "high politics" diplomacy typical of the northern hemisphere or of the major currents of world politics. Its military preparedness has consequently been at a low level for a nation of its size (expenditures about 1.0 percent of GNP), with a largely internal security mission for the armed forces.

The Falklands/Malvinas War. During 1982 and 1983, however, several events abruptly heightened governmental awareness of external security issues and set off a debate on the extent and types of potential future threats and how the nation can best avoid them or respond to them. The first and greatest shock was the Falklands/Malvinas War, which presented several diplomatic and economic rather than military problems for Brazil. The suddenness and violence of the unanticipated engagement of modern weapons, after more than forty years without major armed international hostilities on the continent, jolted Brazilians out of a complacency that regional territorial disputes were unlikely to erupt into war. The performance of the Argentine air force and that nation's subsequent rapid rearmament caused many military and some civilian officials to reflect seriously upon the modernity and adequacy of Brazil's military establishment, even with the current favorable political relations with Buenos Aires.

For Brazil, the security lessons of the Falklands War turned out to be an acceleration of trends already underway, with common purposes of reducing foreign dependency and improving information flow and organization:

1. reaffirmation of the predominantly internal mission of the armed forces and of the role of capable diplomacy and moderation in defusing conflict and preventing war
2. only a slight increase in military spending
3. slight acceleration of plans to create a more autonomous intermediate technology national weapons manufacturing capability rather than purchase fewer and more expensive sophisticated weapons abroad
4. improvement of the land and coastal air defense radar net
5. consideration of an integrated military command to mitigate inter-service rivalries and improve coordination of forces via joint exercises
6. validation of military diversification away from the U.S. and toward Western Europe
7. questioning of the value of alliances, tempered by opposition to a radical restructuring of the inter-American system
8. re-emphasis on keeping political relations with Argentina manageable, so that at worst Buenos Aires could come to represent an annoyance because of erratic behavior rather than a threat because of hostility directed toward Brazil.

Brazil became further involved in controversial political-security issues of interest to itself and others during 1983. First there was the retention of four Libyan planes transporting arms to Nicaragua and then the decision to furnish broad economic and security support to the government of Lieutenant Colonel Deysi Bouterse in Suriname, courted by Cuba and isolated by the United States and the Netherlands. Strong action on these matters, which affected the country directly, contrasted with much less emphatic policies toward the more distant conflicts in Central America.

Libyan Aircraft Incident. The case surrounding the four seized Libyan planes (April 19 to June 7, 1983) provides some insight into national security policy disputes, even though the episode is unlikely to be repeated. Upon learning that the planes were carrying weapons destined for Nicaragua, rather than the medical supplies they had claimed when requesting landing permission, Air Force Minister Delio Jardim de Mattos ordered them detained. Both his position as head of all civilian and military air traffic movements in the country and his role as confidant to President Figueiredo placed him centrally in the ensuing events and sidelined the Foreign Ministry. General Jardim de Mattos, invoking national sovereignty, ordered that the planes could leave Brazil only by flying back to Tripoli, with the military supplies returning separately. (This was the logic of the solution the air force adopted for a British Vulcan bomber which stopped in Brazil on the way to the Falklands during that war.)

Alert to the potential for a deadlock of wills and to the threat to negotiations for major weapons and airplanes sales to Libya, the Foreign Ministry took the view that Brazil was the more vulnerable party and tried to minimize the matter's political ramifications by hewing to the Chicago Convention and a legal approach. It recommended a quick inventory and replacement of the contents, escort of the planes out of national airspace, and a note of protest to Tripoli. General Jardim de Mattos and other military hardliners won the president over to the "point of honor" argument, Qaddafi adamantly refused to accept the "separate return" terms, and the imbroglio was on.

After several false starts and many fruitless diplomatic meetings with lower-level Libyan representatives, governmental pragmatism and the merits of the larger relationship won out. While in Paris at the Le Bourget air show, General Jardim de Mattos met a high-level Libyan military representative and returned to Brasilia with him. Ensuing encounters with this special emissary of Qaddafi, first with Saraivo Guerreiro and then in the presidential palace, resulted in an agreement whereby the planes returned to Libya one at a time with the cargo, and the arms sales negotiations continued. After a long and uneasy interval with intense national press coverage, both the Foreign Ministry and the Air Force Ministry came out of the episode in a somewhat positive light, but it was the military that both unleashed the episode and brought it to solution.

Several issues were at stake in the affair. Conservatives used the occasion to criticize the substantial arms sales to Libya, all the more embarrassing if Brazilian arms had been found in the cargo headed for Central America. At least hypothetically, Brazil had to consider the political implications of its arms sales. Foreign Minister Saraiva Guerreiro, losing influence rapidly in the economic area, now saw initiative of a fait accompli swing to the military and particularly to one of his outstanding critics within government. The essence of the Foreign Ministry's "soft line" eventually prevailed, but the slowness of its acceptance contrasted with the more rapid adoption by the military of Itamaraty's thesis of a slight and cautious tilt toward Argentina in the Falklands War. The negotiations were supervised collectively by the ministers of the National Security Council, the National Intelligence Service, the Air Force, the Military Household, and the Foreign Ministry, a sort of "crisis cabinet," with final decision going to President Figueiredo. Military interest in the case was further enhanced by their national security oversight role in arms, airplanes, and computer sales, already important in the Libyan connection, and in sales of nuclear technology, which is under discussion with that nation.

Suriname. Because of its concern with national security, the military has apparently played a lead role in determining policy toward the Bouterse government in Suriname, which had accepted Cuban aid and advisers. Itamaraty professes less concern than does the military that leftist political developments since 1982 and assassinations of political opponents will lead to Cubanization of Suriname. The chief goal of lending economic and security assistance is preventative, to provide a South American alternative to Cuban influence with the hope of keeping Cuban regular forces and the East-West conflict out of South America, as well as to discourage instability on the borders.

Military officials tend to ascribe an exaggerated geopolitical value to the densely forested border with Suriname and to draw parallels with Central America, probably due to their memories of the Araguaia guerrilla campaign in the Amazon, the only rural guerrilla experience they faced during the military regime. After initial diplomatic groundwork and a visit of Bouterse to Brazil, General Venturini, head of the National Security Council, visited the military government in Paramaribo on short notice in April 1983 as a personal emissary of President Figueiredo, both to show high-level backing for his offers of assistance and to underline firmly a military interest in the relationship. The Foreign Ministry sent a highly regarded ambassador to Paramaribo, and the army is to name a military attaché.

The Suriname case could represent a departure in Brazil's relationships with its smaller neighbors, and an indicator of Brazil's future continental security role in terms of areas of influence. In any event, it represents Brazil's first attempt to supplant Cuba or even to compete politically with Havana. Brazil characteristically avoided public judgment on the internal merits of the regime, but uncharacteristically took a risk in lending a sizable and broad economic and security package under favorable conditions and with clear but publicly unstated political prerequisites. Bouterse accepted the bid and in return lowered his Cuban connections, first partially as a response to Brazil's position and then more thoroughly with expulsion of the Cuban ambassador and most of his staff after the assassination in October 1983 of Grenada's Prime Minister Maurice Bishop, another ministate recipient of Cuban aid.

Should Bouterse or a successor play the Cuban card again, the Brazilian government will be faced with a dilemma in which not only reduction of aid but also intervention will be an option seriously considered. Itamaraty is not given to thinking in national security terms, and the military appear willing to go beyond the diplomats' anti-interventionist orientation should a clear political reversal to the point of a threat occur. Brazil is not experienced in exercising power abroad and regularly disclaims intentions to do so. Yet it is implicitly involving itself in the internal affairs of Suriname and Paraguay, and perhaps others in the future, while not being fully appreciative of where these involvements may lead. Acquired interests and a projection of influence could come to require a projection of power to sustain them.

In other security matters on the northern frontier, Brazil has tilted slightly toward Guyana in its border dispute with Venezuela, to discourage the latter from having recourse to force (perhaps across a strip of Brazilian territory) and the former from requesting Cuban support. The army positioned several pioneer platoon outposts to show the flag along uninhabited stretches of the borders with Colombia and Venezuela. Recent military command and communication reorganizations in the Amazon also signal renewed interest in the region since the Falklands War. Rumors of a development of a rapid deployment capability for the northern borders, however, were officially denied and seem unlikely.

Central America. The Central American conflicts were involved behind both the Libyan and Suriname cases, but the Brazilian tendency has been to downplay that connection to avoid wider political ramifications. Cross-pressures from the U.S. and Latin America and aloofness because of distance from the region have produced calculated ambivalence. Unlike the situation with Suriname, Brazil casts itself here in the role of an interested observer with an attitude more than a policy. Brazil's main interest in both cases is to discourage injection of East-West competition into local problems which would spread the conflict. The military command takes a clearly anti-communist view of Central America, but the official position leans much more to Itamaraty's principled preferences--to support nonintervention and self-determination, to emphasize the internal causes of the conflicts, to recommend negotiated solutions, and to maintain political neutrality sufficient to trade with all parties. (Yet the government shows no interest in reactivating relations with Cuba, a taboo of the military.)

Only during an April 1983 trip to Mexico did President Figueiredo affirm support for the negotiating efforts of the Contadora Group. This occasion was chosen for a full elaboration of Brazil's position to align Brazil more closely with Mexican policy, affirm independence from Washington during the Libyan planes episode, and register views immediately before President Reagan's address on Central America to a joint session of Congress. Yet subsequent requests from the Contadora Group for more concrete support have been turned down, with the explanation that Brazil's political weight in the region is insufficient to justify a serious commitment. Brazil has explicitly refused to support any American military action against Nicaragua, but maintained a low profile during the May 1983 OAS debates on American pressures on Managua, and declined official comment on the July-August 1983 naval exercises off Central America's coasts. Further, it does not interpret American military aid to El Salvador as interference, because it was officially requested.

Future Trends. Some skeptical observers saw the unusual series of security-related issues as merely transitory or random events, but they have been taken as indicators of future trends by enough decision makers in Brasilia to foresee the gradual emergence of a national security component in Brazilian foreign policy in South America and perhaps the Caribbean. Some bolder analysts are questioning the wisdom of Brazil's characteristic avoidance policy of aloofness from regional flashpoints, such as the Beagle Channel (Argentina-Chile) and the Essequibo (Guyana-Venezuela) cases, even though national interests and the local peace are at stake. With peaceful borders on all South American states except Chile and Ecuador, Brazil is a territorially satisfied and noncontentious state whose pro-stability orientation gives it an interest in preventing the eruption of border skirmishes. Because of its status as guarantor of the 1942 Treaty of Rio de Janeiro, for example, Brazil played a constructive mediator role between Ecuador and Peru after a border clash in 1981.

Political competition among South American states could well intensify, with accompanying increases in force capabilities and probabilities of conflict. Brazil is now more disposed to act on its own should its security interests become threatened, but most of these threats will be political rather than military because direct attack is improbable. Doctrinal suppositions are being re-assessed, and an international dimension is being elaborated for national security policy. Brazil is not actively seeking a role as regional hegemon or balancer, however, and still much prefers to consolidate its continental status gradually and in economic terms. Low-key political rather than military solutions will be sought for most of its incipient international security problems in order to resolve matters before they reach the level of a real threat.

As a rule, the military and civilian security establishment will continue to be attentive to matters concerning political stability of neighboring states, border disputes, the control of Brazil's own borders (including the 200-mile maritime limit), and Cuban and Soviet political and military activities in South America, the South Atlantic, and Angola. Argentina will remain the main foreign frame of reference on the continent, but increased attention will be paid to Paraguay, Uruguay, and Bolivia (all with a significant Brazilian presence), and Suriname. Brazil's first expedition to Antarctica in December 1982-January 1983 and accession to the Antarctica Treaty in September 1983 added that continent to the list of priorities in which the military plays a role.

The military will use its withdrawal from politics to catch up somewhat on its capabilities, which have fallen behind national growth. Navy and air force allotments have recently been increased more than the army's, to redress long-standing imbalances. Whereas military garrisons are now located relative to an internal security mission, there will be a future strengthening of the military presence in border areas. Also to be expected are measures to increase armed forces size and professionalization, inter-service rivalries as roles are redefined, and the roles of the National Security Council and the National Intelligence Service in policy formation for continental affairs.

The government's image of Brazil still does not include military strength commensurate with national economic and political size. The military will continue to operate within a modest sense of mission and an acute awareness of self-imposed economic and technical limitations. These conditions, and a narrow definition of national interest, for example, caused the government in 1982 to refuse a UN invitation to be part of a multilateral peace force for Namibia and a Lebanese request to consider similar activity in that country. Cost and mission considerations were also the determining factors in the September 1982 decision not to build a naval base on Trinidad Island, to monitor South Atlantic traffic and aid in coastal defense.

Political-security considerations will soon become evident in arms sales as Brazil becomes a larger market factor, both generally and as an important supplier to countries in conflict, such as Iraq and Libya. An inter-ministerial commission coordinated by Itamaraty examines political implications of sales, belying the supposedly "purely commercial" policy. Refusals of sales to South Africa, Rhodesia, and Somalia have already come to public notice. Sales to Paraguay, Guyana, and Suriname have had domestic and international impact, as yet largely symbolic. Future and broader sales and service relationships, such as the one Brasilia hopes to establish with Nigeria, could be extensive enough to affect the tone of the whole bilateral relationship. Not to be discounted is recipient influence on the seller desirous of continued business, especially if the recipient is an activist state prominent in regional disputes. It will certainly be increasingly difficult for Brazil to ignore political ramifications of arms supply within South America; when this realization occurs, arms sales may come to be accepted as an instrument of influence.

RELATIONS WITH THE UNITED STATES

A number of favorable circumstances converged to produce the U.S.-Brazilian rapprochement, visible in the intense official interchanges of late

1982 into 1983 which opened up new channels of communication and increased mutual responsiveness. The mounting international debt picture, Brazil's reputation for responsible economic policy, its possibilities for longer-term recovery, the size of its debt, the stake of the U.S. banks, American sensitivity to the Newly Industrializing Countries (NICs), Brazil's moderate policies during and after the Falklands War, Argentine unreliability, and the progress of abertura all combined to make the U.S. government focus more on Brazil. Although the Reagan administration did not adopt a remonstrative attitude toward Brazil, in contrast to the Carter administration, Brazil could not identify with the Central American and Cold War focus of Secretary of State Haig's view of Latin America.

With the inauguration of Secretary George Schultz in June 1982, Brazil found an official with concern for economic factors and a knowledge of Brazil. It also received several other signals, from Vice President George Bush and Assistant Secretary of State for Inter-American Affairs Thomas Enders, among others, that Washington was prepared to concede enhanced importance to Brazil, differentiate it from the Central American problem, and open new possibilities. An exchange of presidential visits in 1982 created a strong personal working relationship, with subsequent directives to subordinates to find more compatibilities between the two countries. An activist U.S. ambassador with direct contacts in Brasilia's presidential palace was vital to the tactical engineering of closer relations.

From Brazil's side the U.S. option became attractive for a number of reasons. The overwhelming weight of the debt called for broad solutions, and American banks and officials were considerably more forthcoming than the West Europeans and Japanese. Contrary to the earlier hopes of the Geisel government, the investment and technical assistance which Brazil had expected from other Western partners did not prove as generous as originally envisioned. At the same time, the Third World trade successes of 1981 imploded during 1982. The U.S. market became one of the most promising. Consensus grew in the economic area that relations with the United States had gotten too far out of hand, that they needed to be respected for their significance and managed without polemics. Rapid growth of exports to the U.S. in 1982 and accumulation of a trade surplus confirmed this view.

Rapprochement with Washington came to be supported by widening sectors of the elite as a way of encouraging the U.S. government to underwrite Brazil and to pressure the banks into negotiating more viable terms for the national debt. They hoped in this way to be able to ease up on economic stringency and cover economic growth to avoid loss of political control in presidential succession or as a result of mass action. Much of the opposition became convinced that no other options were open. They were less likely to be thankful for U.S. help, however, because they repudiated the economic policies of the government and saw American policies as a large part of the problem.

The creation of five binational working groups to explore new complementarities in technical areas and avoid old irritations implied a dedication to action rather than merely consultation. If the effort is successful it will put relations on a more positive note and in a more imaginative context. Basically sound mutual attractions appear to have overcome the antagonisms, but a number of cautions are in order as the process moves forward. Because of the changes analyzed above, the relationship will become more complex to manage, with more points of contact and troublesome bureaucratic turf battles on both sides. The relationship is still dependent upon a specific

configuration of officials and could suffer reversals before it is institutionalized. Above all, follow through is needed, particularly by the private sector.
For Brazil, the essence of the matter is extended resolution of the debt issue
in a mutually satisfactory manner. If this is not achieved, a negative backlash
is likely. Brazil is expecting the United States to produce in technical transfer and trade areas as well, activities in which the American government is
saddled by congressional restrictions and lack of control over the private
sector.

Political implications may have some unforeseen consequences for the
United States. U.S. exposure is up in Brazil during a time of economic turn-
down, government unpopularity, and a long presidential election process.
American negotiators are dealing with issues that have a nationalistic content,
such as information policy, foreign bank branches, weapons coproduction, and
trade and finance linkages. Brazil's nationalism has been noncombative, not
systematically anti-American, and quite manageable at the official level.
With converging popular frustrations on the rise, however, and the general
tendency in public opinion to identify the United States unfavorably with the
IMF, foreign banks, and multinational corporations, the United States could
become an easy target in times of growing austerity. The domestic impact of
U.S. policies will be a significant factor in the longevity of the relationship.

Skepticism on the Brazilian side can be traced to past disappointments,
the erratic nature of previous U.S. policies and levels of attention, disparity
of size and levels of development, concerns about political counterparts, and
a sense of national frustration with the end of the development drive and
Brazil's current supplicant role. It is difficult to keep high-level U.S. administrative attention on a single country as other and more accustomed priorities arise. Conflicting pressures from bankers with debt priorities and manu-
facturers with trade complaints cannot be avoided. Treasury requirements
for a trade surplus conflict with the Special Trade Representative's pressure
on subsidized exports, in both U.S. and Third World markets. It is also difficult
for Washington to keep a relationship bilateral, since more general multilateral
policies tend to override the country-specific.

The U.S. is often insufficiently appreciative of the effects of its
domestic interest policies on the solvency of Third World debtors such as
Brazil which take their loans with floating rates. Much of Brazil's current
debt is attributable to compounding high interest rates since 1979. On the
other hand, what appears from the perspective of the Brazilians to be a major
concession on their part commonly passes practically unperceived in the
global view of Washington. Even the greater sophistication with which
Brazilians now deal with Washington does not prevent these irritations from
causing them to express doubts about the long-term dependability of the
United States as a partner. For them, the worth of the newly enhanced relationship will lie with its accomplishments in solving their most pressing
national economic problems and helping Brazil develop its own capabilities.

7
Chilean Foreign Policy: The Pragmatic Pursuit of Geopolitical Goals

Howard Pittman

In the contemporary era there seems to be little interest in Chilean foreign policy in the United States, except in those rare cases where U.S. interests are directly involved. Typical U.S. analyses of Chilean foreign policy have noted such features as Chile's pursuit of a balance-of-power policy (Burr, 1965), its interest in an independent foreign policy, occasional policies of neutrality, and its reputation as a strong supporter of international law (Davis and Wilson, 1975:442). Others have looked at Chile's foreign policy in terms of territorial expansionism, internationalism, and the ways in which Chile has sought to influence the international system in order to aid Chilean development (Cope, 1975:312). Historically, Chilean foreign policy exhibits some unique features and, at certain times, has been an extremely strong influence in regional affairs.

As the title of this work implies, Chilean foreign policy, past and present, has had definite geopolitical goals and continues to pursue new ones. Certain key objectives have been pursued over the years by governments of widely differing composition. In pursuing these goals, Chilean governments have used a wide range of measures, including occupation and colonization, seizure of territory by conquest, membership in regional and extracontinental organizations, negotiations, and accommodation. Once a particular goal, especially a territorial one, has been achieved, it has then been defended patiently and persistently. After the War of the Pacific, Chile resisted attempts by Peru, Bolivia, the United States, and several European nations to deprive Chile of the fruits of victory, until acceptable settlements were secured some twenty-five years later with Bolivia (1904) and fifty years later (1929) with Peru. Pragmatically, while at war with these nations, Chile reached an accommodation with Argentina, relinquishing its claim to Patagonia in the Treaty of 1881 and seeking further accommodation in the Pacts of May (1902), which agreed upon the "Argentina in the Atlantic, Chile in the Pacific" formula.

Chile has always feared the threat posed by a hegemonic power, whether it be by a European nation, the United States, or strong continental rivals, to its own security. Therefore, when its own power has been insufficient to defend national interests, Chilean governments have worked in concert with regional and extracontinental organizations, but always insisting on caveats which would ensure Chilean security and allow a certain freedom of action. For instance, in the Inter-American Treaty of Reciprocal Assistance (TIAR), Chile insisted on provisions which would guard against aggression, not only by extrahemispheric powers, but also by one American nation against another--a hedge against both the power of the United States and the aggressive desires of some of its neighbors.

With these ideas in mind let us review the history of Chilean foreign policy to identify those ideas, concepts, and actions which form the base of contemporary policy.

HISTORICAL BACKGROUND OF CHILEAN FOREIGN POLICY

Chilean foreign policy has an interesting history dating back to its independence movements from Spain which did not come easily. After a brief period of freedom beginning in 1810, the country was reconquered by Spanish forces and only regained its independence with Argentine aid in 1817. Chile in turn fought to secure the independence of Bolivia and Peru--countries which were, ironically, to become Chile's principal future enemies.

Once liberated, Chile rapidly became a regional power, breaking up the federation of Bolivia and Peru and later defeating both of these nations and extracting territorial concessions from them during the War of the Pacific. At the end of this war, Chile had become established as the hegemonic Pacific power in South America, a position it would soon lose with the growth and development of major rival Argentina and the domination of the United States in hemispheric affairs. The opening of the Panama Canal, which replaced the Chilean-controlled southern passages as the primary route between the Atlantic and Pacific Oceans, relegated Chile to relative geographical isolation.

In this century, Chile has been forced into a lesser international position than that enjoyed in the past. Still, Chile has stubbornly retained title to the lands gained by occupation and conquest and has originated new sovereign claims in the sea and Antarctica which are defended with the same tenacity as the territorial claims of the past century. Chile also maintains a remarkably independent foreign policy given its relatively small population and the fact that it is bordered by three often-hostile neighbors, all of whom have grievances against it and who have frequently acted or attempted to act in concert against it in the past. Why and how has Chile been able to maintain an independent foreign policy despite pressure from the outside? The answer to this question includes historic, geopolitical, and pragmatic reasons as well as Chile's continuing adherence to certain irreducible national goals.

One of the reasons for an independent Chilean foreign policy is the geographical isolation of the country. Furthermore, outside pressures and propaganda have tended to isolate Chile politically. Propaganda campaigns and pressures mounted by hostile neighbors in Argentina, Bolivia, and Peru in the last century were aided by the United States and European nations whose interests and investments were affected by the Chilean victory in the War of the Pacific. Such campaigns portrayed Chile as an expansionist power which seized territory from weaker neighbors, obscuring the fact that Chile lost far more territory in Patagonia to Argentina than it ever gained in the north. In recent times, efforts to isolate Chile are found in the critical reactions of the European leftist and Christian Democratic governments to the overthrow of the socialist Allende regime by a military government and the later critical reactions of the United States, reaching their peak in the Letelier case. When these are coupled, as they were in the 1970s, with renewed Bolivian demands for an access to the sea, supported by Peru, as well as Argentine threats and pressures in the Beagle Channel dispute, it is easy to see why Chile is once again politically isolated, leaving it little choice but to maintain an independent stance.

In order to understand how Chile's independent foreign policy developed, it is necessary to examine Chile's international relations in historical perspective. One Chilean authority, Orrego Vicuña, has derived some ten "bases" for the success of Chilean foreign policy in the nineteenth century (from Portales to Balmaceda):

1. Rejection of foreign models and affirmation of internal values.
2. Internal political stability.
3. Economic and commercial development.
4. Military and naval power.
5. Cultural development.
6. Institutional capability.
7. Promotion and protection of private national initiative.
8. Positive national psychological attitude.
9. Pragmatism in foreign policy.
10. Avoiding conflict with great powers (1974:55, 86-87).

Furthermore, he contends that whenever Chile has departed from these tenets, its foreign policy has been adversely affected: ". . . all of the foreign policy failures of Chile coincide with moments in which the country has abandoned some of the basic factors on which the system rests." As an example, he traces the acceptance of "foreign models" beginning with the introduction of parliamentary government in the 1890s, through the subsequent acceptance of foreign ideologies such as socialism, communism, and Christian democracy, to the complete domination of a marxist regime under Allende (Orrego Vicuña, 1974:55-58, 65-67, 73).

Another Chilean scholar (Sanchez, 1977:377) argues that the "outstanding political tendencies," which have characterized Chilean foreign policy over the past 150 years are as follows: "(1) Americanism; (2) Political nationalism; (3) Legalism and the search for a democratic international system; and (4) The alignment and autonomy of Chile during the Cold War and detente."

Let us examine these ideas through historical examples and trace their effects to the present.

AMERICANISM, NATIONALISM AND LEGALISM IN CHILEAN FOREIGN POLICY

The history of Chilean foreign policy has often been portrayed (Encina, 1959; Espinosa Moraga, 1969) as a struggle between competing ideals of Americanism and nationalism. Americanism is the legacy of the Pan-American dream of Latin American unity. Nationalism, on the other hand, is the idea of the strong, self-reliant national state, the balancer of power in the Pacific. Both have played significant roles during identifiable periods of Chilean history. Sanchez (1977:375-376) argues that Americanism and nationalism both contradict and complement each other, an idea which we accept. Legalism, rather than being a primary motivator of foreign policy, has been more of an instrument or tool for supporting both Americanist and nationalist objectives. Let us review the interplay between these concepts in Chilean foreign policy.

Americanism arose early in the liberation era, championed by

O'Higgins, an associate of San Martin, who was instrumental in regaining Chilean independence after the reconquest and who financed and supported the liberation of Peru and Bolivia. Yet, O'Higgins, who was driven from office, partly as a result of his Americanist views, also supported the cause of nationalism, in (1) declaring that Chile must dominate in the Pacific; (2) claiming that Chile extended to the Antarctic; and, (3) from exile in Peru, urging the occupation and colonization of the Strait of Magellan in order to ensure control of the Strait (Fernandez Larrain, 1974)--an act which was carried out in 1843 by the nationalist government of President Bulnes.

Diego Portales is considered the founder of Chilean nationalism. He advocated a strong national government, national unity, and the development of both the country and foreign trade. He counseled against falling under the influence of any foreign power and opposed the Monroe Doctrine, for example, as leading to United States hegemony. He was the originator of power politics and realism in Chilean foreign policy; he was also the author of the balance of power policy which held that Chile must dominate in the Pacific and never allow a union of Bolivia and Peru. According to a biographer, Melo Lacaros, "His ideal was that of a great and powerful Chile, preponderant in the Pacific, but without aspirations of hegemony. Pragmatic and nationalistic he only accepted hemispheric cooperation in economics" (1977:111). In fact, most of the ten bases for Chilean foreign policy listed above rest on Portalian principles.

The third "outstanding tendency" in Chilean foreign policy, legalism and the search for a democratic international system, originated with Andres Bello, a contemporary of Portales, author of the "Bello Clause," which provided for special tariff concessions for other Hispanic American republics as well as the first Chilean book in international law. He is regarded in Chile (Sanchez, 1977:387-390) as the originator of juridical principles designed to safeguard equality among nations and of the nonintervention principle.

Americanists are charged by modern revisionist historians (Encina, 1959; Espinosa Moraga, 1969) with the loss of Patagonia and other territory in disputes with Argentina. On the other hand, nationalists, up through the government of President Balmaceda, are credited with the Chilean policies which led to the control of the Strait of Magellan, the successful exploration, occupation, colonization, and conquest of the Atacama at the expense of Bolivia and Peru and the incorporation of Easter Island as Chilean territory.

In this century, nationalist concepts seem to be behind such actions as the Antarctic claim (1940) and establishment of bases therein (1947), the declaration of sovereignty in the territorial sea (1947), and the definition of the Mar Chileno (Chilean Sea) (1976). Americanism, in turn, is identified with Chile's participation in the Pan-American Union, the Organization of American States, the Inter-American Treaty of Reciprocal Assistance, and various regional integration agreements under the Frei government. The military government since 1973 has returned to a strong nationalism and a balance-of-power policy.

Legalism has primarily served to defend Chilean conquests, territorial accessions, and modern claims to offshore areas. Chile has not fought a war for over a century, relying on legalism, whether through negotiations, arbitration, or participation in international organizations to protect its position. This has not always been favorable to Chile. Although retaining its territorial gains at the expense of Bolivia and Peru, Chile has lost by some accounts (Espinosa Moraga, 1969; Sanchez, 1977), a total of 1,264,600 square kilometers of territory to Argentina in negotiated or arbitrated disputes. The 1977 arbitral award was favorable to Chile, but Argentina has refused to accept the decision.

In another manifestation of legalism, Chile has used treaties and agreements with other nations to protect its own security. In 1848 and 1864 (Bernstein, 1977) Chile entered into pacts with Pacific coast nations against Spanish threats to reoccupy the former colonies. Similar concerns led to Chile's informal "friendship with Brazil" and its adherence to the Inter-American Security Treaty.

So far, this review has concentrated on the past century. Now let us review analyses which focus on Chilean foreign policy during the Cold War and the period of detente.

CONTEMPORARY ANALYSES OF CHILEAN FOREIGN POLICY

Contemporary analyses reflect the fact that Chile is currently diplomatically isolated, but differ on ways to solve the problem. Manfred Wilhelmy (1979) identifies three "subcultures" within Chilean foreign policy, each of which has dominated at certain periods since World War II. The first of these, the "Dominant-Moderate" subculture, governed Chilean foreign policy from 1946 to 1970. A second "Revolutionary" subculture characterized the Allende regime from 1970-1973. The third and current "Traditionalist-Integrist" subculture has been pursued by the military government since 1973, but has proved to be incompatible with the contemporary international system, resulting in a deterioration in Chile's international position. As a solution, Wilhelmy urges the "de-ideologizing" of foreign policy and a return to a pragmatic style of diplomacy emphasizing the continuity of the past.

Heraldo Muñoz (1980) argues that Chile has become isolated in world affairs, due to the establishment in 1973 of an authoritarian domestic regime, a "praetorian-ideological" style of diplomacy, and a belligerent anti-communist foreign policy, in a world of detente. However, he acknowledges that Chile is not economically isolated, having strengthened its ties with international capitalism. Thus, if the world should return to a Cold War situation the position of Chile could be strengthened under the military government. Muñoz advocates a return to internal democracy and a civilian-pragmatic style of diplomacy as the solution to the problem.

Emilio Meneses (1983) believes that Chile is suffering from an "identity crisis" in its international position in a changing world, which has had a tremendous internal impact and has provoked an acute international reaction. The continuity which characterized Chilean foreign policy since 1902 has been broken; Chile's international image has suffered and its prestige has been lowered. Although there have been problems in the style of diplomacy and a confrontation between professional diplomats and political appointees, the real problem is not the style of diplomacy or the origin of diplomatic representatives, but what direction Chilean foreign policy should take. Meneses identifies three possible options or alternatives now under discussion in Chile: (1) isolationism; (2) nonalignment; and (3) a system of alliances and coalitions. Examining the alternatives, he argues that isolationism is implausible, although the geographical isolation and "insular mentality" of Chile cannot be ignored in selecting a policy. Thus, maintaining a "certain distance" within a policy of international participation could be advantageous. He discards nonalignment because of the movement of the nonaligned group towards the Soviet position which is contrary to Chile's pro-western attitude.

Meneses concludes that the basic option for future Chilean foreign policy can only be one of participation in alliances and coalitions, changing them as necessary when the situation demands and always preserving the advantages of Chile's "insular position" on the continent. In designing this new policy, Chilean policy makers must first realize that a serious problem exists; then work toward a solution, based on consensus, which would utilize the salvable parts of Chilean diplomatic tradition and the positive factors of continuity, in addition to new concepts identified above, to create a better future foreign policy.

The above analyses all recognize that for the past decade Chilean foreign policy seems to have been out of step with world opinion and that consequently something must be done to restore Chile's international prestige and image. Wilhelmy (1979) and Muñoz (1980) seem to be calling more for a return to the positions and procedures of the past, rather than for new alternatives and directions. Meneses (1983) takes a more pragmatic and realistic approach, noting that Chilean foreign policy has experienced an abrupt change--a "mutation"--which is derived from a new era in which the rules of the game are still changing and the past formulas on which Chile relied no longer suffice. He urges that a new realistic policy be developed in which Chile enters into alliances and coalitions, while preserving its insular position and utilizing compatible elements of Chilean diplomatic tradition to aid in the process. This is a pragmatic analysis with pragmatic recommendations for reforms.

None of these analyses mention the truly important geopolitical foreign policy goals, with the possible exception of the idea of returning to, or maintaining the status quo. If this means preservation of past territorial gains and maintenance of present claims, such a goal seems to have been relatively unaffected by the decline in Chile's international image or popularity status or by the internal political format of the government at a given time. For example, the initiatives toward an arbitrated settlement of the Beagle Channel dispute with Argentina were made by the Christian Democratic Frei government (1967); the compromise over procedures to be followed was reached during the Allende administration; pleadings before the Arbitral Court (1973-1975) bridged the fall of Allende and the rise of the military government, which accepted the favorable 1977 award and which has continued to defend the Chilean position through bilateral negotiations and threats of war with Argentina and the subsequent Papal mediation. Throughout this period, the Chilean position remained unchanged and its possession of the disputed land and sea territory continued undisturbed. This example alone offers proof that after two traumatic shifts in government, the pragmatic pursuit of geopolitical goals continues, despite the internal composition of the government and its relative popularity in world affairs. Styles and ideologies may change, but the primary objectives remain.

This portion of the study has reviewed certain historical events and concepts, such as Americanism, nationalism, and legalism, which have influenced Chilean foreign policy past and present. Three differing periods of Chilean policy have been traced: (1) an independent nationalist balance of power policy from the 1830s to the 1890s, which covered the periods of Chile's greatest power and principal territorial gains and losses; (2) the period of legalism, accommodation, neutrality, and association with international organizations from about 1902-1970; and (3) the period since 1970, encompassing the socialist Allende regime, followed by a return to an independent nationalist policy, based on Portalian principles, by the military government.

Certain geopolitical goals of the nineteenth century were identified including (1) preventing a union of Bolivia and Peru which would threaten Chilean security; (2) achieving and maintaining a power position in the Pacific; (3) securing the mineral-rich resources of the Atacama for Chile; and (4) controlling the Strait of Magellan and the other southern passages.

Once these goals were attained, especially territorial ones, the emphasis shifted to defending and maintaining them through whatever means were necessary at the time. When its own power would no longer suffice, Chile turned cautiously to association with hemispheric coalitions and international organizations to preserve its position. Patient negotiation and legalism were part of the process, which continued through numerous changes of government and differing political ideologies. Chilean action in the Beagle Channel case illustrates continuity in the pragmatic pursuit of geopolitical goals, regardless of the ideology of the government concerned. This case also provides a link with new geopolitical goals in the sea and in Antarctica; for, as in the past century, Chile has become an initiator of new geopolitical concepts regarding the territoriality and sovereignty of offshore areas.

THE PURSUIT OF NEW GEOPOLITICAL GOALS

In a series of previous studies (Pittman, 1981a, 1981b, 1983) the author has examined the influence of geopolitical theory on government policy in the ABC countries (Argentina, Brazil, and Chile) and the resulting extension of old conflicts in the Southern Cone to offshore areas. Chile has been a leader in the development and application of new geopolitical concepts to the sea and Antarctica and a pioneer in making claims to sovereignty over desirable portions of these areas. Although these claims were made prior to the current renaissance in geopolitics, they were advocated by geopolitical thinkers such as Canas Montalva (1940). Furthermore, geopolitical vision is now attributed to the Chilean presidents involved by analysts such as Buzeta (1978:126-136) who describes President Aquirre Cerda (Antarctic Claim) as "the geopolitician of the integration of national economic space"; President Gonzalez Videla (Territorial Sea Declaration) as "the geopolitician of maritime space"; and President Frei, as "the geopolitician of continental integration."

These identifications may be overstated, but there is no doubt about the credentials of President Pinochet, a former professor of geopolitics at the Army War Academy and the author of the book Geopolítica (1977). His government uses geopolitical analyses to arrive at geopolitical solutions, which are translated into government policy and action (Pittman, 1981a:1339-1378). He has also established "GEOCHILE" (El Mercurio, May 28, 1980), a new institute of geopolitics to train officials in the subject.

Geopolitical goals are established and publicized by the government. Two of the national objectives (Chile, Objectivo Nación, 1975) are: (1) "to preserve Chilean independence and its territorial integrity"; and (2) "to forge a great destiny for Chile." Other goals are more explicit. The National Maritime Policy (Orrego Vicuña, 1977:22-51) defines the Chilean sea and proclaims such goals as "the definitive incorporation of extensive maritime territories with abundant resources into national sovereignty and jurisdiction," and "to definitively and opportunely establish the jurisdictioned maritime boundaries of the country."

Even "Regionalization," the internal administrative reorganization of Chile, was based on a geopolitical concept (Chile, CONARA, 1979; El

Mercurio, January 15, 1979) as announced in the press. This was reiterated in
an address in Uruguay by the head of CONARA (Canessa Robert, 1979), who
explained that "It is necessary to clarify that our process of Regionalization
is not a mere geographic division of our country, but one that arises from
defined geopolitical objectives." This plan was designed to strengthen the
First Region (Arica) and the Twelfth (Magallanes y Antartica Chilena) against
foreign threats. An "Antarctic Province" was established in the latter region.
    Now let us examine the practical measures taken to achieve and main-
tain Chile's new geopolitical goals.

The Chilean Antarctic

    Chilean interests in the Antarctic date back to the time of Bernardo
O'Higgins, but historical events precluded a formal claim for many years. In
1892, the government began to regulate hunting and fishing in Antarctic
waters and in 1906 granted the rights (Fabry- De Todo Hera concession;
Decree 260, February 27, 1906) to the possession and exploitation of the Diego
Ramirez, Georgias and Shetland islands and "Lands to the South" to a group of
Chilean citizens. The decree noted that this was "an enterprise which tends
to secure . . . the dominion of Chile over these abandoned lands" (Pinochet de
la Barra, 1977).
    In 1940 concern over Norwegian claims and the security of Antarctica
in World War II led to the proclamation of the Chilean claim (Decreto Supremo
No. 1747, November 6, 1940) which was defined in these words:

> The Chilean Antarctic, or Chilean Antarctic territory is formed by
> all of the lands, islands, inlets, reefs, and glaciers (pack ice) known,
> and others to be discovered, and to the respective territorial sea exist-
> ing between the limits of the sector constituted by the meridians of
> 53 degrees and 90 degrees west longitude.

    Pinochet de la Barra (1977) indicates these limits were chosen because
the 53 degree boundary was outside the South Orcades (claimed by Argentina)
and coincided roughly with the Tordesillas Line, while the 90 degree limit
coincided with the west boundary of the South American Antarctic Sector.
    Faced with competing claims and installation of foreign bases in its
sector (Pittman, 1981a), Chile established Antarctic bases in 1947. Later,
Chile fought proposals to place the Antarctic under United Nations control
(1948), or under a condominium of interested powers, advocating instead a
freezing of the status quo, a proposal maintained through negotiations until
it was incorporated in the 1959 Antarctic Treaty. Chile continues to maintain
its Antarctic bases; an Antarctic Institute was created in 1963; and President
Pinochet (Presidential messages 1975, 1976) has repeated Chilean determination to preserve its rights and defend its sovereignty in the Antarctic. In
1980, an airfield was constructed at one of the bases. The Chilean Antarctic
claim is related to new concepts regarding the sea as well as the strategic
defense of both areas.

The Chilean Sea

    Although no longer as dominant in the Pacific as in the past, Chile has
maintained a strong strategic position by controlling the southern passages
between the Atlantic and Pacific, which also govern access to Antarctica.

Chile has originated new concepts regarding the territoriality, sovereignty and jurisdiction of sea areas. The Antarctic claim included "the respective territorial sea." The Declaration (maritime jurisdiction) of June 23, 1947, established Chilean sovereignty over the 200nm zone, including the seabed and subsoil thereof. The zone also applied to island possessions, extending Chilean jurisdiction over a 200nm arc around Easter Island and Cape Horn.

About 1950 Argentina, in a new effort to expand to the Pacific, contended that the correct dividing line between the Atlantic and Pacific was the Diego Ramirez meridian, some miles west of Cape Horn. Chileans (Ihl, 1953a) countered with the theory that the waters of the Pacific extended far to the east into the Arc of the South Antilles (Pittman, 1983:21), an idea which was successfully used to thwart the Argentine proposal. Argentina returned to the concept of the Cape Horn divisor, a position it still maintains.

The concept of a Chilean Sea originated in the 1950s. This concept (Ihl, 1953b) visualized a "Mar Chileno" with a northern limit extending from the Peruvian border to Easter Island; thence southeast to the west limit of the Antarctic claim. An eastern boundary would be drawn from the Beagle Channel to the 53 degree eastern limit of that claim. Marull Bermudez (1978) proposed marking the boundaries of the Chilean Sea with buoy markers. He would not claim sovereignty beyond the 200nm limit, but did state that ". . . it does carry, if not full sovereignty, a direct and vital relation and rights of protection between the sovereign state of Chile and her sea with its resources."

The National Maritime Policy (Orrego Vicuña, 1977:23) defines a Chilean Sea extending to Easter Island and Antarctica. Official maps produced by the "Instituto Geográfico Militar" (1978) display the legend "Mar Chileno" along the coast, but no sea boundary is shown. These maps, designated for use in the school system, indicate widespread indoctrination of the public in this concept.

The government has established a new Chilean Pacific Ocean Institute (El Mercurio, May 22-28, 1980) designed to promote "the presence and position of Chile in the Pacific Ocean," a further indication of the desire to project Chilean influence in the vast Pacific.

The Equivalence of Land and Sea "Territory"

The value Chile attaches to sea space is clearly shown in the 1975-1978 negotiations with Bolivia. In reply to the Bolivian request for an access to the sea, Chile offered a land-sea corridor extending to the 200nm limit, which would include "land territory as already described and maritime territory included between the parallels of the furthest ends of the coast which would be ceded (territorial sea, economic zone, and continental shelf)" subject to an exchange of territory in which Chile would receive "a compensating area equivalent to the minimum area of land and water ceded to Bolivia" (Chile, Ministry of Foreign Affairs, December 19, 1975:4d, 4F).

The Bolivian government initially accepted the idea of territorial exchange (land and sea), although it eventually demanded a concession without any exchange (Chile, Ministry of Foreign Affairs, 1978:8-18). Although unsuccessful, these negotiations set a new precedent, the concept that land and sea space can have comparable or equal value. It also confirms the high value attached to sea space by Chile as well as the exercise of sovereignty over maritime "territory."

The Sea Factor in the Beagle Channel Controversy

The crux of the Beagle Channel dispute is not the sovereignty of Picton, Nueva, and Lennox islands, but the control and possession of the waters surrounding them (Pittman, 1981a). The Arbitral Award (Chile, 1977) drew a mid-channel boundary, awarding these islands to Chile which had occupied them since the 1890s. More importantly, it confirmed a new extension of the Chilean Sea. The Chilean government quickly established the so-called "Lineas de Base Rectas" (Straight Base Lines) connecting the Islands, an act which marked its interior waters and created a base line for a new 200nm zone (Brunner, 1977). Chile also appointed "Alcaldes de Mar" for the islands. These acts of sovereignty were strongly protested by Argentina, but Chile has maintained its position through such events as: (1) Argentine refusal to accept the award; (2) subsequent negotiation; (3) the Argentine mobilization and threat of war in 1978; and (4) the subsequent Papal mediation, which was also reported as favorable to Chile (Rouco, 1981).

Argentine objections to Chilean possession of the disputed islands and sea territory are both strategic and economic. General Villegas (1983) warns that if Argentina accepts the decision and cedes the Beagle islands: (1) it will lose the adjacent sea with its resources; and (2) Chile will obtain total control of the Strait of Magellan, Beagle Channel, and the Drake Passage, cutting the geographic continuity between Argentina and its Antarctic Sector, thus weakening a fundamental argument supporting the Argentine claim. He also links the Chilean position with the restored British control of the Malvinas (Falkland) and the Georgia and Sandwich islands, which excludes Argentina from these areas and will weaken the Argentine position when the Antarctic Treaty expires in 1991.

According to recent reports (Washington Times, January 24, 1984), Argentina and Chile have now signed a declaration of "peace and friendship" at the Vatican, in an effort to settle the dispute. New negotiations are to begin, but the terms were not announced. However, Argentine sources indicated that Argentina is willing to give Chile the disputed islands with a twelve-mile territorial sea, with waters beyond this limit under Argentine jurisdiction. If so, this is merely a restatement of the Argentine position. Chile's position was not stated, but it is doubtful that Chile will accept an Argentine proposal that has consistently been rejected in the past. This appears to be a simple agreement to settle the dispute through negotiations, while a definitive solution remains to be determined.

There is no doubt, however, that the Beagle Channel dispute and the conflicting Argentine-Chilean Antarctic claims are linked by the new geopolitical concepts regarding the jurisdiction, sovereignty, and control of sea areas, or that Chile has utilized them to pursue new goals in offshore regions.

The Defense of Geopolitical Goals

Both past and present Chilean foreign policies are characterized by the defense of geopolitical goals. In negotiations, Chile seems to present a persuasive and unvarying line. In fact, the Arbitral Court in the Beagle Channel case noted that while Argentine positions and cartography had varied markedly over the years, the Chilean position was always consistent (Chile, 1977:208-268). One must presume that the same consistency applies under the continuing Papal mediation.

Careful preparation and well-designed proposals designed to protect

Chile's northern flank were also evident in the 1975-1978 negotiations with Bolivia (Chile, Ministry of Foreign Affairs, 1978) where Chile: (1) refused to offer a corridor not contiguous with the Peruvian border, where any transfer required Peruvian consent; (2) insisted any Bolivian access be demilitarized, thus providing a buffer against Peru; and (3) attempted to establish a recognized maritime boundary out to the 200nm limit.

The measures to strengthen Chilean sovereignty over the Beagle islands, the surrounding sea and its Antarctic claim were detailed in the preceding sections. They represent pragmatic steps in the pursuit of the new geopolitical goals proclaimed by the government. Chile also continues to defend its new goals in international forums such as the Organization of American States, the United Nations, and consultative meetings of the adherents to the Antarctic Treaty. The basic Chilean positions regarding the sea, the Beagle Channel dispute, and Antarctica have been maintained by succeeding governments in spite of internal political divisions, international political isolation, and through two abrupt changes in type of government and the style of foreign policy. It seems that Chile is maintaining the same pragmatic defense of its new geopolitical goals that it demonstrated in the past, despite outside threats and pressures and with little support from the international community. This suggests that future Chilean foreign policy, regardless of the type of government or its style of diplomacy, will continue to be oriented toward the pragmatic pursuit of geopolitical goals.

8
Peruvian Foreign Policy
Since the Return
to Democratic Rule

Jennie K. Lincoln

On July 28, 1980, Fernando Belaúnde returned to office as President of Peru--a position from which he had been ousted by a military coup d'etat in October 1968. The military junta which replaced his previous government had been motivated in its actions by a desire to alter radically the domestic and foreign policies of the earlier Belaúnde administration. For the next twelve years under two military generals (Juan Velasco Alvarado, 1968-1975, and Francisco Morales Bermúdez, 1975-1980) the military government implemented policies designed to change the political, economic, and social structures of Peru. Some of the reform policies of the military government were successful, others were not. A sagging economy and growing civilian opposition to the military government prompted the military's return to the barracks in 1980 and Belaúnde's return to the presidency.

The following chapter analyzes the foreign policy of Peru since its return to a democratic political system. What are the foreign policy issues of greatest concern to the Belaúnde administration today? What determines the actions that the Belaúnde administration is taking or is likely to take in response to these challenges? The motivations for the military coup d'etat in 1968 and the subsequent changes in foreign policy promulgated by the military government provide a context within which the Belaúnde administration must act. How is the Belaúnde administration changing or maintaining the foreign policy directions it has inherited from its military predecessors? The following discussion provides a background necessary to answer these questions by reviewing the foreign policy orientation of the military governments which preceded Belaúnde's return to the presidency.

FOREIGN POLICY AND THE TRANSITION FROM MILITARY TO CIVILIAN RULE

In the initial pronouncements of the Revolutionary Government which took power in October 1968 there was a strong nationalistic message which set the stage for the foreign policy decisions which followed. The Revolutionary Government would pursue nationalistic economic policies and would consider its foreign policy orientation to be independent from both West and East bloc inclinations. One of the motivating factors of the military intervention had been the opposition of the military to Belaúnde's policies toward multinational corporations which the military interpreted as less-than-advantageous to the Peruvian national economy. Thus, one of the first acts of the junta, the nationalization of the International Petroleum Corporation (IPC), was an important symbolic as well as economic message: the dominant position of the "imperialist" forces in Peru would no longer be tolerated.

The military government set out to reform virtually every sector of the Peruvian economy by establishing state enterprises to direct the most important sectors of the economy including oil, mining, fishing, and banking industries. The military government relied heavily on restructuring the Peruvian economy in both domestic and international arenas to bring about a fundamental reorientation of society to fulfill the nationalist goals of the revolution: Peru for the Peruvians. Foreign investment in Peru was to be strictly controlled and completely prohibited in some areas. International commerce was expanded as the military government sought to reduce its dependence on the West by increasing international trade with countries outside the Western bloc. International trade was developed with the Soviet Union, the People's Republic of China, Cuba, and other Socialist bloc nations. The establishment of these ties led to diplomatic relations and later to aid for development projects from the Soviet Union.

The military government's political initiatives reflected not only a nationalist orientation of its foreign policy, but also a well-defined concern for improving Latin America's position in the international arena. In other words, the military government's goal of ridding Peru of "imperialist domination" was extended to the Latin American region as well as Peru called for an end to the Organization of American States' blockade of Cuba, sponsored a resolution to relocate the headquarters of the OAS from Washington to Latin America, called for a reorganization of the Inter-American Development Bank, and pushed for the nationalization of the Panama Canal (Gorman, 1981:117). The Revolutionary government of Peru also supported the Nonaligned Movement and a New International Economic Order which would restructure the international economic system to accommodate the needs of the lesser-developed nations of the world (Chaplin, 1976; Cleaves and Scurrah, 1976; Einaudi and Stepan, 1971; Gorman, 1978; Lowenthal, 1975; McClintock and Lowenthal, 1983; Malloy, 1974; Palmer, 1980; Stepan, 1978; Villanueva, 1972; and Werlich, 1978).

Although President Belaúnde set about with great deliberation to dismantle many of the domestic policies of the Revolutionary Government, he did not attempt to restructure completely the foreign policy framework of his military predecessors. For example, President Belaúnde has supported and pursued foreign policies initiated by the Revolutionary Government which expanded the diplomatic and commercial relations between Peru and both Western and non-Western nations; emphasized improved relations within the inter-American system; and supported Peru's participation in the Nonaligned Movement and other Third World organizations.

The following discussion of Peru's foreign policy since the return to a democratic system under the helm of President Fernando Belaúnde will analyze the elements of both change and continuity in foreign policy from the Revolutionary Government until present time. The discussion will be divided into three issue areas which are not necessarily mutually exclusive, but which will provide a framework for the following analysis:

1. economic issues with respect to international trade and foreign debt;
2. political-military issues with respect to the defense of Peru, especially in consideration of historical conflicts with neighbors

Chile and Ecuador; and

3. political-diplomatic issues with respect to hemispheric relations, participation in the Nonaligned Movement, and bilateral relations with nations which might affect political-military issues and/or economic issues.

ECONOMIC ISSUES

When Fernando Belaúnde returned to the presidency in 1980, he faced an ailing economy which had suffered setbacks under the military government due to the phenomenal increase in central government expenditures for development programs and defense. Belaúnde's policy options were limited by fluctuations in prices of Peru's exports and the soaring external debt which Peru began to experience in the late 1970s as a result of both domestic factors and international factors such as the oil crisis and the world-wide recession in the mid-1970s. Lowenthal (1980:185) notes, the revolution "sagged" with foreign debt and inflation outpacing production and exports leaving the Peruvian economy "in shambles."

Beginning with the Velasco regime the military government set out to reduce Peru's economic dependency (principally on the United States) by pursuing a combination import substitution and industrialization/export-led development plan which sought to restructure the domestic economy and to expand markets for Peruvian products (Schydlowsky and Wicht, 1983). To this end the Velasco government sought expanded trade relations with the Soviet Union, Eastern European nations, and other Third World nations. Any nation was a potential market for expansion of commercial relations regardless of political orientation of that nation. The Velasco government believed that the social restructuring of Peru, which would diminish the role of the oligarchy and would control foreign investment in Peru, would also give birth to "new social forces . . . to take advantage of capital importations financed by primary exports" (Gorman and St. John, 1982:182). The problem with this plan was that in order to finance the expansion of export production the government borrowed heavily from foreign commercial banks which set into motion the external debt problem. This problem was compounded by soaring interest rates, falling prices of Peruvian exports, and a vicious cycle of borrowing to pay debt servicing.

By 1975 Peru's foreign debt had reached $U.S. 3.99 billion which equaled 29.4 percent of its GNP (IDB, 1979:97). Peru had fallen into an economic crisis which led to a change in the military government with Francisco Morales Bermúdez assuming the role of president. Morales Bermúdez imposed austerity measures which were increased extensively in 1976 to include devaluation of the sol, wage and price regulations, import restrictions, reduction or elimination of subsidies of consumer items such as gasoline, and extensive cuts in government expenditures for social and development programs (Werlich, 1981). Despite these measures Peru was labeled in international banking circles as a trouble spot. Thus it came as no surprise to observers outside the country when many of Peru's creditors refused to renegotiate in 1977 without the involvement of the IMF which in turn called for even more severe austerity measures (Dietz, 1980:3).

By the time the military returned to the barracks in July 1980, Peru's external debt had grown to over $9 billion and much of President Belaúnde's foreign economic policy had to be concerned with managing the ailing

domestic economy. President Belaúnde's approach to the nation's difficulties
in Peru has been to continue some policies from the military government era
as well as to reverse other policies which had altered Peru's economic framework during the twelve years of military rule.

President Belaúnde has followed the lead of his military predecessors
by continuing to expand the trade horizons of Peru's international commerce.
Japan is rapidly becoming one of Peru's most important trading partners as
Peru trades metals, ore, petroleum and coffee for chemicals, plastics, and
manufactured metal products. One of the current bright spots in Peru's
economy is that trade with Japan increased dramatically since 1978. Exports
to Japan increased from $94.5 million in 1978 to $323.4 million in 1982 and
Peru continues to have a trade surplus ($217.8 million in 1982) with Japan (El
Comercio, April 25, 1983:A17). China (PRC) has also continued to increase
its imports of metals and cotton from Peru and near the end of 1982 Peru
held a trade surplus with China (Expreso, November 21, 1982:3). Belaúnde
has also sought to increase trade within the region through revitalization of
economic cooperation within the Andean Pact (U.S. FBIS, February 4, 1983:J1)
and through increased economic cooperation with neighbors in the region such
as bilateral trade agreements with Argentina, Brazil, and Chile. For example,
the Belaúnde administration has worked closely with the Chilean government
to formulate policies which might facilitate the recovery of the price of
copper (U.S. FBIS, June 30, 1982:V1). Even though Peru has attempted to
diversify its markets the United States continues to be the principal supplier
of goods and services to Peru. Peruvian exports to the U.S. in 1982 equaled
$1.099.4 million while imports from the U.S. totaled $1.116.9 leaving Peru
with a trade deficit even though imports from the U.S. as a percentage of
total imports fell from the high of 35-40 percent of earlier years to 29 percent in 1982 (Business America, February 21, 1983:52).

The most notable deviation of the Belaúnde administration from the
foreign economic policy of the military government actually has roots in
domestic policy and has come as a result of actions of the military government itself. President Belaúnde has systematically begun to dismantle much
of the state enterprise framework which was created by his military predecessors. One by one, 170 state enterprises are being turned over to the
private sector and the significance to the foreign policy arena is that foreign
investment in Peru is once again being encouraged. The explanation for this
shift in policy may be bluntly stated: the Peruvian government cannot afford
to operate the extensive state enterprise system established by the military
government. President Belaúnde's government is faced with an overwhelming
foreign debt situation which can partially be mitigated by divesting itself of
many of these enterprises.

Peru's external debt is a principal issue confronting the Belaúnde
administration. At the end of 1982 the total external debt had reached $11.2
billion which represented a 17 percent increase over 1981 while the gross
domestic product grew by only 0.7 percent. Public foreign debt as a percentage of GNP reached 35 percent and debt service accounted for 46 percent of
Peru's export earnings in 1982 (LAWR, February 4, 1983:7-8). Negotiations
in early 1983 to reschedule much of Peru's external debt bought some time,
but by June 1983 Peru was already behind in payments on loans (totaling $2
billion) which had been rescheduled on a 30-day basis in March (LAWR, June
17, 1983:6). Peru's economy continued to decline in 1983 with a 12 percent
drop in GDP, 125 percent inflation and a 128 percent devaluation of its
currency (LAWR, January 13, 1984:11). By early 1984 Peru's external debt

exceeded $12 billion and negotiations were still underway with the IMF and foreign commercial banks to renegotiate the repayment schedule. The debt issue dominates Peru's foreign economic policy and its impact is felt in other foreign policy issue areas as noted in the following discussions of political-military issues and political-diplomatic issues of Peruvian foreign policy.

POLITICAL-MILITARY ISSUES

When Fernando Belaúnde assumed the Presidency in 1980 he inherited a military which had become one of the most powerful in South America. The military government had allocated a significant increase in central government expenditures to increase the size of the armed forces, to improve training, and to procure weapons to advance the technology and capability of the armed forces. Studies of the Peruvian military suggest that the development of the Peruvian military may be attributed to several factors including: (1) the military's drive for professionalization which necessitates acquiring the most modern weapons systems and accompanying training (Einaudi and Stepan, 1971; Einaudi, 1976); (2) Peru's historical conflicts with neighbors Chile and Ecuador which are perceived as potential arenas for hostilities (Gorman, 1979; St. John, 1977a, 1977b); and (3) the military's drive to modernize before a return to civilian rule (Villanueva, 1980).

Table 8.1 demonstrates the dramatic increase in military expenditures throughout the military governments of Velasco and Morales Bermúdez. Peru greatly outspent the average for Latin America in every category: military expenditures/gross national product; military expenditures/central government expenditures; and military expenditures/per capita. Table 8.2 presents the increase in Peru's armed forces during the years of the military government indicating that the position in 1980 of Peru's 8.5 armed forces/1000 population was almost double the average of Latin American armed forces at 4.9/1000 population.

Not only did the Peruvian military government seek to increase its size and inventory, it also sought suppliers in addition to the United States which had provided the preceding Belaunde administration with substantial military support. The Peruvian military government purchased Mirage fighters, Alouette helicopters, and AMX tanks from France; Canberra bombers, Hunter fighters, and destroyers from Britain; submarines from West Germany; other arms from the Netherlands, Italy, and other suppliers; and a shopping list of hardware from the Soviet Union including: 250 Soviet tanks, 32 SU-22 fighter-bombers and other artillery and helicopters (Pierre, 1982: 239-241). Pierre (1982:240) lends credence to Villanueva's argument that the military was interested in strengthening its position vis-à-vis the upcoming civilian government when he notes that the Morales Bermúdez government ordered two squadrons of SU-22 fighter-bombers just two months before the 1980 presidential election and that a dozen MiG-21's were loaned to Peru by Cuba at the same time. Table 8.3 presents the arms transfers to Peru from 1976-1980 by suppliers from which one can readily see the predominant position of the Soviet Union as a principal supplier.

Much of the military hardware and support equipment which was purchased by the military government continues to be delivered under the Belaúnde administration. Moreover, Belaúnde has not returned to reliance on U.S. military suppliers as was the case in his earlier administration, but has continued significant arms purchases from a variety of sources. Arms

TABLE 8.1
Comparison of Peru/Latin America Military Expenditures by Gross National Product, Central Government Expenditures, and Population

Year	Military Expenditures (ME) ($U.S. millions)	Constant 1979	ME GNP %	Lat. Am. ME GNP %	ME CGE %	Lat. Am. ME CGE %	ME Per Cap	Lat. Am. ME Per Cap
1971	193	330	2.9	1.6	17.2	10.3	23	21
1972	206	339	2.9	1.4	16.8	9.5	23	21
1973	260	404	3.4	1.5	19.2	9.2	27	22
1974	291	413	3.2	1.8	18.9	11.0	27	28
1975	429	557	4.1	1.9	21.5	11.3	35	31
1976	528	651	4.8	1.6	24.0	9.6	41	26
1977	818	952	7.0	1.7	33.1	10.8	58	28
1978	651	708	5.2	1.6	26.5	10.4	42	27
1979	464	464	3.4	1.4	18.1	10.1	27	25
1980	900	816	5.7	1.5	24.4	9.0	46	26

Source: United States, Arms Control and Disarmament Agency, World Military Expenditures and Arms Transfer 1971–1980 (Washington, D.C.: U.S. Government Printing Office, 1983), pp. 35, 63.

TABLE 8.2
Peru Armed Forces, 1971-1980

Year	Armed Forces (1000's)	Armed Forces per/1000 pop.	Latin America/ Armed Forces per/1000 pop.
1971	75	5.4	3.9
1972	75	5.2	4.0
1973	75	5.1	4.0
1974	90	6.0	4.1
1975	95	6.1	4.1
1976	100	6.3	4.1
1977	125	7.7	4.3
1978	125	7.5	4.4
1979	125	7.3	4.8
1980	150	8.5	4.9

Source: United States, Arms Control and Disarmament Agency, World Military Expenditures and Arms Transfers 1971-1980 (Washington, D.C.: U.S. Government Printing Office, 1983), pp. 35, 63.

TABLE 8.3
Value of Arms Transfers, 1976-1980, by Major Supplier

	Total	USSR	U.S.	France	U.K.	W.Ger.	Italy	Others
Peru	1450	900	100	170	10	70	90	120
Ecuador	700		50	390	70	110	5	75
Chile	630		110	170	50	30		265

Source: United States, Arms Control and Disarmament Agency, World Military Expenditures and Arms Transfers 1971-1980 (Washington, D.C.: U.S. Government Printing Office, 1983), p. 119.

purchases from France accounted for over 25 percent of the total $U.S. 2.6 billion of loan contracts signed by Peru in 1982 (LAWR, February 4, 1983:8). Not long after the Peruvian Aeronautics Minister, General Jose García Calderón, denied reports in Washington that Peru had been considering the purchase of 26 F-16's from the U.S. (U.S. FBIS, December 23, 1982:J1), it was announced that Peru would purchase 26 1/2 Mirage 2000 combat jets from France (24 jets plus spare parts and training) with loans from the French government ($610 million at 12% for 10 years, 1 month) and French banks ($74 million, same terms--amount rumored to be the cash down payment)

(LAWR, February 4, 1983:8). Peru is the principal client of the French combat jets in Latin America having purchased 22 Mirage 5's in 1968, 15 Mirage
5's in 1970, and another three in 1981 (U.S. FBIS, December 23, 1982:J1).
Delivery of the Mirage 2000 is expected to begin in the latter half of 1984.
Still another major arms purchase from France under the Belaúnde administration included eight Exocet missiles which the French government refused
to deliver to Peru until the resolution of the Falklands/Malvinas crisis for
fear they would in turn be sold to Argentina (U.S. FBIS, June 8, 1982:J1).
While the Mirage combat jet purchase stands out as the major (and most
expensive) arms purchase, the Belaúnde administration is actively arranging
arms transfers from other sources such as the purchase of 180,000 to 200,000
rifles from Argentina (U.S. FBIS, March 17, 1983:J1); a possible purchase of
helicopters and spare parts from the United States for $60 million (LAWR,
February 4, 1983:8); and $40 million of rifles from Belgium and Brazil (WRH,
November 15, 1983:1).

These arms purchases are all evidence of continued military interaction with Western governments. However, between 150-200 Soviet military
advisers also remain in Peru. The Belaúnde administration hastens to point
out that these advisers are carry-overs from agreements signed by the military government and that they serve needed roles in training and servicing
the military hardware purchased from the Soviet Union during the military
government years (El Observador, March 12, 1983:2). For this reason there
has been no move on the part of the Belaúnde administration to send the
Soviet advisers home.

The motivations of the Belaúnde administration to pursue these and
other arms acquisitions when faced with severe economic problems may be
attributed to the need to appease the military which did overthrow an earlier
Belaúnde regime and did rule for 12 years. While the military did also pave
the way for a return to democracy for Peru, it did so in the shadows of long-
standing conflicts with neighbors Chile and Ecuador.

Conflict with Chile actually stems from the War of the Pacific in the
late 1800s when Bolivia lost its territory on the Pacific Coast to Peru and
Chile. An agreement between Chile and Peru in 1929 established permanent
sovereignty of these two nations over this territory and declared that neither
Chile nor Peru could yield territory to another country without the consent
of the cosignatory of the agreement (St. John, 1977b). Landlocked Bolivia
has continued to press both Chile and Peru for a resolution which would
allow it to have an exit to the sea (St. John, 1977a, 1977b; Shumavon, 1981;
Gorman and St. John, 1982; and chapter 10 of this volume). Although concrete proposals were put forward in the mid-1970s no agreement was
reached. Meanwhile the arms buildup in both Chile and Peru throughout the
1970s and into the 1980s adds to the volatility of the situation in the region.

Peru's border conflict with Ecuador is even more explosive and has
recently involved armed confrontation in the northeast region of Peru.
Although the dispute dates back to the time of independence, a protocol was
negotiated with the assistance of Brazilian arbitration in 1942 which granted
much of Peru's claim to the region. In October 1976 Ecuador demanded a
renegotiation of the 1942 Protocol of Rio de Janeiro (Gorman and St. John,
1982:188) and set into motion a renewed state of agitation. Clashes in the
region became increasingly violent in January 1981 when Peru moved troops
into the disputed territory to secure a portion which had been seized by
Ecuador. "With or without border marks, we know where our border is and we
must safeguard it," President Belaúnde was quoted as saying (U.S. FBIS,

October 31, 1982:J1). Not long after that statement two Peruvian soldiers were killed and one was wounded in a skirmish along the disputed border (U.S. FBIS, January 25, 1983:J1). The situation continues to threaten the stability of the region and contributes to the determination of the Belaunde administration to provide for a strong military in the face of possible war with Ecuador.

In addition, Peru now faces the threat of the operations of a terrorist organization, the Sendero Luminoso, whose revolutionary activities began threatening the countryside in 1980. Violent clashes with Civil Guardsmen and random terrorist acts prompted President Belaúnde to declare the first of many states of siege in 1981. Since that time a death toll of over 1,000 and property damage in excess of $1 billion have been attributed to the activities of the Sendero Luminoso (McClintock, 1983:19). These activities of the Senderistas have prompted arms purchases which are being used by the troops assigned to the Ayacucho region, the scene of the heaviest guerrilla activity (Werlich, 1974:81; Center for Defense Information, 1983:22). For example the Peruvian government recently purchased 16 Soviet-build LI-24 helicopters and went shopping for infrared counter-insurgency equipment (WRH, November 15, 1983:1). This increase in guerrilla activity and the government's seeming inability to control it contributed to rumors of a possible military coup against President Belaúnde in 1982 (WRH, November 30, 1982:3). Rumors flared again in January 1984 when it was reported that the military presented an "ultimatum" to President Belaúnde concerning the need for increased military expenditures in light of possible threats by Sendero Luminoso to the country's power stations (LAWR, January 13, 1984:7). This suggests that Belaúnde must perform a delicate diplomatic balancing act between his government and the military in view of potential threats to national security from inside and outside the country.

POLITICAL-DIPLOMATIC ISSUES

The political-diplomatic orientation of the military government sought to broaden Peru's international horizons. Both Velasco and Morales Bermúdez professed nonalignment and sought to carve a niche for Peru in the politics of the Third World. Relations with the United States which had been such a powerful force in the politics of the governments which preceded the Revolutionary Government were cooled as the military government expanded diplomatic and commercial ties with the Soviet Union, Eastern bloc nations, and other Third World nations. U.S. opposition to the Velasco regime's economic nationalism contributed to the cooling of the relationship as well.

The Belaúnde administration has not abandoned these expanded horizons, but has in fact capitalized on the political-diplomatic ventures initiated by the Revolutionary Government. President Belaúnde has made it clear that the redemocratization of Peru places it solidly in the Western ideological sphere of influence. However, the nationalistic orientation of Belaúnde's foreign policy, coupled with a strong concern for Latin America's role in the international arena, ensures a strong Third World orientation in Belaúnde's foreign policies. The impact of this orientation on Peru's foreign policy under the Belaúnde administration has resulted in:

1. a continuation of the expansion of diplomatic and commercial relations with nations outside the Western hemisphere;

2. active participation in the movement of nonaligned nations;
3. an active role in hemispheric relations including support for Argentina in the Falklands/Malvinas War, a re-establishment of close relations with Bolivia, and an attempt at the revitalization of the Andean Pact; and
4. a volatile relationship with the United States which has included disagreements on the Falkland Islands War, the crisis in Central America, and closer to home--on trade restrictions placed on Peruvian products by the United States.

Following the Revolution in 1968 Velasco announced that foreign policy would be guided by principles of nonintervention and that Peru would not be constrained by East-West divisions. Although the Velasco government did increase diplomatic and trade relations with the Soviet Union, the People's Republic of China, Eastern Europe, and Cuba, these moves were interpreted by the Peruvians as an expansion of trade opportunities for Peruvian markets, rather than as a political statement of alignment with the Eastern bloc.

The Belaúnde administration has maintained the diplomatic and commercial relations originally established by Velasco and the military government. Belaúnde has, however, sought to diversify those relations seen further by emphasizing ties with additional countries such as Spain, Italy, Finland, South Korea, and Japan. For example, in an effort to expand relations with European nations (and perhaps to smooth any hard feelings following the Falklands/Malvinas War), meetings were held in Lima with the Foreign Ministers of Spain, Italy, and Finland. In August 1982 the Prime Minister of Spain, Leopoldo Salvo-Sotelo visited with President Belaúnde and Foreign Minister Javier Arias Stella in Lima to discuss "matters of interest for the development of cooperation between the two countries" (U.S. FBIS, August 11, 1982:J1) which involved Spanish support for technical and cultural projects in Peru. Foreign Minister Arias Stella also met in August with the Foreign Minister of Italy, Emilio Colombo, to discuss the possibility of technical and cultural cooperation after which Italy agreed to participate in economic development projects in Peru and to grant scholarships for the training of Peruvian diplomatic personnel (U.S. FBIS, August 5, 1982:J1). In January 1983 President Belaúnde received a visit from the Foreign Minister of Finland who arrived to discuss energy and health cooperation issues.

Important diplomatic overtures have been made in the Far East with Japan and South Korea. In December 1982 President Belaunde received a visit from South Korean Prime Minister Kim Sang-hyop who also indicated that he would welcome increased cooperation and understanding between South Korea and Peru. Peruvian Foreign Minister Javier Arias Stella returned the favor indicating that Lima would "lend all possible support to South Korea in the international arena" (U.S. FBIS, December 17, 1982:J1). Following that meeting Peruvian and South Korean officials agreed to the development of a bilateral commission on resource cooperation which resulted in the formation of a joint mineral resources cooperation committee to exchange expertise, publications, and manpower. Colombia is the only other South American nation with a similar agreement (U.S. JPRS, June 8, 1983:0087).

President Belaúnde has also maintained Peru's position as a member of the Nonaligned Movement--a position which was strongly supported by his military predecessors. With this commitment Peru continues to support the principles of the Nonalignment Movement and regularly sends delegations to the meetings in the interest of maintaining a position as Foreign Minister

Schwalb put it, "between the two powers on the earth" (U.S. FBIS, January 7, 1983:J1).

Still another point of continuity in Peruvian foreign policy from the military government to President Belaúnde's government is the strong interest in hemispheric relations, even though those interests have been punctuated occasionally with conflicts between Peru and neighboring Chile and Ecuador. President Belaúnde has fostered the development of close relations between Peru and Bolivia as was demonstrated by the award of Peru's Congressional Medal of Honor to President-Elect Hernan Siles Suazo on the day before his inauguration in October 1982 and Belaunde's subsequent travel to his inauguration in Bolivia. These renewed ties do not affect Peru's position on Bolivia's quest for an outlet to the sea, however, according to Prime/Foreign Minister Schwalb who says that Peru still holds by the 1929 treaty and the protocol signed by Peru and Chile (El Comercio, April 30, 1983:A4). Although Peru rhetorically supports Bolivia's claim for an outlet to the sea, it is highly unlikely that Peru would concede any of its territory to ensure such an outlet. Other diplomatic ventures in the region of particular interest include: (1) the discussions between Peru and Venezuela in February 1983 to try to revitalize the Andean Pact; (2) the establishment of diplomatic relations at the Embassy level with Grenada in March 1983; and (3) the continued support for Argentina following the Falklands/Malvinas War in the spring of 1982.

It was the conflict over the Falkland Islands that began an estrangement between the Belaúnde government and the United States. President Belaúnde moved early in the conflict to attempt to mediate between Argentina and Great Britain by proposing a peace plan which involved a cessation of hostilities and a negotiated settlement concerning the future of the islands. President Belaúnde was also in close contact with U.S. Secretary of State, Alexander Haig, who engaged in shuttle diplomacy between London and Buenos Aires. Prospects for a negotiated settlement dimmed early and Belaúnde's position as intermediary was undermined when Argentina rejected Belaúnde's peace proposal following the attack on the Argentine cruiser, the General Belgrano. Although Peru did not enter the actual fighting, Defense Minister General Luis Cisneros Vizquerra reported that the Peruvian army would intervene in support of Argentina should the need arise (LAWR, May 7, 1982:2). Neither the Peruvian peace proposal nor the Argentine military was successful as Great Britain retook the Falklands/Malvinas. Following the unsuccessful attempts at negotiations, the United States supported Great Britain's move on the Falklands which not only undermined U.S.-Argentina relations, but also U.S.-Peruvian relations as well. President Belaúnde said that the U.S. had made a mistake in proclaiming its support for Britain in the conflict over the Falklands/Malvinas and that there should be no doubt about Argentina's rights of sovereignty over the islands (U.S. FBIS, June 21, 1982: V1). Following the crisis President Belaúnde sent a message to President Bignone of Argentina which reaffirmed "the desire of the Peruvian Government to maintain the traditional relations of friendship between our countries and to contribute to the permanent re-establishment of peace" (U.S. FBIS, July 12, 1982:V1). No such message was sent to the United States or Great Britain.

Relations between Peru and the United States have not been as smooth as was originally expected given the return to democratic rule in Peru as well as the return to the presidency of a man well known in U.S. government circles. U.S. Vice President George Bush visited Peru in August 1982 and spoke of a willingness to support development programs in Peru as well as of a desire to strengthen relations between the two countries in the aftermath of the Falklands/Malvinas War (U.S. FBIS, August 12, 1982:J1). However, President Belaúnde's planned trip to Washington, D.C., in November 1982 was abruptly cancelled when it was learned that his trip would coincide with the imposition of countervailing duties on Peruvian textiles by the U.S. Department of Commerce. Prime Minister-designate Fernando Schwalb labeled the act "protectionist" and called on the U.S. and other industrialized nations to be more flexible toward the imports of goods and raw materials from developing nations (U.S. FBIS, December 22, 1982:V1; WRH, November 30, 1982:3).

Still another point of disagreement between Peru and the United States concerns U.S. involvement in Central America--particularly attempts to threaten the government of Nicaragua. Belaunde has been quoted as saying that Peru "fully and categorically condemns any military intervention" of the U.S. military in Central America (U.S. FBIS, October 26, 1982:V1). President Belaúnde has repeatedly voiced Peru's support of the efforts of the Contadora Ministers (Colombia, Mexico, Panama, and Venzuela) to find a negotiated settlement to the crisis in Central America (El Comercio, April 30, 1983:A4).

PERUVIAN FOREIGN POLICY: FUTURE DIRECTIONS

The foreign policy of President Belaúnde's administration is being formulated today in response to a complex set of factors which include external stimuli as well as internal demands to generate policies which will contribute to the development and well-being of all Peruvians. The social and economic reforms set into motion by the military government which preceded President Belaúnde contributed to the decline in the economy, but they also established popular demands that the government continue to improve the standard of living for a wider number of Peruvian citizens. As a result the Peruvian government today finds itself in serious economic difficulty and at the mercy of the international banking system. It appears that while the military government was driving to eliminate Peruvian dependence through policies of economic nationalism, it actually transferred that dependence to the International Monetary Fund, the Inter-American Development Bank and a host of private lenders in Europe, the United States, and the Eastern bloc. The result is that foreign policy in Peru today is clearly determined to a large extent by the financial commitments made by its military predecessors.

Two other factors are also important to consider in reviewing the foreign policy of Peru since the return of democratic rule, however, which also have antecedents in the foreign policy of the military government. First, the Peruvian armed forces began a program of development for the military itself which led to an accelerated arms procurement. This policy continues to be pursued as evidenced in the purchase of the Mirage jets--a purchase which accounted for almost 25 percent of the total debt incurred in 1982. The Belaúnde administration has also followed the military government's lead in diversifying arms suppliers. This active arms policy may be attributed to a perceived need for defense in the region, or in response to the increased guerrilla activity now threatening Peru. It is most likely, however, that this policy is determined in part by the need for the civilian government to appease the military predecessors whose proclivity for intervention has been a fact of Peruvian political life for generations.

The second important aspect of Peru's foreign policy today which also has antecedents in the military government is the extension of Peru's diplomatic and commercial relations both within and beyond the region. Whereas the Belaúnde administration of the 1960s was intimately tied to the United States in many ways, this Belaúnde administration has actively sought to expand its diplomatic and commercial horizons with nations of Europe and the Third World. One cannot ignore the significance of the political and economic relationship between the U.S. and Peru, but one must note in analyzing Peru's foreign policy that the Belaúnde administration is actively seeking an identity in Latin America and in the Third World which is less tied to the dominance of the U.S.

With these issues in mind it is likely that Peruvian foreign policy will continue in directions of diversification of diplomatic and commercial relations within the region of Latin America as well as beyond the region to the continents of Europe and Asia. President Belaúnde has made it clear that while his government rests comfortably in the ideological camp of the West, Peru's national development mandates an expansion of diplomatic and commercial ties in both the Western bloc and the Eastern bloc. Peru's future foreign policy choices are going to continue to be affected by its efforts to repay its albatross-like foreign debt and by military pressure to maintain high levels of defense expenditures to protect Peru from threats to national security from both inside and outside its borders.

9
The Foreign Policies of Venezuela and Colombia: Collaboration, Competition, and Conflict

William A. Hazleton

During the past two decades, Latin American states have become more actively involved in international relations. This is due in part to changes in the international environment providing expanded opportunities for weaker states to act, and in part to enhanced domestic capabilities enabling them to better pursue national policy objectives, both at home and abroad. However, countries like Venezuela and Colombia that have made substantial progress toward socioeconomic and political development find themselves in the paradoxical situation where greater internal resources, plus increased flexibility and choice in formulating foreign policy strategies, have not significantly enhanced their independence from external constraints. The conditions leading to greater international participation by Latin American states are not unique to the region, but are rather serious world-wide problems such as rising energy costs, slowing economic growth, accessing scientific and technological achievements, halting environmental deterioration, and promoting popular participation (Urquidi et al., 1978:6-18). Given the complex nature and extensive scope of these problems, it is not surprising that even with more sophisticated and varied foreign policy approaches, the capacity of Latin American states to affect international developments remains relatively weak.

To appreciate not only the accomplishments but also the ironies, paradoxes, and conflicts arising from the expanded international roles of Venezuela (generally recognized as an international actor) and Colombia (viewed as a potential or emerging international actor), their foreign policies need to be examined outside the narrow and deterministic confines of both the realist paradigm and dependencia. While no attempt is made to develop an alternative analytical framework, it is the author's contention that valuable insights into the motivations and actions of larger Latin American states can be derived from a more open-ended approach that draws upon several recent concepts from the international relations literature. They include: "complex interdependence" (Koehane and Nye, 1978:24-29), "intermestic politics" (Manning, 1977:309), "political adaptation" (Rosenau, 1981), "dependence" (Caporaso, 1978:18-21), and "unorthodox dependency" (Dominguez, 1978:106-108). These concepts take differences in foreign policy behavior into account, both over time and between issues, by recognizing the inter-relationship between internal and external factors as well as the relative capabilities of states to act. Venezuela and Colombia are not locked into a set of foreign policy responses; nor do their current governments, which strive for new policy alternatives, see the situation that way. By assuming these states "make" foreign policies, it becomes necessary to employ concepts that eschew prescribed courses of action and to look instead at how these states seek to adjust to or change their international environment.

Venezuela and Colombia provide interesting case studies for illustrating the variety of factors involved in determining the foreign policy behavior of Latin American states. This chapter focuses on (1) the position of Venezuela and Colombia in the international system, (2) their foreign policy interests and expanded scope of international concerns, and (3) the strategies they employ to promote and protect their national interests. The chapter concludes with a brief examination of foreign policy initiatives by Venezuela and Colombia in the circum-Caribbean region and their efforts to move out from the shadow of the United States through closer collaboration with the Third World and the nonaligned bloc. As is so often the case of major international actors that are unable to blend the different elements of their foreign policy into a coherent whole, the decisions and actions taken by Venezuela and Colombia reflect a constantly evolving relationship between ends and means in which foreign and domestic factors compete for the government's attention and limited national resources.

VENEZUELA AND COLOMBIA AS INTERNATIONAL ACTORS

All Latin American and Caribbean nations have foreign relations; most do not, however, have true foreign policies. Foreign policy implies purposive behavior, not simply the ability of a state to react to external events. The minimum objective of any state is to ensure its continued survival and advance the nation's well-being. However, most states have neither the organizational capacity nor the range of alternatives necessary to make foreign policy decisions and implement them. While no state can fully guarantee its security in the nuclear age, the fact remains that the ability of states to affect their international environment varies greatly, resulting in a hierarchical international system composed of "superpowers," "secondary powers," "middle powers," "small states," and "ministates." The traditional basis for distinguishing among states has been the size of their land area, population, and gross national product (GNP), along with assessments of their relative military capabilities. Neither Venezuela nor Colombia are small from the standpoint of size: Venezuela, with a land area of 911,680 square kilometers is almost four times the size of the United Kingdom, and Colombia's land area of 1,139,600 square kilometers is nearly twice the size of France and Spain combined. While the interior portion of each country is largely undeveloped and sparsely populated (see Robinson, 1971:179-246), the current population estimates for Venezuela and Colombia are a substantial 15.2 million and 26.7 million, respectively. Both are considered less developed countries, but a per capita GNP of $3,630 for Venezuela and $1,180 for Colombia place them among the middle-income countries, ranking 91st and 66th respectively out of 125 states surveyed by the World Bank (1982:110-111). As for military preparedness, Venezuela's armed forces number 40,500, with an estimated defense budget of $U.S. 1,142 billion in 1982, while Colombian forces total 70,200, with an estimated $U.S. 420.3 million expended on defense in 1982 (IISS, 1983:108 and 114-115). The point is that while neither of these states is particularly small, both have usually been placed in the residual category of "small states" that is reserved for the militarily weak, economically disadvantaged, and parochial; in other words, those countries which are more often acted upon than actors in international relations.

Because of their position of relative inferiority, "small states" were assumed to have no foreign policy. But just as population, geographic size, and economic wealth may not be accurate indicators of a state's international standing, assumptions concerning the passive foreign policy behavior of "small states" have been called into question. The problem of defining "small state" behavior is not one of identifying physical differences between states, but the subjective nature of the process itself. As Rosenau (1981:104) points out, the boundaries between categories of superpowers, middle-range powers, and small states are defined not by objective criteria, but rather by the concerns of foreign policy analysts wishing to compare the relative capabilities and national policy objectives of large numbers of states. One alternative to placing countries like Venezuela and Colombia in a category so diverse that it ranges from Italy to ministates is to distinguish between states according to their degree of participation and influence in international arenas. While the superpowers would be classified as "system-determining," smaller states would be either "system-affecting" (i.e., able to exert some influence through collective action) or "system-ineffectual," namely, those states for whom foreign policy is adjusting to external reality (Keohane, 1969:296). Such distinctions become important, especially when assessing the relative influence and involvement of states in the circum-Caribbean region.

Certainly, one factor determining a state's ability to prosper and survive is its national situation, namely, the combined features of a nation's internal strength and the external environment in which it must operate. Not only does this mean that there will be some obvious limitations placed on Latin American and Caribbean countries, but also that some of these countries are destined to fare far better than others because of differences in their internal and external settings. However, one trait that most states, large and small, share is that their domestic structures are becoming increasingly sensitive to actions taken by outside centers of decision-making authority. This "stress sensitivity" increases with the level of national development creating the need to divert more resources to the sphere of foreign policy as the country advances domestically (McGowan and Gottwald, 1975:475-76). Foreign policy, therefore, is not simply a luxury of developed nations, but rather a necessary part of the on-going development process in an age of complex independence.

With the exception of Argentina, Brazil, Mexico, Venezuela, Cuba (whose overseas involvement constitutes a unique case), and Colombia, it is hard to conceive of Latin American states as independent actors, even within their immediate locality. The reason is most have yet to achieve the degree of internal economic strength and national integration needed to formulate and support a true foreign policy. Venezuela's stature in international affairs, for example, has been greatly enhanced by its oil wealth and stable democracy, while Colombia's somewhat more tenuous standing among influential American states is due in large measure to its lack of unifying national goals, continued outbreaks of internal violence, and the government's inability to secure the resources necessary for long-term internal development policies.

While national situation determines a state's relative capacity to respond to external challenges, the exact nature of the response depends primarily on the government's foreign policy objectives--its sense of purpose. Most often, these objectives reflect not only national ambitions but also particular images of the outside world and the role that the state should play in international affairs. All Latin American states do not share identical

world views, nor do they necessarily have similar aspirations. Rather, each
nation's definition of its international position tends to be unique in that it
embodies the subjective judgments of political leaders who confront the difficult task of reconciling national objectives with internal and external realities. Thus, an important psychological dimension must be incorporated into
the study of small-state behavior, for the lack of conviction that their individual and collective efforts will substantively change external conditions is
a major obstacle that most small states have yet to overcome (Rosenau, 1981:
105-106).

Traditionally, Latin American leaders have been reluctant to invest the
necessary national resources to maintain an active foreign policy role.
Because of a long history of foreign penetration, United States hegemony, and
second-rank status, Latin Americans tend to have a hostile vision of the outside world--a world in which their nations have been primarily the victims of
powerful external forces, and in which they have had little or no opportunity
to shape major international events (Milenky, 1975:101-103). Today's Latin
American leaders remain acutely aware of their countries' weaknesses as they
confront escalating domestic demands and serious international constraints.
If a government hopes to retain popular support through national development
strategies, it must act as a mediator between these forces, a role which
clearly requires both domestic and foreign policies.

For countries with such long histories, the emergence of clearly identifiable foreign policy goals is a rather recent development in Venezuela and
Colombia. Venezuela became active in hemispheric affairs following the
overthrow of the Perez Jimenez dictatorship in 1958. The establishment of a
competitive political system, along with rising petroleum earnings, gave the
Acción Democrática administration of Romulo Betancourt both the confidence and opportunity to begin speaking out in defense of democracy and
reform in Latin America. In Colombia the process has taken even longer.
After World War I conservative President Marco Fidel Suarez set the basic
tone of Colombian foreign policy by enunciating the doctrine of the "polar
star," namely, that Colombia should always look northward and cast its
fortunes with the United States. The development of an indigenous foreign
policy received a serious setback after World War II, when la violencia and its
legacy of internal problems pushed foreign relations aside (Bushnell, 1975:
410-412). Until the 1960s Colombian leaders clung to the belief that a low
international profile and a foreign nonpolicy served the country's best interests, thus turning their Andean nation into the "Tibet of South America" in
order to escape from potentially dangerous foreign competition (Drekonja-
Kornat, 1983:229). Indeed, only after abandoning this outlook of resignation
and helplessness did Colombia begin to develop a semiautonomous foreign
policy and open its doors to the rest of Latin America and the world.

The level of a state's activity in the international system is a function
of three important variables: (1) internal resources, (2) psychological outlook,
and (3) external conditions. The first category would include such factors as
a state's military and economic resources, as well as the government's organizational and leadership capacity to marshall and direct these resources
toward the achievement of specific ends. Venezuela and Colombia, albeit in
varying degrees, enjoy a distinct advantage over most of their Latin American
counterparts in terms of foreign policy capabilities because of their democratic orientation, domestic stability, bureaucratic capacity, and quality of
leadership. Secondly, the willingness to sacrifice resources in order to affect
change in the external environment requires self-confidence and a sense of

purpose on behalf of any potential actor. If Latin American states are to assume a larger role in international affairs, their world views must support such actions, as in the case of Venezuela and, more recently, Colombia, the costs of making foreign policy commitments must be seen as being outweighed by the potential benefits. Finally, it goes without saying that the character-istics of the international system, and especially the nature of relations among its most powerful members, have a decided impact on the role Latin American states can play. Thus, the rise of small-state participation in the 1960s and 1970s accompanied by increased multipolarity, reduced superpower tensions and, specifically in the case of Latin America, the decline of U.S. hegemony in the region. What these changes did in effect was not so much weaken the dominant position of the superpowers but widen the limits of permissibility for the foreign policy actions of Latin American states.

Of the three variables, the external environment is often considered to be the most important. In academic circles the tendency to focus on East-West conflict and North-South relations is understandable given the lack of information available to observers concerning the capabilities and attitudes of individual states. However, unless the internal resources and predisposition to act are present in Latin American states, major changes in the inter-national system will likely have little or no bearing on their passive or ineffectual foreign policy orientations.

Reliance on external observations has led, for example, to classifying small states by their actions or, more precisely, their foreign policy approaches. Small states are said to: (1) have a narrower geographic and functional range of concerns; (2) stress multilateral diplomacy through parti-cipation in international conferences, regional associations, and the UN; (3) downplay the use or threat of military force, relying instead on legal instru-ments, moral arguments, and economic means of influence when available; and (4) strive to avoid behavior and policies that would either alienate or offend more powerful nations. Venezuela and Colombia have certainly employed all of these approaches, as have much larger states outside Latin America; but Caracas and Bogota have also transgressed these bounds of appropriate small-state behavior when their interests or the occasion demanded a different course of action.

Whether or not small states strictly adhere to these approaches is not as important as understanding the overriding implication of applying "rational" behavior models to examine the foreign policies of small states. As will be seen with dependencia, internal conditions and perceptions are largely ignored in favor of externally based notions as to what constitutes an appropriate or rational response for states with limited resources and little potential for affecting change in the international environment. Ironically, the use of the rational policy paradigm assumes that small states have the necessary organi-zational and leadership skills to formulate rational policies, that their weak-ness is somehow confined only to their military arsenals and/or national treasuries and does not impair the decision-making process. As East (1973: 557-560) has illustrated, the lack of organizational capacity in small states can contribute to high-risk behavior or actions that otherwise might be labeled "irrational" by outside observers. Moreover, it is possible to miscal-culate, as the Argentine armed forces apparently did in the Malvinas crisis. Or the absence of foreign policy options due to limited resources and/or external constraints could back a small country into a corner from which it felt there was no way out but to make a great national sacrifice for a losing cause. Quite simply, we must accept the reality that small states think and act differently than large states writ small (Rothstein, 1968:1).

Dependencia theorists also fall into this trap of overemphasizing the role of external factors in shaping a small state's foreign policy. In this case, international economic relations establish patterns of "structural" dependence for Latin American states, thus explaining their "peripheral" position and lack of influence in the world. Dependency involves a complex set of relationships incorporating less-developed countries (LDCs) into the global division of labor. The result of LDCs is the absence of state autonomy, penetration by foreign or transnational interests, severely limited development alternatives, and a distorted domestic economy structured to serve the needs of foreign export-ers. Brazilian economist Roberto Campos (1978:82) rejects the notion that dominant-subordinant economic ties govern all aspects of small-state behav-ior, charging that dependencia "appears to relegate policy makers and admin-istrators within developing countries to the humiliating position of puppets or idiots." But while Rosenau (1981:116-117) and others contend that an internal consensus in support of strong national leadership can bring about innovative attempts to reduce small-state dependency, dependencia theorists see exter-nal conditions as beyond the control of small-state actors. Consequently, their social, economic, and political development will be distorted by an enduring and penetrating structural relationship.

In actuality, Latin American countries that are very dependent eco-nomically and militarily on the United States have repeatedly demonstrated their noncompliance with the latter's wishes (VanKlavern, 1982:19-20). Some exponents of dependencia do concede that several Latin American states have been able to exert some bargaining leverage to win concessions from northern industrialized nations (Muñoz, 1981:24). Consequently, dependencia has been revised by incorporating the "strategic" dependence of developed nations on the raw materials, export markets, and cheap labor of certain states on the periphery of the international system. This relationship of "strategic" depend-ency appears closely akin to dependence, except that the latter lacks the attraction of clear ideological distinctions between winners and losers, between the wealthy and their victims. Dependence is a pattern of external reliance, a highly asymmetrical form of interdependence (Caporaso, 1978:18). The degree of dependence/independence varies from one state to the next, from one issue-area to another. The important distinction between depend-ency and dependence is that the latter is a relative, rather than a fixed condi-tion, thus permitting the use of bargaining models to explain interactions between unequal, but relatively autonomous, international actors.

In the short run, and on a case-by-case basis, the foreign policies of Venezuela and Colombia, especially with regard to the United States, clearly indicate a dependent relationship, but certainly not one in which they have no independence or control over their external actions. Indeed, their foreign policies are designed in large part to lessen their dependence on the United States by diversifying their foreign relations, thus enhancing their bargaining position vis-à-vis the U.S. Yet, while Caracas and Bogota may undertake independent initiatives, even at the risk of Washington's displeasure, there is also a certain convergence of interests and a coincidence of policies between these two countries and the United States that is readily apparent over the longer run. In a study of the foreign policy of dependent states, Moon (1983) concludes that the dependency model accounts for the pro-U.S. orientation of LDCs in that structural penetration has affected the foreign policy-making processes of nations just as it has their economic, political, cultural, and social relations. At this point if one thing is clear, it is that defining the role of Venezuela and Colombia as international actors depends largely on the perspective employed by the observer, and not simply on a list of objective criteria.

FOREIGN POLICY INTERESTS AND NATIONAL DEVELOPMENT

Because of their limited resources, Venezuela and Colombia focus their foreign policy efforts on select functional and/or geographic areas. The salience of these areas fluctuates with changes in the international and domestic environment, resulting in shifts of emphasis and direction as well as in the level of activity. While it is possible to differentiate between military, political, economic, and geopolitical objectives in their foreign policies, national objectives are often closely interrelated in a given set of circumstances. Therefore, externally oriented goals are perhaps best understood in the broader context of foreign policy interests. For example, Venezuela's and Colombia's interests in national economic development and the stability of the circum-Caribbean region comprise a variety of different, and not always compatible, objectives. Foreign policy capabilities as well as the range of interests help to determine the scope of their activity in international affairs. Their participation can be on several different planes, with Venezuela and Colombia pursuing foreign policy interests at the global (e.g., NIEO and Nonaligned Movement), regional (e.g., OAS and SELA), subregional (e.g., Andean bloc and Contadora Group), and bilateral levels.

To operate simultaneously at different levels and pursue multiple interests requires a set of guidelines and controls for making policy choices as well as for overseeing their implementation. Unfortunately, most Latin American states have not developed a coherent foreign policy framework and fall into the category of Colombia, which is described as still "learning the foreign policy process" (Drekonja-Kornat, 1983). Venezuela, despite far more experience in this area, has yet to articulate a set of principles to guide its foreign policy makers, and consequently, a clear delineation of specific Venezuelan policy priorities remains elusive (Martz, 1977:158-159). Part of the problem is that the Venezuelan diplomatic service is small and its quality uneven, although efforts are being made to upgrade the level of professionalization (Martz, 1982:142; Bond, 1982:190). Another is that the foreign policy-making process is weak and diffuse. In both Venezuela and Colombia, the foreign ministry shares its responsibilities with a number of competing agencies engaged in planning, finance, and trade (Martz, 1977:194; Bond, 1977:253-254; Kline, 1983:121). Under these conditions, the personal leadership of the president becomes critical in that foreign policy matters are often resolved at his desk, and activist presidents like Venezuela's Carlos Andres Perez tend to become their own foreign minister. Still, in most cases, decisions are made on an ad hoc and incremental basis, which not only deprives Venezuela and Colombia of consistent and cohesive foreign policies but also consumes additional resources that they can ill afford to waste.

One factor inducing Latin American states to become more active in international relations is the "intermestic" nature of the problems confronting them. However much governments would like to control or eliminate the adverse impact of external developments, it has become increasingly difficult to separate outside influences from important aspects of national life. For LDCs the compartmentalization of foreign and domestic policy began to break down with large-scale efforts to promote national development (Rothstein,

1977:128-129). The causes of and remedies for their pressing economic needs
were seen as coming from a common source--external dependency. Blame
was placed on a history of colonial exploitation and foreign penetration of
local economies, and the solution was found in increased foreign assistance,
the diversification of trade, and the adoption of the New International Economic Order (NIEO).

For example, Venezuela's foreign policy is explainable only in terms of
the domestic political and economic development strategy pursued by political
elites after the ouster of Perez Jimenez. According to Robert Bond (1982:
189), Venezuela's development goals include the (1) consolidation of a competitive, democratic system; (2) nationalization of the petroleum industry
(achieved in 1976); (3) diversified economic growth; and (4) greater equity in
the distribution of economic benefits. Central to their accomplishment was
the maximization of government oil revenues, from which the country earned
97 percent of its foreign exchange in 1982. In addition to diversifying the
economy through the "sowing of oil revenues," development goals have been
pursued through Venezuela's endorsement of the NIEO, massive foreign
borrowing, and efforts at accommodation with the United States.

A recent example of intermestic politics can be found in debt-ridden
Venezuela's decision to sidestep an agreement with the International Monetary
Fund so as to avoid the imposition of IMF austerity measures that could bring
about political unrest (LAWR, December 8, 1983:2-3). Another example of an
intermestic issue is the highly profitable illicit production and trafficking in
Colombian cocaine and marijuana that threatens corruption at home and
creates tensions with the United States (Craig, 1983, 1981; LAWR, February
11, 1983:5). Intermestic politics, then, means having to address major
national problems on two fronts, foreign and domestic.

For Venezuela and Colombia, foreign policy is an instrument for
achieving greater national autonomy. Their major interests are economic
development and political stability, and these two goals are assumed to be
interconnected in that democracy is a necessary condition for development
and development in turn will contribute to political stability. While their
foreign policies attempt to inhibit external forces which pose a danger to
domestic political and economic structures, their main outward thrust is in
the area of diversifying political contacts and expanding export markets.
While it would be wrong and misleading to look at Latin American foreign
policy interests solely in terms of domestic ambitions, it must be realized
that the primary motivation for Venezuelan and Colombian participation in
the international arena is the desire to find ways of alleviating their internal
weaknesses.

FOREIGN POLICY STRATEGIES: PRINCIPLES AND ACTIONS

Since a state's foreign policy is usually designed to achieve several
distinct, yet interrelated, ends it is natural that, even in the case of small
states, a number of foreign policy approaches would be employed. Limited
economic and military capabilities lead Latin American states to rely heavily,
though certainly not exclusively, on foreign policy instruments that avoid
explicit threats or the use of physical coercion. Although their foreign policies are often described as either defense reactions or taking advantage of
external opportunities, states like Mexico, Venezuela, and Colombia are at
times innovators, seeking to promote change in what they see as new and

positive directions. A fairly wide range of options, or foreign policy strategies, are available to Latin American states, if they have the resources and capabilities to effectively utilize them. While not mutually exclusive, these strategies tend to take the following general forms: (1) internationalism through expanded bilateral political and economic contacts, (2) special relationships with a larger power, (3) regional and subregional integration, and (4) multilateral diplomacy and cooperation on a regional and global scale.

Because of the varying costs and benefits associated with each of these options, Latin American states have either alternated between different strategies or, more commonly, employed several strategies simultaneously. Flexibility, however, exacts a toll in terms of policy coherence. The objectives being pursued may not be compatible or the actions may appear to contradict other foreign policy objectives. For example, Venezuela's efforts to stabilize the situation in the Caribbean basin through international mediation is said not to apply when the issue is the recovery of national territory from neighboring Guyana (Ewell, 1982:311-312). Or in the mid-1970s, Perez's energetic diplomacy sought to portray Venezuela as "the voice of Latin America, OPEC, the Third World, and Western democratic nations," causing no end of confusion as different aspects of these positions came into conflict (Bond, 1977:223-229). Martz (1977:158-159) characterized Venezuela's actions as a series of pragmatic responses to particular issues that were unfortunately taken in the absence of any overall policy-making framework or clearly articulated guiding principles. The result is that foreign policy priorities become elusive because governments wish to avoid being trapped by "absolutist" positions on important international issues. Rather, they much prefer to employ flexible approaches or what is commonly referred to as "pragmatic opportunism"--taking advantage, when possible, of whatever opportunities may exist (Milenky, 1977:95-96).

In the past, Latin American power elites were concerned with preventing challenges to the status quo and therefore favored static foreign policies aimed at preserving regional alliances and maintaining good relations with major trading partners (Astiz, 1969:5-7). In the 1980s, however, it is with enhanced national capabilities, greater self-confidence, and an increased willingness to experiment that politicians and técnicos in Latin American countries like Venezuela and Colombia confront each other, the United States, and the rest of the world (Drekonja-Kornat, 1983:243-245; Ewell, 1982:296). For instance, in negotiating trade agreements with the United States, which can have enormous consequences for Latin countries in terms of employment levels, economic growth, price stability, and debt-servicing, Colombia, along with Mexico and Argentina, was cited (Odell, 1980:217-218) as winning important concessions through advanced preparation, the presentation of technical arguments, and a sophisticated strategy of making allies with "friendly" groups and agencies inside the United States.

Despite indigenous efforts at modernization and reform, autonomous national development remains an elusive goal for Latin American states. If dependence in some form is a reality, then the question becomes how to manage it. For Latin Americans, one way to enhance their relative independence is to avoid exclusive dependence on a single export market or source of investment (e.g., the United States). Quite simply, the aim of this approach, known as the "new internationalism," is the diversification of Latin American economic and political relations on a global scale. Expanded bilateral commercial contacts with Western Europe, Canada, Japan, Korea, Taiwan, the Soviet Union, and the Eastern bloc will, it is assumed, not only open up new markets and sources of capital and technology, but also lessen Latin America's vulnerability to adverse economic trends (Fontaine and Theberge, 1976). This deliberate process of diversifying trade ties could be seen in Colombia in the 1960s and early 1970s (Drekonja-Kornat, 1983:235-237). Today, both Colombia and Venezuela are looking northward to the Caribbean basin for new and untapped export markets that will hopefully encourage greater capital investment at home. Moreover, Colombia has broken ranks with much of the Third World and joined the liberalized trading arrangement of GATT (Premo, 1982: 113).

Another measure to reduce external dependence is to diversify the national economy so as to avoid overreliance on a single export. In Venezuela, where oil accounts for over 60 percent of its exports, the government has struggled to secure a long-term future for petroleum exports, while promoting diversification of the economy and the increased export of manufactured goods (Black, 1982:74). Recently, Venezuelan economic experts have argued that the significant drop in the country's petroleum export earnings, estimated at almost $U.S. 1 billion in 1983, would necessitate more rapid diversification and expanded growth of non-traditional exports (U.S. JPRS 83159:78-79). Colombia faces similar problems regarding its heavy dependence on coffee exports. Colombian industrialists have certainly not been satisfied with government efforts to promote the export of their products and services as indicated by this report in El Tiempo (U.S. JPRS 82094:27):

> As long as we do not possess a competent, stable, skillful, and well-supported negotiating team in international forums, Colombia will continue to be a dark, insignificant, and grey country in the international concert. Right now, we only think about coffee, and that is because we have always had the same people representing us and because we are the second largest producer in the world.

Latin America's new internationalism is not necessarily designed to play one state or power bloc off against another. However, there is always the possibility that expanded diplomatic and economic relations could be used to counterbalance the strength of a neighboring country. Venezuela, for example, has sought to check growing Brazilian power by promoting ties with the U.S., Europe, and Japan (Blank, 1982:78). In other cases, Latin American states hope to break out of their localized role by getting out, speaking out, and being heard in foreign capitals and international forums. Recently, both Colombia and Venezuela have assumed a much larger role in addressing the problems of the circum-Caribbean region as well as taking a more active part in the Nonaligned Movement for reasons that include enhanced international recognition and prestige.

While broadening their diplomatic and economic horizons, Latin American states cannot help but be mindful of the awesome presence of a global giant in their midst. In the past, there was frequently a strong urge among small states to cooperate with the great powers, known as "pilot fish" behavior or staying close to the shark to avoid being eaten. In the case of the United States, Latin American states have participated in a series of inter-American arrangements in hopes of constraining this regional hegemon by channeling its tremendous power and wealth into potentially useful directions. Today, "special relationships" with great powers have fallen out of favor for obvious domestic reasons. Yet, in response to charges from political opponents, former Colombian Foreign Minister Lemos Simmonds (U.S. FBIS,

July 27, 1982:F1), who does not "think it is a disgrace to be a friend of the United States," asserted that the Turbay government followed an independent foreign policy in that it neither consulted with Washington nor asked its permission on key decisions. Given the dangers of neglect and the existence of similar foreign policy concerns, an ongoing dialogue with Washington is considered an important and necessary part of the foreign policies of Venezuela and Colombia. Consequently, both pursue a policy of accommodation, if not at times outright "friendship," toward the United States because it serves their political and economic interests.

Concern over external dependence and the desire to insulate one's economy from free-wheeling global competition has resulted in Latin American efforts to coordinate their economic development and growth through the creation of regional and subregional associations. These attempts at economic integration have included: the Latin American Free Trade Association (LAFTA), which died a peaceful death in 1980; its replacement, the Asociacion Latinoamericana de Integracion (ALADI); the Andean Pact; Central American Common Market; and the Caribbean Community and Common Market. While the benefits of pooling resources and developing common economic policies may seem apparent from a technical and regional standpoint, the governments involved have been slow to respond. Two of the major stumbling blocks have been (1) strong resistance by the contracting parties to surrender any meaningful control over their national economies to international agencies and (2) out-spoken opposition from special interest groups within these countries that fear the adverse consequences of increased external access to their markets and internationally imposed restraints.

Colombia was an early proponent of regional economic integration. When Bogota became disillusioned and impatient with LAFTA's lack of progress, it helped to establish a subregional group, the Andean Pact, in order to eliminate trade restraints at a faster rate (Bushnell, 1975:404). Meanwhile, much to Colombia's displeasure, Venezuela delayed joining the pact until 1973, mainly because of the opposition from domestic pressure groups which feared higher-priced Venezuela goods would place them at a disadvantage (Ferris, 1981). Outside the adoption of common trade policies and the elimination of certain tariff barriers, little has been accomplished through economic integration. Most recently, the momentum has swung in the opposite direction, with the Andean Pact suffering from a wave of protectionism and retaliatory measures as members have sought to lessen the impact of a worldwide economic slowdown. These developments caused one high-ranking Venezuelan official (U.S. JPRS 82634:15) to remark that the Andean Pact had become an "integration anxiety," and that more patience and understanding were required if the organization was to eventually succeed. And despite the renewal of more modest efforts toward subregional integration at the end of 1983, the five member-governments reportedly remain pessimistic about the Andean Pact's future (LARR, November 11, 1983:8). The irony of this situation is that the need to cooperate continually brings states like Colombia and Venezuela together, but the differences between them are still great enough for localism and nationalism to keep them apart.

Multilateral diplomacy remains an attractive alternative to regional integration, for it allows greater flexibility on the part of individual states while still holding out potential benefits from mutual cooperation. Even as practiced by small states, multilateral diplomacy can assume several different forms, be pursued for numerous purposes, and be employed as a convenient backstop for promoting national policy objectives. Latin American efforts at multilateral diplomacy have focused mainly on common economic concerns and been directed largely at extra-regional targets (e.g., the United States and the rest of the industrialized world). To coordinate these efforts, Latin American states consult on common policies through such agencies as Comite Especial Coordinadora Latinoamericana (CECLA) and Sistema Economico Latinoamericano (SELA). Venezuela, who along with Mexico was an initiator of SELA, has proposed a political counterpart to that organization, an alternative to the OAS that would exclude the United States and English-speaking nations of the Caribbean (LAWR, August 13, 1982:5; U.S. JPRS 81696:86). Colombian President Belisario Betancur (U.S. FBIS, May 16, 1983:F1) has also talked of restructuring the OAS and turning it into a Latin American UN.

Other examples of multilateral diplomacy involving Venezuela and Colombia are not hard to find. Both have endorsed the establishment of the NIEO and assumed more active roles in the Group of 77 and the nonaligned bloc. Within the region they, along with six other South American states that have an interest in the Amazon Basin, have begun to cooperate in the region's development, though progress on this front remains clouded by lingering concerns of Brazilian hegemony (Bond, 1981). Both countries have joined the Organización Latinoamericana de Energía (OLADE), which is intended to promote the production, conservation, and distribution of energy resources in the region, and Venezuela is a founding member of OPEC. In the Caribbean Basin Mexico and Venezuela have jointly underwritten the San Jose oil export agreement to supply the petroleum requirements of small states in the region on favorable terms, and Colombia has joined Mexico, Venezuela, Canada, and the U.S. in what is known as the New York Group, to coordinate the giving of foreign assistance to Caribbean and Central American nations. More importantly, the Contadora Group, composed of Mexico, Colombia, Venezuela, and Panama, has been working for a negotiated settlement to the Central American conflicts.

Internal discord and national rivalries pose a constant threat to any type of multilateral cooperation, as the lack of progress in most of the aforementioned examples painfully illustrates. Nevertheless, these setbacks have apparently not diminished the enthusiasm of Venezuela and Colombia for cooperative ventures and associational ties. According to Bond (1982:190), Venezuela's preference for building institutional arrangements within which differences between countries can be settled is a direct outgrowth of the conciliatory style that characterizes its domestic politics. From the Venezuelan perspective, developing a network of institutionalized contacts provides ways to disaggregate as well as resolve international conflicts, thus preventing specific issues or the adversarial aspects of a relationship from impeding opportunities for cooperation elsewhere.

As seen in each of these strategies, the foreign policies of Venezuela and Colombia focus almost exclusively on questions relating to their national security, which is most often defined in broad terms of political and economic development. Cooperative international ventures, for whatever purpose, have little chance for success if their activities are deemed threatening to these objectives. More importantly, from the standpoint of all Latin American states, continental solidarity, regional integration, and bloc action are seen first and foremost as strategies for national advancement. Consequently, collective action is considered to be an expanded form of self-help by the participants, with only secondary concern being shown for the welfare of the group as a whole. In the case of Venezuela, this contradiction between purpose and practice reflects a discrepancy between its pragmatic approach to conflict management through institution building on the one hand and its undaunted Bolivarian idealism on the other. Former President Luis Herrera Campins, both in the OAS (1981-82:13) and the UN (1981:2-3), continually stressed the theme of unity, be it Latin American solidarity or Latin America's unity with Africa and Asia. Yet, focusing on unity as "an indispensible key" to resolving regional as well as North-South problems ignores two important realities: (1) assumptions of common aspirations and international solidarity do not provide a sound basis for Venezuelan foreign policy, either on the regional or global level, given the marked absence of unity in the past; and (2) Venezuela sees unity as a means of strengthening its own independence, economic development, cultural identity, and aspirations for leadership in Latin America and the Third World.

REGIONAL ROLE IN THE CARIBBEAN BASIN

The increased involvement of Venezuela and Colombia in the circum-Caribbean region serves as an excellent illustration of the range of their foreign policy interests and the strategies used to pursue them. Both Venezuela and Colombia have gradually been moving away from the United States position in the current Central American conflict by initiating their own economic assistance programs for the region and pressing efforts for a negotiated settlement. At first glance, these moves may appear to be an attempt to meddle in the United States' backyard by Venezuelan and Colombian politicians anxious to capitalize on growing anti-American sentiment. But this view ignores the fact that Venezuela and Colombia are both Caribbean states, and as such, they have a number of concrete reasons for wanting a voice in determining the region's future. The scope of their interest ranges from border disputes and economic self-interest to a genuine concern for regional stability that will accommodate socioeconomic and political change in those countries needing reform. To achieve these ends, Caracas and Bogota have stressed the importance of regional collaboration and peaceful settlement; yet, they also recognize that the potential for international conflict is constantly present, especially when dealing with such a volatile situation against a backdrop of escalating East-West tension.

In the last decade, the circum-Caribbean region has become a major area of interest for Venezuela and Colombia, both of which have traditionally been considered Andean countries. Prior to the early 1970s, Venezuela's main concern in the Caribbean had been attempts by Castro and Dominican dictator Trujillo to undermine its democracy; otherwise, the foreign ministry concentrated on a South American policy to contain Brazilian expansionism. It was Brazil's effort to extend its influence northward through Guyana and into the Caribbean by way of preferential agreements with Trinidad-Tobago that forced Venezuela to venture into the region as a diplomatic countermove. There is no question of the Caribbean's strategic value to Venezuela in that the islands off its shore are vital in guaranteeing the safe passage of oil to U.S. east coast ports. Despite the pressures of growth, the interior regions of both Venezuela and Colombia remain undeveloped because of the enormous obstacles and costs involved in settling them. Moreover, to the south of Venezuela lies Brazil. Thus, development of the Atlantic coast and northward expansion into the circum-Caribbean region became an attractive alternative in that it seemed to offer the path of least resistance.

The political instability of the Caribbean basin is a major security concern for Venezuela and Colombia. If open warfare should break out between Nicaragua and its neighbors, both Caracas and Bogota believe that they would be quickly drawn into the conflict, most likely as members of an inter-American peacekeeping force (LAWR, July 29, 1983:2-3; August 26, 1983:24; U.S. JPRS 80597:7). Betancur (U.S. FBIS, August 18, 1983:F1) and Herrera Campins (U.S. FBIS, June 18, 1983:L1) have both warned that "Central America must not become the backyard for an East-West confrontation." Therefore, one of their primary goals became to resolve the conflict, de-emphasize its East-West nature, and neutralize the region, making the Carib-bean, in the words of the Venezuelan government (U.S. JPRS 80878:1), "a zone of peace," free from "the global strategies of domination by hegemonic super-powers."

In the broadest sense, what concerns Venezuela and Colombia the most is safeguarding their own democracies from radical currents and repressive militarism, from either the right or the left. To accomplish this, they pro-mote the ideals of pluralism and reform via competitive democratic parties and electoral solutions. This link, some argue, is at the heart of President Betancur's Contadora peace initiative for Central America in which he has tried to eliminate the causes of subversion, while holding out the promise of negotiations and democratic guarantees--the same strategy he has so far been unsuccessful in implementing at home with regard to the M-19 terrorists and Fuerzas Armadas Revolucionarias Colombianas (FARC) (LAWR, August 26, 1983:2-4; LARR, July 29, 1983:1-2).

Another major interest is the region's economic potential as a market for nontraditional exports. Colombian sources estimate the size of the Caribbean market to be roughly $U.S. 1 billion a year (U.S. JPRS 83394:5). Furthermore, it has the advantage of not being saturated with competing products, as is the case of Europe, the U.S., Japan, and the Andean bloc. The Herrera government was also interested in expanding Venezuela's Caribbean export markets, particularly as an incentive to reverse declines in internal investment in the private sector (Martz, 1982b:34).

Finally, the international prestige that comes with regional influence is very important to each country. For example, ex-Foreign Minister Lemos Simmonds (U.S. FBIS, July 27, 1982:F1) talked of Colombia serving as a model for "development within a democratic system" in the Caribbean basin. Vene-zuela has already firmly established itself as a regional power, and Colombia soon hopes to attain this status, but not for the sake of honor alone. Colom-bia's entry into the Caribbean was prompted in part by the rising prominence of Venezuela and Nicaragua, just as Venezuela's expanded presence was said to be partly an attempt to emulate Mexico's foreign policy. Both Caracas and Bogota also wish to gain added prestige and influence within the region in order to enhance their own bargaining position in several outstanding disputes. Venezuela, of course, desires to advance its claims for recovering what amounts to about two-thirds of present-day Guyana and to secure a favorable settlement to its maritime boundary dispute with Colombia. Meanwhile, Colombia is involved in another emotionally charged territorial dispute with Nicaragua over the islands of San Andres and Providencia.

In their efforts to help resolve the crisis in Central America, Venezuela and Colombia have adopted a twofold approach. First, they have provided much needed economic assistance. Venezuela has clearly been a major donor, with the Ministry of Energy and Mines (U.S. JPRS 81696:91) claiming Vene-zuela and Mexico provided $U.S. 1 billion over two years in their energy cooperation program, while the Reagan administration's Caribbean basin initiative only accounted for $U.S. 350 million in assistance. While Colombia has supplied relatively little in economic aid, it has established a financial corporation to funnel Colombian investment into Central America and the Caribbean in order to increase trade (U.S. JPRS 81439:17). Oil-rich Venezuela has relied heavily on economic instruments, a "petroleum diplomacy," to enhance its influence in the region. However, Central America's growing ideological polarization and militarization has raised serious doubts as to whether economic assistance alone can bring about long-term stability in the region (Bond, 1982:188).

The formation of the Contadora Group marks a second, and more recent, approach of stepping up efforts to achieve a negotiated settlement to the conflict. Advocating "autochthonous" solutions to subregional problems (LARR, January 14, 1983:5), the Contadora foreign ministers drew up, in the summer of 1983, a twenty-one point proposal for peace to be ratified by states in the region. Furthermore, ex-Venezuelan Foreign Minister Zambrano Velasco (U.S. JPRS 83644:78) and Colombian UN Ambassador Rodríguez (LARR, October 28, 1983:4) made it clear that they wanted to limit the scope of the conflict, and thus maximize their nations' role, by not having the situation debated in the United Nations or negotiated in other forums outside the region. At the same time, the Contadora Group called for international support of its peace bid, and Colombia's Betancur (LAWR, July 15, 1983:11) asked the European Community to launch a program of economic and social aid to alleviate inequalities and injustices in Central America.

The Contadora peace initiative has been stalled by counterproposals calling for a survey of troop and military installations that would require the concurrence of Salvadoran guerrillas, and Guatemalan demands for the repatriation of its nationals who have sought refuge in Mexico (LARR, January 13, 1984:8). U.S. support has also weakened. Secretary of State George Schultz, while in Caracas for President Jaime Lusinchi's inauguration, claimed that the group ignored Soviet-Cuban activities in the region and failed to criticize Nicaragua (LAWR, February 10, 1984:4-5). Schultz's remarks were interpreted as part of an administration move to concentrate attention on the recommendations of the Kissinger Commission Report. Nor has all been well within the Contadora Group. Policy differences between Mexico, Venezuela, and Colombia continually threaten to divide the group, and as Mexico and Venezuela have become more occupied with their internal economic problems, Colombia's Betancur has emerged as the group's spokesman. Evidently, Lusinchi believes that the limelight has been too easily stolen by the Colombian president, and he wants Venezuela to play a more visible part in the process (LARR, January 27, 1984:4-5).

Elsewhere in the Caribbean region, Venezuelan and Colombian relations with Cuba have yet to be normalized. In the case of Venezuela, relations between Caracas and Havana became strained in the wake of a 1976 incident when Cuban exiles carrying Venezuelan passports sabotaged a Cuban airliner, with the loss of seventy-three lives. Relations further deteriorated in 1980 when disenchanted Cubans sought diplomatic asylum in the Venezuelan embassy in Havana and Castro refused to allow them safe passage off the island resulted in a mutual recall of ambassadors. But when Venezuela and Cuba adopted convergent positions on the South Atlantic conflict, verbal hostilities noticeably lessened. Shortly thereafter, Cuba endorsed Venezuela's admission into the Nonaligned Movement and spoke out against third-party intervention in the Essequibo dispute between Venezuela and Guyana (LARR, July 23, 1983:8). With most leading figures in COPEI and Acción Democrática favoring normalized relations, Herrera Campins (U.S. FBIS, June 30, 1982:L2) began to seek a rapprochement with Havana in 1982. Early indications are that President Lusinchi will normalize relations with Cuba, and then work to bring Castro back into the Latin American fold at a later date (LARR, January 20, 1984:6).

Colombia's current relationship with Cuba is no less complicated. Relations soured in 1979 when Colombia sought to block Cuba's election to the UN Security Council. Two years later, President Turbay broke relations because of alleged Cuban support for M-19 terrorist actions. With the election of Betancur, relations have improved. No doubt this was due in part to Castro's personal appeal and Cuba's help in gaining the release of the president's brother, Jaime Betancur, held by Ejército de Liberación Nacional (ELN) guerrillas. In return, Betancur and Spain's Felipe Gonzalez were instrumental in repatriating Cuban causalties and prisoners after the U.S. invasion of Grenada (U.S. FBIS, January 12, 1983:F1). Reportedly, there is an agreed-to plan for restoring diplomatic relations, but it "will not be hurried," since elements in the Colombian military remain strongly opposed to the move (LARR, January 27, 1984:3). For the moment at least, relations between Bogota and Havana are very good, causing Colombian Foreign Minister Rodrigo Lloreda Caiceda (LARR, December 16, 1983:3) to remark: "It is better to be courting than to be married."

Nicaragua's Sandinista regime has been another controversial subject in Caracas and Bogota. Having pursued a policy of "democratization of the continent," Venezuela sought to encourage pluralism within Nicaragua by helping the government and aiding political groups opposing the Sandinistas. Specifically, the COPEI administration of Herrera Campins wanted to enhance the role of the Christian Democratic party in Nicaragua. But as the Sandinistas turned toward Cuba, and the regime became more anticlerical, anti-democratic, and repressive, Venezuela's aid diminished and relations with Managua cooled (LARR, July 29, 1983:2-3). It was notable then that Sandinista leader Daniel Ortega was the first head of government received by President Lusinchi following his inauguration (LAWR, February 10, 1984:5). While it is too early to assess the full significance of this event, there is a strong possibility that the new Acción Democrática administration will be more accommodating toward Nicaragua.

Colombia has continued to maintain diplomatic and trade links with Nicaragua despite an unresolved dispute that dates back to 1803 over the status of two Caribbean islands, San Andres and Providencia, and the uninhabited keys of Quinta Sueño, Roncador, and Serrana (Kline, 1983:132-133). When the new Sandinista regime showed interest in these territories, the Colombia military reinforced its presence with a new naval base on San Andres, and without informing the foreign ministry, the military entered into secret discussions with the Pentagon concerning the granting of access rights to the United States (LARR, January 27, 1984:3). Betancur, like his new Venezuelan counterpart, seems to want to maintain good relations with all states in the region. But the military appears worried that the president's independent foreign policy line will distance Colombia from the U.S., thus denying the country the only support it would count on should Nicaragua attempt to assert its claim to these territories by force of arms (LAWR, February 3, 1984:5).

Venezuela is currently involved in a potentially more volatile dispute over the Essequibo region with Guyana. Until recently, Venezuela had applied diplomatic pressure to get its neighbor to enter into bilateral negotiations and strongly opposed what it saw as Guyana's attempt to "inter-nationalize the conflict" by seeking the Nonaligned Movement's censure of Venezuela for alleged aggression (U.S. FBIS, June 21, 1982:L1). But when the nonaligned states merely reaffirmed the necessity of reaching a peaceful solution in accordance with the 1966 Geneva Agreement, Caracas reversed its position on direct talks, and along with Guyana, agreed to accept UN Secretary General Perez de Cuellar's mediation in selecting a method for resolving their dispute (U.S. FBIS, April 5, 1983:L1). This is where the dispute currently stands, with the Lusinchi government giving its consent to the UN's mediating role and a permanent solution to the Essequibo claim nowhere in sight, because both sides remain divided on the procedures for peaceful settlement as well as on the substantive issues involved (Martz, 1984:77).

Finally, Venezuela and Colombia have several unresolved problems. Already mentioned, an incipient trade war reflects a rise in protectionist policies on both sides of the border. A second issue relates to some 1.4 million Colombians living in Venezuela. Since many of these illegal aliens live in the border region, there is a fear of fifth column activity that might result in the seizure of Venezuelan territory (Ewell, 1982:308). Betancur has responded to the problem by creating a Secretariat for Border Affairs, which will aid in the development of border areas to stem the flow of immigrants and work toward agreements with neighboring states regarding natural resources and environ-mental protection (U.S. JPRS 83950:48B). The major outstanding conflict between Venezuela and Colombia, however, is over their maritime boundary in the Gulf of Venezuela. At stake are potentially great petroleum deposits and maritime resources extending out into the Caribbean. Between 1970 and 1980, several unsuccessful attempts were made to negotiate an off-shore boundary. More recently, Colombia was very critical of Venezuela's refusal to sign the Law of the Sea Treaty, charging that Caracas feared having to accept mandatory international mechanisms for the exploitation of maritime resources and the solution of boundary conflicts (U.S. JPRS 81416:17).

Because of the December 1983 Venezuelan presidential elections, many of these issues had been put on hold. In the case of the Venezuelan-Colombian off-shore boundary, the Lusinchi government has already expressed interest in renewing direct talks. Moreover, the new Venezuelan Foreign Minister, Isidro Morales Paul, is a leading expert on the law of the sea, which indicates the question will receive serious attention (LARR, January 27, 1984:7). With regard to the Caribbean basin, Morales Paul has stated that the Venezuelan government places a high priority on the region, with a firm commitment to democracy and representative government, and that it intends to pursue a "pluralist" foreign policy with no exclusions (i.e., Cuba and Nicaragua) (LARR, January 20, 1984:6). The general foreign policy orientation of the Lusinchi government appears likely to coincide with that of Colombia's Betancur. While these two leaders will no doubt find areas of compatible interest for cooperative endeavors, a strong sense of rivalry will also be present as both countries pursue their national policy objectives and attempt to enhance their international prestige.

AN INDEPENDENT FOREIGN POLICY?

Through the actions of the Contadora Group and other initiatives in the Caribbean basin, Venezuela and Colombia have attempted to distance themselves from the Reagan administration's policies and avoid the stigma of being simply junior partners of the United States. The 1982 Malvinas crisis, particularly in the case of Venezuela, appears to have been a major stimulus for this shift in policy. When the South Atlantic war broke out, Venezuela expressed its support for Argentina in the UN and OAS and halted commercial relations with Great Britain. Venezuelan Foreign Minister Zambrano Velasco (U.S. FBIS, May 3, 1982:L1-2) accused the United States of encouraging the aggression, claiming that Washington's support for its NATO ally contravened the spirit and letter of the Inter-American Reciprocal Assistance Treaty. Herrera Campins (U.S. FBIS, May 8, 1982:L1) sent a letter to President Reagan stating that Latin America was "surprised, pained, disillusioned, and frustrated" by the U.S. position on the Malvinas. Venezuela charged that in siding with the British the Reagan administration had shown its disregard for Latin America, though many believe what upset Caracas more was the fact that the U.S. had moved so decisively in opposing the use of force to resolve a territorial conflict since Venezuela also claimed to have been "the victim of territorial usurpations by colonial powers" (U.S. FBIS, April 6, 1982:L1).

Initially, Colombia did not support Argentina's claim, and the Turbay government's position of resolving the dispute through peaceful means coincided in large part with that of the United States. While the Argentine junta reacted by recalling its ambassador from Bogota for consultations (U.S. FBIS, May 3, 1982:F1-2), Turbay refused to condone Argentina's actions lest he help establish a dangerous precedent regarding Colombia's outstanding territorial disputes with Nicaragua and Venezuela. Colombian policy on the Malvinas changed after Betancur's election. At the 1983 meeting of the Group of 77 in Buenos Aires, Colombia supported Argentina's position and attacked "decaying colonialism" (U.S. FBIS, April 7, 1983:134-135), thus concurring with the pronouncement of Venezuelan Delegate Perez Guerrero (U.S. FBIS, April 11, 1983:B2-3) that "Argentina's sovereign rights over the Malvinas Islands are a Latin American cause."

As indicated by the references to colonialism, the Malvinas situation is actually seen as part of some much larger issues that divide the United States from Latin America and the rest of the Third World. Beginning in the 1970s, Venezuela's Carlos Andres Perez had embraced the Third World's cause and advocated North-South dialogue in the UN and other international forums. Today, Colombia takes much the same view. Indeed, when President Reagan visited Bogota in late 1982, Betancur (U.S. FBIS, December 6, 1982: F1-3) used the occasion to personally lecture him on the region's severe economic problems, the danger of the U.S. closing its markets to Third World manufactured goods, and the waste incurred in the nuclear arms race. It is from this broader, North-South perspective of socioeconomic development that one can see how the Reagan administration's emphasis on the East-West nature and military aspects of the Central American crisis diverges from the positions of Venezuela and Colombia. For these two Latin American states, while advocating the negotiation of an intra-regional political settlement, continue to link many of the problems in the Caribbean basin to those generally afflicting the Third World.

Concern over these issues has also led to diplomatic activity on other fronts. U.S. support of Britain in the Malvinas conflict caused Venezuela to announce (U.S. FBIS, July 7, 1982:L1) that it was considering formal membership in the Movement of Nonaligned Nations. Colombia soon followed in Venezuela's wake, with President Betancur making the announcement that his country would also seek admission during his attendance at the inauguration of Bolivian President Siles Suazo. In an impassioned plea for Latin American unity, Betancur (U.S. JPRS 82242:56) charged that the Malvinas conflict had "demonstrated that in the eyes of the major powers we are merely something to be disdained." Later when asked what he saw as the advantages of Colombia joining with the nonaligned, the president (New York Times, January 9, 1983:E5) responded:

> Our proposal to join the nonaligned group is an affirmation of sovereignty and a search for new forums, for new partnerships with those who have problems similar to Colombia's. It's a question of not being a satellite of any one power center and of maintaining our own power of decision. Given the complexity of international relations with its effect on the internal life of nations, the minimum a government can do is to take advantage of all means of information and direct participation to be an active witness and not a dangerously passive one to everything that occurs at every moment in the world. That's what we are looking for.

There was little doubt that in the Nonaligned Movement Colombia and Venezuela hoped to find greater independence of action and increased international support for their national policy goals. Trying to assure more international support, or at least making sure it was not lined up against them on a major foreign policy issue, was an important consideration, particularly in Colombia's case. As Colombian Foreign Minister Lloreda Caicedo (U.S. JPRS 82410:30) explained:

> The importance of joining the Nonaligned Group is obvious: it is enough to point to the election of Nicaragua as a member of the United Nations Security Council thanks to the support it received from the movement, which is made up of some 100 countries. . . . Had the Dominican Republic been a member of the movement, which it is not, perhaps it would have had more votes than it obtained.

Unfortunately for Venezuela, Guyana is a member of the Nonaligned Movement, and it successfully blocked the former's application. Evidently, Guyana was willing to lift its veto if Venezuela signed a document foresaking its claim to the Essequibo territory, but Venezuela decided to neither accept Guyana's terms nor challenge the right of consensus on membership questions, and instead to simply continue its observer status at nonaligned conferences. Meanwhile, Colombia encountered no opposition from Nicaragua in joining. The Betancur government consequently complied with the seemingly necessary ideological requirements of nonaligned membership by announcing the withdrawal of its consular mission from South Africa and endorsing the call for a Palestinian homeland.

Interest in participating in the nonaligned bloc is primarily a tactical move on the part of both countries in that they will not, and really cannot, realign their positions in any major way. Indeed, in response to charges that nonaligned membership would upset Colombia's traditional ties with the United States and Western Europe, Lloreda Caicedo (U.S. JPRS 82131:23) claimed it would not "in any way interfere with Colombia's relations with friendly countries and, conversely, could be helpful in difficult situations." Therefore, this shift by Colombia and Venezuela does not entail any fundamental change in ideology or commitment, but rather is a further attempt to provide themselves with more room to maneuver on important issues, which is not the same as foreign policy independence. Most certainly, they will have to seek continued accommodation with the United States, especially if Washington's increased preoccupation with events in Central America leads to policies of conflicting interest and threatened cooperation.

While Betancur (U.S. JPRS 83093:71) is proud of Colombia's transformation from "a passive to an active role in world affairs," economic storm clouds line the horizon, threatening to divert his government's attention to domestic affairs. In neighboring Venezuela, the soaring burden of foreign indebtedness and deteriorating internal economic conditions had already brought about a relative decline in foreign policy activism before the end of Herrera Campins' term of office (Martz, 1984). Given existing realities, increased foreign policy activity, though it may show enhanced capabilities to influence external events, does not guarantee the ability to either achieve or sustain an independent policy in the case of Latin American states likes Venezuela and Colombia.

10
Bolivian Foreign Policy: The Struggle for Sovereignty

Waltraud Queiser Morales

FOREIGN POLICY AND GEOPOLITICS

Geopolitics is about winning (Jay, 1979).

Bolivian foreign policy has traditionally been considered as a function of domestic conditions: civilian versus military regimes, political stability, and economic development. Dependency, an alternative approach, has emphasized the external restraints upon Bolivian diplomacy and economy, particularly the dominant influence of the United States and the uncontrolled vagaries of the international tin market and multinational credit sources. Geopolitics, as a third approach, readily subsumes other analyses and has become the guiding logic of contemporary Bolivian foreign policy under Hernan Siles Suazo, the first civilian and popularly elected president in eighteen years. Geopolitics as the central determinant of Bolivian foreign policy captures the essence of the country's past, present, and future; for few countries has geopolitics been as important and constant as in the Bolivian struggle for political and economic sovereignty.

The origins and the destiny of Bolivia are rooted in its unique geographic position in the very heart of the South American continent, and the political consequences of that geographic position. Bolivia has been perceived by many as a geographical anomaly, an unnatural geographical state, and a nation unable to channel its cultural diversity into national unity. Geopolitics for Bolivia is at the heart of the ongoing struggle to overcome the disintegrative forces of regionalism, race and culture, climate, and political and economic dependency. If for some countries geopolitics may imply a study of expansionary foreign policy goals, contemporary Bolivian geopolitical goals, with the exception of the campaign to regain lost Pacific coastal territories, have been reactive. Bolivia is, and has traditionally been, a zone of intense intra-regional rivalry and conflict. With the exception of the independence victories of Sucre and Santa Cruz, geopolitics for Bolivia has been concerned with the consequences of losing in diplomacy and war. Geopolitics, as epitomized in the ceaseless campaign to regain sovereign access to the sea, has been the constant factor in Bolivian foreign policy and has provided diplomatic continuity regardless of the political coalitions and ideologies of domestic regimes. Geopolitical factors further conditioned Bolivian dependency, not only because all its economic exchanges are impeded by its land-locked position, but because geography delivers the country to a potential stranglehold by its neighbors and narrows options of ideological and diplomatic alignment within the international system of nations.

Geopolitics has been defined as "geopolicy, or the dynamic aspects of those combined geographic and political factors that influence the options and strategies of a nation's foreign policy" (Roett, 1975:95). This study surveys these geographic and political factors which have determined past and present patterns of international relations and which will continue to influence the future of Bolivian foreign policy in its attempt to make geopolitics about winning.

GEOPHYSICAL STRUGGLE

Bolivia is a country of immense geographic, climatic, and cultural diversity. The land and climate includes three regions: the Andean, the transitional sub-Andean, and the lowlands. The Andean consists of the arid highlands or altiplano; the sub-Andean of the mild to lush intermountain valleys, or yungas; and the lowlands, the rich subtropical grasslands and tropical rainforests, or the oriente. Each region is relatively autonomous; although traditional population centers are found on the high plateau, the newest population expansion has been concentrated on the subtropical plains of Santa Cruz. Each region has a different climatic and ecological base with the highlands barely supporting subsistence agriculture of potatoes, corn, and wheat, the valleys producing coffee, citrus, vegetables, and coca leaves, and the eastern plains sugar, cotton, and cattle ranching.

The economies of each region are no more integrated than the cultural and ethnic bases of the peoples. While Bolivia is generally described as an Indian country--and indeed Bolivia has one of the largest Amerindian populations in Latin America, perhaps 60 percent--this does not imply cultural and ethnic homogeneity nor the absence of racial barriers. The largest Indian groups in the highland are the Aymara, comprising approximately 20-25 percent of the population, and the Quechua, with perhaps 37 percent of the population. Each has their own language and a history of racial and economic oppression by the "white" Spanish settlers and mestizo (or mixed) offspring. Lowland, forest Indians are often overlooked in evaluating Bolivia's indigenous heritage because so few tribes have survived. Although these ethnic and cultural factors are not, strictly speaking, a component of geography, they become important since ethnic differences coincide with the three geographical regions of the country and intensify geophysical barriers.

Tremendous geophysical obstacles to transportation and communications infrastructure complicate the divisive forces inherent in socio-cultural patterns. The Andean mountain ranges, the Cordillera Occidental to the west bordering Chile, and the Cordillera Real bordering Peru in the northeast contain the country physically (and psychologically) within the continental land mass. These two ranges seal off the highland from the Pacific coast and the rest of Bolivia. The Cordillera Real divides into the Cordillera Central and Cordillera Oriental insulating the valley towns of Cochabamba, Sucre, and Tarija from each other, the highland, and the lowlands. Within the lowlands most communication is by river systems which generally flow northeastward away from the population bases of the country and toward Brazil. In short, except for the altiplano, no region is well integrated as a region much less with the rest of the country. This situation has influenced commentators to characterize Bolivia as a "land divided," and three nations, not one.

A rich and diverse resource base has further conditioned Bolivian relations with the outside world and its internal development pattern. While rich
in mineral and natural resources including gold, silver, tin, nitrates, petroleum,
and natural gas, the Bolivian treasury is bankrupt and burdened by a foreign
debt approximating $U.S. 4 billion. External exploitation by Spain, terri-
torial conquest by neighbors, internal economic and political rivalries,
denationalization of wealth by an international group of tin barons, and
extreme economic dependency are primarily to blame for the "development
of underdevelopment" of Bolivia. These geophysical constraints have produced
distinctive political responses including a Bolivian foreign policy delimited by
key geopolitical factors.

GEOPOLITICAL DETERMINANTS

Bolivia is the heartland and geopolitical center of the South American
continent bordering Argentina, Brazil, Chile, Paraguay, and Peru, and dividing
the continent into northern tier and Southern Cone, and Atlantic versus
Pacific coast powers. Bolivia belongs to the three major regional systems of
the continent--the Andean, Amazonian, and River Plate. It has served as a
traditional buffer state in bilateral and multilateral interactions of nations
and regional subsystems. Although the sixth largest of the nineteen Latin
American nations (424,152 square miles), Bolivia is sometimes perceived as a
"small" country, perhaps because of the impotence of its foreign policy in
realizing its core goal--sovereign access to the sea--and the dependency of
its policy on outside actors. Isolation, imposed by a landlocked geography,
and sparsely and unevenly populated frontiers clearly have contributed to its
relative ineffectiveness in foreign affairs. Ironically the failure to achieve
foreign policy objectives has been the result of Bolivia's inability to break out
of its geopolitical encirclement--the very condition which its foreign policy
has sought to change. Bolivian foreign policy has been aggressive, innovative,
and initiatory despite the absence of economic, military, and political power
and despite the key geopolitical factors of centrality, regionalism, landlocked
status, and dependency, which have worked to determine it.

Centrality

As the geographical "heart" or center of South America, Bolivia
becomes the "natural" object of the geopolitical aspirations of its neighbors.
From a Brazilian perspective, political (if not physical) expansion into
Bolivia would increase Brazilian influence in the Andean region and among
the Pacific coast nations, perhaps even furthering a Brazilian goal of "manifest destiny" toward the Pacific coast (Schilling, 1978; Pittman, 1982;
Selcher, 1982). For Brazil, expansion into Bolivia would also mean increased
economic and mineral assets in iron ore, oil, and natural gas. Similarly for
Argentina, Bolivia has been an object of northward expansion, and might
figure as a long-range route (versus the short-range access through the
Beagle Islands) to the Pacific and as a balancer in the geopolitical rivalry
with Brazil and Chile. Historically such geopolitical forces were at work when
Brazil seized Bolivia's rubber-rich Acre territory in 1903, and when newly
independent Argentina, coveting the silver of Potosí, sent four military
expeditions to "liberate" Bolivia and incorporate the country into the
Audiencia de la Plata between 1810 and 1817 (Klein, 1982).

Historically Peruvian designs upon Bolivia have been no less threatening. The Bolivian independence struggle was as much a struggle to assert the
right of national self-determination from its rapacious neighbors as independence from Spain. Incorporated into the viceroyalty of Lima since colonial
days, Bolivia had limited judicial and administrative autonomy as the Audience
of Charcas or Upper Peru by 1561, but was reorganized into the Viceroyalty
of Buenos Aires in 1776 to combat the growing political independence of the
highland from Lower Peru. In the "Fifteen Years War" Bolivians fought the
royalist armies sent from Lima to achieve independence. The fact that
Bolivian national independence was not achieved until the liberation of Lima
and Buenos Aires and then maintained only in armed opposition to both power
centers, is one clear example of Bolivia's historic impotence in foreign relations with its neighbors.

The Peru-Bolivian Confederation, the first attempt by the new Bolivian
state to expand its influence, was a failure. Established in 1836, the unifica-
tion of Peru and Bolivia under Marshall Andres de Santa Cruz threatened the
geopolitical interests of Chile, which sent an army that destroyed the confederation in 1839. The historical irony is that the Bolivian expansion was
facilitated by the political rivalry and internal division of Peru. Although the
union brought relative prosperity and peace to Peru and Bolivia, the expanded
state was a potential great power rival that would not be tolerated by Chile
or Argentina. This "balance of power" principle remains valid today, threatening even modest attempts by Bolivia for access to a territorial coast. Both
Argentina and Chile established another practice which has equally become a
geopolitical principle in their dealings with Bolivia--direct or indirect intervention in Bolivian internal affairs by supporting domestic opposition movements and by manipulating Bolivian interest groups. A divided and politically
unstable Bolivia, made even more so by external interference, was no match
for these geopolitical pressures. Although the dissolution of the confederation ensured the legal status of Bolivia as an independent nation, it left but
an impotent buffer soon to lose its outlet on the Pacific.

Landlocked Status

The loss of the Pacific coastal provinces in 1879 has hampered Bolivia's
economic development and intensified its geopolitical containment. In part
geopolitical forces contributed to the loss of the littoral initially; largely
unsettled, isolated from the highland, and rich in nitrate deposits, the coastal
province of Atacama was a valuable economic prize. Chile, which would
make the grab, was also intent on dominating the Pacific coast and monopo-
lizing expanding European trade links. Excluded from influence on the
Atlantic coast via Patagonia in 1878, Chile asserted political hegemony in the
Pacific by seizing the Bolivian territories after a long-standing boundary dispute, lasting from 1857-1879, erupted into war. Bolivia was militarily and
diplomatically unable to defend its sovereignty. Despite Peruvian assistance
and Argentinian sympathy, the balance of power game was won by Chile.

The loss of major Pacific ports left Bolivia permanently contained by
its neighbors. Future access to the sea would depend on limited port facilities, duties, and regulations controlled by its neighbors, who shared a common
interest in maintaining the geopolitical status quo. Bolivian foreign policy
was directly and immediately affected as the central diplomatic goal of all
governments has been the revindication of Bolivia's sovereign access to the
sea. Salida al mar diplomacy embittered and compromised Bolivian relations

with its neighbors, monopolized national energies, and provided the rationale for the Chaco War with Paraguay as a means of breaking through to the Atlantic coast in the east. The Chaco War would be the last expansionary foreign policy campaign dictated by the drive to the sea. The Gran Chaco was a desolate waste area where rival territorial claims of Bolivia and Paraguay intersected. Bolivia believed that it could and would win a war with its weaker neighbor, and it manipulated war fever to quell growing domestic unrest as then President Salamanca used foreign policy to generate internal patriotism and unity. Of course, success in war demanded the very unity that Bolivia lacked. For Bolivia the war was an unmitigated disaster which proved once again that the Bolivian state was only semi-sovereign and unable to assimilate all its peoples and territories. Some 60,000 Bolivians died and about 94,000 square miles of national territory were lost. Bolivia's geo-politics of failure was only partially due to the expansionism of its neighbors; its extreme disunity and regionalism were equally instrumental.

Regionalism

Geography and local ethnic traditions have resulted in an extremely decentralized and regionalistic nation. Disparities of resources and a history of internal "colonialism" by the highland governments ensured that the low-lands with 70 percent of Bolivian territory were virtually ignored except for "what they could do" for their country, namely the central government in La Paz. The regional dominance of the highland also explains why Bolivia with two-thirds of its territory in the Amazon Basin has been generally described as an Andean country. Lowland populations traditionally have sought the socio-economic opportunities of Brazil and Argentina, creating streams of outmigration. Recent internal migration into the lowlands is reversing the pattern and may erode traditional Bolivian regionalism. Historically low-landers have identified with neighboring countries; particularly strong have been the secessionist movements in Tarija and Santa Cruz. The underdevelop-ment and weakness of the Bolivian state, and its traditional dominance by highlanders, contributed to decentralization and facilitated interference by Argentina, Brazil, and other neighboring countries.

In the first century and a half as a nation, Bolivia lost 46,233 square miles of territory to Chile; 189,353 square miles to Brazil; 65,924 square miles to Argentina; 96,527 square miles to Peru; and 94,018 square miles to Paraguay (Alexander, 1982:2). Bolivian internal divisions and regionalism were partially to blame, but had geopolitical conditions been different Bolivia might not have been the victim. Bolivian foreign policy under Siles Suazo has attempted to redress this geopolitical imbalance by reaching out to neighbor-ing states through bilateral and multilateral diplomacy and cooperative development agreements. With the exception of Chile, Bolivia has sought to emphasize functional cooperation through trade agreements, communications networks, and oil and gas contracts to woo the surrounding countries to the Bolivian cause. While the civilian government has broken the diplomatic iso-lation and ostracism which limited the maneuverability of its military prede-cessors, this foreign policy may be no more effective than others in breaking the geopolitical forces which have contained Bolivia in the past as in the present. Clearly the policy assumes that "good regionalism" is not only "good geopolitics" but the way to diminish Bolivia's own internal regional problems (Jay, 1979:485).

Dependency

Most Latin American countries have experienced economic and political dependency, so that dependency is not unique to Bolivia. However, geopolitical constraints have made it more difficult for Bolivia to offset economic and political dependency particularly through unilateral foreign policy initiatives. Although not a "small" country in territorial size, dominant external influences on Bolivian politics make it a "penetrated" system with limited options for an independent foreign policy posture. The definition of economic dependency formulated by Dos Santos, as a "situation in which the economy of certain countries is conditioned by the development and expansion of another economy to which the former is subjected," can equally be applied to a concept of geopolitical dependency, whereby the internal politics of a country is conditioned by the ideological, class, and interest group alignments in other countries to which the former is subjected (Dos Santos, 1970:231).

Economic dependence in Bolivia dates back to the Spanish conquest and the imperial policy of mineral exploitation, which continued to provide the main source of government revenues for the independent states. After 1880 most capital for development was tied to the large tin interests which were controlled by European, Chilean, and American investors. Until 1929, the state was dependent for 90 percent of government revenues upon a small portion of taxes levied reluctantly on the mining companies, and mining interests literally "owned" legislators, generals, and often presidents. The revolutionary military governments of Colonel David Toro and Colonel German Busch attempted to redress this economic stranglehold between 1935 and 1939, with little success. Structural changes awaited the 1952 national revolution.

The post-revolutionary situation has not reversed economic (or political) dependency despite attempts to regulate foreign investment by Decision 24 of the Andean Pact, a regional effort in economic integration and development by Bolivia, Chile, Colombia, Ecuador, Peru, and Venezuela (Mytelka, 1979). The Andean regional integration scheme sought to encourage foreign investment but under national economic control and to offset dependency relations by a common and unified policy. In certain industrial sectors, for example metalworking, Bolivia remained extremely vulnerable to manipulation by multinational investments (Mytelka, 1979:166-167). Efforts in economic cooperation by the Andean Pact nations, however, "spilled over" into common diplomatic postures, particularly in Central America, where the group has been critical of the militaristic approach of the Reagan administration in El Salvador and Nicaragua, continuing a tradition of mediation begun during the 1979 Nicaraguan revolution.

Although Bolivia is less dependent upon tin for national revenues since 1970, tin production continues to account for 30-60 percent of Bolivian exports, having risen after the slump in petroleum exports after 1975. Moreover, Bolivia has been economically dependent on the United States for finance capital and trade. The United States generally has consumed around 50 percent of Bolivian tin production. The General Services Administration (GSA) regularly sells large quantities of tin from the U.S. strategic stockpile on the international market, depressing tin prices and pushing the Bolivian government into an economically induced instability. These sales are made with little consultation with the Bolivian or the other international tin producers (Morales, 1980:86-87). Since over 30,000 Bolivians work in tin mining and smelting, with over 70 percent of the industry state owned, such U.S. policy has had devastating impact on the Bolivian economy. The December

1981 decision by GSA to sell 20,000 tons of tin on the international market caused several strong Bolivian protests, and Bolivia's June 1982 withdrawal from the International Tin Council, which had long been criticized as dominated by the importing nations against the interests of the producers (WRH, July 13, 1982:8; April 6, 1982:6).

Osvaldo Sunkel has emphasized another aspect of dependency--distribution of benefits from socio-economic development. "Access to the means and benefits of development," he noted, "is selective; rather than spreading them, the process tends to ensure a self-reinforcing accumulation of privilege for special groups as well as the continued existence of a marginal class" (Sunkel, 1972:519). Bolivian economic development models have attempted to follow a socialist or _dirigista_ model, dominated by the state and the public sector. U.S. involvement has attempted to stifle these tendencies and strengthen the laissez-faire forces, largely by the manipulation of aid. Since the 1952 revolution, North American aid has so dominated the Bolivian state and society that a situation of neo-imperialism and economic dependence was established and perpetuated.

The Eder Mission and the Agency for International Development (AID) established administrative checks and controls over Bolivian development policy as well as exercising the financial power of the purse (Whitehead, 1969, and 1974:94-95). Radical economic development policies and distributive programs of reform were systematically vetoed by North Americans in favor of "conservative" development schemes, which eventually stalled and reversed the socio-economic achievements of the revolution. Per capita U.S. aid to Bolivia was the highest in Latin America between 1960 and 1964 (Morales, 1984). Ironically, economic assistance for the purpose of Bolivian development served to weaken and inhibit the emergence of autonomous decision making and sound planning (Thorn, 1971; Wilkie, 1971:223; Patch, 1960). Military assistance was another major avenue for the development of influence networks and maintenance of dependency.

Through military assistance the U.S. government has preferred military presidents in Bolivia--with the exception of General García Meza. With the Bolivian political situation one of the most chaotic in Latin America, military regimes have been better able to control dissent and ensure the proper investment and ideological climates. With a few exceptions, U.S. relations have been relatively cordial with these military governments and their consevative political and economic policies. During these periods the economy was opened up to multinational corporate capital, and foreign aid--especially from the U.S.--was dramatically increased. Under Banzer, loans and grants for 1973 and 1974 tripled over those made previously by the U.S. to other Latin American governments (Burke and Keremitsis, 1982:226-227). The U.S. influence network is especially strong in the military sector, which has virtually dominated Bolivian society and which takes perhaps half of the government's budget (Burke and Keremitsis, 1983:226).

U.S. influence has been exercised on the military through extensive training programs in addition to millions in military assistance. Table 10.1 indicates the linkages that may exist between the U.S. military and Bolivian officers through the training program conducted by the School of the Americas at the Southern Command in Panama. Of the South American countries, Bolivia has a ratio of one graduate from the School of the Americas for every seven military men. This is the highest ratio in the region and compares starkly with Bolivia's two major regional influencers--Brazil and Argentina--which have one graduate for every 1,233 members of the armed forces and one

TABLE 10.1
South American Graduates of SOUTHCOM in Relation to Total Armed Forces and Population

Country	Armed Forces (Thousands)	Graduates	Population (Millions)	Armed Forces (Per 10,000 population)	Graduates (Per 10,000 population)	Ratio of Number of Graduates to Number in Armed Forces
Argentina	160	613	27.7	58	0.2	1:290
Bolivia	24	3,573	5.3	45	6.7	1:6.7
Brazil	455	349	122.0	37	0.03	1:1,233
Chile	115	2,130	11	105	1.9	1:55
Colombia	65	4,097	24.8	26	1.7	1:15
Ecuador	35	3,124	8.0	44	3.9	1:11
Paraguay	15	1,039	3.2	47	3.3	1:14
Peru	150	3,585	17.6	85	2.0	1:43
Uruguay	29	920	2.9	100	3.2	1:31
Venezuela	58	3,134	17.3	34	1.8	1:19

Source: Combination of World Military Expenditures and Arms Transfers, 1971–1980 (Washington, D.C.: U.S. Arms Control and Disarmament Agency, March 1983); and Christopher Dickey, "'Southcom' Hub of U.S. Latin Role," Washington Post, May 23, 1983, pp. A1 and A15.

for every 290 men, respectively (World Military Expenditures, 1971-1980;
Washington Post, April 23, 1983:1, 15; Child, 1980b).

Today dependency is expressed both through dependence on aid and on
finance capital from the World Bank, International Monetary Fund, and
private, North American-controlled banking interests. In July 1980, President
Carter cut all U.S. aid to Bolivia as an indication of displeasure over the
"cocaine coup" of General García Meza. With a $2.3 billion foreign debt and
inflation at over 50 percent, the new military government of Celso Torrelio
was forced in September 1981 to court U.S. assistance for a $220 million IMF
loan to keep the treasury afloat (WRH, December 1, 981:4-5; October 20,
1981:2). By August 1982 Bolivia faced a default of $400 million on its $4
billion foreign debt due over 70 private foreign banks (WRH, September 7,
1982:6). When Siles Suazo took office in October 1982 the country needed
$540 million to pay private bankers, and had already defaulted on September 9
on a $10 million debt payment to a consortium of international banks led by
Bank of America (WRH, October 19, 1982:1, 6).

The withholding of U.S. aid funds ultimately brought down the repressive government of García Meza, and aid has been used to encourage Bolivian
control of the cocaine traffic under the military governments of Torrelio and
Vildoso and the civilian government of Siles Suazo. The delay in U.S. aid
commitments in early 1983 was used to moderate the influence of Communists
in the cabinet of newly elected President Hernan Siles Suazo (Economist,
February 26, 1983:58). External pressure through aid and finance capital
intensified in 1983 because of severe droughts and floods. Already bankrupt
because of military corruption, the country faced estimated disaster damages
from $250 to $350 million. In June Bolivia received $23 million in food aid
from the United States (New York Times, June 2, 1983:A8). Since 1978
Bolivia has recieved U.S. PL 480 Title II (Food for Development) aid to
address the problems of poverty and starvation. Although alleviating desper-
ate conditions of starvation in 1983, Bolivia's dependence on these aid shipments increased the political vulnerability of the government to U.S. policy
pressures. Foreign policy under Siles Suazo has sought--as have most
Bolivian governments--to escape the negative consequences of geopolitics
by an independent, neutralist stance. But the unstable domestic political
environment has made this difficult.

FOREIGN POLICY AND DOMESTIC POLITICS

. . . a united people always win.   Siles Suazo.

A Chilean diplomat once commented during the "heat" of a new salida
al mar offensive by Bolivia, that Bolivia's greatest liability was its lack of
national stability and unity. Although geopolitics and domestic instability
may not be so easily unraveled, a corollary of international relations has held
that ineffective internal control frequently translates into ineffective foreign
policy. In the past, Bolivia has manipulated external foreign policy difficulties, particularly the issue of a Pacific seacoast, to impose artificial political
tranquility and national consensus.[1] Siles Suazo seems to be utilizing the
same approach. The representative to the Organization of American States
(OAS) referred to this interpretation. "They have said that the external policy
could be the major factor of national unity to save the country" (Boletín
Informativo Semanal, June 30, 1983:9). This dependence on external factors

to provide unity has been the central fallacy of Bolivian foreign policy, dooming military as well as civilian regimes and especially hindering the effectiveness of Bolivia's diplomats. No Bolivian government has been free of intense domestic constraints upon foreign policy; "linkage politics," or the overlap of the domestic with the external, has been a chronic Bolivian dilemma which is especially apparent now with the government of Siles Suazo (Shumavon, 1981:179-190; Holland, 1975; Lincoln, 1981:5-6). Cabinet instability and turnover every 3-5 months resulted in three different ministers of foreign relations in 1983 alone. This domestic instability has made it nearly impossible for Bolivia to negotiate vital refinancing of the national debt with the World Bank.

Domestic constraints on foreign policy have generally included extremely partisan politics, ideological polarization, and chronic military intervention. The Siles Suazo government is plagued by all of these in addition to the threat of economic collapse. Payment of the interest on Bolivia's debt alone accounts for 70 percent of export earnings, and the inflation rate is over 300 percent; perhaps over one million people face hunger and destitution through natural disaster, while in the cities workers face declining buying power. Work stoppages, protests, and political terrorism have raged through 1983. The governing coalition of the Popular Democratic Unity (Unión Democrática Popular, UDP) and the Revolutionary Movement of the Left (Movimiento Izquierda Revolucionario, MIR) have been in constant conflict. On December 2, 1983, the cabinet resigned upon the threat of parlimentary censure, leaving only the weaker political groupings, the left-wing of the MNR, the Christian Democrats (PDC), and the Communist Party (PCB), willing to form a government. Ministries are split along partisan lines in an elaborate spoils system which duplicates services and spreads suspicions. The national legislature is divided between the parties of the "left" and of the "right" with the MNR, and the National Democratic Action (Acción Democrática Nacionalista, ADN) of former President Banzer in vocal opposition. Vice President Jaime Paz Zamora (leader of MIR) aspires to the presidency and reportedly plots with the military. Coup threats are constant, leaving President Siles Suazo with periodic appeals to the nation's power groups to join in a government of conciliation (WRH, October 19, 1982; December 27, 1983:1; Presencia, December 8, 1983:1; December 27, 1983:1).

Domestic politics have influenced the direction and success of Bolivian foreign policy. Although more or less consistent in overall foreign policy objectives, domestic political alignments have caused diplomacy to shift between two distinctive approaches: a pro-United States stance and a neutralist, nonaligned position which attempts to distance itself from U.S. influence. Siles Suazo has had to contend with major domestic constraints and U.S. disapproval of his nonaligned foreign policy. In addition the geopolitical alignments in Latin America, especially in the Southern Cone, have shifted, stimulating--as in the past--a realignment of Bolivian internal forces in accord with external ones. Democratic governments are seizing the initiative with the inauguration of Raul Alfonsín in Argentina and growing popular unrest against the military governments of Uruguay and Chile. These democratic forces have given vital support to the civilian Siles government in the foreign, as well as domestic, policy arenas. The result has been a mixture of continuity and change in key foreign policy areas: the salida al mar diplomacy, United States-Bolivian relations, inter-American relations, and South-South relations.

Salida al mar

A constant and central foreign policy goal of Bolivia has been the recovery of the lost seacoast. In 1974 an important initiative was taken in the Ayacucho Declaration with Chile which recognized the importance of a sea outlet for Bolivia. In December 1975 a Chilean proposal provided a Bolivian outlet to the sea north of Arica in exchange for Bolivian territory equal to the area ceded in the corridor and the land equivalent of the two hundred mile extension of territorial waters. This historical breakthrough occurred because of the convergence of several geopolitical and domestic forces.

President Salvador Allende had been overthrown by a brutal military coup in Chile, and the successor government of Augusto Pinochet found itself diplomatically isolated because of its abysmal human rights record. Bolivia's initiative was well received as a vehicle for improving Chile's image in Latin America. The military governments of Ernesto Geisel in Brazil and Francisco Morales Bermudez in Peru provided regional support to the military links between Pinochet and Bolivian General Hugo Banzer Suarez. However, as domestic conditions changed in respective countries, the breakthrough and diplomatic opportunity were lost (Holland, 1982). Chile was soon "rehabilitated" through United States recognition and international aid, despite human rights criticism. There was now little incentive to continue to "humor" the Bolivians by reconsideration of the maritime question. Peru eventually put forward its own proposal, which was duly rejected by the Chileans (Holland, 1982:134-137). The difficulty centered in Bolivia where the Chilean offer was rejected by the major political power groups, while political instability aborted the very initiative begun by Banzer.

Bolivians rejected in principle territorial compensation, while the Chileans would consider a sovereign seacoast for Bolivia only in territorial exchange. Banzer's diplomatic efforts over three years gained him little domestic "political capital" and the vociferous criticism in the press and opposition camps demonstrated the absence of unified internal support for his policies. Further the domestic debate generated over the maritime question grew into popular demands for a return to constitutional government. Holland suggests that the seacoast question, instead of unifying domestic forces for a faltering regime, can also become a potentially destabilizing domestic issue (1982:139). The diplomatic failure demonstrated the close relationship between internal instability and lack of foreign policy success, as well as the fundamental differences that separated the Bolivian, Chilean, and Peruvian governments on the maritime issue. The three, like-minded, military governments of Banzer, Pinochet, and Morales Bermudez were no more able to surmount these national differences than the earlier, aborted initiatives between the socialist governments of Salvador Allende and Torres. The three-year process came to an abrupt end by 1977 with further domestic dissension. By 1978 Bolivia had again interrupted diplomatic relations with Chile, as had occurred from 1962 to 1975 (Shumavon, 1981:184-189).

The Siles government has continued this non-recognition policy, exchanging only consular representatives with Chile. Full ambassadorial exchange will be reinstituted only when Chile promises to reconsider the problem of Bolivia's landlocked status (Boletín Informativo Semanal, March 9, 1983:7). The government has recently sought the diplomatic isolation of Chile, and been more successful than in the past with this strategy because of the domestic unrest within Chile and the shift of the Southern Cone countries to democratic forms of government. Bolivia has further sought to regionalize

and multilateralize its "drive to the sea" by supporting the Argentinian territorial claims in the Falklands and eliciting the support of the Andean bloc,
the La Plata group of nations, the OAS, and the Nonaligned Movement in the
Bolivian cause.[2] The diplomatic offensive for a sovereign seacoast without
territorial concessions continues and must continue for Bolivia since only a
coastal outlet can mitigate the tremendous obstacles to national development
and the traditional encirclement of Bolivia's neighbors. Ironically, the United
States, which has been so influential in Bolivian affairs, has never particularly
championed this Bolivian cause, thereby ignoring one clear issue which would
turn many a Bolivian pro-American. Instead the major issues in U.S.-Bolivian
relations have been tin and cocaine, and a desire for docile, pro-U.S. foreign
policy.

United States-Bolivian Relations

The North American minister to Bolivia commented in the 1890s that
"Bolivia is as yet the only remaining country in South America not in the hands
of England" (Fifer, 1972:245). However, North American capital and trade
soon moved into this void created by geopolitics, since as one British representative commented, "Bolivia has no seaboard, we should have no means, in
the last resort, of forcing redress" (Fifer, 1972:241). This did not stop the
U.S., which by the end of World War I had no rival in the country and controlled the major northern hemisphere source of tin which was vital to industrial expansion. The major tin company, Patino Mines, was incorporated in
Delaware in 1924, and the second largest group, the Caracoles Tin Company,
was established by the Guggenheim family in 1922 (Fifer, 1972:246).
The strategic importance of Bolivian tin for U.S. industrialization and
defense and the inordinate poverty and weakness of Bolivia became the bases
for a long-standing dominance by the U.S. Due to geopolitical conditions,
Bolivia was unable to play the neutralist game in the Cold War or in World War
II and instead found its foreign policy increasingly dictated by the U.S.
(Green, 1971; Parkinson, 1974). Favoring Axis interest briefly in 1943, Bolivia
soon redirected its foreign policy under U.S. diplomatic and economic pressures and declared war on the Axis. Nonrecognition was used to determine
the political coalition in the December 1943 coup and to oust the members of
the National Revolutionary Movement (Movimiento Nacionalista Revolucionario,
MNR) from the governing coalition of Villarroel. Bolivia further was pressured to break diplomatic relations with Peronist Argentina, which had refused
to sever relations with Nazi Germany in proper alignment with U.S. policy.
The inflow of U.S. economic and military assistance in late 1941 encouraged
the government of General Penaranda to settle with Standard Oil whose
properties had been confiscated by previous military reformers in 1937. In
January 1942 the Bolivian foreign minister agreed to a $U.S. 1.5 million
indemnification to Standard Oil; the next day the U.S. announced a $U.S. 25
million economic aid program for Bolivia (Green, 1971:51). Between 1942 and
1968 American aid to Bolivia was the highest per capita in the world. This
pattern of economic carrot and stick continued after the 1952 Revolution to
influence Bolivian internal and foreign policies.
Relations with the United States were close during the governments of
Barrientos and Banzer (1964-1969 and 1971-1978), especially contrasting with
the independent, neutralist foreign policy of the last years of the MNR government of Paz Estenssoro (1960-1964). In 1960, when the Eisenhower administration would not give economic aid to state-owned enterprises, Bolivia

threatened to apply to the Soviet Union. Soon after an American credit of
$U.S. 2.7 billion was granted to the Bolivian National Petroleum Company
(Yacimientos Petroleras Fiscales de Bolivia, YPFB) (Parkinson, 1974:114).
Bolivia (along with Chile, Mexico, and Uruguay) did not support severing diplomatic and economic relations with Cuba nor its expulsion from the OAS in
1964, until pressured by the U.S. (Connell-Smith, 1966:186 and 253). During
the 1962 Cuban missile crisis, Bolivia (together with Brazil and Mexico) submitted reservations to U.S.-sponsored resolutions condemning Cuba in the OAS
(Connell-Smith, 1966:258-259). Tito of Yugoslavia visited Bolivia in 1963--
as did another Yugoslav president in 1983 under Siles Suazo. In 1963 Foreign
Minister Fellman Velarde argued that "we must maintain the respect of our
people, and this we cannot do if there is any suspicion that the United States
has a hand in our foreign policy" (Parkinson, 1974:179-180). Tito, as a distinguished founder of the Nonaligned Movement, represented an equidistant
position for Bolivian foreign policy between the two superpowers and ideological blocs.

U.S. relations with Bolivia also became strained during the governments
of Ovando and Torres, but by 1968 the shift had already begun with the
Barrientos regime. Although cooperating closely with the United States to
rout out the Cuban guerrilla foco of Che Guevara in 1967, by January of 1968
Rene Barrientos invited the Soviet Union to open trade with Bolivia and in
February 1969 (after the 1968 reformist military coup in Peru nationalized the
holdings of the International Petroleum Corporation) Barrientos sought Soviet
assistance to the Bolivian oil sector. His foreign policy also proposed accredi-
dation of Cuba in the OAS (Parkinson, 1974:231-237). In a sense, therefore,
the brief military governments of Generals Ovando and Torres continued a
nationalist and independent foreign policy posture initiated by Barrientos
before his death.

The radical-reformist government of General Ovando Candia replaced
the brief civilian government of Adolfo Siles Salinas, Vice President under
Barrientos in September 1969. Although Bolivia had recognized the Soviet
Union since 1945, ambassadors had not been exchanged until Ovando sent a
Bolivian ambassador to Moscow in early 1970. Ovando also sought Soviet aid,
and in August 1970 the Soviets extended a $U.S. 27.5 million loan. In the
Peruvian pattern, Ovando nationalized Gulf Oil holdings in November 1969,
while General Torres attended the Nonaligned nations conference in Lusaka
as the Bolivian observer in September 1970. Further Bolivian diplomatic relations were reestablished or upgraded with the Eastern European governments
of Poland and Hungary (Holland, 1975:354). However, domestic chaos and U.S.
economic and diplomatic pressure gradually moderated this neutralist foreign
policy agenda, symbolized by a $U.S. 78 million compensation to Gulf Oil
(Parkinson, 1974:231-237). "Independent neutralism" as a foreign policy position ultimately was abandoned when General Hugo Banzer assumed office in
August 1971, reversing most of the foreign policy overtures of the previous
governments. For example in March 1972 over a hundred Soviet diplomats
were expelled. The U.S. felt that with the Banzer coup, "international confidence in Bolivia had been restored" and that the possible "creation of an
international front of left and left-inclined governments stretching from Chile
via Bolivia to Peru and Ecuador" had been thwarted (Parkinson, 1974:237;
Holland, 1975:348-354).

Between July 1978 and July 1980 Bolivian foreign policy suffered
through severe domestic instability as military and civilian governments,
changed hands in rapid succession. On July 17, 1980, General Luis Garcia

Meza, notorious for his blatant involvement in the cocaine traffic and gross
violations of human rights, began his 14-month rule. The U.S. isolated this
government diplomatically in a relatively easy maneuver given its international reputation. In Latin America García Meza maintained cordial ties only
with Argentina, which reportedly had assisted him to power (WRH, November
16, 1982). President Carter suspended U.S. aid and did not reappoint an
ambassador to La Paz. The Reagan administration continued this "nonrecognition" policy in spite of the private "bets" of the cocaine generals, who
believed that the conservative administration would be quick to establish full
relations. Interior Minister Luis Arce Gomez had so flaunted his disrepute
that U.S. pressure with the termination of the U.S. drug control assistance
program caused his dismissal from the cabinet by García Meza in February
1981 (WRH, November 16, 1982). After sixteen months of severely restricted
and chilly relations, and only after General Torrelio had replaced Garcia
Meza in September, did Edwin G. Corr arrive as the U.S. ambassador to
Bolivia in November 1981.

In December speeches Ambassador Corr emphasized the altered U.S.
position on normalization of relations with Bolivia and collaboration in
democratization and drug control (Soberanía, May 1-17, 1982). Former
Assistant Secretary of International Narcotic Affairs, Corr spearheaded a
policy of crackdown on the narcotics trade--a central issue in U.S.-Bolivian
relations since 1980. Although the military governments of Torrelio and
Vildoso half-heartedly cooperated in drug control and coca eradication projects, they were too politically vulnerable and dependent on a military institution riddled by drug corruption to serve as entirely effective policemen.
Popular unrest over the failure to constitutionalize the country after the 1980
elections erupted after a relaxation of government repression with the fall of
García Meza. Given the U.S. pressure to control drugs, the economic crisis,
and constant political unrest, Torrelio quickly was removed by General Vildoso
in July 1982. Within two months Vildoso was replaced by the constitutionally
elected president, Siles Suazo, who confronted the U.S. with another leftist
political coalition and neutralist foreign policy program.

The foreign policy approach of the Siles Suazo government is an obvious
departure from that of García Meza's government which had criticized the
French and Mexican mediation efforts in El Salvador as intervention (WRH,
April 4, 1983:7). However, it marks a continuation of the independent
policies pursued during periods of the MNR, Barrientos, Ovando, and Torres.
Siles Suazo has vigorously sought to control the drug traffic from Bolivia and
has arrested and prosecuted members of the military and previous governments implicated in the trade, but despite these efforts U.S. pressure to clamp
down even more on the cocaine traffic continues making the military
extremely restive and eager to remove Siles (WRH, November 30, 1982:4).
Siles Suazo has also granted French and West German requests for the extra-
dition of Klaus Barbie--requests which had been refused by the Banzer
government in 1972 and 1974 (WRH, December 14, 1982:1; Miami Herald,
October 27, 1982:8A; Latinamerica Press, March 31, 1983).

Various government spokesmen have described the new foreign policy
direction as "a policy of closer relations with all the countries of the world,
respecting ideological pluralism . . . and affirming the principles of self-
determination and nonintervention" (Boletín Informativo Semanal, May 18,
1983). For Bolivia this has meant a foreign policy that minimizes external
dependency and establishes balanced relations with the global poles of power
(Boletín Informativo Semanal, February 2, 1983:22). Translated into practice

Bolivia has recognized Cuba, the Polisario Liberation Movement, the Palestine Liberation Organization, and has forged closer ties with the Soviet Union. These actions have not endeared the government to the Reagan administration. Although Washington has extended $216 million in aid to Bolivia since 1982, and AID officials announced that U.S. aid to Bolivia will reach $300 million through 1987, these actions may not be enough to sustain the Siles government in the face of the growing economic chaos (Presencia, December 10, 1982 and December 23, 1982:1). The Reagan administration has failed to intercede on behalf of Bolivia with the World Bank and the IMF to curtail stringent austerity measures--measures which will only feed labor unrest and speed government collapse. Such aggressive intercession has not been forthcoming because, although Washington favors the return of democracy in Bolivia as a means of controlling the drug traffic, its "leftist" foreign policy has generally antagonized the U.S. administration, which would as soon prefer a more moderate civilian government. Although the United States and the international bankers have the Bolivian economy by the tail, Bolivian foreign policy is attempting to balance this dependence by seeking broad multilateral support for its domestic and external programs among the inter-American community and the nonaligned countries.

Inter-American Relations

Given its geopolitical position in the center of South America, Bolivia lacks the option used by Cuba, Chile, and Nicaragua of turning to the Eastern bloc to decrease U.S. influence. To redress the imbalance of U.S. domination, Bolivia has strengthened bilateral and regional relations with its South American neighbors. In the past this option often has been precluded by traditional rivalries--such as that with Chile--or shifting inter-American military and ideological blocs. Despite the relatively constant principles of Bolivian foreign policy--sovereign access to the Pacific, expansion of economic development assistance, trade diversification, and more independent foreign relations--changing regional and ideological alignments have influenced how the various Bolivian governments historically pursued these goals (Ferguson, 1975:7-8).

From the War of the Pacific until 1969 Bolivian foreign policy generally gravitated toward Argentina, despite the latter's support of Paraguay (along with Chile) in the Chaco War. Only Brazil and Peru permitted free transit of Bolivian war material. Argentine complicity in the December 1943 coup against Enrique Penaranda and in support of Gualberto Villarroel is well known (Davis et al, 1977:232; Callcott, 1968:414-417; Green, 1971:142-152; Child, 1980b:59-61). The Villarroel government admired Peronism and was sympathetic to the Axis cause. Argentina used Bolivia and Uruguay (and their desires for nationalistic and independent foreign policies) to organize an anti-U.S. bloc during the war years. Argentina supported the Bolivian nationalization of Gulf Oil and financing for a gas pipeline in 1969. With the death of Barrientos in 1969, Bolivian foreign policy began a gradual tilt toward Brazil under Ovando and Torres. The Banzer government came to power through a Brazilian-supported coup in August 1971, and extensive Brazilian political-military ties and economic penetration followed until 1978. The Mutun iron ore and gas exploitation projects were carried out largely in favor of Brazilian economic interests. In 1972 Banzer and Brazilian President General Emilio Medici signed several financial and technical assistance agreements (Holland, 1975:352; Alexander, 1982:135).

During this period the Banzer government experienced difficult relations with Allende's Chile, which had supported the nationalization of Bolivian Gulf by Ovando. The Bolivian government had shifted to an ideologically conservative, military regime, while Argentina and Chile had remained under the more radical and independent policies of Perón and Allende. For example in 1971 Argentina and Chile signed a declaration accepting "ideological pluralism" of regimes. Argentina supported Allende's hosting of UNCTAD III in April-May 1972, while the U.S. and Brazil objected. Argentina also formally associated itself with the Andean Pact countries effectively isolating Brazil. Therefore, when the Torres government fell in Bolivia, Brazil was the logical ally for Banzer (Ferguson, 1975:7-8). Brazil at this time also actively supported Bolivia's maritime diplomacy as an avenue for its own expansion toward the Pacific (Ferguson, 1975:7). With the rise of General Pinochet in Chile, of course, these alignments shifted, and Chile, the traditional rival of Argentina and Peru, was drawn into the Brazilian orbit.

Another foreign policy realignment occurred with a coup against Banzer's selected successor, Juan Pereda Asbun, who had won carefully manipulated elections in 1978. After a coup in November 1978 the new government of General David Padilla Arancibia redirected policy back toward Argentina and improved relations with Peru (Gorman, 1979:51). The Argentine connection persisted under General Jorge Videla's government, which assisted Garcia Meza to office in 1980 (Selcher, 1982:11). A high in Bolivian-Argentine relations was realized and continued under Siles Suazo with Bolivia's support of the Argentine position in the Malvinas War and in its territorial claims against Britain (Boletin Informativo Semanal, October 14, 1983:2-12). Declarations of solidarity, disaster assistance, and refinancing of the $600 million debt with Argentina exemplified continued Argentine-Bolivian cooperation (Boletin Informativo Semanal, March 9, 1983:40; and October 14, 1983:2-12). At the inauguration of Alfonsín in Buenos Aires good relations between the two nations were personally furthered by Siles (Presencia, December 10 and 11, 1983:1).

However Siles Suazo has also attempted to balance Bolivia's relations with the two giants on its borders without antagonizing either one. The strategy appears to be working. In October the Bolivian and Brazilian foreign ministers met to explore closer cooperation and strengthening of relations (Boletin Informativo Semanal, October 14, 1983:16). At the meeting of the La Plata Basin nations in Brasilia in December 1982, Brazil, Argentina, Paraguay, and Uruguay supported the return to democracy in Bolivia and the maritime issue. At a meeting of the group in Asunción in late 1983, economic development assistance, cooperative projects, and disaster relief for Bolivia were approved by the members. In Asunción the Bolivian Foreign Minister, Jose Ortiz Mercado, revealed the broad regional strategy in which the Bolivian seacoast campaign was being placed by the Siles Suazo government. "We believe," declared Ortiz Mercado, "that one day not far distant, my country will be able to serve as the conduit between the Atlantic and the Pacific Oceans" (Presencia, December 3, 1983:1). Siles Suazo and government spokesmen considered the Southern Cone nations as a growing fulcrum for democracy and inter-American integration and cooperation with Bolivia as somewhat of a centerpiece (Boletin Informativo Semanal, August 26, 1983:29).

This regionalism is "good neighborliness" which has been fostered by Bolivia in all the inter-American forums of which it is a member. In the meeting of Bolivarian governments (Bolivia, Colombia, Ecuador, Panama, Peru, and Venezuela) to celebrate the bicentennial of the birth of the liberator, Bolivar, in Caracas on May 25, 1983, Bolivia elaborated a foreign policy of Latin American unity and solidarity, seeking cooperation with the Latin American nations in economic development and in "multilateralizing" the seacoast issue. Bolivia interpreted this meeting as a success for its campaign to generate broad inter-American support for its domestic and foreign policies (Boletín Informativo Semanal, July 29,1983). Bolivia has been active in a movement to animate the Amazon Pact nations, and will be the seat of the Council of Amazonian Cooperation (Consejo de Cooperacion Amazonica, CCA) for 1984 (Boletín Informativo Semanal, July 29, 1983:45-56). Similarly within the Andean Pact Bolivia has gained broad regional support for policy in general and special consideration in development assistance and disaster relief at major meetings in May 1983 (the fourteenth anniversary of the signing of the Cartagena Agreement), July (with Ecuador), and December. The Andean Development Corporation (Corporación Andina de Fomento, CAF), the financial organ of the Andean group, granted Bolivia a $U.S. 10 million loan in December and through an agreement of cooperation with the European Economic Community (EEC) extended most-favored-nation status to Bolivia (Presencia, December 16, 1983:1). Bilateral relations with Latin American countries have also been supportive of Bolivian foreign policy objectives, particularly those with Ecuador, Panama, and Colombia. President Belisario Betancur of Colombia proposed his country as a future site for a Bolivian-Chilean meeting to reconsider Bolivia's maritime problem (Presencia, December 10, 1983:1).

Bolivia's inter-American relations, especially with the two South American "giants," have been heavily conditioned by geopolitical forces: natural resources, political and ideological affinities, balance-of-power blocs, and territorial disputes. Various patterns have emerged: (1) a pro-Argentinian tilt, (2) a pro-Brazilian tilt, (3) a balance between the A and B powers, (4) the balancing of Argentina and Brazil through cooperation with Chile and/or Peru, and (5) integrated regional strategies--Andean Pact, Southern Cone, Bolivarian nations, and Amazon Basin Pact. The strategy of the Siles foreign ministry appears to be emphasizing the latter approach in its attempt to coordinate a coalition of Latin American democracies, as expressed in the "Declaration of Boyaca" by the Bolivarian nations (Presencia, December 16, 1983:1). This foreign policy program contrasts with Bolivia's position during 1979-1981 when the Andean Pact countries, especially Ecuador, Colombia, and Venezuela, sharply criticized Bolivia's human rights record. Bolivia threatened to leave the Andean Pact and for diplomatic and economic support gravitated toward a purely Southern Cone, pro-Argentinian policy.

Multilateralization of Bolivian foreign policy strategies also has occurred in other forums. In the Organization of American States (OAS) and in the economic and financial forums (IMF, World Bank, IDB, GATT, and UNCTAD) Bolivia has regionalized and then multilateralized common problems. For example, the debt crisis--particularly acute for Bolivia--is characterized as a Latin American crisis and as a crisis of political economy between developed and developing nations (Boletín Informativo Semanal, July 29, 1983:13). This tendency is especially apparent in Bolivia's South-South strategy, or its relations with the Third World.

South-South Relations

Bolivia's sympathy with the nonaligned nations is a natural outgrowth of a foreign policy attempting to distance itself from the East-West confrontation and to focus instead on issues of development and international economic reform. The roots of this "neutralist" foreign policy date back to the reformist, post-Chaco era when Bolivian forces of economic nationalism began to surface. The tendency expressed itself in the 1940s with support for Peronism and revolutionary Bolivia's identification with other reformist movements in Guatemala and especially Cuba. At the San Jose Conference of the OAS nations in August 1960 Bolivia, with Mexico and Venezuela, emphasized the principle of nonintervention and strongly identified with the "popular" revolution in Cuba (Parkinson, 1974:84). At Punta del Este in 1962 Bolivia did not support the OAS resolution which would use U.S. forces to remove the missiles in Cuba nor the resolution that would exclude Cuba from the OAS (Washington Post, October 24, 1962:a; Connell-Smith, 1966:12). The Siles Suazo foreign policy position has reinforced this neutralist stance and has championed the cause of Cuba in inter-American and global international organizations, specifically arguing for the reintegration of Cuba into the inter-American community of nations. The government has open and warm diplomatic relations with Cuba.

Bolivia's relations with revolutionary Nicaragua have also improved under Siles Suazo. In 1980 and 1981 the Nicaraguan delegation provided the Bolivian delegation of the exile government of Siles Suazo a seat with their delegation in the United Nations so that the Bolivian opposition could denounce the human rights abuses of the Garcia Meza regime. Bolivia formally thanked Nicaraguan Foreign Minister, Miguel D'Escoto, for the assistance of the Nicaraguan delegation in those critical years of political protest. Bolivia has been critical of destabilization action by the United States against Nicaragua and has repeatedly emphasized the principles of self-determination, national sovereignty, and nonintervention which are the core of the Nonaligned Movement (as well as the OAS charter). With the Contadora Group of nations, Bolivia has favored mediation efforts in Central America. It was in Managua at the meeting of the coordinating committee of the Nonaligned Movement that Bolivia signed a protocol renewing diplomatic relations with Cuba, explaining the action as nonideological, but as an integral position of Bolivian foreign policy to maintain official relations with all countries. In return the nonaligned members affirmed Bolivia's internal democratization and supported Bolivia's campaign for a maritime coast (Boletín Informativo Semanal, February 2, 1983:2-4).

Bolivia has used the nonaligned movement to multilateralize its foreign policy position as well as a springboard for criticism of the OAS. Disenchantment with the OAS is becoming a general mood in Latin America, and Bolivia's disaffection lies with the organization's dominance by the U.S., exclusion of Cuba, and especially neglect of socioeconomic development. Bolivian policy appears to interject "Third World" policies of anti-imperialism into the more conservative OAS forum, as a new rallying point for an inter-American forum which will be more independent of the U.S. (like the Economic System for Latin America, SELA) and as an effort to link the Latin American region more closely with Third World alignments and issues. Bolivia has been outspoken over the global economic crisis and has identified the Bolivian plight with that of the developing world. Bolivian solidarity with the nonaligned nations-- the majority of the world's population--is an attempt to universalize and popularize Bolivian problems. As one of the Vice Presidents of the Nonaligned Movement, Bolivia hopes that the organization will be a vehicle for greater diplomatic support in the seacoast question. At the nonaligned meeting in Nicaragua, Bolivian Foreign Minister Velarde stated that "one day the cause of Bolivia's seacoast would be a global cause" (Boletin Informativo Semanal, February 2, 1983:2). Nonalignment is a way to expand the collective effort toward resolution of Bolivia's landlocked status; the Third World nations have been receptive to Bolivia's plight, especially in acting as a power bloc in the United Nations.

Bolivia also hopes that the majority forces of the nonaligned nations may succeed in a restructuring of the global financial and economic organizations, especially the World Bank and International Monetary Fund. Bolivia's economic history has been one of extreme dependency. As a result the Third World movement's emphasis on neo-imperialism, exploitation, and great-power dominance finds resonance in the Bolivian reality. In an address to the nation celebrating national independence, Siles Suazo argued that Bolivia's economic crisis was not purely domestic, but a specific consequence of the structural crisis in the global economy. Bolivia, like all Latin America, faced "a situation of external financial strangulation" by Western-dominated financial institutions. The global recession which has imposed such hardship on the Bolivian people was the direct fault of the economic policies of the developed countries. Economic crisis and democracy in Latin America and the world were interlinked (Boletin Informativo Semanal, August 26, 1983:27-32). Reform in the economic order was a prerequisite to the persistence of democracy. Certainly the Latin American debt crisis will stimulate other Latin American nations (for example Venezuela is planning membership in the Nonaligned Movement) to opt for more independent and neutralist foreign policies.

Prognosis for the Future

> . . . how are nations to improve their capability positions and to modernize their societies while preventing inordinate influence in their economies and political systems? (Lincoln, 1981:14).

To balance and coordinate the conflicting tensions and policies of the Southern Cone, the Andean Region, the Amazon Basin countries, the River Plate grouping, the inter-American community and the OAS, the United Nations and the Nonaligned Movement will certainly demand a highly innovative and flexible Bolivian diplomacy. The key to a successful foreign policy largely remains within Bolivia, and unless Bolivian domestic politics are stabilized it is more likely that its foreign policy will draw Bolivia into the vortex of these conflicting regional and global pressures. In 1984 the prognosis is not favorable due to the immense domestic and international problems which plague the country. Geopolitically Bolivia must confront continuous outmigration of Bolivians into neighboring countries. There is constant pressure to develop national resources and to protect these resources and the national territory from economically aggressive neighbors. The international cocaine traffic continues to hold the country in its grip fueling rampant inflation and general corruption. Access to a sovereign port to break Bolivian geographical isolation and economic dependence eludes Bolivia's leaders and people. The natural disasters of drought and flooding, astronomical international debts, the threat of military intervention, extreme political instability, and external intervention in Bolivian affairs complicate all of the above.

Will the Siles Suazo government be able to sustain these pressures? It is essential for the ultimate political reform and stabilization of Bolivia that the democratic form of government be supported and the cocaine mafia eliminated from Bolivian society. It is ironic that a country which grows 80 percent of the world's demand for coca, processed into cocaine, sustains massive food shortages and starvation. It is in the interests of the United States as well as Bolivia's regional neighbors to assist the democratic forces in Bolivia in strengthening and stabilizing "the vulnerable center of the South American continent" (Fifer, 1972:250).

Classical Greek history reports the words of the Athenian General to the Melians, who refused to surrender to the Athenian armies, preferring devastation to dishonor: "The strong do what they can and the weak do what they must." Geopolitics and domestic instability have often placed Bolivians in the position of the Melians. Bolivians have been the first to recognize their nation's weaknesses of internal instability and external dependence. One Bolivian philosopher observed that Bolivia "is sustained by the opposition of the elements that comprise it" (Pike, 1977:78). Domestic instability has been a constant and significant factor in Bolivian national weakness and suscepti- bility to foreign influence. Writers have also urged the Bolivian people to secure their own frontiers, to "conquer Bolivia by the Bolivians," to "march towards the national frontiers," and to win a sovereign coast (Valencia Vega, 1982:355, 364, 366). Geopolitical forces thus have been a constant and critical dimension of Bolivia's national weakness. Bolivian foreign policy traditionally has struggled to escape the debilitation of domestic and geo- political forces and to achieve full national sovereignty. External relations under the Siles Suazo administration have served to forge national strength through broad solidarity with Latin American neighbors and to expand coop- eration and interests with the international community. Multilateralization of Bolivia's problems and foreign policy goals in regional and global forums has been an effort to avoid the Melian dilemma--the dilemma of the weak and the dependent nations to do what they must.

Bolivia's continued weakness has been in the interest of its neighbors. Bolivia is the "ultimate" buffer, and as the Bolivians say, "if Bolivia did not exist, it would be necessary to create it" (Fifer, 1972:252). Bolivia's future demands a change in the geopolitical status quo, while the nation's very existence is predicated upon its continued weakness and maintenance of that status quo. Fifer argued that "at political and economic levels, and in all the varied sectors of continental exchange, it remains to be seen whether Bolivia is prepared, or able, at last to come to terms with both the liabilities and the assets of its location" (Fifer, 1972:263). Can geopolitics and foreign policy in Bolivia's case ever be about winning? The shifting power realign- ments in Latin America and the world and the emergence of greater foreign policy independence and neutralism of powers like Brazil and Argentina may offer new opportunities for Bolivia. Also important is the enlightened role of the United States and the continued support of the international community, which could change the Bolivian experience from losing into one of coopera- tion and development. Although internal unity is a crucial key to the future success of Bolivia's domestic and foreign policy, Bolivia does not hold all the cards in this geopolitical struggle for sovereignty any more than the ancient Melians did.

NOTES

1. This has been a popular Chilean argument used to dismiss Bolivian diplomatic initiatives. See Tomasek (1967).

2. For example Bolivia introduced the issue of an outlet to the sea in the IX, X, XI, and XII Regular Sessions of the OAS in 1979, 1980, 1981, and 1982 respectively. It was brought up at the XIII Foreign Ministers Meeting of the La Plata Basin group in Brasilia in December 1982; at the Bolivarian meeting celebrating the bicentennial of Bolivar's birth in Caracas in May 1983; when Siles Suazo visited the United Nations in early 1983; at the meeting of the Andean Pact parliament in March 1983; at the Seventh Summit meeting of the Nonaligned Movement in March 1983 in New Delhi;   at the meeting of the Coordinating Committee of that movement in Managua during January 1983; and at the Fifth Meeting of the "Group of 77" in Buenos Aires in April 1983. The issue has been pressed successfully in bilateral talks with France, Spain, Argentina, Brazil, Panama, and Yugoslavia to mention major cases (Boletín Informativo Semanal, February 2, 1983; March 9, 1983; June 16, 1983; July 29, 1983; and August 12, 1983).

Part 3

Central America:
Challenges of Revolution

11
Central America:
Regional Security Issues

Jennie K. Lincoln

Throughout the history of the Western hemisphere the politics of the small nation-states of Central America have rarely made a splash in the international political arena. Two events in 1979, however, turned the attention of the world to this region: (1) the overthrow of the dictatorship of Anastasio Somoza in Nicaragua by a group of rebel forces, the Sandinistas; and (2) the overthrow of the military government of Humberto Romero in El Salvador by a group of young military officers. Since that time the dynamics of the politics of this region have commanded the increased attention of the neighbors of those countries, the hemisphere, and the world.

In between the continents of North and South America lie a group of small countries which are referred to as Central America. With some regularity the nations of Central America are lumped together as if they comprised a homogeneous entity which merited the label. Ralph Lee Woodward Jr.'s historical treatment of the region (1976), which reviews the common historical roots of these nations as part of the Spanish empire, is even titled Central America--A Nation Divided. This heritage laid the foundation for authoritarian rule, social class divisions, and an agro-export economy in each of the nations which became the sovereign states of Central America. To some extent the identification is applicable when one considers the experiences with dictatorial politics, the low level of economic development, and the equally low level of quality of life experienced by the majority of people in this region. Historically, oligarchic control of the land supported by military repression has prevented any significant redistribution of resources among the masses which account for the largest percentage of the population.

On the other hand there are social, economic, and political differences in the region which account for and contribute to the conflicts in the region today. Guatemala has a large Indian population, while El Salvador, Nicaragua, and Honduras have a majority of mestizos (mixed Indian and Spanish descent). Costa Rica has a population of over 90 percent mestizo with a strong European cultural heritage. Panama and Nicaragua both have significant black or West Indian populations. Literacy varies in the region as is noted in Table 11.1 from a low of 48 percent in Guatemala to a high of 90 percent in Costa Rica and Nicaragua.

Economically these countries vary in the degree to which they are dependent upon primary products for export and in levels of industrialization. The basis of the economy in Guatemala is principally agriculture with exports of coffee, cotton, bananas, and sugar cane. A large percentage (55%) of

TABLE 11.1
Socio-economic Indicators, 1981

	Pop. (millions)	External Debt as % GNP	GNP Per Cap ($U.S.)	Literacy*	% Labor Force* in Agr.
Guatemala	7.5	8.0	1140	48	55
Honduras	3.8	47.1	600	60	63
El Salvador	4.7	19.0	650	62	50
Nicaragua	2.8	80.2	860	90	43
Costa Rica	2.3	92.6	1430	90	29
Panama	1.9	12.6	1910	85	27

Source: World Bank, World Development Report 1983 (New York: Oxford University Press, 1983), pp. 148, 149, 152, 153, 178, 179, 188, 189. *indicates data from 1980.

Guatemala's work force is in agriculture (see Table 11.1) and per capita income barely exceeds $1000. The Honduran economy is similarly based on agricultural products with exports of bananas, corn, and beans. Honduras has the largest percentage of labor force in agriculture (63%) in Central America and has the lowest per capita income ($600) of those nations. Although El Salvador's economy is based principally on the export of coffee and cotton, there has been an attempt to establish processing and manufacturing industries in El Salvador. El Salvador still has a large percentage of its labor force in agriculture (50%) and the per capita income figure of $650 in 1981 is likely to be lower now as a result of the continued civil war. The war in El Salvador has crippled the economy with vast destruction both of crops and of the infrastructure which supports the country's export economy. Nicaragua, like the other Central American nations, has an economy based on agricultural exports of coffee, cotton, and sugar cane. Nicaragua's high percentage of its labor force (43%) in agriculture and its low per capita income ($860) reflect the many years of control of the economy by the Somoza family.

The economies of Costa Rica and Panama differ from those of their neighbors in the region with much lower percentages in agriculture (29% in Costa Rica and 27% in Panama) and higher per capita incomes ($1430 in Costa Rica and $1910 in Panama). Coffee continues to be Costa Rica's leading export, but manufacturing and services are growing in significance to its economy. Panama does export some primary products including bananas, sugar, and coffee, but over half of its economy is based on revenues from the Panama Canal.

The overwhelming dependence of the economies of these nations on primary products in international markets which have seen most of these prices plummet has been troublesome. The prosperous era of the 1950s and 1960s which saw rapid economic growth and the development of the Central American Common Market gave way to an era of economic deterioration as a result of both the political turmoil of the Soccer War between El Salvador and Honduras in 1969 and the world economic crisis which stemmed from the oil crisis in the early 1970s. Consequently, although the nature and composition of the economies of the nations of this region may be varied, the impact of the economic deterioration of the 1970s has been felt drastically in each of these nations. Table 11.1 also illustrates the large external debt in Central America which has resulted from these economic disruptions. The debt burden felt by Honduras (47% of the gross national product), Costa Rica (80%) and Nicaragua (93%) threatens the economic stability of those countries. El Salvador's burden would indeed be even higher if it were not for the economic aid from the U.S. which totaled $182 million in 1982 and $242 million in 1983 (U.S. Library of Congress, 1984:Table 9).

Politically, there is a range of regime structures in Central America which include a military dictatorship in Guatemala; a democratically elected president in Honduras who lives in the shadow of a military veto power; a president in El Salvador who was chosen by an elected Constituent Assembly, but who also must deal with a strong military organization and powerful paramilitary organizations; an elected president in Costa Rica following a tradition of democratically elected regimes since 1948 where there is no military organization by law; a ruling directorate in Nicaragua which ousted the dictatorship of Anastasio Somoza and which is building the largest military organization in Central America; and a president of Panama who was elected by the National Assembly but who also must contend with the veto power of the National Guard.

The intra-regional relations among these nations are evolving into an alignment which posits most of the nations in the region against the Sandinista regime in Nicaragua. This regime has become increasingly characterized as a security threat to the region due to its military buildup, its support for the Salvadoran guerrillas, and its relations with Cuba. The Honduran border with Nicaragua has become an armed camp of Honduran and U.S. military troops. Costa Rica, a country without a standing army and with a commitment to "neutrality," is preparing measures to secure its border with Nicaragua. El Salvador is seeking extensive military aid from the United States to continue its battle with the guerrilla opposition which it alleges is being supported by the Sandinistas. Guatemala, too, is seeking U.S. military aid which was cut off in 1977 due to human rights violations. Now Guatemala suggests that the U.S. must come to the aid of Guatemala which is threatened by guerrilla groups and which may fall prey to the "international communist conspiracy" designed for Central America. Panama, too, has joined the opposition to the Sandinista regime as evidenced by its moves to defend its borders and its concern for Costa Rica's national security.

The nations of Central America today individually and collectively face economic and security problems which have a direct impact on their domestic and foreign policies (Dickey, 1984; Diskin, 1983; Feinberg, 1982; Riding, 1983). Economic adversity fertilized the seeds of revolution in El Salvador and Nicaragua which resulted in changes in those governments in 1979. The impact of economic adversity was also felt in Guatemala where guerrilla activities increased and in Honduras where pressure mounted for the military to allow a civilian government to assume power. It may be argued that a nation's response to economic adversity and its subsequent shifts in political and/or governmental frameworks are matters of domestic policy. However, when the impact of economic deterioration and subsequent changes in governmental structures bring substantial involvement of external actors, the lines between domestic and foreign policy become blurred. The utilization of foreign policy as an extension of domestic policy-making, especially in times of economic deterioration, is widely discussed in the case of Latin America (Atkins, 1977; Chilcote and Edelstein, 1974; Cochrane, 1978; David and Wilson, 1975; Ferris and Lincoln, 1981; Hellman and Rosenbaum, 1975). Consequently, an analysis of the foreign policies of the nations of Central America today reflects governmental responses to the economic downturn of the 1970s and the political instability in the region which followed. The threatened economic situation and political instability in this region have had a direct impact on the foreign relations of these nations whose individual concerns for national security have become a hemispheric concern for the regional security of Central America.

National security is usually understood in terms of defense of the national boundaries of soverign territory. The concept has been translated into governmental policies "which justify the maintenance of armies, the development of new weapons systems, and the manufacture of armaments" (Brown, 1984:340). In a broader sense, however, national security implies more than a military protection of a nation's population and territory. It also implies protection "of vital economic and political interests, the loss of which could threaten fundamental values and the vitality of the state" (Jordan and Taylor, 1981:3). This expanded definition is quite appropriate in Central America where national security is translated by both civilian and military government into policies to protect economic development and political stability from internal threats as well as to protect national boundaries from external threats.

The national security concerns and subsequent foreign policy actions of all the nations of Central America have been directly or indirectly affected by the conflicts in El Salvador and Nicaragua and the U.S. government's response to those conflicts. The impact of the political turmoil in these two nations has regionalized the conflict as guerrilla activity and subsequent refugee migration have affected all of the Central American nations. Guatemala and Honduras have both experienced increased guerrilla activities which have threatened the legitimacy of existing governments. The migration of refugees and subsequent increases in tension along the borders have become more frequent throughout the region with uninvited refugees from Guatemala, El Salvador, and Nicaragua relocating in Honduras, Costa Rica, and Mexico. Costa Rica, the only country in the region with an uninterrupted history of democratic governments in the past 35 years, has given political asylum to several political leaders who have actively called for the overthrow of other governments in the region. Every country in Central America is affected by the political unrest and violence which are prevalent in the region and which have reached crisis proportions not just for Central America, but for the hemispheric neighbors of Central America as well.

This chapter presents an overview of the regional security issues and the foreign policy actions of the governments of Central America as they face the present crisis in the region. In a broad sense the "crisis" here is understood to mean violence, unrest, and threats to political stability of the various governments in the region. More specifically two distinct, yet intertwined, crises occupy the forefront of Central American politics: (1) the continued threat to the existence of the government of El Salvador from guerrilla

organizations and political opposition groups which do not accept the legitimacy of the recent elections and which continue to attack militarily the armed
forces of the present government of El Salvador; and (2) the political and
military activities of the Marxist-oriented Sandinista regime in Nicaragua
which is perceived by others in the region as an expansion of Cuban (hence
communist) influence in the region and military activities of the contra forces
which are determined to overthrow the Sandinista regime.

Although these crises pertain to distinct political entities which are
not even geographically contiguous, the linkage of Sandinista support for the
guerrillas of El Salvador has tied these two crises together and regionalized
the crisis. There is concern in the region that a "spillover effect" will add to
the guerrilla operations which already exist in Honduras and Guatemala; thus
the entire Central American political arena has become a potential powder
keg. A review of the speeches of the leaders of the region and of the editorials from the newspapers of the region refer to the entire area as a potential war zone. Former Minister of Foreign Relations of Costa Rica, Gonzalo
Facio, suggested that it was unlikely that there would be an isolated war
between Honduras and Nicaragua (Interview, San Jose, Costa Rica, April 14,
1983). Instead he talked of "war in Central America" which encompassed the
entire region. The conflicts in both El Salvador and Nicaragua have led to an
increased militarization of the region with a buildup of military forces including foreign troops and a substantial increase in arsenals of weapons in the
region. At the same time, regional and international commerce in the area
have been disrupted which also has had an adverse impact on the economies
of all the countries in the region. Taking these factors into consideration, it
is understandable that the foreign policies of the Central American nations
today are most concerned with preserving national security which is essential
to both national economic development and regional political stability.

How did Central America become such a war zone and what are the
prospects for peaceful resolutions of the conflicts in the region? What are the
dynamics of the politics of the region which may facilitate or impair the
peace process? The following sections address these questions by looking at
the foreign policies of Guatemala, Honduras, El Salvador, Costa Rica, and
Panama as they deal with the regional security issues of the present crisis in
Central America.

GUATEMALA

Following an attempt to restore the democratic political process in
Guatemala, military intervention placed a governing junta in command of the
government in March 1982. One of the generals in that initial junta was
General Efrain Rios Montt, a career army officer, who later dissolved the
junta and declared himself to be not only the chief executive of the state, but
also the Defense Minister. Rios Montt did not become chief executive at the
request of the Guatemalan people. Rios Montt became chief executive
through military manipulations of the government following elections which
were accused of being fraudulent by the three unsuccessful contenders and by
the military. A group of young officers took control of the government in a
bloodless coup on March 23, 1982, although reports from insiders in Guatemala
at the time suggest that two different juntas were established during the day
before the ultimately successful junta was established. On June 9, 1982, Rios
Montt dissolved that junta and consolidated the powers of chief executive and

commander-in-chief of the armed forces into his own position in a move which was seen as an attempt to defuse the possibility of a coup which might oust him (WRH, June 29, 1982:1). Rios Montt indicated at that time that he would remain in office until at least 1984 and he declared that he was "trying to operate the government on Christian principles" (LAWR, June 18, 1982:7). These Christian principles, however, included a declaration of a state of siege, the suspension of civil liberties, and prohibition of activities of labor unions and political parties.

The Rios Montt government did enjoy, however, the support of the U.S. government which became evident with the proposals of the Reagan administration to renew U.S. military arms sales to Guatemala. U.S. military aid and arms sales had been suspended under the Carter administration in 1977 because of human rights violations. This ban did not prevent U.S. commercial and "nonmilitary" sales of approximately $8 million of small weapons and ammunition, spare parts, trucks, trailers, and light aircraft to Guatemala between 1978-1981 (Montealegre and Arnson, 1983:304-305). In January 1983, however, the Reagan administration announced the decision to sell $6 million of helicopter spare parts and communications equipment to the Guatemalan Air Force to service another $25 million of Bell helicopters which have been sold to Guatemala in violation of the arms sales restriction (WRH, January 23, 1983:3).

Another reason that Rios Montt enjoyed U.S. support was that he viewed the crisis in Central America in very simple terms: guerrilla groups threaten the stability of the countries of the region and must be dealt with militarily. Guerrilla groups have been fighting in Guatemala since the 1960s but Rios Montt's government attempted to militarize the countryside with "civil defense patrols" in a move to strengthen national counter-insurgency strategy (New York Times, September 12, 1982:3). Rios Montt viewed the leftist groups as part of an international conspiracy threatening democratic institutions in Central America. Resolution of this conflict would come only through military victory over the insurgents which would be facilitated by restoring military cooperation and arms sales from the United States (Schoultz, 1983).

Rios Montt was less concerned with regional conflict than with two issues of national concern which had foreign policy implications: (1) the territorial dispute over Guatemala's claim to two-thirds of the territory of the nation-state of Belize; and (2) the problem of guerrilla operations against the government of Guatemala. The dispute over Guatemala's claim to territory of Belize has been going on since the nineteenth century. Negotiations broke down again in January 1983 which prompted the Belizan Ambassador to the United Nations to comment that he saw the "threat of a Guatemalan attack as real as ever" especially given the resumption of U.S. military arms sales to Guatemala (WRH, February 8, 1983:6).

Guatemala's second arena of conflict prompted governmental actions to combat the guerrilla groups in Guatemala which Rios Montt attributed to the efforts of a superpower trying to make Guatemala into an experimental field operation. Military operations to combat guerrilla activities have had repercussions on the foreign relations with Guatemala's neighbors--especially Mexico. Estimates of Guatemalan refugees who have fled to Mexico now number over 100,000 according to the UN High Commissioner for Refugees (Ferris, 1984; Aguayo, 1983). In addition the Mexican government has repeatedly protested incursions into Mexican territory by Guatemalan military troops in counter-insurgency operations in the border regions.

Although Rios Montt held views similar to his counterparts in the region concerning the threat of guerrilla activity, his often erratic behavior prompted other Central American leaders to view him with suspicion and to some extent to isolate him. For example, regional meetings which were held to promote "democracy in the region" specifically excluded Rios Montt. This occurred at the meeting in January 1982 in Costa Rica in which the foreign ministers of Honduras, El Salvador, and Costa Rica met to proclaim the creation of the Central American Democratic Community and again at the meeting in October 1982 in Costa Rica of the foreign ministers of Belize, Colombia, El Salvador, Honduras, Jamaica, Costa Rica, the Dominican Republic, and the United States to call for the creation of a regional association to support a "forum for democracy." Guatemala supposedly was excluded from the January meeting of the Central American Democratic Community because of its human rights record, but subsequently was given observer status in July 1982. The Forum for Democracy which met in October included Belize, which in turn precluded the participation of Guatemala given the bilateral conflict between those two nations.

An example of mixed support for Rios Montt in the region was the arrangement with President Suazo of Honduras for President Reagan to meet with Rios Montt in Honduras in December 1982 reportedly because President Monge (Costa Rica) did not want such a meeting to take place in Costa Rica (New York Times, December 5, 1982:E1). Only hours after meeting with President Reagan, Rios Montt announced his intentions to try to meet with Nicaraguan leaders to ease tensions in Central America. Rios Montt appeared to be looking for increased contact with the Nicaraguan leaders--a move which was looked upon with skepticism by other leaders in the region including the Nicaraguans themselves (Interview, Embassy of Nicaragua, Washington, D.C., January 14, 1983). For some time Rios Montt's only ally in the region appeared to be the President of Honduras as evidenced by talks held with President Suazo in January 1983 which resulted in Suazo's announced support for Guatemalan participation in the Forum for Democracy (LAWR, January 21, 1983:12). However, a new proposal of peace talks in the region came from Costa Rica which included the Foreign Ministers of Costa Rica, Honduras, El Salvador, Nicaragua, and Guatemala as well as observers from Panama, Mexico, Venezuela, Colombia, Belize, Jamaica, and the Dominican Republic (New York Times, March 6, 1983:1). This proposal was significant for several reasons: (1) notably absent was an invitation to the United States (neither as participant nor as observer); (2) both Guatemala and Belize were invited (with Belize in observer status, however); and (3) Nicaragua was invited as a full participant.

In the months which followed, however, Rios Montt lost political control and was not the active political negotiator in the Central American region that he may have thought he could be. A coup d'état in August 1983 replaced Rios Montt with General Oscar Mejía Victores whose foreign policy views concerning the crisis in Central America mirrored those of the Reagan administration and eased the way for restoration of U.S. military aid to Guatemala. In his first days in office, Mejía referred to the Sandinista government in Nicaragua as "not only a threat to Guatemala, but to the whole continent" (New York Times, August 13, 1983:3). In this light, Mejía supported Guatemala's participation in the revitalization of the Central American Defense Council, CONDECA, which had been formed in 1964 by Guatemala, Honduras, El Salvador, and Nicaragua with U.S. assistance and with Costa Rica and Panama as observers. Although the initial meeting of the defense ministers of Guatemala, El Salvador, and Honduras with the commander of the Panamanian National Guard and the chief of the U.S. Southern Command to discuss the revitalization of CONDECA took place on October 1, 1983, an emergency meeting was called on October 27, 1983 (following the U.S. military rescue/invasion of Grenada) after which it was reported that "there is an invasion plan for Nicaragua and it is supported by CONDECA" (LAWR, November 4, 1983:12). Guatemala is pursuing a strong militaristic policy with respect to its foreign relations in Central America. Mejía subscribes to the domino theory of former U.S. Secretary of State, Alexander Haig, which suggests that the Marxist orientation of the Nicaraguan government and the renewed interest of Cuba in Central America threatens the national security of Guatemala. Even though Guatemala is still subject to the ban on security assistance from the U.S. because of its human rights record, President Reagan has responded to a request for renewed assistance to Guatemala with a proposal for $10 million of military sales credits and $250,000 training funds for FY1984 (U.S. Department of State, 1983c:6).

Closer to home Guatemala's relations with Belize are still not resolved. It is ironic that as Guatemala seeks to regain military aid from the U.S., the U.S. is now sending military aid to Belize also. In September 1983 Great Britain announced its intentions to withdraw its forces (between 1400-1800 troops supported by Harrier Jumpjets, Puma helicopters, tanks, and Rapier missiles) which it could no longer afford to maintain in the aftermath of the Falkland Island war (LAWR, October 7, 1983:12). The U.S. is beginning to fill the security gap by allocating $600,000 in FY1984 (U.S. Library of Congress, 1984:Table 9) in military assistance to Belize. While this is a modest amount, U.S. policy makers have pledged to support a stable and democratic government in Belize (U.S. Department of State, 1983c:7) which perceives its security still to be threatened by Guatemala.

HONDURAS

The election of Roberto Suazo Cordova in Honduras on November 29, 1981, marked the return to civilian rule after 18 years of military governments in Honduras. Roberto Suazo Cordova, a candidate of the Liberal Party, was seen by Hondurans as anti-communist, conservative-oriented, and pro-U.S. In a press conference the day before his election, Suazo declared that "the United States is the defender of democracy and liberty in the world" (New York Times, November 29, 1981:4)--a clear statement of his perspective then and a harbinger of closer relations with the United States. Suazo Cordova took office in January 1982 and by all rights should serve a four-year term. However, given the historical role of the military in Honduras and the present state of agitation in the region, Suazo Cordova's position is secure only to the extent that the military is satisfied with his actions as chief executive (Rosenberg, 1984; Volk, 1981). The contradiction between Suazo Cordova's foreign policy pronouncements in his inauguration speech which called for a Honduras which would maintain principles of self-determination and nonintervention in the affairs of others and the increasing drive toward military confrontation with Nicaragua indicate a lack of control over foreign policy-making by the new president. "Suazo Cordova has allowed the military to control national security policy and foreign affairs policy making particularly at the regional level" (Rosenberg, 1983:14). Analyzing the current situation in Honduras, John Booth (1983) agrees that the military has considerable influence in the foreign policy making arena. "Greatly increased military assistance from the United States has encouraged the Defense Minister (Alvarez) to be active in foreign policy making and to reduce President Suazo's effective range of options externally" (Booth, 1983:2).

Suazo Cordova interprets the "crisis in Central America" in terms of regional conflict which goes far beyond individual domestic or bilateral conflicts. No doubt this perspective may be attributed in part to the fact that Honduras borders Guatemala, Belize, El Salvador, and Nicaragua which has meant that conflicts in all of those areas have spilled over onto Honduran territory. Suazo Cordova has attributed the instability of the region to a series of internal and international factors which threaten the region as a whole (Tiempo, September 19, 1982:13). He sees Honduras threatened from all sides as refugees flood the border regions near El Salvador and Nicaragua. The Office of the UN High Commissioner for Refugees estimates (U.S. Department of State, 1983b:5) that 32,000 Salvadorans, 36,000 Nicaraguans, and 800 Guatemalans have sought refuge in Honduras, and that 10,000 Hondurans have been displaced within their own country. Suazo Cordoba's response to this threat was to pursue joint military operations with the U.S. in July 1982 and again in January 1983 and to call on the United States "to send troops to Central America (no country specified) to 'defend democracy' and 'to reduce tension in the region'" (LAWR, August 20, 1982:12). The strong influence of the military may be clearly interpreted from this action as well as from the increased interaction between the armed forces of Honduras and the U.S.

U.S. military operations in Honduras are more extensive than the adviser role of the U.S. military in El Salvador. Operation Big Pine I (Ahuas Tara I) in January 1983 which took place 10 kilometers from the Nicaraguan border included 4,000 Honduran troops with 900 U.S. troops and 600 support troops in Panama. According to the U.S. Department of Defense, the objective of the exercise was to "include assisting Honduras in developing techniques and exercising logistical support of a field force" (LAWR, January 28, 1983:11). Operation Big Pine II which began in August 1983 expanded the scope and duration of the exercises begun under Big Pine I. Big Pine II (Ahuas Tara II) involved the training of three Honduran infantry battalions, an amphibious battalion and an artillery battalion (approximately 4,000) in addition to the U.S. training of Honduran and Salvadoran soldiers already being trained by U.S. Special Forces. In addition to training, Operation Big Pine II also involved the construction of military airfields at Trujillo and San Lorenzo as well as the construction of a military access road across La Mosquitia, the eastern region of Honduras which borders the Caribbean and Nicaragua (La Tribuna, August 16, 1983:24). During the operation of Big Pine II, the U.S. military demonstrated a show of force with the positioning of U.S. aircraft carriers and the battleship USS New Jersey operated off both coasts of Nicaragua and a mock invasion was carried out on the coast of Honduras. After six months of Operation Big Pine II, Operation Big Pine III (Granadero I) has been announced to continue the training and joint exercises which have been in place in Honduras for the past year. The continued military presence of U.S. troops in Honduras has been assured by the Pentagon which is seeking funds to support a permanent U.S. military base in Honduras (Washington Post, January 11, 1984:1). Support for such a plan has been voiced by General Gustavo Alvarez who wants to improve the Honduran defense capability "against the threat of the communist penetration in Central America by the Sandinista regime in Nicaragua" (La Nación

Internacional, December 29, 1983-Janaury 4, 1984:20). The strength of the
military buildup in Honduras supported by Operations Big Pine I, II, and III
clearly define the foreign policy defense posture of Honduras as preparing
for an all-out war with Nicaragua.

Suazo Cordova is well aware of the position that Honduras has played
militarily in other conflicts in the region. Honduras served as the staging
ground for the CIA-supported coup which overthrew Jacobo Arbenz in Guatemala in 1954 (Immerman, 1982; Kinzer and Schlesinger, 1981). Also, Swan
Island, off the coast of Honduras, was used as a communications center during
the Bay of Pigs invasion of Cuba in 1961. In addition Honduran troops were
also involved in the "Inter-American Peacekeeping Force" that invaded the
Dominican Republic (Volk, 1981:35). It appears that the present buildup of
the military capability of Honduras and the presence of a significant number
of U.S. troops on Honduran soil demonstrate a clear commitment to prepare
for a military solution to the crisis in the region. Before the extensive buildup of military operations in Honduras, Suazo Cordova's approach to the crisis
in the region did involve a modest diplomatic path of meetings with his
Central American counterparts. In June 1982 Suazo met with Alvaro Magana,
President of El Salvador, after which a joint communiqué was issued condemning the arms race in the region and promising to promote better relations
among all the nations of the region (LAWR, June 18, 1982:12). In December
1982 Suazo hosted President Rios Montt of Guatemala during the Reagan
visit and again in January 1983 Rios Montt and Suazo conferred. Since that
time, however, the diplomatic approach to the resolution of conflict in the
region has been relegated to a distant second place to the military preparedness Honduras is building. While Suazo Cordova voices support for the diplomatic efforts of the Contadora Group, his Defense Minister Alvarez deepens
the commitment of Honduras to a level of military preparedness for war.

COSTA RICA

Costa Rica is the only Central American nation to have maintained
uninterrupted regular elections since 1948 when the military was in effect
disbanded (Ameringer, 1982, 1979; Arias Sanchez, 1976; Bell, 1971; Denton,
1971). Since that time successive governments have declared the "neutrality"
of Costa Rica, referring to Costa Rica as the Switzerland of Latin America.
In international law neutrality is understood as "the legal relationship that
exists between states which take no part in the war on the one hand, or the
belligerents on the other" (Bishop, 1953:651-652). In theory, nations which
declare a "neutral" position "proclaim themselves in advance desirous of
avoiding participation in any war at any time" (Brecher, 1962:224). Costa
Rica's governmental actions have not always reflected the purity of these
definitions of neutrality. However, the unstable situation in Central America
right now and Costa Rica's proximity to the arenas of conflict threaten the
very existence of a neutral foreign policy doctrine.

In the election of February 1982 Luis Alberto Monge, a co-founder of
the social democratic National Liberation Party (PLN), emerged victorious
following a fierce anti-communist campaign. Monge was inaugurated on May
8, 1982, and six weeks later he visited Washington, D.C. where he asked for
$10 million in security assistance to "combat terrorism." During that visit
with President Reagan in June 1982, Monge declared in a joint news conference that Nicaragua "is converting itself into a totalitarian dictatorship with

the strong support of Cuba" (WRH, July 13, 1982:3). Monge's request was "symptomatic of Costa Rica's identity crisis in choosing between a traditionally independent posture in regional affairs, and growing concern for its own political and economic survival amidst spreading Central American turmoil" (WRH, July 13, 1982:3). The U.S. responded to Monge's request for military aid with $2 million of military equipment accompanied by trainers sent to Costa Rica to strengthen the Civil Guard in October 1982 (Los Angeles Times, October 16, 1982:4). This security assistance was increased in 1983 to $3 million which included training, communications equipment, four-wheel drive vehicles, and basic items such as uniforms, tents, boots, and canteens (U.S. Department of State, 1983c:7).

President Monge does not see any conflict with the request for security assistance from the U.S. and the neutrality doctrine of Costa Rica's foreign policy which he formally reaffirmed in a proclamation which was transmitted by satellite to other nations on November 17, 1983 (La Nación Internacional, November 17-23, 1983:2). Having wrestled with the relationship between neutrality and national security President Monge has pursued a path of "active neutrality" which aligns Costa Rica with the U.S. and the democratically elected governments in the region. Active neutrality has meant that Costa Rica supports diplomatic efforts to protect its national security and to resolve the crisis in the region through a variety of mechanisms including: (1) multilateral negotiations designed by the Contadora Group; (2) bilateral negotiations between the guerrillas and the government of El Salvador; and (3) unilateral efforts such as the actions by the U.S. government in appointing a special ambassador to the region, Richard Stone, and a special commission to study the problems in the region, the National Bipartisan Commission on Central America--better known as the Kissinger Commission. The airport at San Jose has operated as a revolving door with diplomatic missions flying into and out of Costa Rica regularly. The Costa Rican interpretation of neutrality under President Monge does not preclude participation in international forums such as the United Nations or the Organization of American States. It does, however, prohibit a reinstatement of the military establishment which was outlawed in 1948 (La Nación Internacional, November 24-30, 1983:5). This widely acclaimed neutrality, however, has not diminished the concern about threats to Costa Rica's national security as a result of the current instability in the region. President Monge had said during his campaign that he supported the Mexican and Venezuelan position with regard to a negotiated settlement in El Salvador (LAWR, February 12, 1982:2). During his visit to the U.S., however, Monge stated that he understood that "the U.S. must conduct a global policy concerned with preventing the expansion of communist forces throughout the world" (Weekly Compilation of Presidential Documents, 1982:827). President Monge's views toward Nicaragua were less than tolerant as he accused Nicaragua of mounting an "international communist campaign" against his country following statements of Sandinista leaders about human rights in Costa Rica (LAWR, August 13, 1982:11). The concern of a security threat from Nicaragua is understandably greater given that Costa Rica borders Nicaragua, not El Salvador.

While pursuing security assistance for Costa Rica on the one hand, President Monge has actively promoted diplomatic cooperation among the democratically elected governments in the region. His life-long experiences in labor union leadership no doubt influenced his proclivity toward face-to-face negotiations which he attempted to bring about with his support for the Central American Democratic Community and his role as host of the "Forum for Peace and Democracy" in October 1982. The Forum for Peace proposed an organization to provide technical (and financial) assistance to governments in the region who wish to reform or modernize their electoral systems. According to sources at USAID, one result of this proposal was a transfer of funds from the United States to the Inter-American Institute of Human Rights in San Jose for the purpose of establishing a series of seminars to discuss the issue of strengthening democracy through free elections. These funds were part of "Project Democracy," an $85 million communication and education program announced by the Reagan administration on February 23, 1983 (WRH, March 22, 1983:5). The meetings and subsequent proposals concerning election funds pointedly did not include neighboring Nicaragua. Among his diplomatic ventures President Monge also met with President Reagan three times between June-December 1982. At each meeting President Monge reaffirmed the common goals of the two administrations: "a Central America where not just some but all countries are democracies, where institutions are based on free and regular elections in an atmosphere of political reconciliation . . ." (Weekly Compilation of Presidential Documents, 1982:1575). Again, the political alignment of Monge was quite clear at this point even though "neutrality" was a fundamental tenet of Costa Rica's foreign policy. President Monge continued the diplomatic path and later proposed regional meetings to discuss conflict resolution which did in fact include Nicaragua. In an interesting turn of events this proposal specifically excluded participation by the United States (New York Times, March 6, 1983: 1). Monge attempted to increase his role as a balancer in the region by suggesting that all nations in Central America and interested parties from the northern part of the South American continent should be included in a regional effort of conflict resolution. From one standpoint this contradicted Monge's seemingly close relationship with the United States. On the other hand this was seen as an effort to reaffirm Costa Rica's position of neutrality in the region.

President Monge's foreign policy actions in the past year have been curiously varied. Monge appears to be redefining the "actively neutral" stand that Costa Rica has taken under previous administrations which granted political asylum to exiles from many Latin American countries. It is well known that Costa Rica provided more than sanctuary for many of the leaders of the FSLN as they plotted the downfall of Somoza in Nicaragua in the 1970s. Under President Carazo there was open sympathy for the FSLN which freely operated training grounds and launched attacks on Nicaragua from Costa Rica. Military supplies were easily run through Costa Rica for the Sandinistas. Costa Rica broke diplomatic relations with the Somoza government in October 1978 and in May 1979 recognized the FSLN as a revolutionary government of Nicaragua in exile (Ameringer, 1982; Booth, 1982; Seligson and Carroll, 1982). President Monge is now faced with a similar situation only this time it is the very Sandinista regime that Costa Ricans had supported which is now under attack by a group which splintered from the original junta led by Comandante Cero, Eden Pastora. It was in the name of neutrality that Eden Pastora was expelled from Costa Rica soon after Monge's inauguration. However, not only was Pastora allowed to return to Costa Rica a few months after his expulsion but several other former Sandinista leaders have been granted political asylum in Costa Rica including former Nicaraguan businessmen, Alfonso Robelo and Arturo Cruz, as well as former Nicaraguan Ambassador to the United States, Francisco Fiallos. The political activities of the Revolutionary Democratic Alliance, ARDE, one of the principal contra groups operating against the Sandinista government, are quite visible in San Jose, the location of ARDE's headquarters. The military activities of this group are being directed by Eden Pastora in the northern part of Costa Rica.

The government of Costa Rica has been deeply concerned about border violations especially in the area of the San Juan River where Costa Rican nationals have been harassed and commerce has been interrupted in that region. Costa Rica does not have a standing army and most Costa Ricans openly oppose reinstituting one (Hoivik and Solveig, 1981). Costa Rica's only security forces include: 5,000 Civil Guards, the principal police force in San Jose and other cities; 3,000 Rural Guards in the countryside; and the 647 Judicial Police (OIJ) who have been trained outside the country in criminology, ballistics, and intelligence (Edelman and Hutchcroft, 1984:9). However, as the conflict in Central America deepens, the Costa Rican government has moved to professionalize its Rural and Civil Guards with training at the U.S. training facility in Panama and has asked for increased security assistance from the U.S. Much of the security assistance obtained from the U.S. has been used to provide basic supplies and training for the Rural Guard in the Costa Rica/Nicaragua border area where Costa Rican fishing boats have been detained or seized on the river by Sandinista patrols. These incidents have been frequent as the contra activities of Pastora increased following his formal declaration of war against the revolutionary directorate of Nicaragua on April 15, 1983.

Pastora's group has moved in and out of the northern provinces of Costa Rica with minimal hindrance--especially in the area of Los Chiles where Pastora has family ties. Such operations draw criticism from those who prefer a genuine neutrality for Costa Rica. Pastora's visa has been revoked from time to time, but President Monge stated in a visit to the U.S. in December 1983 that he would not seek an all-out expulsion of anti-Sandinista forces "since to do so would violate their right to political asylum" (Edelman and Hutchcroft, 1984:11). The sanctuary for anti-Sandinista forces in Costa Rica is beginning to pose domestic problems for Costa Rica as the number of refugees from Nicaragua has increased dramatically in the past year. The UN High Commissioner reported an estimated 15,000 refugees in Costa Rica including 2,000 Nicaraguans in the early part of 1983 (Taran, 1983:7). However, according to Costa Rica's Deputy Foreign Minister, Ekhart Peters, over 25,000 Nicaraguans (and a similar number of Salvadorans) had taken refuge in Costa Rica by the end of 1983 (U.S. Department of State, 1983b:5). This influx of refugees prompted the Costa Rican government in February 1984 to refuse approximately 200 Pastora supporters permission to enter Costa Rica on the ground that the increase of immigrants to Costa Rica with intentions of joining Pastora's battle threatens Costa Rica's position of neutrality (La Nación Internacional, February 3-9, 1984:5 and February 9-15, 1984:14).

It is increasingly evident that neutrality has become problematic for the Costa Rican government in the present state of affairs in Central America. Differing perspectives concerning Costa Rica's neutrality have become quite apparent with open disagreements in the Cabinet. Foreign Minister Fernando Volio, who had been known for his hard-line position concerning Nicaragua and who had opposed Costa Rica's vote in the UN condemning the U.S. invasion of Grenada, resigned in November 1983 (La Nación Internacional, November 17-23, 1983:10, and January 6-13, 1984:3). The Minister of Government, who commands the Rural Guard, and the Minister of Public Security, who commands the Civil Guard, have openly disagreed about a proper governmental response to Pastora's operations in the north. This disagreement came to a head in February 1984 when President Monge intervened to support the Minister of Public Security's demand that in the name of Costa Rican neutrality Pastora's troops should not be admitted through immigration to Costa Rica (La Nación Internacional, February 9-15, 1984:14). President Monge has attempted to satisfy various factions by pursuing his own "two-track policy." The first track involves a diplomatic path as evidenced by the numerous meetings during the past year which either took place in Costa Rica--such as the attempt to bring together the representatives of the guerrilla factions in El Salvador with representatives of El Salvador's government--or involved Costa Rica's direct participation or consultation such as the meetings of the Contradora Group and the recently revitalized Central American Defense Council, CONDECA. The second track involves Costa Rica's increased requests for security assistance from the U.S. and the suggestion by the former foreign minister of Costa Rica of the possible necessity of a peace-keeping force in Costa Rica from the Organization of American States (La Nación Internacional, July 21-27, 1983:12-13). The Monge government has been openly supportive of the report from the Kissinger Commission which targets substantial U.S. aid for democratic Costa Rica. Both of these tracks indicate the growing concern for Costa Rica's national security which jeopardizes even Costa Rica's expanded definition of the concept of neutrality.

EL SALVADOR

In 1932 workers and peasants revolted against the tyranny of the coffee oligarchs in El Salvador which resulted in the deaths of approximately 30,000 people. In an attempt to restore political stability the coffee oligarchs negotiated with the military to run the government. This led to military rule for the next 57 years with periodic "elections" which were subject to military veto. Over the years roots of the revolution in El Salvador grew underground as various opposition groups formed to oppose the military repression which frequently invoked state of siege, censored the press, closed the university, and denied personal liberties to the people (Anderson, 1971; Armstrong, 1983; Armstrong and Shenk, 1983; Arnson, 1982; LeoGrande and Robbins, 1980; Montgomery, 1982; North, 1981; Woodward, 1976).

Today social and economic conditions exist which have fed these roots including factors such as (Inter-American Development Bank, 1982; World Bank, 1983):

1. 2% of the population owns 60% of the land, 90% of the arable land;
2. 5% of the population receives 38% of the national income, while 40% receives 7.5% of the national income;
3. per capita GNP is only $650 with 50% of the population having a per capita income of only $100;
4. 75% of the children under age 5 suffer from malnutrition;
6. per capita calorie supply as percentage of daily requirements reaches only 84%; and
7. life expectancy at birth is only 62 years.

These social and economic conditions, aggravated by the legacy of military repression, set the stage for the military revolt in 1979 in which a group of

young officers overthrew the dictatorship of Carlos Humberto Romero and
set up a junta which included civilians from center groups. Repression continued, however, with the university closed, the press censored, no civil right
to assemble, and the operation of paramilitary death squads which accounted
for nearly 1,000 deaths per month (Anderson, 1971; Arnson, 1982; Montgomery,
1982; and North, 1981).

In January 1980 civilian members of the junta resigned forcing several
reorganizations before choosing Jose Napoleon Duarte, a civilian politician,
as president. Duarte was clearly subject to the veto of the military members
of the junta which continued state of siege policies. In March 1980 Archbishop
Romero was assassinated while saying mass and the Catholic Church was
targeted by the government as supporting guerrillas in opposition to the
government. As political instability continued to threaten El Salvador, the
government charged that the national security of El Salvador was being
threatened by external subversive forces which were being directed from
Havana.

Until this point several guerrilla organizations had been calling for
social and economic reforms in El Salvador throughout the countryside using
various strategies ranging from political demonstrations to terrorist tactics.
In the spring of 1980 these guerrilla organizations joined together to coordinate their political and military activities. Civilian opposition leaders from
a variety of groups banded together in the Frente Democrático Revolucionario
(FDR) and chose Guillermo Ungo, a Social Democrat who had been Duarte's
running mate in the 1972 election which was overturned by the military, as
President of the Front. The military guerrilla organizations loosely organized
under the Frente Farabundo Martí para la Liberación Nacional (FMLN). The
leaders of these organizations called for a major offensive in January 1981--
"a final offensive." The assault did not succeed in overthrowing the government, but did gain control of nearly one-third of the countryside including
areas to the north near the Honduran border and to the east toward the Gulf
of Fonseca. The government of El Salvador recognized the growing threat of
the somewhat unified opposition and initiated a course of action which
became its principal course of foreign policy: to seek political, economic,
and military assistance from the United States to preserve El Salvador's
national security from the growing guerrilla insurgency.

Following President Reagan's inauguration in January 1981 the government of the U.S. began to define the civil war in El Salvador in terms of an
East-West conflict which suggested that the guerrillas of El Salvador were
being directed and supported by Cuba and other communist sources. El Salvador's requests for assistance from the United States were immediately
answered with 55 military advisers and an initial allocation of $100 million
in emergency aid to El Salvador. U.S. aid to El Salvador has increased
dramatically from that initial allocation as may be seen in Table 11.2

Despite the millions of U.S. dollars El Salvador has received in military
training and equipment, the civil war in El Salvador has not subsided and the
power of the guerrillas to disrupt the economy has not even been diminished.
The destruction of the country's infrastructure has been estimated at approximately $600 million in damage to power stations, bridges, roads, transporta-
tion vehicles and crops (Riding, 1984:680).

According to the U.S. government the number of guerrillas operating
in El Salvador (approximately 6,000 frontline guerrillas and slightly more than
6,000 in local militias) has not changed in the past two years while the
amount of U.S. aid has more than doubled in that time. Still the Salvadoran

TABLE 11.2
U.S. Economic and Military Assistance to El Salvador (in millions of $U.S.)

	U.S. Fiscal Year					
	1979	1980	1981	1982	1983	1984
Economic Aid	8.6	72.0	136.5	182.2	242.2	197.2
Military Aid	--	6.3	35.5	82.0	81.3	64.8
Total	8.6	79.3	172.0	264.2	323.5	262.0

Sources: For 1979-1981: Cynthia Arnson, El Salvador--A Revolution Confronts the United States (Washington, D.C.: Institute for Policy Studies, 1982), p. 106. For 1982-1984: information on U.S. aid to Central America from Table 9 in U.S. Library of Congress, Congressional Research Service, Foreign Aid Issues in the 98th Congress--Issue Brief Number IB83084. Updated January 6, 1984.

Note: The total for 1984 does not include the supplemental allocation proposed by the Kissinger Commission.

armed forces (which number approximately 37,500) have been unable to control the guerrilla threat. The foreign policy response of the Salvadoran government has been to request more aid from the U.S. The recommendation of the Kissinger Commission notes that a successful counter-insurgency campaign may require a 10 to 1 manpower advantage which would mandate a significant infusion of additional military assistance for El Salvador (Bipartisan Commission on Central America, 1984:98). The Commission did not specify an amount, but Pentagon sources estimated that $400 million would be needed in fiscal years 1984-1985 "to break the military stalemate" (Congressional Weekly, January 14, 1984:40).

The government of El Salvador also sought political support from the U.S. for its elections in March 1982 which established a Constituent Assembly and diplomatic support from the other Central American democratic regimes for its war with the guerrillas. The Constituent Assembly in turn chose Alvaro Magaña, a Salvadoran businessman, as president. President Magaña and the Constituent Assembly have maintained very close relations with the United States as evidenced by the yearly increases in economic and military aid sent to El Salvador by the U.S. In addition, President Magaña has participated in regional fora which have met to discuss the present instability in El Salvador and Nicaragua as well. Any suggestions from these regional meetings that the government should negotiate with the guerrillas has been met with stiff opposition, however.

El Salvador continues to face a serious threat to its national security from the guerrilla operations in the countryside and its government has become completely dependent upon U.S. economic and military support to wage war against that opposition. It is doubtful that the presidential election scheduled for March 1984 will have much affect on this condition. There

seem to be two possible scenarios for an end to the conflict in El Salvador:
(1) an all-out military victory by one side or the other; or (2) a negotiated
settlement which would call for a cease-fire and an extension of the governing process to include representatives from the various opposition groups. At
this point in time, neither scenario is close to a reality and the civil war in
El Salvador continues to devastate the country.

PANAMA

   Although Panama is located in that isthmus which connects the North
and South American continents, its identification has varied from Central
America, to Caribbean, to a separate national identification all its own.
Panama has the highest per capita income ($1910) of the Central American
nations and one of the highest literacy rates (85%). But income is not well
distributed and there are high levels of unemployment and underemployment.
Political instability and violence have characterized Panamanian politics and
have prompted the National Guard to intervene in domestic politics repeatedly.
   Following a coup d'état in 1968, Omar Torrijos became the strongest
political figure in Panama and proceeded to dominate Panama's domestic and
foreign policies until his death in 1981. Torrijos will be most remembered in
Panama and in Latin America for the negotiations with the U.S. to turn the
rights to the Canal over to Panama. The Panama Canal Treaty signed in 1979
abolished the Canal Zone, which had essentially been U.S. property, and
approved the return of the Canal to Panama by the year 1999. In the meantime the U.S. would share administration of the Canal, would continue to
receive revenue from the Canal, and would train Panamanians to assume the
operations of the Canal. The return of the Panama Canal was symbolic of
the foreign policy of Panama under Torrijos which was Third World-oriented
and supported the Nonaligned Movement.
   Since his death, however, the leaders of Panama have been systematically dismantling "torrijismo--the political structures and ideas of the late
General Omar Torrijos" (LARR, March 25, 1983:6). The forging of a new
political path without Torrijos has prompted contradictory foreign policy
actions which on one hand may support Third World orientation of Panama
under Torrijos, but on another hand may be seen as moving closer to a pro-
U.S. position. The clearest case of this contradiction is evident in Panama's
position concerning the conflict in Central America. Panama was a charter
member of the Contadora Group (Mexico, Colombia, Venezuela, and Panama)
which was formed in January 1983 in an attempt to provide reasonable solutions to the crises in Central America by interested governments within the
region, i.e. not including the U.S. The Contadora ministers have met frequently since January 1983 and have traveled extensively throughout the
region to offer a diplomatic vehicle for conflict resolution. The Contadora
Group has proposed removal of foreign troops and a cessation of the arms
buildup in the region. The 21-point Contadora proposal was ratified by all
the Central American nations (including Nicaragua). However, while the
Panamanian government actively supported and participated in the Contadora
meetings, the head of Panama's National Guard, General Ruben Dario Paredes,
proposed a peacekeeping force to "back up the Contadora Group" and suggested that in terms of regional security, "Panama's frontier was not in
Chiriqui, but on the dividing line between Costa Rica and Nicaragua" (LAWR,

July 15, 1983:12). In another hard-line move, General Manuel Antonio Noriega, who succeeded Paredes as head of the National Guard, attended the meeting on October 1, 1983, in Guatemala which proposed the revitalization of the Central American Defense Council (CONDECA). Although he attended as an "observer," his presence signalled an inclination on the part of the National Guard to consider the military option rather than a diplomatic option for resolution of the crisis in Central America.

CENTRAL AMERICA: CHALLENGES FOR THE 1980S

The 1980s have brought serious challenges to the survival of the governments and economies of the nations of Central America. Political instability and economic insecurity have dominated both domestic and foreign policy making of each of these nations. The governments of these nations have in turn sought military and economic assistance from external sources to promote national security and national development which are inextricably linked. In so doing, however, the existence of outside actors in the domestic policy-making arena--on whatever level--has contributed to the instability in the region.

The politics of the two countries which turned the attention of the world to this region in 1979--El Salvador and Nicaragua--still command international attention as conflicts in those countries rage on. El Salvador continues to experience a civil war which has engaged the support of the U.S. on the side of the government and several U.S. allies on the side of the guerrillas. The Sandinista government of Nicaragua, facing serious threats from the U.S.-supported Somocista contras in the north and the Pastora contra group in the south, has sought aid from Cuba, the Soviet Union, the Eastern bloc as well as Western European and South American nations. The fear of the "spillover effect" which suggests that the conflict in these two countries will spread throughout the region has motivated Central American governments such as Guatemala, Honduras, and Panama to commit scarce national resources to additional arms purchases and increased levels of military preparedness. Even Costa Rica, the nation without an army, has sought additional security assistance from the U.S. and is training special forces to secure its northern border. U.S. military exercises in and around the region have grown in number of troops committed and length of operations as a reminder of U.S. strategic interests in the region. The message from the U.S. has been clear: the U.S. will not tolerate a Cuban (which is therefore interpreted to be Soviet) base of operations on the isthmus.

The challenges facing the Central American nations in the 1980s, therefore, extends beyond the problems which accompany the quest of Third World nations for economic development. The Central American nations confront that quest in an atmosphere of armed conflict which permeates the region and which involves significant influence on the part of external actors. How each of the Central American nations responds to these problems will depend on the perspectives of their leaders as they formulate policies to preserve national security and promote national development. The dynamics of the politics of this region involve efforts to resolve as well as efforts to sustain conflict in the region. The foreign policy choices of these nations ultimately will decide which efforts prevail.

12
Mexico's Foreign Policies: A Study in Contradictions

Elizabeth G. Ferris[1]

Mexican president Miguel de la Madrid faces his greatest foreign policy challenge in Central America. While relations with the U.S. and with international financial institutions continue to occupy center stage, the difficulties in formulating consistent policies toward Central America underscore recurrent structural problems in Mexico's foreign policy processes. De la Madrid and his foreign policy team must struggle with the contradictions in Mexico's national interests in the region--contradictions brought into sharp relief by the policies of his predecessor, José López Portillo.

Central America was vitally important to López Portillo's overall foreign policy and his government was successful in cultivating an image of Mexico's progressive posture in the region. Where the U.S. saw Cuba and Soviet forces instigating Central American revolutionary movements, Mexico's leaders stressed domestic social and economic inequities and political repression as the causes of regional turmoil. Indeed, armed revolution in El Salvador might be necessary, claimed Jorge Castaneda, Mexico's foreign minister. While the U.S. accused Nicaragua of spreading revolution and unrest in the region and saw Nicaragua as already lost to Soviet domination, Mexico continued to extend substantial moral and financial support to the revolutionary regime. While the U.S. became increasingly bellicose in Central America, Mexico sought to find peaceful solutions to the violence. Furthermore, Mexican president José López Portillo apparently accomplished the almost impossible task of maintaining personal friendships with both Ronald Reagan and Fidel Castro. Since de la Madrid's assumption of the presidency, Mexico has continued its role as regional peacemaker. Under Mexican leadership the Contadora Group (composed of the presidents of Venezuela, Mexico, Colombia, and Panama) has sought to avert armed conflicts between Central American nations and has repeatedly called for dialogue, negotiations, and compromise between Central American governments, the United States, and Cuba. Mexico's increasing regional activism and its progressive policies in Central America--its "natural" area of influence--have increased Mexico's prestige and power on the international scene. Clearly, Mexico continues to be an important force in efforts to resolve the Central American conflicts.

Such a portrait of Mexico's Central American policies, although common in both U.S. and Mexican media coverage, obscures the many contradictions and inconsistencies in Mexico's policies. These contradictions are symptoms of deeper crises in Mexican political and economic institutions and reveal a great deal about the different national interests and the conflicting pressures on Mexico's foreign policy makers. Furthermore, these

213

contradictions shape the foreign policy choices confronting de la Madrid. It should be noted that the foreign policies of <u>all</u> governments are contradictory to some degree as they are developed in response to different national interests and to pressure from different groups. The demand for consistency in foreign policy is also a call for rigidity in policies. Yet, while policy contradictions may be inevitable, national leaders present their policies as consistent, coherent, and congruent with national foreign policy traditions. Mexico is no exception.

Taken together, the five contradictions discussed here illustrate the gap between revolutionary myths and political reality in contemporary Mexico. Mexico's "enlightened" foreign policies have been neither as "enlightened" nor as "foreign" as the political myths would have us believe. Mexico's foreign policies have largely been formulated to meet domestic political needs and to increase domestic political support for the system--a system increasingly in crisis.[2] At the same time, Mexico has legitimate foreign policy interests in the region which seem to conflict with U.S. goals for the area. As the U.S. reformulates its Central American policies in light of changes in political and military events, Mexico's policies will become more important to the United States. And as Mexico's economic crisis worsens, pressure will intensify for the government to re-evaluate its policies in the region. With limited economic capabilities, it will be more difficult for Mexico to exercise a leadership role in the region.

THE CONTRADICTIONS

1. The Mexican government is revolutionary abroad, but increasingly conservative at home.

This has become an almost commonplace assertion in studies of Mexican foreign policy (e.g. Hanratty, 1982; Williams, 1981). While the government openly (albeit symbolically) supports revolutionary movements in El Salvador and extends substantial financial support to the revolutionary Sandinista government in Nicaragua, efforts to change the Mexican political system are carefully and sometimes brutally smashed. The same month that López Portillo presented Mexico's much-heralded peace plan for Central America (February 1982), his government effectively crushed independent labor movements of school teachers, telephone workers, and workers in the Ruta 100 bus company. De la Madrid has continued in the same tradition, forcefully discouraging challenges to official labor unions while talking of the need for revolutionary change in Central America. While conditions in the countryside remain poor, agrarian reform through redistribution of land has ended. Redistributive social measures are largely palliative and reforms to open up a political system based on PRI's octopus-like manipulative domination are not taken seriously by an increasingly cynical population. In short, the Mexican revolution survives almost exclusively on a rhetorical level and cynism is the dominant political attitude. Economic and political conditions portend a further drift toward conservatism in the future. Yet Mexican support for revolutionary movements in Central America which increased substantially under López Portillo continues under de la Madrid's regime.

2. The image of Central America as Mexico's "natural" area of influence obscures the fact that for over a century, Mexico has virtually ignored the region and that even today Mexico has much less of an economic stake in the region than it did in the 1940s.

A brief history of relations illustrates this point. Mexico achieved its independence in 1821, and for a short eleven-month period, was the dominant power within an empire which included the Central American nations. Once the Central American republics broke away from Mexico, Mexico's Central American policies were largely limited to defining its southern border with Guatemala. Indeed Mexico paid more attention to threats from its southern border than to challenges from the north (erroneously so, as events in the mid-1800s proved). Mexican diplomatic relations with Guatemala in particular show a surprising replication of Mexican-U.S. relations in the nineteenth century. While Mexico refused to acknowledge Texas independence in the 1830s, arguing that the needs of the nation as a whole overrode the will of the inhabitants of one particular area, Mexico acquired the Soconusco region--long disputed with Guatemala--by arguing that the region's residents had the right to make the ultimate decision. Mexico intervened in Guatemalan politics on several occasions though such actions never reached the degree of U.S. intervention in Mexico. Letters from the Mexican ambassador to Guatemala reveal a paternalistic attitude toward Guatemalan politics--a paternalism also evident in U.S. attitudes toward Mexico. However, this seeming restraint was due as much to lack of resources as to lack of desire to intervene.[3]

During the reign of Porfirio Díaz (1876-1910), Mexico's interest shifted dramatically toward the U.S. Relatively little attention was paid to Central America and Mexico's political, economic, and cultural life came to be dominated by the U.S. As the U.S. presence in the Central American region increased, as evidenced by repeated military incursions, Mexico occasionally challenged U.S. dominance in the region by trying to assert its independent leadership. But these efforts were limited due to Mexico's economic dependence on the U.S. Thus under Mexican president Calles, the Mexican government extended asylum to Sandino, the Nicaraguan revolutionary, although (in accord with U.S. wishes), it ensured that he did not establish a base of operations in Mexico. For the most part, however, Mexico paid little attention to Central America and indeed, until 1966, no Mexican president had ever even visited a Central American nation.

Until the mid-twentieth century, economic ties between Mexico and Central America were minimal. However during World War II, trade increased due to U.S. preoccupation with the war. Sixteen percent of Mexico's trade was with Central America. By 1950, U.S. dominance had been resurrected and Mexico's commercial ties with Central America declined (from $9.7 million in 1946 to $8 million in 1950) (Warner, n.d.). In the mid-1960s Mexican president Díaz Ordaz saw the possibility of increasing Mexican exports to the region and his economic hard-sell was accompanied by diplomatic overtures. Presidential visits were exchanged, trade agreements were signed, Mexican credits were extended to encourage Central American purchases of Mexican goods, and Mexican investors turned slowly, haltingly, to Central America. Under Luis Echeverría, the trend of signing economic agreements with Central America continued. But in spite of the rhetoric about Mexican economic interests in Central America, Mexico's trade with the region amounted to only one percent of its total trade in 1980. Although the argument is occasionally made that while this was a relatively unimportant percentage for Mexico, it was very important to Central America, the figures simply do not bear this out. Mexico's trade with Central America ranges from less than one percent of El Salvador's trade to a high of three percent for Guatemala's total trade.[4] Tourism and investment figures from Central America make up a similarly low percentage of Mexico's total. And with the current political instability in Central America and the economic crisis in Mexico, Mexican investment in and trade with Central America are not likely to increase in the near future.

During the 1960s and 1970s, Mexico sought to increase its economic ties with Central America, but its political relations in the region remained low-key. Mexico's traditional adherence to nonintervention inhibited Mexican leaders from criticizing the Mexican dictatorships while its progressive image made Mexican leaders cautious about aligning too closely with Central American governments. President Luis Echeverría (1970-1976) clearly sought an activisit leadership position for Mexico in world affairs, but his efforts were concentrated on the global level and Central America did not play a central role in his foreign policy strategy.

In this context, and despite Mexican efforts to stress Mexico's "historic" ties with the region, the talk of Mexico's "natural" interests in Central America rings a bit hollow. While the Mexican government is aware of the strategic importance of Central America, given the region's geographical proximity, its foreign policy orientations have been overwhelmingly involved with the U.S. Within Latin America, Mexico's ties have been more with the large South American powers than with the Central American republics (as evidenced, for example, by its membership in Latin America integration schemes, and Echeverria's initiatives in creating the Latin American Economic System, SELA). López Portillo's dramatic entry into Central American affairs, particularly the break in relations with the Somoza government in May 1979 and the August 1981 joint declaration with France in support of the Salvadoran revolutionaries, violated Mexico's cherished principles of nonintervention. The Mexican government explained that neither of these actions was interventionist and yet both marked a Mexican judgment about the unacceptability of particular Central American regimes--judgments the Mexican government was unwilling to make earlier (at least in public). Earlier repressive governments in Central America did not provoke Mexico's suspensions of diplomatic relations or efforts to encourage opposition forces. Mexico's Estrada doctrine, for example, which mandated automatic recognition of other governments, underscored Mexico's conviction that diplomatic relations should not be dependent on ideological compatability. By breaking relations with Nicaragua, Mexico's Central American policies under Lopez Portillo did not represent continuity with Mexico's past relations with the region.[5] The myth was that Mexico was continuing a long-standing foreign policy tradition. The interesting point is that the Mexican government felt compelled to present its policies in such a fashion. De la Madrid is developing his policies toward Central America within the same myth of Mexico's historical tradition, while trying to carve out his own unique leadership role in the region.

3. Mexico's symbolic support for the revolutionary forces in El Salvador stands in sharp contrast to its lack of support for revolutionary movements in Guatemala.

The headquarters of the FMLN/FDR (Frente Farabundo Martí para la Liberación Nacional/Frente Democrático Revolucionario) are in Mexico City and the Mexican government has provided both political asylum and material support for some representatives of Salvadoran revolutionary groups. Furthermore, Mexico has championed the cause of the revolutionary movements at considerable cost to itself. The negative reaction of other Latin American nations to the Franco-Mexican initiative, continual conflicts with the U.S. over these policies, and the risk of losing status should Mexican peace efforts fail are some of the costs of Mexico's support for revolutionary movements in El Salvador.

Although Guatemala's government is undeniably repressive and the level of violence there has reached crisis proportions, the Mexican government has done little to encourage revolutionary activity. In fact, the government has gone to great lengths to stress the friendly relations between the two governments. Even before taking office Miguel de la Madrid stated "I express my firm conviction that the friendship and cooperation with our sister republic of Guatemala should be increased as corresponds to the political and affective desires of our people. We will not permit circumstantial differences that occasionally arise in the relations between two neighboring countries, as between members of a family, to affect the solid friendship of Guatemala and Mexico" (Excelsior, January 8, 1982:2). Indeed, there have been joint military maneuvers and secret meetings between military leaders of the two countries. Mexico's support for revolutionary movements is decidedly selective. Even when Mexico's border was repeatedly violated by Guatemalan troops pursuing (presumed) guerrilla forces, the Mexican government put off a confrontation with the Guatemalan government as long as possible. Why El Salvador and not Guatemala or Honduras? Clearly there are other factors which are more important to Mexico's foreign policy makers than revolutionary solidarity. As will be discussed below, the existence of a common border is a major factor determining relations between the two countries.

4. While Mexico protests the treatment of its undocumented workers in the U.S. and newspapers dwell on the human rights abuses of these workers, the Mexican government has expelled thousands of illegal Central American migrants from its territory.

Mexico has long prided itself on its tradition of offering asylum to refugees from political repression, but this asylum--like support for revolutionary movements--has been selectively offered. South American intellectuals are more welcome in Mexico than Guatemalan peasants fleeing the random and systematic violence in their country. The specter of hundreds of thousands of Central American refugees flooding into Mexico where unemployment already reached 30 percent is a frightening one to Mexican politicians. In fact, Mexican receptivity to political exiles has never been as warm and open as the Mexican ideal has implied. In a summary of editorials of the nation's principal newspapers, one study noted only one editorial favorable to the influx of South American exiles in 1975. These refugees, primarily Chilean and Argentine professionals, were viewed as competitors to middle-class Mexicans (Marquez, 1977).

Mexico may indeed have legitimate reasons for excluding, even expelling the Guatemalan refugees that are flooding into the already-troubled states of Chiapas and Tabasco. While Mexican immigrants to the U.S. find jobs and many return to Mexico after acquiring funds, the Mexican economy is not capable of absorbing the hundreds of thousands of Central Americans fleeing the political violence and economic hardship of their countries. Nonetheless, there is an apparent contradiction between Mexico's policies toward Guatemalan immigrants and its protests of U.S. policies limiting Mexican workers from freely immigrating to the U.S. There is also a contradiction between condemning the violence of the Salvadoran government while refusing to admit (legally) the thousands of victims of that violence. In fact, Mexico deports between 600 and 1000 illegal Central American immigrants weekly (del Muro et al., Johnson and Williams, 1981:8).

5. Finally, there is the contradiction between the traditional bedrock of Mexico's foreign policy--nonintervention--and what can only be described as its open and direct (albeit well-intentioned) intervention in Central America.

Mexico's suspension of relations with Somoza in May 1979 was justified as an exceptional case of intolerable brutality. Yet just two years later, Mexico had clearly chosen sides in the Salvadoran conflict through its insistence that the revolutionary groups be included in direct negotiations and its frequent condemnations of the government's repression. The López Portillo regime was obviously stung by the condemnation by nine Latin American governments of its joint declaration with France supporting Salvadoran revolutionary groups. The Mexican government responded by describing its policies as noninterventionist in that Mexico still maintained relations with the Salvadoran government and did not recognize any of the parties as "belligerents." Yet Mexico's verbal support for the revolutionaries is countered by the fact that through the Acuerdo de San José, Mexico is selling oil to El Salvador on terms that effectively amount to a $73,000 per day subsidy of the Salvadoran government (LARR, November 20, 1980). Foreign Minister Castañeda hotly rejected suggestions that Mexico reduce its oil sales to El Salvador, saying that would be intervention. The July 1983 decision by Venezuela and Mexico to renew the Acuerdo de San José ensures that this contradiction will continue.[5]

The question of what constitutes intervention becomes increasingly difficult as Mexico moves into a more activist role in Central America. Intervention in the sense of trying to influence political decisions within another country is, of course, a matter of degree. Nonintervention is only possible when a government adopts low-key, passive foreign policies. Once governments become active and assertive in their policies--as Mexico has been doing for the past decade--then nonintervention becomes increasingly difficult. Clearly Mexico is intervening in Central America (indeed not to intervene and to continue business as usual constitutes support for repressive regimes). Although its policies are always couched in terms of a continuity with Mexico's foreign policy independence of the past, the lines between Mexico's traditional noninterventionism and its new activism are becoming increasingly unclear in Central America.

UNDERSTANDING THE CONTRADICTIONS

The contradictions in Mexico's Central American policies can be understood in terms of: (1) the conflicting demands on foreign policy makers, (2) the crisis of the Mexican system, (3) the decreasing ability of leaders to use effectively revolutionary rhetoric in legitimizing the system, and (4) the tensions engendered by the nation's economic dependency on the United States.

The Mexican foreign policy machinery has been under both internal and external pressure to change its policies toward Central America. The most obvious and most sensitive pressures have come from the U.S. government to follow its lead in the region. U.S. officials have pressured the Mexican government to moderate its policies. In the midst of Mexico's August 1982 financial crisis when Mexican officials were involved in negotiating a mammoth loan package from international bankers, Latin America

Weekly Reports reported that "[a] recently leaked State Department position paper recommended letting Mexico sweat a little to secure greater amenability to U.S. policy aims in the region" (August 20, 1982:10). Furthermore, Mexican intellectuals and journalists have been quick to see U.S. pressure regarding Central America in a variety of seemingly unrelated U.S. actions. The Reagan decision to crack down on undocumented workers in May 1982, for example, was regarded by many Mexicans as further pressure on Mexico to change its policies in Central America. The U.S.-Mexico-Central America triangle is fraught with tension. Mexico and the U.S. are simply too important to one another to risk a break in relations over Central America (Bagley, 1981:386). Even though their Central American policies appear diametrically opposed to one another, Mexico and the U.S. treat each other with caution and subtlety. The stakes are too high for either nation to push for confrontation, though this confrontation tactic has higher political payoffs for Mexico than for the U.S.

Domestically, the Mexican government has been under continual pressure from both leftist opposition groups pushing the government to adopt more revolutionary policies and from the conservative business coalition, which shares Washington's view of a communist conspiracy in Central America, and has pressured the government to be more moderate in its policies. Finally, there is always pressure from an increasingly cynical, dissatisfied population for the government to do something and show that it is not simply serving the status quo interests of the conservative and corrupt powers that be. This pressure is manifest in the national press. Right-wing publications such as Impacto subscribe to the domino theory of Central America while Proceso and Unomásuno have been critical of the government's economic policies with editorials calling for more open support for the revolutionaries and more open admissions policies toward the refugees.

Within the government there have been conflicting pressures on foreign policy-making. Foreign policy making has traditionally been the exclusive domain of the president and there were strong personal political reasons for López Portillo's open sympathy with (at least some of) the revolutionary movements in Central America. Such sympathy responded to his desire to be remembered as a statesman, to distract attention away from Miguel de la Madrid's campaign, and to remove himself from the negative consequences of the almost catastrophic economic situation. While Echeverría sought a place in history for his Third World activism, López Portillo sought the same objective through his innovative Central American policies. De la Madrid, in turn, has tried to develop regional foreign policies which set him apart from Lopez Portillo's initiatives while building on the tradition of Mexican support for progressive social change in the region. But all Mexican presidents face pressures from within the government which make foreign policy making still more difficult.

Bureaucratic and political pressures on López Portillo come from the Partido Revolucionario Institucionalizado (PRI), from opposition parties, and from members of the government itself. Sectors of the PRI, according to Excelsior columnist Buendía, reportedly were dismayed by the Franco-Mexican initiative and extended only lukewarm support to López Portillo's Central American policies (LAWR, January 22, 1982:1, 2). The growing strength of the conservative opposition party, the Partido de Acción Nacional (PAN), in municipal elections has placed pressure on de la Madrid to adopt more conservative policies. The Secretariat of Gobernación, charged with handling refugee cases, is riddled with policy contradictions and factional splits. While the leadership of Gobernación has steadfastly maintained that "not one single exile--whether or not his papers are in order--will be sent out of Mexico" (Buendía, 1982), other officials with different interpretations effectively sabotage those principles by expelling refugees left and right. The Secretariat of Foreign Relations is also more disposed to grant political asylum than is Gobernación. Current estimates are that as many as 250,000 Central American refugees are currently in Mexico.[6] Most of the refugees are Guatemalan campesinos fleeing the political violence at home and looking for jobs in Mexico. While the Guatemalan refugees are concentrated in rural areas along the border, Salvadoran refugees have migrated to urban areas where they generally live without legal recognition. There are very few Nicaraguan exiles in Mexico; given Mexican support for the Sandinista regime, Nicaraguan dissidents generally prefer to seek sanctuary elsewhere. Their presence (often illegal) aggravates existing social tensions by putting still more pressure on the government to provide jobs and services--jobs and services the government is hard-pressed to provide for Mexicans.

While de la Madrid maintains firm control over foreign policy formation, there are signs that the Mexican Senate is becoming more concerned with foreign policy issues. As a result of López Portillo's political opening, there are now some progressive senators in office who are exercising more of a voice in foreign policy matters, particularly with refugee issues. Furthermore, the presence of so many refugees in the southern states of Chiapas and Tabasco has led to more social discontent there and consequently to a more prominent role for the military.

The military is becoming ever more visible in Mexican politics, particularly in the southern states. There are increasingly frequent charges of Guatemalan military incursions into Mexican territory (presumably in pursuit of Guatemalan guerrilla forces)--resulting in several formal Mexican protests to the Guatemalan government. Troop movements have increased in southern Mexico. In December 1980 the Mexican army carried out large-scale maneuvers in Chiapas involving 40,000 men (out of an army of 95,000). Furthermore, the new governor of Chiapas, Absalán Castellanos Dominguez, is a former military general. The Central American revolutions have brought a sense of renewed mission to the military and a realization of the importance of putting down guerrilla movements in the Mexican countryside. In 1980 alone, the combined budget of the army and air force increased by 85 percent. Although this increase was unusually high and, in comparison with other Latin American countries, Mexican military expenditures remain relatively low, Mexico's military budget is growing, and the military is becoming more active in civic action operations. Thus, the military was visible in the cleanup and rescue operations following the eruption of the Chichonal volcano. While rumors of a military coup in Mexico were largely unfounded, under López Portillo the military came to exercise an increasingly important role in foreign policy formation. The military has continued its activist role under de la Madrid.

Preoccupation with the political and economic fallout of the 1982 economic crisis have occupied center stage during the first years of the de la Madrid administration. The tasks of implementing unpopular austerity measures, of holding the line on wage demands, and of securing necessary international agreements for the economy have demanded considerable political acumen and skill from the de la Madrid team. Contradictory pressures on and within the Mexican government added to the systemic crises in creating Mexico's contradictory Central American foreign policies.

THE CRISIS OF THE MEXICAN SYSTEM

For years, political scientists (non-Mexican observers at least) have pre-dicted the upcoming failure of the Mexican political system (e.g. Hellman, 1978; Johnson, 1978; Cockroft and Gandy, 1981). In spite of these dire pre-dictions, however, the Mexican state has managed to survive. Today (as in 1976), the economic chaos triggered by unexpectedly sharp devaluations, austerity measures, and public lack of confidence in political institutions and leaders all lead to further pessimism about the ability of the Mexican system to survive in its present form. However, unlike the situation of 1976, there will be no oil saviour this time to restore order and to inspire hope in the system. The oil bonanza was able to provide a million new jobs a year for the hordes of unemployed and to provide a rising standard of living for the middle classes. Ominously, it also raised public expectations about what government can and should do for the people. With declining oil prices, governmental revenues have fallen dramatically and the government is unable to meet those expectations. Inflation was estimated at 78 percent for 1983 while 60 per-cent of Mexico's population was estimated to be unemployed and under-employed (LAWR, December 9, 1983:8). Cuts in public expenditures will have far-reaching effects. No new jobs are expected to be created in the public sector and major construction projects (including the 52-story Pemex headquarters building) have been halted in mid-stream. According to the Consejo Coordinator Empresarial, at least 50 percent of all companies will have to sack at least part of their work force in 1983 (LARR, May 6, 1983: 7-8).

With the government seriously overextended and with the international oil glut limiting governmental revenues, it seems clear that oil cannot save Mexico this time. In fact, the raised expectations, coupled with the poorly executed devaluation, have made the fall even harder and the crisis even more acute. The mounting pressures on the capital city (growing at a rate of 1800 migrants per day), the rapid population growth (2.9 percent), the spiral-ling public and private debt (estimated at $85 billion in 1983), and above all, the growing alienation of ever more Mexicans from the political system have created pressures on government which can only be described as critical. While the economic crisis of the Mexican system has been exacerbated by recent events, there are long-term structural causes of the crisis. Food pro-duction simply has not kept up with the population increases and Mexico, a corn-producing nation, now imports tortillas. In 1979, Mexico had a $750 million balance of trade surplus for agricultural products, but by 1981 it imported some $800 million more agricultural goods than it exported. The rural-urban disparity in living conditions continues to stimulate migration to the cities and to the U.S.

The oil money increased the degree of corruption within the govern-ment and correspondingly popular cynicism about intentions of government officials. At the same time, López Portillo's 1977 political reform made it easier for opposition parties to organize and campaign for office. Seven parties fielded candidates in the 1982 presidential elections and while there was little doubt that PRI candidate Miguel de la Madrid would win, the increased competition put still more pressure on government. The Mexican system has been in crisis before, but most long-time observers of the system agree that confidence in government is lower now than at any time in recent years. While Echeverría was very unpopular in the business community, he was, as Mexicans today frequently point out, a strong leader. López Portillo's mea culpas and talk of a "devalued president" greatly increased popular perceptions of a political crisis. While de la Madrid has not faced the vociferous personal attacks suffered by López Portillo, there is still a sense of uncertainty about the system as a whole. As Latin America Weekly Reports states, it "is wrong to think that the crisis has been overcome. Indeed for most Mexicans it is only beginning. Unemployment has yet to rise dramatically and real wages have yet to fall sharply" (May 6, 1983:7-8). The crisis of the Mexican system has made it more imperative that revolutionary elements be coopted, that further economic pressures (such as those presented by Guatemalan refugees) be avoided, that the military be kept occupied and satisfied, and that popular attention be directed to governmental successes abroad.

THE REVOLUTIONARY IMPERATIVE

Traditionally, the Mexican government has been able to compensate for its fundamentally conservative policies at home through support of progressive governments abroad. There is substantial popular sympathy for revolutionary movements in Central America given Mexico's own revolutionary heritage and its own isolation following that revolution. Mexico's tradition of nonintervention--developed largely in reaction to centuries of U.S. intervention in its affairs--and its policies toward Cuba set it apart from other Latin American nations. Mexico, the only Latin American nation to maintain relations with Cuba from 1964 to 1970, used these policies to moderate leftist opposition at home. Mexico's leftist foreign policies are frequently explained in terms of the regime's need to coopt leftist opposition and this seems to play a large role in Mexico's policies toward Central America as well. In comparison with the Nicaraguan and Salvadoran revolutions, Mexico finds its own revolutionary credentials looking a bit insipid. Association with the more dynamic Central American revolutionary groups clearly adds to Mexico's prestige in progressive circles.

The flattering words of Nicaraguan and Cuban leaders are used to counteract domestic criticism. Fidel Castro in April 1982 referred to the Mexican revolution as the "father of all Latin American revolutionary movements." A Sandinista leader visiting Mexico in 1981 recently was asked to respond to the charge that Mexico was the perfect dictatorship (a characterization by Mario Vargas Llosa carried on the front pages of Mexico's newspapers). "Yes, Mexico is the perfect dictatorship," he responded gallantly, "because it is a dictatorship of the majority and the people are happy." [7] Clearly these statements are soothing balm to the Mexican government's efforts to cover up the gaping inequalities and the mass discontent with the Mexican political system. The Nicaraguan and Cuban leaders also find it useful to shore up Mexico's revolutionary credentials for domestic consumption as well. Mexico's diplomatic support is much more acceptable and more easily explained when it is seen as coming from a fellow revolutionary government rather than from the conservative society it has become.

Revolutionary politics abroad then legitimize the government's revolutionary heritage and give Mexico a humanitarian, progressive, statesmanlike image which inspires in Mexicans a pride in their government not easily found in other sectors. Furthermore, since Mexico's Central American policies seem to conflict with those of the United States, the government can use them to demonstrate its independence from its northern neighbor--always a popular theme in Mexico.

Mexico fears direct U.S. intervention in Central America which would further destabilize the regime and which would increase Mexico's geopolitical weakness. Although governmental leaders dismiss domino theories of Central America--rightly noting that Mexico is very different from other Central American nations--they are also aware of the direct threat posed to their regime by revolutionary upheaval.[8] With the crisis in the Mexican political system and the abysmal economic forecasts, particularly the diminished job-creation possibilities, the likelihood of revolutionary violence and increased governmental repression is not too far-fetched.

Thus, the crisis of the Mexican system makes it imperative that the government pursue foreign policies that reduce pressure on the system and that at the same time emphasize the government's revolutionary heritage. These pose contradictions: the flow of Central American refugees must be limited and Central America must be stabilized. For Mexico, this means preventing U.S. direct intervention, pragmatically supporting those revolutionary movements (as in Nicaragua and El Salvador) which are going to succeed and discouraging those where the risk of revolution is too threatening to Mexico's borders (as in Guatemala). At the same time, the Mexican government needs to encourage Central American revolutions to satisfy leftist opponents at home. It is difficult to achieve such a balance, and especially so when the final explanatory component is added: the tensions of dependency.

THE TENSIONS OF DEPENDENCY

As a nation economically dependent on the United States to an embarrassingly high degree, Mexican presidents have always sought a degree of independence and the appearance of independence through their foreign policies. Although many hoped that Mexico's new-found oil wealth would increase its independence, it seems merely to have produced a different form of dependence. The need for sophisticated oil technologies and access to an astronomical amount of credit together with reliance on the U.S. as oil market in times of world surplus have meant that Mexico continues to be economically dependent on the U.S. And Mexico's chances for reducing that economic dependency on the U.S. in the future are limited. Efforts to diversify its oil exports (now accounting for 78 percent of Mexico's total exports) have been only moderately successful and Mexico's manufacturing and tourism industries continue to depend heavily on the U.S. The severe financial straits in which Mexico finds itself increases the nation's reliance on international monetary institutions and makes it even harder to reduce its dependence on the U.S. The astronomical debt demonstrates the limits of Mexican independence. Given the fact that the costs of reducing Mexican economic dependence on the U.S. are so high, it is more politically expedient for Mexican administrations to demonstrate their political independence of Washington. And when the government pursues policies which are obviously opposed by Washington, opposition forces publicly unite behind the president in his defiance of the U.S. After the Franco-Mexican declaration, for example, newspapers were filled with advertisements proclaiming allegiance to the Mexican president.

The myth of foreign policy independence is a strong legitimizer of the Mexican government and has been skillfully used in times of domestic difficulties. López Portillo's heralded Central American peace initiative was announced in Managua on February 21, 1982, only four days after the first devaluation of the Mexican peso. With the devaluation touching off an avalanche of discontent, speculation, and rumors, the peace plan enabled the government to present itself in a more positive light. Instead of the uncertain, disorganized, out-of-control entity it appeared to be with the unanticipated fallout from the devaluation, the Central American initiatives presented a statesman-like government which was developing plans and not merely reacting to serious problems. But this strategy of using foreign policy issues to overcome discontent with domestic economic crises seemed to run out of steam under López Portillo. De la Madrid has adopted much more low-key foreign policies and has been much more reactive in his policies toward Latin America than his predecessor. Indeed, his regional peace-making efforts through the Contadora Group serve to "share the risk" and to defuse possible criticism at home and abroad. As popular cynicism continues to increase and as the dimensions of the economic crisis become ever more grave, it is going to take more than foreign policy issues to produce a domestic consensus in support of the government.

If Mexico is in an ambiguous position with respect to its Central American-U.S. policies, it is also in a difficult role with respect to the Third World. Mexico sees itself as a Third World leader and, increasingly, as a member of a select group of "important" Third World nations which can exert significant influence on global events (Pellicer, 1980). But Mexico's Third World credentials are not unquestioned. Mexico's refusal to join OPEC, its traditional close relationship with the U.S. and (until recently) its passive foreign policy have not convinced everyone that Mexico's Third World priorities are high. Mexico needs the Third World--economically as a potential market for its exports and more importantly as a political tool to combat continued dependence on the U.S. Consequently, Mexico is courting the Third World. The Cancún summit (Fall 1981) displayed López Portillo's statesmanship to the world although it garnered little public support for his leftist opposition at home. The March 1983 decision to follow OPEC's pricing policies bolstered Mexico's Third World image. But it is primarily Mexico's Central American policies which were designed to show the world, and especially the Third World, that Mexico is indeed a progressive, if not revolutionary government and one which is capable and willing to exercise independent leadership in defiance of U.S. preferences in the region. While there will be strong pressures on de la Madrid to continue his predecessor's symbolic support for Central American revolutionary movements, the nation's diminished economic capabilities will make Mexican influence in the region more difficult. Major loans and grants are harder to justify in times of domestic economic recession than in times of oil-fired prosperity.

Mexico and the U.S. share a set of preferred outcomes for the region (Bagley, 1980; George, 1981). They both want stable, reformist governments which will not provide havens for exporting revolution to Mexico or to other Latin American nations. Both governments recognize the threats that Latin American revolutions pose to Mexico's southern provinces. Although the U.S. expresses its fears for Mexico's safety more openly, the Mexican government is taking both domestic and foreign policy actions toward the same goal. Increased military activity and increased governmental spending in the south of the country are indications of Mexico's concern, as are Mexican policies supporting the Guatemalan government. For both governments, the need for Mexico's political and economic stability is the single most important determinant of their Central American policies.

Mexico has been much more pragmatic than the U.S. in its policies

toward the revolutionary states of the region. Believing that in both Nicaragua and El Salvador (though not in Guatemala) revolution is inevitable, the
Mexican government has tried to influence--to moderate--the nature of the
revolutionary governments which emerge. Mexican pressure, much more
subtly and skillfully applied than U.S. pressure, on Nicaragua to moderate
radical positions is clearly in U.S. interests. The activities of the Contadora
Group throughout 1983 stand as an example of moderation and reliance on
negotiation by Mexico which contrasts with Washington's militaristic policies.
Central America is of strategic importance to both the United States and
Mexico although the way in which those strategic interests are defined varies
in accord with the ideologies of the current governments and the different
political traditions of the two countries.

The Acuerdo de San José brings together two contending regional
powers (Mexico and Venezuela) who have traditionally pursued very different
Central American policies. Through this agreement, effectively subsidized
oil is made available to Central American and Caribbean nations which helps
relieve some of the awesome economic pressures on Central American
governments. This subsidy indirectly helps maintain the status quo and also
partially relieves the U.S. of the need to extend increased economic aid to
the region. Williams estimates that the Acuerdo de San José means financial
aid to Latin American and Caribbean nations of $300 million per year with
70 percent of the benefits going to conservative governments in the region
(Costa Rica, Dominican Republic, El Salvador, Guatemala, Haiti, Honduras,
and Jamaica) (1982:159). Mexican policies toward the nonrevolutionary
governments of the region--Costa Rica, Honduras, and Guatemala--are
clearly directly congruent with U.S. interests. Most important, and most
directly, the central goal of both Mexico's domestic and foreign policies--to
prevent social discontent from boiling over at home--is basic to U.S. national
interests.

The policies of both the U.S. and Mexico toward Central America are
undergoing considerable change. The initial militancy of Alexander Haig's
tenure as Secretary of State was followed by lower-key U.S. policies. U.S.
foreign policy makers seemed diverted by foreign policy issues elsewhere,
particularly the Middle East and issues of defense and arms control vis-à-vis
the USSR. However, the failure of elections to eliminate human rights violations in the region together with a deteriorating military situation in El
Salvador and a regionalization of the conflict led the U.S. to increase the
level of its military aid and advisors to El Salvador and Honduras. U.S. pressure on Costa Rica has also increased. The Reagan administration is well
aware that opposition to more-militant U.S. actions in the region could
quickly develop--opposition which might damage the party's fortunes in the
1984 elections. Reagan's appointment of a bipartisan commission to rally
support behind his policies reflects that domestic political pressure.

De la Madrid faces a different set of pressures. Mexico's economic
woes make it increasingly difficult to exercise economic leverage in Central
America. The generous aid packages to Nicaragua have diminished. Yet
domestic economic problems also increase pressure on the Mexican president
to find dramatic issues for diverting public attention from those woes by
emphasizing Mexico's revolutionary heritage and for underscoring Mexican
independence from the U.S. De la Madrid undoubtedly wants to carve out his
own foreign policy approach and not merely follow in López Portillo's foot-
steps. He needs to dramatize his differences from López Portillo in foreign
(as well as domestic) policy while at the same time responding to many of

the same pressures that all Mexican presidents must face.

Central America, particularly Guatemala, will be one of the most difficult foreign policy challenges facing de la Madrid throughout his term of office. The stakes are very high and unlike Mexico-U.S. relations, Mexico's policies toward Central America can be fundamentally re-directed by a new administration. The contradictions in Mexico's policies toward Central America reflect those conflicting national interests. While Mexico's policies toward the region are certainly much more progressive and realistic than those of the United States and of other Latin American nations, they fall short of the myth of Mexico's revolutionary, independent policies in the region. That myth is designed primarily for domestic consumption and as the economic-political crisis in Mexico deepens--as it surely will--even more contradictions between the myth and the reality will become apparent.

NOTES

1. Research for this study was conducted while the author was a Fulbright professor at UNAM (Universidad Nacional Autónoma de México) in Mexico City, 1981-1982. Thanks are extended to Irene Zea, Marco Aurelio Guzmán, and Judith Matloff for their comments on earlier versions of this manuscript.

2. Many authors have stressed this point including Olga Pellicer de Brody, 1980, 1981; Mario Ojeda Gómez, 1974, 1970; Grabendorff, 1978; Bagley, 1981; Hanratty, 1982.

3. Personal interview, Irene Zea, Colegiode Mexico, 1982.

4. Trade data were compiled by the author from International Monetary Fund, 1960, 1970, 1980.

5. This interpretation conflicts with that of many well-known scholars such as Olga Pellicer (1980, 1981) and Mario Ojeda (1974, 1976) who see Mexico's Central American policies as following the Mexican tradition of nonintervention. Mexico has traditionally been isolated in Latin America, they argue, citing the cases of Mexican recognition of Cuba through the 1960s, opposition to U.S. intervention in Guatemala, and opposition to the Dominican Republic invasion in 1965. In 1954, for example, Mexico opposed U.S.-instigated efforts in the OAS to condemn Guatemala, arguing that to do so was to intervene in Guatemala's internal affairs. But there is a fundamental difference between these cases and the current Mexican posture. While Mexico argued that it could not break relations with Cuba because to do so would be interventionist in that it would imply a Mexican judgment about internal Cuban affairs, in 1979 Mexico was unable to continue business as usual with Nicaragua under Somoza. And in 1981, Mexico made an official statement about its view of Salvadoran internal politics in calling for the inclusion of revolutionary groups in the process. When Alexander Haig made a statement that he thought de la Madrid was the best candidate for the Mexican presidency, the newspapers were full of Mexican officials chastizing him for his intervention in the Mexican political process. Yet Mexican officials continued to condemn the Salvadoran junta.

6. Accurate estimates of the number of refugees are notoriously difficult to obtain. These figures are based on the assessments of the United Nations High Commissioner for Refugees in Mexico City as well as the estimates of governmental and nongovernmental organizations working directly with the refugees.

7. Radio news programs, Mexico City, April 1982.
8. Personal interviews, Mexico City, 1982-1983.

13
Nicaragua's Foreign Relations: The Struggle for Survival

Max Azicri

INTRODUCTION

The new Nicaragua built since July 19, 1979, is the product of both profound domestic political and socioeconomic changes and of equally transformed international relations. The exercise of revolutionary power by the Sandinista National Liberation Front (FSLN)--in conjunction with a coalition of labor, social, political, and economic sectors which together form the Council of State (parliament)--made it possible for the government to develop comprehensive social engineering policies which have transformed the Nicaraguan polity. To complement these domestic changes, a new regional, hemispheric, and even world outlook in foreign policy was needed. The reasons for a new foreign policy direction were compelling. From the outset, the Sandinista leader understood that international isolation is an inherent danger of revolutionary politics which they wanted to avoid. The government eagerly sought outside support and was rewarded by technical assistance, credits, trade agreement proposals, military equipment, and political support from countries and organizations representing different political orientations.

In addition to sensitive national security concerns, the difficult economic and financial conditions inherited from the Somoza regime and the destruction of the country's infrastructure that took place during the war of liberation made it apparent that the revolution's foreign policy would play a critical role for the survival of the regime, especially since a hostile and aggressive U.S. administration came to office in 1981. President Reagan's obsessive notion that the traditional United States' hegemonic control over the region had to be re-established was translated by the end of his first year in office into a $19 million covert operation campaign aimed at destabilizing the Sandinista revolution.[1] Moreover, the remaining $15 million of the $75 million loan granted under President Carter--primarily for the private sector-- was frozen just a few days after Reagan's inauguration.

Inasmuch as the revolution placed the country at center-stage in the world's political arena, its international relations have become complex. The scope of diplomatic activity was expanded and Nicaragua became an important member of international organizations, most notably the Nonaligned Movement.[2] Today, Nicaragua is acting and speaking with a newly gained independence and assertiveness developed under the rationale of Sandinista political principles and ideology. The FSLN National Directorate, working as the highest decision-making organ of the revolutionary regime, determines policy guidelines for both domestic and foreign policies. The regime is

particularly concerned with the role model that Nicaragua plays internationally, especially for other developing nations (see Booth, 1982:183-214; Azicri,
1982:364-365; and Walker, 1981:90-102).

According to Sandinista revolutionary thinking, the new foreign policy
is meant as a total break with the past and is intended to obliterate finally
those long years in which Nicaragua acted in a subservient role vis-à-vis
successive United States' administrations. This new diplomatic path has been
undertaken in a calculated and well-planned fashion which in many ways
parallels the domestic change process. The fact that this social engineering
process is happening in the midst of extremely difficult national and international conditions provides an explanation (though not a justification) for
some of the policy failures.[3] Nicaragua's foreign policy is, then, a vital
expression of a renewed national will and thus represents an offensive strategy. It is also a protective shield preventing the regime from losing needed
political and economic support, while providing the military equipment and
assistance needed for national defense (politically, economically, and militarily a defensive strategy). This chapter examines the rationale behind
Nicaragua's policies toward Latin America, and the context in which these
policies are developed. Nicaragua's relationships with Cuba and more recently
with the Contadora Group on both a bilateral and a multilateral level are discussed. Finally, the always sensitive relationship with the United States is also
examined, including its affected strategic interests, client regional regimes,
paramilitary and counter-revolutionary sponsored groups, and diplomatic
initiatives.

BREAKING THE OLD HEGEMONIC MOLD

The cardinal principle of Sandinista revolutionary ideology is its anti-
imperialism. In addition to the bizarre episode of William Walker proclaiming
himself president of Nicaragua and attempting to reinstitute slavery in 1856,
the United States interfered in Nicaragua's internal affairs in other cases
before the end of the century. The long years of U.S. political, military, and
economic intervention in the twentieth century left indelible marks painfully
recorded in the collective memory of a deeply troubled nation. Augusto
Cesar Sandino led an anti-colonialist struggle in Las Segovias from 1927 to
1933 against the country's occupation by U.S. Marines (which followed a
previous U.S. occupation which lasted from 1912 to 1925). Sandino was
assassinated by military officers of the National Guard on February 21, 1934,
acting under orders from General Anastasio Somoza García, who by then was
in charge of the newly organized military force. The Somoza family dynasty
controlled the country for over forty-five years in a symbiotic relationship
with the United States. These facts constitute some of the major ingredients
of the nation's pathos which provide the bedrock upon which a new national
ethos is being created.[4]

Nicaragua's nationalism, as reasserted by the Sandinista regime, is
intimately and definitely based on a collective, deeply felt anti-imperialist
sentiment. This sentiment is heightened by Reagan's anti-Sandinista covert
war policy which unifies the public behind the government in defense of the
nation. Thus, Nicaragua's anti-imperialism is not a passing political fad, but
rather a central component of a new revolutionary identity which engulfs the
nation and defines its emerging political culture. In the words of the first
government program of July 1979 it was decided that:

An independent foreign policy based on nonalignment and the openness of relations with all countries willing to collaborate with our people in a framework of mutual respect and cooperation will be the policy of our government (Nicaragua, JGRN, 1982:16).

From the outset, the government moved quickly to develop the revolution's foreign policy. After what amounted to a joyous welcome in Havana in celebration of the Cuban revolution's July 26 anniversary, only a few days after the Sandinista victory, the Nicaraguan leaders returned to Cuba two months later, this time to attend the Sixth Nonaligned Summit Meeting. According to Commander Daniel Ortega, presently head of the Government of National Reconstruction, by joining the nonaligned countries Nicaragua expressed its principled foreign policy based on solidarity with the struggles of people throughout the Third World against imperialism, colonialism, apartheid, racism, and other forms of oppression. Thus by official actions and pronouncements Nicaragua's foreign policy was cast from the beginning as anti-imperialist, anti-colonialist, committed to nonalignment, and decisively pro-Third World. Altogether it represented a striking departure from traditional Central American internal and external political practices. The contrast between the Sandinistas' and neighboring countries' international relations was sharp and led to confrontational politics.[5]

It was in this ideological context that two bases were developed to serve as the legal foundation of the nation's independent foreign policy: (1) genuine national sovereignty (not only symbolically expressed, but manifested in practical terms exuding political independence), and (2) effective self-determination (a logical corollary from a nation's legal and political independent status). Predictably, the exercise of these rights was translated into political decisions that are still unacceptable by the military and political establishment of most Central American nations which maintain largely pro-Washington positions. From this Sandinista central policy came a national defense and military preparedness program with far-reaching international repercussions (Dickey, 1984:661-662; Motley, 1984:1-4). The U.S. intensified an unprecedented military buildup in Central America. This buildup may have been in direct response to the Sandinista initiative, or may stem from a previously decided anti-Sandinista strategy reinforced by Sandinista actions, or may have represented a response to requests made by conservative regimes in the area who were concerned with Nicaragua's defense activities. Whatever the motivation, the U.S. buildup was most apparent in the quasi-permanent war games and joint military exercises in Honduras. This was possible because of the decisively militaristic, and militantly anti-Nicaraguan posture of the Honduran armed forces commander, Division General Gustavo Alvarez Martinez. It should be noted that U.S. military aid to Honduras, one of the poorest countries in Latin America, increased from $3.98 million in 1980 to $41 million in 1984, with additional security-supporting assistance totaling $36.8 million in 1982 and $48 million in 1983, and $40 million more programmed for 1984.[6]

Twelve different United States military training maneuvers have been held in the Central America-Caribbean area since 1981. The joint U.S.-Honduran Ahuas Tara, or Big Pine I and II, military exercises were held in 1983 with a 19-ship battle fleet stationed off the coast of Nicaragua. Granadero I will include Salvadoran, Guatemalan, and probably Panamanian troops in exercises scheduled for the summer of 1984 involving 6,000 Honduran and 5,000 U.S. troops. Approximately 600 to 800 U.S. troops are to be left behind

in 1984 in a semi-permanent deployment. The trend toward institutionalization of these joint United States-Central American military exercises is
evident in that further joint maneuvers are being programmed for the next
three years, with the possibility that they might be held at least annually for
the next twenty years (New York Times, February 24, 1984:4 and February 29,
1984:23).

Meanwhile, U.S. military support for the Salvadoran government in its
counterinsurgency campaign against the FDR-FMLN forces increased from
$6.7 million in 1980 to $64.8 million in 1984, with $312 million more requested
for 1984. The region as a whole would receive $259 million in additional
military aid in 1984, with $256 million being considered for 1985. The train-
ing and financing of counter-revolutionary groups by the U.S. Central Intelligence Agency, operating from Honduras and Costa Rica against Nicaragua,
continued unabated at a cost to the U.S. taxpayer of $73 million in less than
two years (from March 1982 to the beginning of 1984). Nicaragua has
suffered economic losses in the conflict of more than $200 million as well as
1500 of its citizens kidnapped, wounded or killed. The Costa Rican border
is increasingly militarized as it is from here the counter-revolutionary leader
Eden Pastora and his 2,000 men are launching their attacks against the
Sandinista regime (Boletín Semanal, February 4, 1984:7-9).

In spite of superb diplomatic skills, Minister of Foreign Affairs Miguel
D'Escoto's efforts to ameliorate the conflicts by allaying Honduran fears
proved to be formidable--especially given the Reagan administration's anti-
Nicaraguan, overtly hostile stance. This conflict underlines Nicaragua's
present vulnerability and illustrates a fundamental foreign policy dilemma.
The present political and economic conditions in both the region and in the
world at large raise questions about the viability of the Sandinistas' foreign
policy orientation as timely or even viable; that is, can the country afford--
economically or otherwise--this kind of international relations? On the other
hand, could the revolution afford not to have the foreign policy it has chosen
as its own, understanding that anything else would seriously compromise its
image abroad while raising identity questions at home?

The decision to move toward a diversification of international relations
on the basis of national sovereignty and self-determination proves to be a
more pragmatic approach than implied by ideological statements. Inasmuch
as a revolutionary Nicaragua seeks new friendships and relations the world
over, the Sandinistas' political posture could provide a cost-effective rationale
for pursuing national goals in the international arena. This would include (1)
political relations: with different degrees of diplomatic relations; (2) economic relations: including fostering trade exchanges, international credits,
and technical assistance from both socialist and market economies; and (3)
military relations: including receiving military hardware for self-defense
purposes, as well as basic military training and assistance in the planning and
construction of a national defense infrastructure, without formalizing military alliances with other countries.

NICARAGUA'S NONALIGNED FOREIGN POLICY

In addition to joining the Nonaligned Movement countries, Nicaragua's
foreign policy has been determined within a nonaligned framework which has
included: (1) establishing a voting record at the United Nations expressing
its principled international political posture; (2) acquiring observer status and

participating in the Socialist International, while developing political ties with political parties associated with this strategically significant international political organization; (3) initiating contacts that would broaden the nation's commercial, diplomatic, and financial relations; and (4) renegotiating the international debt inherited from the Somoza regime in more favorable and realistic terms for an economy weakened by the war of liberation, 1978-1979.

Voting at the United Nations

As the contras' (counter-revolutionaries') war gathered momentum after 1982, Managua utilized the United Nations as the most suitable forum for denouncing and seeking other nations' condemnation of such actions which were in violation of international law and the UN charter. Significantly, even after maintaining the country's membership in the Organization of American States (OAS), the Sandinistas carefully avoided this diplomatic forum in those confrontations in which the United States' responsibility supporting the contras' illegal actions came under a condemnatory scrutiny in 1982 and 1983. The main idea behind this voting record was to enforce strictly a policy of nonalignment which included: (1) endorsing Third World issues such as protecting human rights; (2) limiting the arms race; (3) supporting the struggles for decolonization, the movements of national liberation, and Namibia's right to self-determination; (4) endorsing multilateral agreements regulating international trade, i.e., the new international economic order; and (5) condemning the practice of apartheid in South Africa, and any form of political hegemonism in international relations (by any superpower). Moreover, the Sandinistas went on record supporting all countries' rights to self-determination by endorsing the UN's Declaration of the Inadmissibility of Intervention and Interference in the Internal Affairs of the Member States.

In most cases Nicaragua found itself voting with other Third World nations. Sometimes it voted for resolutions supported by the Soviet Union, while disagreeing with others. Nicaragua voted differently from the United States in many cases, but agreed in others. For example, Nicaragua voted in favor of the suspension of nuclear experiments, while the Soviet Union abstained. On the reconstruction of Chad after its devastating war and the installation of United Nations facilities in Nairobi, Nicaragua and the United States both voted favorably, while the Soviet Union voted against those measures. In the case of UN condemnation of the Soviet invasion of Afghanistan, Nicaragua abstained, but made a plea for world peace. By distancing itself on this resolution from most Third World countries, the overwhelming majority of whom voted in favor of the resolution, Nicaragua allegedly rejected the East-West connotation built into the United States-sponsored resolution condemning the Soviet Union for its military occupation of that country.

Nicaragua took the issue of the crisis in Central America to the UN when Junta Coordinator Commander Ortega presented a resolution on October 17, 1981, seeking a political solution to the armed struggle in El Salvador. According to Ortega, the most effective way to reduce tensions in the area would be to allow effective political participation by all the actors involved, including the FDR-FMLN. Although it was not presented before the UN as such, Nicaragua also supported the Mexican-French presidential declaration in 1981 for a negotiated settlement in El Salvador recommending national (by the Salvadoran regime) and international (by the world's nations, particularly the United States) recognition of the political forces grouped under the FDR-FMLN, which were characterized by both heads of state as representative of legitimate political persuasions. On September 27, 1983, Ortega returned to the UN for the third time in four years (having twice denounced the contras' war against his country) and proposed that the General Assembly ". . . consider (now) the Central American question as urgent before the growing danger of a war in the region." He also mentioned Nicaragua's increasing alarm due to ". . . the (war-like) policy being promoted by President Ronald Reagan's administration" (Barricada Internacional, September 26, 1983:6 and October 3, 1983:1; La Nación Internacional, December 29, 1983-January 4, 1984:7).

The Socialist International

As the leading political body in revolutionary Nicaragua, the FSLN's pursuit of an active form of internationalism brought new associations and responsibilities to the revolutionary regime; inspired by the FSLN's observer status in the organization, the Socialist International gave an enthusiastic endorsement to the Sandinistas which reflected its socialist position regarding Central America as a whole. Under the leadership of West Germany's Social Democratic party's Willy Brandt, and with the support of such social democratic parties as France's Socialist party and Venezuela's Democratic Action Party, during the Fifteenth Post-War Congress held in November 1981, the Socialist International stated that: ". . . the victories and achievements of the Nicaraguan revolution reflect the hopes for social change in the whole region" (Black, 1982:176). This broadly based international support for Nicaragua soon faced a serious test from quarters opposed to Sandinista revolutionary politics which exerted pressure against such support from within as well as from outside the Socialist International. Trying to isolate Managua from any Western support, the Reagan administration insisted that there was a contradiction between the politics of social democracy (acceptable to Washington) and what was characterized as a totalitarian state under the Sandinistas (unacceptable to Washington). The relative political advantage derived from this antagonistic position was sharply reduced when the Nicaraguan elections, originally scheduled for 1985, were set for November 4, 1984 (two days before the U.S. presidential elections). Commander Ortega announced this important decision in Managua's Revolution Square, during the commemoration of the 50th anniversary of Sandino's death, on February 21, 1984 (Barricada Internacional, February 27, 1984:1; El País, February 27, 1984:4).

Despite U.S. pressure to the contrary, Nicaragua's relations with political leaders and heads of state associated with the Socialist International increased rather than decreased. This included a meeting in Lisbon between the Minister of the Interior, Commander Tomás Borge and Portugal's Prime Minister, Mario Soares, in September 1983 and an invitation was extended to the FSLN leader to attend the Socialist Congress held later in the month. More recently, in January 1984, in one of the most politically significant visits to Nicaragua by a head of government since 1979, Swedish Prime Minister and Vice-President of the Socialist International, Olof Palme, paid a 48-hour visit as part of a trip to the region that also took him to Mexico and Costa Rica. In the city of Rivas, he publicly stated in Spanish: "We want to defend Nicaragua's right to independence and consider it unacceptable that the territories of small countries be attacked" (La Nación Internacional, February 17-22, 1984:3). Also, he announced that a shipment of 7,100 tons of wheat was arriving shortly at the port of Corinto, affirming the

continuation of Swedish aid and of his support for the revolution's social programs. Both in Mexico and Nicaragua, Palme expressed his preference for a
"policy of dialogue and understanding that could be carried out through the
Contadora group" (Barricada Internacional, February 27, 1984:3). The inauguration of Venezuela's newly elected president, Democratic Action Party's
Jaime Lusinchi, became a work session focusing on the Central American
crisis with Commander Ortega joining other heads of state in what was
characterized by the Nicaraguan press as a "mini-summit." French President
François Mitterand's ambassador-at-large for Latin America and the Caribbean, Antoine Bianca, visited Managua in February 1984 and stated that ". . . a
state's sovereignty must be respected" (Barricada Internacional, February 27,
1984:3). In a stopover in Madrid while returning from the funeral of Soviet
leader Yuri Andropov, Commander Ortega, traveling with Cuban President
Fidel Castro, met with Felipe Gonzalez, Spain's socialist Prime Minister. The
European press characterized it as a meeting of "great political content" (El
País, February 20, 1984:1).

In addition to relations with the heads of state associated with the
Socialist International, the FSLN joined the permanent Conference of
Political Parties of Latin America (COPPAL) sponsored by Mexico's ruling
Institutional Revolutionary Party (PRI). Other FSLN ties with individual
political parties include the communist parties of Cuba and the Soviet Union.
As part of this broad spectrum of international political relations, delegations
representing the European Parliament and the Latin American Parliament
(Parlatino) visited Managua separately in 1984. Nicaragua's Council of State
(parliament) is a member of the International Interparliamentary Union which
recognized the work accomplished by Nicaragua's broadly based revolutionary
parliament during its first session (1980) and admitted Nicaragua into its ranks
during the Union's 1981 Manila meeting. A delegation representing Nicaragua's
Independent Liberal Party, one of the three political parties which together
with the FSLN form the Patriotic Revolutionary Front (FPR), a political
coalition which supports the current revolutionary process, attended the meeting of the Liberal International held in Canada in 1983.

Diversifying External Relations

Largely due to its new internationalism, Nicaragua's foreign relations
have become highly diversified under the revolution. While maintaining most
of the diplomatic relations which existed before 1979, and strengthening some
of these ties, Nicaragua has established new relationships with countries
from every continent, representing different political systems and ideologies.
In the words of a Nicaraguan diplomat, ". . . diversity in diplomatic relations
figures as a keynote of the revolution's foreign policy" (Bendaña, 1982:323).
New diplomatic relations were established with the Soviet Union and its
European socialist allies; African nations including Algeria, Angola, Mozambique, Tanzania, Zambia, and Zimbabwe; and Asian nations including India,
the People's Republic of China, and Vietnam. In Latin America, Cuba became
a new close ally, as did Grenada (until the 1983 U.S. invasion).

However, in 1982, three years after the Somoza regime had been overthrown, 30 percent of Nicaragua's exports still went to the U.S., 30 percent to
Europe, and 20-25 percent to Latin America, including Central America. The
rest was divided between Japan, Canada, and other countries. Exports to
socialist countries were minimal. But with respect to imports there were
important changes. Imports from the United States dropped from 36 to 27

percent of the total between 1977 and 1980, and imports from Central and South America grew from 36 to 54 percent in the same period. Given present U.S. policies, commercial relations between Nicaragua and the United States became increasingly difficult. Two 1983 Washington decisions further aggravated this situation: the cancellation of 52,800 short tons of raw sugar, 90 percent of the total previously sent by Nicaragua to the United States; and the State Department request that Nicaraguan consular personnel leave the United States, resulting in the closing down of the Nicaraguan consulates. This action was taken in reprisal for the expulsion of three U.S. diplomats by Managua for allegedly plotting to assassinate Foreign Minister D'Escoto. Altogether, Reagan's anti-Sandinista commercial policies were seen by some political analysts as a campaign in which ". . . the United States has used its considerable leverage in the international financial community to enforce a credit embargo designed to strangle the war-torn Nicaraguan economy" (PACCA, 1984:64).

It is precisely in the area of credits and financial assistance where most significant changes have taken place. Loans received in the 1979-1980 period reached a total of $1,200 million, with $260 million in grants of both currency and materials (Agencia Nueva Nicaragua, 1982:104-107). The sources for this support were 49.4 percent from Third World countries; 32.1 from capitalist countries; and 18.5 percent from socialist countries, including Cuba. Paradoxically, while the U.S. economic embargo added further pressure on Nicaragua, it also helped to justify Sandinista policy-making principles. Applying the same rationale used for diplomatic relations to commercial relations, the overall strategy has been to diversify Nicaragua's traditional dependence on the United States by directing it toward other nations--primarily non-aligned countries in Latin America. The explanation for this change is that under different political conditions, the nature of its international obligations would change and, therefore, so would its impact on the revolutionary process itself.

Renegotiating the External Debt

As a consequence of the expansion of international trade relations, Nicaragua was able to derive substantial assistance in terms of donations and credits. Nicaragua was also able finally to renegotiate the enormous external debt inherited from the Somoza regime, which amounted to $1.6 billion. After coming to power in July 1979, the Sandinista regime faced an enormous task of reconstruction. The damage to the nation's economy and infrastructure was estimated at approximately $480 million. Additionally, the government had to face a staggering debt from credits received and misappropriated by Somoza, who had used the monies for self-enrichment while the country was left deeply indebted to international banks and lending institutions. Nicaragua exemplified at that very moment the extremely difficult condition of many Third World countries in today's politically and economically troubled times: unable to face the immediate repayment of principal and interests for debts incurred by their corrupt and frequently tyrannical regimes, they are also unable to afford the international credit freeze that would ensue if they default on their payments. Yet in spite of the difficult circumstances, Nicaragua was still able to arrive at a financial settlement.

In what were rather difficult negotiations, Nicaragua did not yield on its fundamental principles. The revolution's commitments to internal income redistribution and social reform were not hampered by either the debt itself, or by the final settlement. Requests by private banks for immediate repayment of past-due interest were rejected and the troublesome involvement by the International Monetary Fund prior to a negotiated solution was also rejected. A resolution adopted by the United Nations General Assembly which unanimously recommended assistance to Nicaragua was particularly helpful at such a critical moment, providing moral strength to what otherwise was a vulnerable bargaining position.

The role of the U.S. was critical in determining the ultimate agreement. Under the Somoza dynasty, the United States was Nicaragua's main trading partner, and the source of its international credit. At the same time, the U.S. attitude on this issue weighed heavily on the international banks' decision-making strategy, particularly on how much were they willing to ease payment conditions, as requested by Managua. Fortunately for the Sandinistas, this happened while President Carter was still in office. Even though there were serious concerns in Washington regarding events in Managua, they did not yet resemble the level of animosity reached during the Reagan years. In September 1980 an agreement was reached with approximately 100 multinational banks which were represented by a thirteen-bank steering committee: Managua agreed to repay its debt in a twelve-year period at reduced interest rates, with an additional five-year grace period. Hence, Nicaragua committed itself to face in years to come the multiple challenges of rebuilding its war-torn economy, restructuring its society, modifying its political institutions, and transforming its international relations, while still having to make heavy debt payments. But at least, as a matter of national pride and a reservoir for future transactions, it had retained in good standing its credit with the international lending community (Black, 1982:176).

NICARAGUA AND LATIN AMERICA

The Sandinistas came to power at a very special moment in the history of the Americas. Several factors account for this phenomenon. First, throughout the 1970s during its post-Vietnam and post-Watergate political period, the United States went through an introspective phase in which its traditional grip over Latin America, and particularly over Central America and the Caribbean, was somewhat relaxed. Second, the emphasis on human rights in President Carter's foreign policy had a salutary overall effect in the region, but especially in Nicaragua, where a revolutionary struggle against the Somoza dynasty had been brewing for years. Third, the country's internal political dynamics changed once an arms embargo was put into effect by Washington in response to Somoza's horrible record of human rights violations (Booth, 1982:128-130; Walker, 1981:111-112).

In the face of what was generally understood as a withdrawal of the historic U.S. backing of his regime, the dictator became increasingly isolated at home. Most of the middle and upper class support traditionally associated with him vanished and he was left virtually alone with his own military structure, the National Guard. A broad anti-Somoza coalition materialized as middle class professionals, businessmen, industrialists, landowners, and others joined the political groups that had been fighting the dictatorship for years. Nevertheless, because of the sacrifice and dedication of its members, the organizational capability and the will to carry out the military and political struggle, and, above all, for having been for years the vanguard of the revolutionary forces fighting against Somoza, the FSLN was recognized as the institutional leader of the revolution and of the emerging new Nicaragua.

Nevertheless, just before the revolutionary victory, the Carter administration used its power and leverage in the Organization of American States to
try to prevent what by then was inevitable: that the Sandinistas would become
the real political power in a post-Somoza Nicaragua. Washington had no
interest in saving Somoza (the man), but it was concerned with saving the
system (Somocismo), so Nicaragua would continue to be in the future, as it
had been in the past: a good place for U.S. private enterprise. The U.S. also
sought to prevent the country from slipping out of Washington's sphere of
influence and to avoid the establishment of a political and economic system
combining political pluralism with a mixed economy (Ramirez, 1983:7-11).

In June 1979 Washington proposed in a seven-point draft resolution presented at the Seventeenth Foreign Ministers Consultative Meeting of the
Organization of American States, that ". . . the governments of the member
states be prepared to provide an OAS peacekeeping presence as may be
requested. . ." in order to ". . . call for a halt to the armed conflict which is
causing such human suffering." The Latin American representatives defeated
this proposal. They understood it for what it was: a last minute attempt to
control further damage to U.S. hegemonic interests in the guise of solving the
crisis--basically trying to minimize political losses. Instead, they voted on
June 23 for a resolution stating "that the solution of this serious problem is
entirely in the hands of the Nicaraguan people" (seventeen votes in favor; five
abstentions; and two against including Nicaragua--still representing the
Somoza regime--and Paraguay) (Granma - Weekly Review, July 1, 1979:3).

That was an unique moment in the history of the inter-American
system of Latin American unity in support of a nascent revolution. For
Nicaragua it represented the high-water mark of Latin American support.
Although the record of Nicaraguan-Latin American relations has been a
largely satisfactory one, the initial level of unity and support has diminished.
The contradictions between a sense of common hemispheric destiny and differing perceptions of national interest and political realities has created
different Latin American attitudes toward revolutionary Nicaragua. Mexico
and Cuba have relentlessly supported the Sandinista revolution, while Venezuela has been highly supportive albeit less committed. President Belisario
Betancur's Colombia and, more recently, President Raul Alfonsín's Argentina
have expressed support for Nicaragua's government. The multilateral four-
country Contadora diplomatic initiative has been particularly significant in
its level of moral support in Latin America and in the United Nations.

Logically, the most immediate impact of the Somoza downfall was
felt in Central America (a region in which events in one country always affect
the others), as well as in the Caribbean. It is in this region that the Sandinistas' victorious popular revolution had, and still has, a broad, rippling effect.
Political observers (as well as U.S. State Department and Pentagon Latin
American watchers) could not fail to notice that in the space of a few months
two revolutionary regimes had come to power in the region. First, on March
13, 1979, in the small English-speaking Caribbean island of Grenada, Maurice
Bishop and his New Jewel Movement ousted the dictatorial Eric Gairy in a
bloodless coup; Nicaragua followed only four months later. A revolutionary
wave seemed to be building, right in the "American backyard." Stopgap and
damage control measures were immediately put into effect, with short-term
beneficial results for U.S. interests. A successful coup organized by allegedly
progressive military and civilian leaders in El Salvador in October 1979 was
supported by Washington as a pragmatic way of avoiding "another Nicaragua"

(even though progressive elements in the junta walked out in protest a few
months later). This was followed by the October 1980 Jamaican elections in
which Michael Manley's pro-Cuba, pro-Third World administration (although a
strict observer of the parliamentary Westminster political model at home)
was replaced by the pro-United States Edward Seaga administration after
months of turmoil and bloody electioneering (Manley, 1983:7-9 and 45-47;
Dam, 1983:1-4).

It was the presidential election in 1980 of Republican candidate Ronald
Reagan, however, which put into motion the present interventionist and
militaristic U.S. policy toward Central America--a policy which has had far-
reaching effects on Nicaraguan-Latin American relations, particularly
Nicaraguan relations with its neighbors. President Reagan came to office
determined to halt what he understood as Soviet-inspired interventionism in
the Western hemisphere, first in Cuba and then in Nicaragua. Thus came the
U.S.-supported Argentine military experts stationed in Honduras training
anti-Sandinista Nicaraguans; the increased economic and military support to
the Salvadoran regime, so it could carry on with its anti-FDR-FMLN counter-
insurgency campaign (notwithstanding the ever-present and active death
squads, an embarrassment to Washington); the buildup of the Honduran military, and the utilization of Honduras by the U.S. as if it were a virtual U.S.
military base in the middle of Central America; the support of Nicaraguan
contras (allowing them, for example, to use military training facilities in
Florida and California, in violation of American neutrality statutes), including
first the Somocista Nicaraguan Democratic Front (FDN), and later former
Sandinista leader Eden Pastora's Democratic Revoluionary Alliance (ARDE);
and the invasion of Grenada on October 25, 1983, after the assassination of
Bishop by Bernard Coard and Unison Whiteman's New Jewel Movement
faction. In addition, the development of the Caribbean Basin Initiative (CBI)
was meant to serve as the economic development counterpart of the above
listed policies, reinforcing democratic institutions while the military side of
the policy would reduce the level of the communist threat supported by Cuba
and Nicaragua (Dam, 1983).

When Washington decided to increase the number of contras from a
few hundred in 1981-1982 to approximately 15,000 by late 1983, it was justified in terms of what is called "symmetry" (in parallel political situations).
This means that what the FDR-FMLN guerrillas have allegedly been doing to
the U.S.-supported Salvadoran government--i.e., destroying the country's
economic and military facilities, attacking the military and civilian population, etc.--is now being done to the Sandinistas by U.S.-supported contras.
The assumption behind this policy is that it will force Managua to pay a very
high price for exporting its revolution and to modify its internal policies.
Also, it just might oust the Sandinistas from power altogether. To justify this
policy, administration spokesmen said that there was no reason for anyone,
particularly in Washington, to rescue the Sandinistas from their own people's
opposition. The intention clearly was to make the contras look as if they
were homegrown, like a purely indigenous movement. Furthermore, the prevailing expectation was that counter-revolutionary forces would soon be
controlling territory along the border area of nearby Honduras. In fact, the
forecast given in the summer of 1983 was that by December the FDN would
be close to Managua. This proved to be wrong, however, in spite of increasing U.S. and Honduran military support for the contras (Dickey, 1984:668-671;
Kenworthy, 1983:181-200).

Washington and Tegucigalpa have escalated their involvement with the

240

anti-Sandinista forces from initial covert support and advice, to in-the-field coordination and direction, and currently to an even closer alignment in which Honduran military advisers are allegedly participating directly in the contras' actions. Meanwhile, U.S. military personnel are involved in monitoring the size and movement of the Nicaraguan forces and are passing the information to the FDN command (Barricada, July 15, 1983:1; Newsweek, August 1, 1983:12-17; New York Times, October 6, 1983:1). For Honduras, the consequences of this policy have been more than just becoming the contras' main Central American ally. Its territory has become militarized by the United States, with several airports and naval and military installations built for the benefit of the U.S.-Central American war and diplomatic policy (Update Latin America, February 1984:1-12).

It is in this difficult and conflictive political context that Nicaragua must formulate and implement a foreign policy which is designed to de-emphasize Washington's and its allies' polarization of Central American politics. For the Sandinistas it has been difficult to assume a diplomatic and professional demeanor in the face of constant provocation and aggression and to talk peace in the face of war. It is difficult to maintain confidence in the Contadora diplomatic effort in the face of the Kissinger report, which was seen in Nicaragua and elsewhere as a politically expeditious rationalization of policies already in effect. Managua's response to such hostile policies was articulated by Foreign Minister D'Escoto: "We wish to be friends (with the United States), but we will never sell out, nor will we ever compromise in our sacred task of building a new, free, and sovereign Nicaragua." His statement, in a nutshell, summarizes the main themes of Sandinista's foreign policy (Bendana, 1982:326).

From Managua's standpoint, if the United States would stop using its surrogates to pursue its anti-Sandinista policy, regional conditions would improve. Perhaps even relations between Nicaragua and Honduras would improve under such a condition. Currently the two countries are on the verge of a war which neither needs nor wants. The process of restoring normal relations between Nicaragua and its southern neighbor, Costa Rica, may be more likely. A small improvement has already been realized as evidenced by Costa Rican President Luis Alberto Monge's statement in the fall of 1983 reiterating his country's policy of effective neutrality. This policy shift followed the resignation of Foreign Minister Fernando Volio, who supported an active anti-Sandinista policy favorable to Pastora's ARDE (Barricada Internacional, November 28, 1983:7; and La Nación Internacional, November 17-23, 1983:8 and November 24-30:5).

From the United States' and its allies' standpoint, however, the overall conditions in the region will improve if Cuba first, and then Nicaragua, were to cease intervening in the Salvadoran civil war and to stop their arm shipments to the FDR-FMLN guerrillas, and elsewhere in the region. The White Paper issued by Washington in early 1981 accused Nicaragua of precisely those actions. Since then, however, the document has been widely discredited, and Washington has furnished no substantive new evidence supporting its charges. Nevertheless, even without substantive evidence, policies have been developed to respond to Nicaragua's perceived intervention in other nations. U.S. policies in Central America have had the effect of deepening the adversarial relationships within the region. Nicaragua's position against the political and military forces threatening the Sandinista regime is becoming more entrenched and the relationship appears both irreconcilable and irreversible. Nevertheless, in spite of this deplorable situation, Nicaragua has been

241

able to maintain diplomatic relations with all Central American countries.

Relationships within Central America today are the product of intra-state and inter-state political dynamics which are influenced by outside powers' interference in the region's affairs. The result is that adversarial positions have become hardened and, in turn, have caused further tension in the region. The Sandinistas believe that the reaction to their revolution by their own bourgeoisie and by conservative political leaders and the military establishment in neighboring countries is largely determined by the United States. U.S. influence is made possible by the region's dependence on the U.S. which is particularly evident in ties of regional militaries to the U.S. Not only do the region's armed forces receive military hardware from the U.S., but their proven anti-communist stance as demonstrated by a long record of repressive anti-leftist and counterinsurgency campaigns provides an ideological compatibility. By early 1984, the political and military hardliners seem to have gained the upper hand in most Central American countries. As discussed in Chapter 11 of this volume, governments of all Central American nations have been forced to respond to the conflicts in the region. The efforts of the Contadora Group, the formation of CONDECA, the buildup of military forces throughout the region, the growing intensity of border incidents, and the ever more visible U.S. military presence in the region are indications of the growing internationalization of the conflict and place additional pressures on the Nicaraguan government.

NICARAGUA'S THREE-TRACK OFFENSIVE

A complex policy articulating internal and external issues and challenges under a comprehensive umbrella is the revolution's response to the anti-Sandinista threat, which is increasingly putting the survival of the regime in serious danger. It is not a question of faltering internal support. Internal support for the regime has increased in the face of the anti-Sandinista threat. However, it is true that internal political allegiances have become increasingly polarized, primarily along class lines with younger and traditionally poor sectors of the population providing a higher level of support for the Sandinistas. The counter-revolution simply will not go away; in fact, it is like having to fight the U.S.-directed 1961 Bay of Pigs invasion against the Cuban revolution over and over again. Even in light of growing opposition to U.S. involvement in Central America from Congress and the public, the Republican-dominated Senate is keeping the contras' war financially alive. Also, under General Gorman's hawkish leadership as current chief of the U.S. Southern Command in Panama, the militarization of Central America continues relentlessly--virtually turning the area into a U.S. military base. In addition to the contras, the U.S. is applying other pressures, as discussed above-- including political and diplomatic isolation and economic sanctions designed to limit the regime's financial capabilities.

Yet, even when faced with this threat, there still is an energetic and imaginative Sandinista response which has so far proven successful in maintaining the revolution. Nicaraguan initiatives and policies can be analyzed in terms of a three-track policy: (1) a military and national defense preparedness program; (2) the political and legal process institutionalizing the revolution; and (3) a focus on intra-regional relations in view of the present crisis in the region.

National Defense

Nicaragua has been accused by the Reagan administration of building an army and military facilities beyond what its natural defense needs would suggest. In doing so, it was charged, Nicaragua is endangering the security of neighboring states, particularly Honduras. Cuba and the Soviet Union have been accused of being the promoters and main suppliers of this effort, with Havana working as a Soviet conduit of communist penetration and control over the Sandinistas. Cuba has acknowledged providing military expertise to Nicaragua, and the Sandinistas have said publicly that they will accept military help from any quarter, providing that there are no obligations (politically or otherwise) attached to it. The Soviet Union and other socialist countries have provided military hardware and technical advisers to Nicaragua but a precise dollar amount is unknown to U.S. sources. Western diplomats estimate that Soviet economic aid to Nicaragua will equal $100-$150 million in 1984 "aimed more at filling emergency needs, like oil (and wheat), than providing long-term developmental assistance" (New York Times, March 28, 1984:1). In addition, an estimate of fewer than 100 Soviet civilian advisers are located throughout the Nicaraguan bureaucracy, but there are no known Soviet military advisers stationed there. Soviet diplomats have, in fact, downplayed the importance of bilateral relations with Nicaragua and have suggested that Nicaragua "may not be ready for a socialist revolution in Soviet terms" (New York Times, March 28, 1984:4).

Strengthening the military, however, has been a priority for the Nicaraguan government. The military strength of the Sandinista People's Army (EPS) is reinforced by the Sandinista People's Militia and the national conscription program instituted under the Patriotic Military Service. It was precisely the vocal opposition to conscription by the church hierarchy that caused major new problems between the Sandinistas and the Catholic church in the last months of 1983, which added to a relationship already strained from the Pope's visit early in the year. The Sandinista Police and the state security apparatus are contained in the Ministry of Interior. The Sandinista Defense Committees, organized nationally on a block by block basis in every city and town, mobilize the population into the national defense program. All of this represents a respectable military force, which so far has proven successful in fighting the contras. With a standing army of 50,000, the militias several times larger, and a national network of civilians ready to defend the revolution, the major military weakness of the Sandinistas seems to be in its miniscule navy and virtual lack of an air force.

The Institutionalization of the Revolution

The process of institutionalizing the Nicaraguan revolution is taking place under extremely difficult war conditions, which make a normal process of state-building almost an impossibility. Nevertheless, it is moving forward. The paradox here is that while the FSLN and supporting political forces might profit from the institutionalization process, they can certainly survive without it. On the other hand, the forces opposing the institutionalization--under the banner that it is not democratic enough--have much to lose in the process and very little to gain, regardless of how open the process might be. The dramatic announcement on February 21 that the elections will be held sooner than expected, was a clear act of revolutionary pragmatism. Rather than being opportunistic, it was a principled decision which respected the revolution's historical commitments.

Furthermore, on November 4, 1984, when the people elect a president, a vice-president, and 90 deputies for a Legislative Assembly which will be drafting a new constitution during the following 24 months, the political outcome might prove to be devastating for the opposition political parties and economic sectors. Rather than gaining, they might regress from their present level of representation under the Council of State. As it is, there is a guaranteed participation to opposition political parties--with the exception of those organized after the Council of State was established in 1980. Also, such economic groups as the Superior Council of Private Enterprise (COSEP) will not have direct representation in the Legislative Assembly, as they do today in the Council of State. While the law of approved political parties gives legal recognition to ten political parties (four in opposition to the Sandinista revolution), it is the electoral law that decides the number of deputies allotted to minority political parties, under proportional representation or some other system.

The four-party Patriotic Revolutionary Front (FPR), including the FSLN and three other political organizations, most likely will continue as the dominant political force, competing with other political parties, after the elections. This will bring the Sandinistas closer to Mexico's Revolutionary Institutional Party (PRI) than to Cuba's Communist Party (PCC) which functions in a single party system. Where Mexico and Nicaragua depart, however, is in the latter's commitment to social justice and income redistribution. Although it functions with a mixed economy, Managua has pursued in its five years of revolution a policy favoring basic popular needs for education, health, employment, and other social benefits, comparable only to the policies pursued in this area by the Cuban revolution.

Finally, the nation's political, economic, and social institutions will be determined by a Legislative Assembly which will be the product of national elections in which opposing political parties have competed with one another for popular support. It is most likely that the forthcoming constitution will establish as permanent features of the political system the present model combining political pluralism with a mixed economy--although the specific rules governing the system will have to be decided. It seems paradoxical that the FSLN as a revolutionary leadership is presently fighting for the survival of a system in which the private sector, albeit under state control, will have a guaranteed place and an important role to play.

Intra-regional Relations and Peace Proposals

The third component of Nicaragua's three-track offensive is its Central American focus which is implicitly and explicitly related to the other two tracks discussed above. This is not to say that either Nicaragua's military might, or its process of political institutionalization are being used directly as bargaining chips by the Sandinistas. Instead, it is the regime's viability-- as guaranteed by its defense program and the further legitimization of the revolution gained through its institutionalization--that strengthens the Sandinistas' diplomatic initiatives.

The overall Nicaraguan Central American policy involves different political initiatives undertaken by assorted political actors. Within the framework of its foreign policy toward its neighbors, the U.S., and the Contadora process, Nicaragua's peace proposals form a significant component of its regional foreign policy. In some cases, these initiatives originate in Managua;

in other cases, Managua reacts to other states' individual or collective diplomatic undertakings. This policy includes: (1) bilateral relations in the region; (2) reactions to initiatives such as the Contadora proposals (as well as the Mexican and French peace proposals) and such U.S. initiatives as Reagan's special envoy to Central America and the Kissinger Commission; and (3) Nicaragua's own regional peace proposals including relations with Cuba.

    Bilateral Relations. Through a complex political and diplomatic mechanisms Nicaragua still has diplomatic relations with all of its neighbors, as well as with the United States. This political phenomenon suggests how deceiving a state of formal diplomatic relations may be. Having ambassadors in each other's capitals has not stopped Washington from waging a covert war against Managua--nor has it stopped Honduras, or even Costa Rica, from willingly or unwillingly contributing to Reagan's military plan.

    Neither national (U.S. law) nor international (international law and treaties) legal constraints have stopped the Reagan administration from waging a covert war. The Boland Amendment, a 1982 federal statute, forbids the U.S. government from engaging in actions aimed at overthrowing the Sandinista regime. Article 2 of the OAS Charter and Articles 18 and 19 of the UN Charter oppose any act of force against the territorial integrity of any member state. The 1933 Inter-American Conference's Convention on the Rights and Duties of States (Montevideo) stipulates the "principles of equality of states, nonintervention, and the inviolability of territory and the renunciation of force" (Booth, 1982:58). As members of these international organizations, all Central American states, and the United States, are bound by their legal norms. However, the region is presently confronting a near collapse of international law as a set of norms governing international behavior.

    United States' interference in Central American inter-state relations is a major reason for this situation. Military advantages for the U.S. might explain its unconventional behavior, but do not justify its illegal covert actions against Nicaragua. Although the joint U.S.-Honduran exercises are officially held for the purpose of training the Honduran army it appears that U.S. troops are equally trained in these exercises. In fact, it may well be that the principal beneficiaries of the exercises are U.S. military personnel. According to U.S. military officials, current maneuvers are helping the United States militarily to improve combat readiness in Central America. Meanwhile, in the opinion of Honduran military personnel their troops are training by association, and are helping their American patrons in their familiarization and orientation in the region's terrain.[7]

    Managua has sent formal protests several times, with little or no results, to Tegucigalpa, the U.S. and various international organizations. Demonstrating its concern, the Nonaligned Movement condemned these actions, but did not name specifically any country as the culprit. The Sandinistas see the joint military exercises as being held to intimidate them and to prepare for major acts of aggression in the future. Although both the war and the diplomatic processes continue, it seems that expanding the Big Pine exercise series is a direct attempt by the U.S. to embrace all of its Central American allies in a single military framework under CONDECA.

    Meanwhile, Costa Rica formally protested a border skirmish on February 15, 1984, in which units of the Sandinista Popular Army (ESP) fired mortars and other artillery against a Costa Rican Rural Guard patrol. San Jose protested this military action, recalling its diplomatic representative in Managua for consultation. A protest was filed with the four Contadora foreign ministers (Venezuela, Colombia, Panama, and Mexico) and the

Organization of American States. The incident was used to portray the Costa Rican northern border as being in imminent danger of attack by Sandinistas. According to the chief of Costa Rican Civil Guard, Colonel Oscar Vidal, new precautions were taken to restrict movement of persons in the so-called "critical sectors" (La Nación Internacional, February 17-22, 1984:4). Whether this was a passing incident or it was being utilized by internal and external forces in order to draw Costa Rica closer to a Honduras-like anti-Nicaraguan position is not clear yet.

San Jose's 1983 neutrality declaration is being criticized for not being as neutral as it claims to be (leaving in its text enough room for what is called an "active neutralism," which is understood as providing the needed grounds for justifying future attacks against Nicaragua). President Monge, however, speaking to national and foreign businessmen, stated that Costa Rica is "an example of a silent revolution," adding that his country "does not need the (U.S.) Marines. . . ," as long as "it is not armed by its own decision, and whose security rests on the vigilant attitude of its citizens, the natural intelligence of its police, and the organs of the inter-American system" (El Día, February 22, 1984:3).

From the standpoint of the contras' military actions, it is possible that Nicaragua's southern border may become a more peaceful place in the future, more than what has been in a long time. Many of Pastora's men asked for refuge in Costa Rica, after stopping fighting their guerrilla war (it is not sure whether this is temporarily or permanently); and one of his closest associates, Alfonso Robelo, stated that they would like to participate in the electoral process just inaugurated by the Sandinistas using ARDE as their own political party (Excelsior, February 22, 1984:3).

Contadora. Begun in January 1983, Contadora is an unusual diplomatic initiative that stands as a positive development in what otherwise is a worrisome and difficult international political period in the Western hemisphere. The nature of its four-country membership (Venezuela, Colombia, Panama, and Mexico) and its proclaimed purpose of searching for peaceful political solutions--opposing the militarization of the region which heightens the danger of a war among the countries involved in the dispute--reflect a new will and assertiveness among Latin American countries. This indicates a political maturity and a sensitive awareness of responsibility in handling their own affairs. This attitude seems to be a product of the Falklands/Malvinas War and the ensuing unified Latin American opposition to the United States support of England against Argentina in 1982. Despite its earlier role training counter-revolutionaries in Honduras, Nicaragua supported Argentina's position throughout the war. Although Argentina's involvement with the contras declined considerably after the war, the Argentine government did not end its participation in an advisory capacity for the Somocista forces until the inauguration of civilian President Alfonsín in January 1984 (Dickey, 1984:669).

With the pragmatic recognition of the U.S. being the superpower that it is--there has been, nevertheless, a clear intent of preserving Contadora as a Latin American diplomatic undertaking. The Contadora Group has reached out, however, not only to the Organization of American States, but to the United Nations as well. The latter provided the conduit for the overwhelming support given on a worldwide basis to this regional effort, whose final outcome is very much in the balance. All along, the ambivalence built into the U.S. response to Contadora's peaceful efforts has been disruptive in deeds even if supportive in words and rhetoric, confirming early Latin American reservations and suspicions regarding Washington's real intentions. Reagan's Central American war/diplomatic policy is a negation of Contadora's political aims, which strive for the coexistence of Sandinista Nicaragua with its neighbors. The United States public position in support of Contadora is largely determined by the support given to it by practically every country in the world, making very difficult for Washington to reject it offhand. President Reagan, however, has his own agenda.

As expected, the National Bipartisan Commission on Central America's report, handed to President Reagan in January 1984 by Henry Kissinger and the other members of the commission, provided a handy rationalization for both the policies of the administration already in place, and their continuation with the legitimizing aura of being the product of a bipartisan effort. In presenting the new military and economic aid package based on the report, the administration enlisted the diplomatic representatives of its four Central American allies as well: Costa Rica, El Salvador, Honduras, and Guatemala, who participated in the selling of the proposal to the U.S. Congress. Despite the criticism raised in the United States, Latin America, and elsewhere about the Kissinger report, Washington is using it as it had planned all along. Mexico's President Miguel de la Madrid explained, "While the Kissinger report continues to regard (military force) as a possibility the Contadora Group has tried to eliminate it, because we don't believe that economic and social development can take place in the middle of a war" (Pittsburgh Press, February 10, 1984:8).

While the Contadora process is an ongoing effort, so is the U.S. militarization of Central America with the building of CONDECA as a regional military structure; the emergence of Honduras as a military power in the area; Costa Rica's inching under pressure toward a frontline position against Nicaragua; and the CIA-trained, -financed, and -directed contras as Reagan's condottieres in the region. In the middle of all of this, Reagan's special envoy to Central America, Richard Stone, presented his resignation after visiting the region five times between the summer of 1983 and the winter of 1984. Altogether, the appointment of a special envoy was a noneventful diplomatic initiative tailored more to satisfy the critics of the administration at home than to bring forward effective solutions. His successor, Harry Schlaudeman, brings very poor credentials indeed for a better performance. Having been the second highest U.S. diplomat in Chile in 1973 and secretary of the Kissinger Commission, he is not expected to fare any better in Central America than Stone did.

Nevertheless, the Contadora foreign ministers found encouraging signs in their February 1984 Panama meeting including plans for elections to be held in the region and increasing international cooperation to help find solutions to the area's social and economic problems from the International Labor Organization, Central American Social and Economic Development Committee, Pan American Health Organization, and others. Upon receiving a report from its technical staff, formed by the four member states and the five Central American representatives, the Contadora foreign ministers concluded in their thirteenth meeting in over a year that there are possibilities for finding a peaceful solution to the problems in the region and for perhaps a peace treaty in 1984 by the Central American countries (La Nación Internacional, January 26-February 1, 1984:4 and March 1-7, 1984:4).

Peace Proposals. Nicaragua recognizes the positive effect that Contadora has had in the region. In fact, given present conditions in the area, the efforts of the Contadora Group have probably been one of the major factors preventing a regional war and/or a U.S.-led invasion of Nicaragua or El Salvador. Both in a reaction to Contadora's efforts and on its own initiative, Nicaragua has presented its own peace proposals designed to find a nonviolent solution to the Central American crisis. The timing and content of these proposals have played an important part in the Sandinistas' strategy to prevent the different hostile forces from launching a major attack against Nicaragua.

The summer of 1983 was a period in which both Contadora and Nicaragua frantically searched for peace in the region. On July 17 the presidents of the four Contadora states issued the Cancun Declaration after their summit meeting in that Mexican resort. Miguel de la Madrid of Mexico, Luis Herrera Campins of Venezuela, Belisario Betancur of Colombia, and Ricardo de la Espriella of Panama asked all countries in the region to end hostilities, to promote a peaceful atmosphere, and to oppose the installation of military bases in the region by outside parties. Two days later, on July 19, during the festivities held in the city of Leon in commemoration of the fourth anniversary of the triumph of the revolution, Commander Ortega responded positively to the Cancun Declaration with a six-point plan. Nicaragua agreed to begin multilateral negotiations under the auspices of the Contadora Group to further the peace process. This represented a change in Nicaragua's previous position asking for direct (bilateral) talks with Honduras and the United States. However, this concession did not impress the United States or Honduras, nor did it bring them closer to the negotiating table with Nicaragua.

Commander Ortega's six-point peace proposal included the following: to end any war situation; to stop supplying weapons to the forces in El Salvador; to end all military support to forces opposing any of the regimes in the region; to respect all countries' right to self-determination and to noninterference in their internal affairs; to stop economic aggression; and to have no foreign military bases nor military exercises using foreign troops. Washington's response was to announce the beginning of the massive, six-month Big Pine II exercises in Honduras, thus demonstrating that Washington's agenda for Central America was substantively different from any peace proposal made by either the Contadora Group or Nicaragua. Regardless of the concessions that the Sandinistas made or were willing to make, early that summer Washington had decided what its course of action would be, and has followed it ever since--that is, the increasing militarization of the region.

Nevertheless, continuing its policy of constructive engagement through peace proposals, Managua presented a more elaborate plan on October 15, 1983, that could be carried out within the framework of the Contadora process. This included four draft treaties: (1) Draft Treaty to Guarantee Mutual Respect, Peace and Security between the Republic of Nicaragua and the United States of America; (2) Draft Treaty of Peace, Friendship and Cooperation between the Republic of Honduras and Nicaragua; (3) Draft Treaty to Contribute to the Peaceful Solution of the Armed Conflict in the Republic of El Salvador; and (4) Draft Treaty Concerning the Maintenance of Peace and Security and Concerning the Relations of Friendship and Cooperation among the Republics of Central America.[8] Nicaragua's draft treaty proposals had no impact whatsoever on the Honduran government or the U.S. government's hostile political and military policies--nor were they welcomed by the Salvadoran regime. Nevertheless, the Contadora Group provided a receptive audience which seemed to appreciate Nicaraguan efforts. Managua was more successful here due to its active and productive participation in the regional diplomatic effort. Its contribution went beyond such formalities as attending meetings and presenting position papers responding to the issues under discussion. The Sandinistas came forward with elaborate and serious peace proposals and draft treaties on their own. Also, by engaging themselves constructively in the peace-making process, they had a positive impact in such critical political forums as the Nonaligned Movement (which held a meeting in Managua early in 1983); the Socialist International (a source of much needed political and economic support); and the United Nations (a forum used and preferred by the Sandinistas, who frown on the OAS), and others. All along, Managua demonstrated that rather than behaving like the intransigent party that its hemispheric foes claim it is, it can actually be a constructive partner, cooperating in the search for peaceful solutions to the problems faced by Central America.

CONCLUSIONS

The study of the Latin American foreign policy of a small, developing nation like Nicaragua underlines two major factors. First, a country's potential for creative policy making can be attained once a nation exercises genuine national sovereignty and effective independence. Second, the costs of such independence can be high. As in the case of Nicaragua, whenever the small, developing nation's internal and external politics are not approved by the regional superpower, the latter subjects it to endless reprisals. Hence, the Sandinistas' foreign policy represents both the politics of exercising independence and of struggling for the nation's and the regime's survival.

Managua uses a sophisticated foreign policy which is characteristic of a major power. By pursuing a policy of active internationalism the regime has been able to establish new diplomatic relationships, to develop closer ties with both the Nonaligned Movement and the Socialist International, and to renegotiate its foreign debt. For Nicaragua and for Central America, the Sandinista revolutionary victory on July 19, 1979, was a turning point. The election of Ronald Reagan as President of the United States in 1980, and his efforts to re-establish U.S. hegemony in the Central American-Caribbean area, led to a logical political outcome: a Central American war and diplomatic policy. Nicaragua's internal and external revolutionary politics became the politics of regime survival. While developing several peace proposals and draft resolutions for consideration by the Contadora Group, the revolutionary regime built up its military national defense program and moved to institutionalize the revolution. It is in such a geographical, political, and military setting that the Sandinistas' policies toward Central America are now developed.

One of the most damaging aspects of Reagan's anti-Sandinista policy is the support for counter-revolutionary forces waging war against Nicaragua from Honduras and Costa Rica. This policy has brought death and destruction to the country when it was just emerging from the terrible devastation of the war years, particularly 1978-1979. It is a policy which damages the region, too, undermining fragile Central American civilian and constitutional political institutions. Pragmatic policy makers are being replaced by ideological hard-liners, who support the ongoing militarization of Central America. Reagan's anti-Sandinista policy is equally harmful to the United States. Besides being highly divisive internally, by pursuing a policy supportive of a covert war the United States is breeching national and international law. Washington sees national security as the supreme value for U.S. society; yet, is the security of the United States or of the Central American countries really endangered by the Sandinistas? Are indigenous revolutions produced by decades of social, political, and economic exploitation the product of communist subversion? It is the misconception of the U.S. and its misguided policies and not the Sandinista revolution that are dangerous for the security of the United States and Central America. The internal logic of Reagan's policy will lead to direct U.S. military intervention in Nicaragua, El Salvador, and most likely the rest of Central America, in a costly and deadly regional war. Meanwhile the Sandinista regime continues to survive and to develop creative foreign policies to ensure its future survival. As the Nicaraguan people celebrate the July 19 revolutionary anniversaries, a popular tune reflects the notion that those anniversaries are being watched rather closely: ". . . y el imperialismo ya los va contando. . . ."[9]

NOTES

1. Commander Jaime Wheelock Roman, Minister of Agriculture and Agrarian Reform of Nicaragua, denounced the policy on March 4, 1982, at the Washington meeting of the Latin American Studies Association (LASA). This was received with skepticism by the media and political circles, official and non-official. Eight months later Newsweek's "exclusive report" was published (November 8, 1982:42-46, 48-49, 53, 55). Since then, it has been a publicly known fact the world over.

2. See Bendana (1982); Nicaragua, Dirrección de Divulgación y Prensa de la Junta de Gobierno de Reconstrucción Nacional (1982); and Black (1982).

3. Commander Tomás Borge, Minister of Interior of Nicaragua, member of the FSLN National Directorate, and the only survivor of the original FSLN founders, stated regarding the Miskito question (which has been used against the revolution for political propaganda purposes, as well as for counter-revolutionary actions), "The Somoza dictatorship never made the slightest effort to bring education or health to its population. Tuberculosis decimated lives and illiteracy blotted out minds. Neglect was the policy toward the Miskitos. We wanted to resolve this historic backwardness, having a great deal of will, but with little knowledge. We committed errors, many errors; many times no account was taken of the cultural particularities of the Miskitos. . . . Such errors were committed in good faith; they were taken advantage of by the bad faith of the counter-revolution" (emphasis added) (The Militant, January 27, 1984:10-12). See the special issue of Nicarahuac on "La Costa Atlantica," (October 1982). For official documents from the Nicaraguan Government of National Reconstruction concerning the Sandinista human rights policy see: Nicaragua y los Derechos Humanos (n.d.) Managua, Nicaragua: Centro de Investigaciones Juridicas y Politicas, Ministerio de Justicia.

4. See Fonseca (1982:169-199); Balcarcel (1980:112-119); Selser (1983) and Ramirez (1980).

5. See Toriello Garrido (1983); Nicaragua, Ministerio del Exterior (1982); Ramirez (1982).

6. See Central America Alert, October-November 1983:1-2; Central America Alert, February 1984:2; Honduras Update, October 1983:1-6; Update Latin America, February 1984:1-12.

7. See Latinamerica Press, March 8, 1984:1-2; Washington Post National Weekly, February 13, 1984:19; Mexico City-The News, October 2, 1983:7; Guardian, November 9, 1983; Excelsior, October 2, 1983:1, 18, 32;

<u>Central America Alert</u>, December 1983:1-2.

8. Nicaragua, Junta de Gobierno de Reconstrucción Nacional (1983); Nicaragua, Ministerio del Exterior (1983); <u>Barricada Internacional</u>, October 31, 1983:4 and January 16, 1984:3; <u>Pensamiento Propio</u>, March-April 1983:5-7.

9. "and the imperialists are keeping tabs. . . ."

14
Cuba's Foreign Policy in Central America and the Caribbean

Juan del Aguila

INTRODUCTION

Struggles unfolding in the Caribbean Basin[1] are being examined and described from perspectives that, for a variety of reasons, were not utilized during much of the 1970s. The tools of "revolutionary" analysis are used in describing processes of change in Central America (Ungo, 1983), conflicts are also perceived as manifestations of local struggles potentially "spilling over" into entire regions (Grabendorff, 1983), and a new literature describing the dynamics of "political breakdown" and "transition" is emerging (Baloyra, 1982). In practical terms, a perception that a period of protracted instability can affect regional security arrangements, possibly shifting local balances, has activated intense diplomatic activity and military preparedness which have escalated regional tensions.

Policy makers as well as academic practitioners are divided on the extent to which involvement by outsiders is likely to produce final outcomes, but the view that local actors control their own destiny is increasingly discredited. Much of the debate focuses on the means through which political change can be affected and whose purposes are served if change takes a radical, evolutionary, or reformist character. In effect, the area's struggles invite involvement from several quarters, and outcomes may once more legitimize the means used to attain political goals, or to vindicate one strategy over another. The use of force in various forms indicates how high the stakes are and how unwilling to risk compromise the contestants have been, partly out of a belief that a perpetuation of the status quo is preferable to running the risks of political accommodation.

In Central America, instability results from the clash between forces seeking to preserve order and hegemony and sectors committed to wider economic and political participation. This is particularly true in El Salvador, Guatemala, and Nicaragua, despite the fact that the character of the political regime is different in each case. The struggle is further intensified by the external support which local contestants receive and by the openly absolutist aims of some violence-prone factions of the left and right. Historically a crossroads for imperialist ambitions, the Isthmus continues to be shaped by the contest for influence among local rivals and their foreign allies, though intra-regional competition overshadows most other forms. It is thus not surprising that external intervention is a complicating factor in regional politics, and that East-West as well as North-South features are present in the region's politics. In a nutshell, the perspective of East-West relations, the "national breakdown" approach, and the North-South "inter-dependence" focus assign varying degrees of importance to the role of external actors. But none is sufficiently capable of adequately assessing how influence is exerted or how specific objectives are formulated. Insofar as linkages between external actors and domestic groups or governments are assumed to exist, these are taken to be sensitive to <u>central</u> direction and manipulation, rather than conceived as relations which may be mutually beneficial.

This essay rejects both the globalist approach focusing exclusively on geopolitical rivalries, as well as the "indigenous" crisis view which minimizes the role played by revisionist states, thus properly framing Cuba's behavior in regional politics. Cuba is viewed here as a "regionally intrusive power," namely a nation exhibiting "politically significant involvement" beyond its borders, an involvement determined in turn by its very "objectives, power, motivation, location and international position" (Cantori and Spiegel, 1973). Cuba's involvement thus "produces participation in the balance of power of the subordinate system (in this case the Isthmus) and may affect the dominant system's balance as well" (in this case, the Basin as a whole). Often, such participation entails economic or military aid, formal alliances, troop commitment, or any agreement causing the external power (Cuba) to behave "in ways which resemble the types of actions that would ordinarily be taken by a country indigenous to the region" (Cantori and Spiegel, 1973:349). From this perspective, Cuba's regional objectives in political, ideological, and military terms, its strategies in pursuit of these objectives, the means used in expanding its influence, and the set of constraints which Cuba faces are examined in this chapter.

FOREIGN POLICY OBJECTIVES

Goal-induced behavior among states seeks to preserve or achieve multiple, related, and often incompatible objectives. One can certainly distinguish among fundamental, middle-range, and "specific-immediate" goals, and establish relationships among means, capabilities and desirable policy goals (Wendzel, 1980:42-46). In complex fashion, the pursuit of foreign policy goals is invariably affected by a state's assessment of its will and capabilities, as well as by its perception and estimates of its adversaries. In conflict or crisis situations, specific-immediate objectives may give way to advancement of longer-term goals, insofar as the nature of the conflict may introduce new opportunities or expand the prospects for greater gains. In any case, whether a crisis is perceived favorably--as an event in which one's goals may be achieved--or unfavorably, as a period where caution is in order, attaining desired goals involves rational calculations of one's assets and the initiation of measures designed to frustrate real or potential nega-tive responses.

Properly framed, an objective is "essentially an image of a future state of affairs and future set of conditions that governments through individual policy makers aspire to bring about by wielding influence abroad, and by changing or sustaining the behavior of other states" (Holsti, 1983:124). In accordance with means, prevailing conditions in the disputed system, practicality and achievability, objectives are often stated in viable political, strategic, military, and ideological terms. Thus, foreign policy objectives ultimately reflect an actor's view of the forces at work in the immediate arena, as well as broader global considerations and perhaps its dominant world view. For instance, the marked activism of Latin American states in regional politics reflects discomfort with the present structure of the regional system. The behavior of states like Mexico, Venezuela, and Colombia is intended to bring about the reordering of the regional system through new alignments, tactical alliances among less powerful states, and repeated political challenges to declining U.S. hegemony. More specifically, Cuba, regionally isolated but in the vanguard of the activist-revisionist faction of the Non-aligned Movement (NAM) and supportive of numerous Third World demands, is also aware that activism in North-South issues enhances its prospects in Central America. In addition, the retreat of the hegemonic power (the U.S.) from overt intervention due to the considerable costs of implementation improves Cuba's probabilities for goal attainment, since its Latin American adversaries prefer accommodation rather than confrontation with Havana. As long as new security arrangements do not emerge in the Basin and the prospects of direct military intervention are less than appealing for status quo powers, Cuban moves are probably designed to frustrate the former (new security arrangements) and increase the costs of the latter (intervention). In such a context, its intrusions may well lead to considerable gains.

THE CONTEXT OF CUBA'S INVOLVEMENT

Disintegration in Central America and the opportunity to strengthen ties with several Caribbean nations have drawn Cuba into various regional struggles, turning these into multilateral competitions among states with different and often rival interests in the region. As an intrusive power aligned with the Soviet bloc (despite its prominent role in the Nonaligned Movement), Cuban objectives appear predicated on the view that the reluctance of the traditional hegemonic power to set clear limits on what it will or will not accept is unlikely to be reversed. Opportunities still exist for expanding Cuban influence, especially in Central America, but the demise of Maurice Bishop's revolutionary regime in Grenada is clearly a major setback for Cuba's overall regional standing.

All along, Cuba's goals have been to guarantee its own survival, preserve its territorial integrity, and maintain its domestic belief, political, and economic systems from externally imposed change. But its freedom of movement in the region has been affected by political defeats in the Eastern Caribbean and by a more aggressive U.S. posture. Still, apparently confident in its ability to cope with aggression or diplomatic isolation, Cuba has embarked on a policy designed to secure longer-term goals. Always a messianic state, its view now is that "historic processes" unfolding due to the irreconcilable contradictions in dependent capitalist societies deserve a "push," namely the encouragement of revolutionary violence and ideological warfare, especially in El Salvador and Guatemala. In contrast, Cuba now appears to have realized that further radicalization in Nicaragua may be counterproductive and may in fact further reduce the support given to the Sandinistas from "friendly" states in Europe and Latin America. Thus, Cuba is supportive of measures taken by the Sandinistas intended to improve the regime's relations with its opponents in the Church, the business community, and with non-Sandinista labor unions. But Cuba has not reduced its military presence in Nicaragua, though 1,000-2,000 of its nonmilitary personnel did leave in late 1983.

Several factors have qualitatively altered the balance between the forces desiring stability in the region and those determined to introduce radical change. Among the former, one finds the difficult transition to viable politics in El Salvador, declining guerrilla activity in Guatemala, the restoration of democratic rule in Honduras, the Monge administration's strong anti-Marxist stand, and greater regional assertiveness by the U.S. which is intended to strengthen friendly governments considered vulnerable to subversion or destabilization. On the other hand, armed insurgents in El Salvador are not close to being defeated by the military. The Sandinista military buildup continues unabated, arms continue flowing into El Salvador from Nicaragua, peace initatives flounder because conflict is believed to offer greater payoffs, and violence is viewed as a legitimate means of settling disputes.

In addition, persistent debt problems, negative growth rates for several Central American economies, disinvestment, capital flight, high inflation rates, and the resulting unemployment and displacement dampen prospects for regional prosperity. For instance, a recent report documents the extremely poor economic performance of Caribbean Basin economies in 1982-1983, estimating that all of the Central American nations, Guyana, Jamaica, and the Dominican Republic will have negative GDP growth rates for 1983 (Miami Report, 1983:35). A climate of economic deterioration is further exacerbated by political inertia and by the failure of several diplomatic proposals such as that of the Contadora Group, or those presented by Managua to the U.S., to move beyond platitudes calling for "a political solution" or "negotiated settlements." If at some point Contadora's agenda is agreed upon, it offers a solid starting point for an eventual democratization and demilitarization of the region, as well as for ending state-sponsored insurgencies. But so far, Mexican and Colombian unwillingness to escalate pressures on Managua means that the Sandinistas can defer having to subscribe to what in effect are a series of regional treaties. In the meantime, suspended in a permanent crisis in which combatants prefer conflict and diplomatic minuets to reconciliation, the area's vulnerabilities rapidly multiply, and the area remains at the mercy of external forces. In a nutshell, beyond economic dislocation, political conflict and foreign intrusion,

> There is the depressing dimension of the region itself, where the struggle for power seems more critical than the battle of ideas, where personalities are more important than principle. . . . It is a region where only the short term exists for the tens of thousands who die violently each year, and the long term is only marginally less bleak (Riding, 1983:643).

CUBA'S VIEW OF THE REGION

Despite poor economic performance, annual Soviet subsidization of some $3 billion (25 percent of GDP), permanent austerity, an external debt of some $4 billion to Western creditors, and a marked dependence on sugar, Cuba's leaders consistently claim that compared to dependent capitalism, developmental socialism is a superior model. From the Cuban leadership's perspective, the outbreak of violence in Central America is attributable to the persistence of poverty, illiteracy, economic oppression, and exploitation, all resulting from the preservation of capitalist orders dominated by a few oligarchs and their military allies. As Castro himself stated:

> The revolutionaries exist precisely due to the repression and the historic socio-economic problems of those countries: poverty, misery,

political tyranny, centuries-old colonial exploitation, neo-colonialism, imperialism. And imperialism and neo-colonialism are to blame for the appalling misery in which those countries live (Granma, December 13, 1982:4).

This has consistently been Cuba's diagnosis, and there is little question that it views armed revolution as the means through which fundamental change can be achieved. Speaking to the uninitiated, Castro also denies that there is an East-West dimension to the conflict in Central America, describing as "ridiculous, absurd and incredible" (Granma, December 13, 1982:4) efforts to attribute the violence to Soviet-Cuban intervention. According to Castro, in the late 1970s the Soviets did not know any of the leaders of the revolutionary organizations in Nicaragua, El Salvador, and Guatemala, except those from the constituted communist parties. On the other hand, Castro was on good terms with many of these leaders, and in fact Cuba did provide assistance to several Central American guerrilla movements in the 1960s and 1970s. Well-known differences between assorted radical movements and established communist parties created opportunities for Castro and gave Cuba's foreign policy a great deal of flexibility. According to Aguilar, it is precisely because Castro "tried to leave a door open for unorthodox Marxists, radicals, and populists, refusing to limit his relations to the Communist parties," that he "could play the role of ideological guide and unifier for many of those movements" (Aguilar, 1983:117). In short, the inclusion of communist parties in guerrilla movements such as the Frente Farabundo Martí de Liberación (FMLN) in El Salvador is partly due to Castro's insistence and partly to the realization among orthodox parties that the once derided theory of "armed struggle" now offers the best opportunities for acquiring at least a share of political power.

Havana is certainly aware that insurgents in El Salvador, for instance, are apparently willing to settle for less than total gains in order to acquire the political foothold that has so far eluded them. Consequently, Havana supports calls for negotiations without any prior conditions between the insurgents and the government in El Salvador and lowering tensions between Honduras and Nicaragua through a pragmatic realization that a regional war might break out if border hostilities, ideological acrimony, and open-ended militarization do not cease. Evidently, Havana's assessment of the military situation in El Salvador is that the insurgents cannot win a total victory, that withdrawal of U.S. support for the government is unlikely, and that a military stalemate can be converted into a limited political victory through negotiation. In the meantime, psychological warfare, hit-and-run attacks, raids against military installations and assorted targets by the insurgents continue, combined with an international propaganda offensive designed to further discredit the government, erode its support, wear down its resistance, and capitalize on its unwillingness to negotiate. With little doubt, while the prospects for negotiation are held out to the Salvadoran government and its Washington sponsors, Havana, and presumably those in the FDR-FMLN committed to that strategy, tailor their military strategy in a way that increases their political leverage.

On the other hand, Havana's position is not new, nor are its calls for political solutions (which do not include the electoral road that the U.S. and Salvadoran governments prefer). In 1982, Castro approved former Mexican President López Portillo's call for lowering tensions in the region, though Castro then as now identifies the government of the U.S. as the source of all problems today which affect Latin America and the Caribbean. Writing to López Portillo, Castro pledged his government's collaboration "in the most noble efforts which you (JLP) have delineated in Managua in order to bring to the region the atmosphere of peace, mutual respect and necessary transformations, to which we too aspire," but with the caveat that the United States refrain "from aggression against its neighbors, end its threats, cease to supply arms and finances in support of genocidal regimes, and cease its illegitimate subversive activities" (Granma, February 22, 1982:1).

One year later, Cuban Foreign Minister Malmierca reaffirmed his government's support (Granma, January 17, 1983:12) for "honorable and political solutions for Central America's conflicts." This was in line with the Franco-Mexican declaration of August 1981, FDR-FMLN proposals released in Mexico City in 1982, and subsequent Mexican-Venezuelan efforts aimed at moving beyond declarations or public pronouncements. Still, Malmierca asserted that "the forces of imperialism and zionism are on the move (se concitan) against the people of Central America as they did against the Arab peoples." At the time, imperialism conspired "against Grenada and Suriname for their independent position," something which merits "militant solidarity" from the Nonaligned Nations Movement (NAM). Completing Havana's view, Malmierca attacked violations of the Torrijos-Carter treaties by the U.S., the latter's refusal to recognize the inalienable right of the Puerto Rican people to independence and self-determination, the illegal occupation of the Guantanamo Naval Base, the blockade, and "various threats against Cuba making the Caribbean Basin a focal point of tension which can only be eliminated through respecting the people's freedom and self-determination."

Havana's insistence on blaming the U.S. for the region's failure to achieve relative peace is natural, given its political alignments and its leader's world view. But its approach to goal attainment in the Basin is incremental, i.e., featuring a willingness to frame limited political aims with a conviction that larger gains may come once some priorities are secured. For instance, a military stalemate in El Salvador is propitious for a settlement, especially if the will of the government to resist is subject to pressures from moderates and influential sectors in the U.S. pushing for dialogue with the left. It thus appears that Cuba's aims have changed from what they were in late 1980--a quick push for total victory by the insurgents--now taking into account "systemic referents" and modifying its "goal aggregate in light of environmental restraints and opportunities" (Hanreider, 1971:118). Such an assessment, though, is subject to change if Cuba and its allies on the left perceive that greater gains are possible either through a reversal of their position, changing the terms prior to negotiations themselves, or from the emergence of factors improving the "correlation of forces."

So far, Havana's policies in El Salvador and Guatemala have focused on uniting splintered leftist groups, providing weapons to insurgents as well as sanctuary and training for leftists in transit, and various forms of political guidance, support, and sympathy (U.S. Department of State, March 1982). These are not insigificant contributions, and Havana's commitment may grow depending on how it perceives responses to its behavior, the extent to which the various factions subordinate their parochial interests to the attainment of a common goal, and the political assets Havana can claim as its just reward. Undoubtedly, the presence of a strong, "friendly" regime in Havana, with proven logistical capabilities for subversion[2] throughout the Basin is a major asset for the region's radical forces notwithstanding periodic tactical differences between these and Havana. What is also evident is that Castro is informed of ongoing diplomatic efforts, that he sees factionalism as politically sterile, and that his support is avidly sought. For example,

Guillermo Ungo visited Havana December 1982, discussing with Castro the latest proposal for a dialogue put forth by the FDR-FMLN. Echoing Castro's line in declaring that a solution to the confict depended largely on the attitude of the U.S. government, since the latter had no other option but to "intervene broadly and massively," Ungo asserted that "the international correlation of forces supporting a solution favors a dialogue and a lowering of tensions." Upon leaving, Ungo stated that Castro had agreed with the merits of the FDR-FMLN proposal, and that he had found Castro's attitude "frank, open, and understanding" (Granma, December 20, 1982:6). Castro's role thus is crucial, continuing a cherished tradition in regional politics, namely that conflict resolution depends as much on personal involvement by leaders as on established procedures and mechanisms. In a region where hatching plots and conspiracies is legendary, focusing exclusively on the empirical referents of crisis management obscures how the personal motivation, temperament, and outlook of leaders directly affect the process of conflict resolution.

ROLES AND CONSEQUENCES: PROXY OR INDEPENDENT ACTOR?

Havana's activist behavior in the Basin stems from its deeply felt need to challenge U.S. hegemony in the region, but to do so in a manner that neither jeopardizes Cuba itself, nor frontally assaults U.S. security interests. Caution and circumspection characterize Havana's regional policies while always searching for opportunities to increase its power. Exploiting vulnerabilities in shaky regimes (El Salvador), consolidating ties with radical ones (Nicaragua), and taking into account the interests of potential rivals like Mexico and Venezuela--rather than major military moves such as in Angola-- are typical of Havana's incremental approach. Likewise, capitalizing on traditional Latin American nationalism in order to strengthen its Latin identity, and driving wedges between the U.S. and important Latin nations are also evident in Havana's behavior. In that aspect, Havana's policies serve longer-range goals, namely fragmentation in the regional security system and the gradual isolation of the U.S. Havana's actions during the Falklands War illustrated how the prospects of capitalizing on Latin American nationalism for its own political warfare against the U.S. energized its policies. Havana's behavior was entirely rational in the sense that ideological incompatibility with Argentina's odious authoritarian regime did not preclude transient political collaboration in pursuit of more fundamental, essentially anti-U.S. goals.

As a member of the socialist bloc and as a leader of the Nonaligned Movement's radical faction, Havana brings proper credentials and additional leverage to bear on its relations in the Basin, skillfully using its outspokenness to disguise its fundamental alignment to the Soviet bloc. Its role in the Nonaligned Movement paid off handsomely in earlier African campaigns. Cuba's ability to integrate Third World themes into its regional policies creates the perception that its behavior is autonomous, i.e., free from substantial superpower influence, when this is clearly not the case. Even if Cuba's economic or political models are found lacking because of its "institutional-organizational and functional-behavioral traits of a Soviet-type system" (Jorge, 1983:227), its quintessential anti-Yankeeism mesmerizes radicals in the region. More than any objective feature of its polity or society, Cuba's appeal lies in its ability to galvanize messianic urges into concrete political acts.

In addition, what appeals to nationalistic revolutionaries as well as leftist "moderates" in the Caribbean Basin is Havana's uncompromising radicalism, its permanent defiance of the U.S., its defense of Marxism-Leninism as an ideology of change and social progress, and its ability to camouflage dependency and satellization into a credible form of autonomy and national sovereignty. That the facts may suggest otherwise is not as important as the phenomenon that Cuba's credentials with the sectarian left are "pure," almost beyond question, and nourished through a crafty use of symbolism, imagery, and public relations. For example, invitations to visit Cuba for artists, writers, and intellectuals from the region, the holding of cultural congresses which close with ringing "anti-imperialist" declarations, and the passing out of literary rewards from Casa de las Americas have for some time been common practices with foreign policy implications. Consequently, a good number of Latin American intellectuals admire all that which is autonomous, indigenous, and national in the Cuban system and purposely disregard patently obvious totalitarian and Stalinist features.

In reality, Cuba's position in the socialist bloc, its hyperbole regarding the "wonderful achievements of the socialist fatherland" (the Soviet Union), and its routine support for Soviet foreign policy goals (from Vietnam's invasion of Cambodia to the "proper" incarceration of irksome counterrevolutionaries in Poland), raise questions regarding its ability to act independently of its superpower patron. Horowitz has described this condition as "authenticity without independence," namely the conversion of an "authentic revolution into a dependent counter-revolution." Even in the Basin, Havana's moves are necessarily circumscribed and:

> diplomacy is charged up with rather than divested of the crusading spirit. Objectives of Cuban foreign policy are defined in terms of Soviet national interest rather than Cuban national interest. Worse yet, the two are considered forever identical. Cuban diplomacy lacks the antonomy to look at the political scene from the perspective of other nations; indeed, it is probably the clearest example in the western hemisphere of small-power chauvinism (Horowitz, 1981:4).

Castro himself, deriding efforts by the Reagan Administration designed to test Cuba's ties and loyalty to the Soviets, reaffirms Cuba's position in the following terms: "We are prepared to live in peace, in mutual respect, but we shall never break our ties (vínculos) with the Soviet Union. Those imperialist gentlemen should well understand that we are not among those who break with their friends in order to become allies of their enemies" (Granma, December 13, 1982:4).

As long as Havana's behavior is totally supportive of Soviet goals, whether at the UN, in the Horn of Africa, in Afghanistan, or in the Middle East, Cuba cannot escape the charge that it is only a Soviet proxy. In the Basin, Cuba acts as a way-station, and a contact and transit point for assorted revolutionaries seeking various types of Soviet assistance. Even if economic, financial, and developmental needs force Basin countries to maintain links with Western donor countries, Cuba's ideological appeal and political connections are major assets for the Soviets. According to Duncan, the proliferation of "trans-state ties of revolutionary governments in the region" is notable, as are the "types of opportunities available to the Soviets," especially if trends point toward increasing U.S. isolation (1982:23-24). In short, what has been established is a set of mutually supportive linkages between the Soviet Union and Cuba in diplomatic, political, and military matters, with Cuba exercising some initiatives, preserving its tactical flexibility, and yet carefully avoiding overt moves that might compromise Soviet interests.

CUBA AND NICARAGUA: AN ASIDE

The overt radicalization of the Nicaraguan revolution, its leaders' acceptance of Marxism-Leninism as the driving force shaping "the new society," the manifest encroachments on pluralism designed to concentrate political power in Sandinista-dominated bodies, and the establishing of party-to-party agreements between the FSLN and the Soviet as well as other East European Communist parties signal that the original populist, social democratic project has been indefinitely shelved. Logically, Managua's ties to Cuba are quite strong across the board. Cuba is a key component of "an impressive network of ties" among Nicaragua and Soviet bloc countries, and its own influence continues to expand via Cuban personnel involved in politico-ideological, military, security, and intelligence tasks (Rothenberg, 1982:176).

To dissaffected, nationalist-minded democrats like Eden Pastora, Alfredo Cesar, and Arturo Cruz, tightening domestic controls and strengthening relations with radical states constitute a de-legitimation of the Revolution, a willingness to duplicate the Cuban model, and an unwise, ill-advised challenge to Nicaragua's own neighbors. Interestingly enough, Pastora's assertion that "if Soviet imperialism is not stopped in time, we are going to be very sorry, and not only Nicaraguans" (La Nación Internacional, April 16-22, 1982:8), suggests that he attaches geopolitical significance to Nicaragua's internal and external policies, even as others, Castro included, make every effort to dismiss East-West factors from any analysis of contemporary Nicaragua.

Short of a successful U.S. military move against Nicaragua, which is unlikely despite contentions by the Sandinista leadership that an invasion "is imminent," Havana has realized a major objective, namely the establishment of a strong ally and ideologically kindred regime in Central America. To have achieved that at relatively low cost, without compromising either its own security or secondary interest speaks of Havana's tactical flexibility, clearly superior to that of other regional actors who have chosen a nonconfrontational strategy. Moreover, it is clear that since 1979, Cuban influence has grown tremendously, to the detriment of Venezuela, Costa Rica, Mexico, and Panama. Cuba's influence appears to be extensive in ministries and parastate organizations charged with political control, internal security, and ideological coercion, but its assistance in education and health services is also substantial.

One who has little doubt regarding the extent of Cuban influence is Pastora. When asked, "Which of the nine (Sandinista) majors is really in charge?" Pastora answered that in reality, "the comandante who is really in charge is Fidel Castro. In Nicaragua, what is done is what Fidel feels must be done." More specifically, Pastora contends that one of the most powerful men in Nicaragua is the Cuban ambassador, a man "who participates in many meetings of the government," and whose assistant "is in charge of Nicaragua's intelligence service" (La Nación Internacional, February 24-March 3, 1983:9). Pastora obviously feels that Havana is a crucial player. Despite his well-founded apprehensions regarding Cuba's willingness to participate in a meaningful dialogue, Pastora established direct contact with Cuban officials in

1983 in order to explain his organization's (ARDE) objectives. Subsequently, Pastora explained that he had broken off talks with Cuba, accusing the latter of sowing divisions within ARDE (LAPR, November 18, 1983:1-2). He has since resumed his guerrilla campaign against the Sandinista regime, which he views as Cuba's satellite.

It is difficult to assess the extent to which Cuban advisers in Nicaragua are directly involved in the policy-making process as actual decision makers rather than influencing that process collaterally, from less-central roles. One's impression is that close collaboration exists among Nicaraguan policy makers and technocrats from the socialist bloc, especially in technical, planning, economic, and financial matters, but that overall policy trends are set by the Sandinista directorate and managed through the pertinent bureaucratic units.

Without restating the obvious difference between exercising influence and attaining control it is evident that the former is magnified when the primary objective of a regime is consolidation through centralized decision making. No sector is entirely autonomous, nor are parallel mechanisms which could potentially exert counter-influences upon the regime's core likely to prove effective, least so in political arrangements. It is often argued that if Havana's long-term objectives are known, then its ability to deliver material assistance (economic or military) to friendly governments is limited by its own poor economic performance. Obviously, Cuba cannot be a major donor, but it can help in other ways. For instance, doctors, nurses, teachers, and construction workers involved in delivering medical, educational, or social services in a period of national reconstruction is commensurate with Cuba's ability to aid friendly governments. It is wrong to assume that these are non-political tasks, strictly service-oriented contributions offered by Cuba altruistically for humanitarian purposes which the host government defines. Cuban technocrats or skilled personnel assigned to "internationalist missions," often at personal cost and sacrifice, constitute a critical foreign presence which aids the process of nation-building, reconstruction, or the necessary transformations preceding the creation of "a new society."

What is often misunderstood is that there is no such thing as a non-political task in bilateral assistance, and that role differentiation obscures the eminently political purposes of such programs. Cuban missions abroad represent the system which sent them; in fact, collectively and individually, Cuban contingents serve as "ambassadors" whose mission is to represent the achievements of Cuban socialism. Insofar as their presence makes a contribution to health, welfare, education, and national defense, a legitimation of revolutionary, Marxist-Leninist ideas and practices may follow. Competence as well as on-the-job performance and an ability to "blend" into the local environment are additional assets, but the critical dimension is that a positive correlation be found between the level of contributions from Cuba and Cuba's social system.

In situations where efforts are underway to transform the political culture, as is the case in Nicaragua, Cuba's ideological and political assistance is transmitted by personal contact as well as through institutional and structural means. Aggregate levels of financial aid, therefore, prove to be distorted measures of influence, since the latter pales when compared to political and ideological support, which has a considerable impact on the process of changing values. Cuba's nonconventional aid is often more critical for a revolutionary government than weapons or money, since it focuses on processes of value-transformation and cultural change, making a direct impact on early, adolescent, and adult socialization (Wriggins, 1968; Stephen, 1980). But one must not overstate the impact of education on political or individual attitudes, especially in a context where total regimentation does not yet exist. The point here is that Cuba's efforts in this area strengthen friendly governments in ways that arms, material, or technical help does not and that in the final analysis may be more durable since political loyalties and attachments to "the new order" are bound to emerge over time. In sum, Cuba's role is multifaceted, involving a struggle of ideas, of ways in which society is organized and values shaped, of systematically stripping away the ethical underpinnings of "bourgeois" society and advancing its very antithesis on all fronts. Those who choose to resist such overt penetration have a formidable task on their hands.

Not only in Nicaragua, but wherever there is a considerable Cuban presence, its collective behavior may be understood in political terms, i.e., carrying forward a particular conception of what constitutes "the good society," a counter-model to either desarrollista or statist-reformist approaches. If socialist authoritarianism inevitably produces concentration of power in an elite, monolithic rather than corporatist or pluralistic arrangements, an all-encompassing ideological ethos, and a necessary reliance on coercion rather than persuasion in order to shape behavior and force compliance, such are but "unwelcome" outcomes of the process of political change (Cuzan and Heggen, 1982).

In Nicaragua, questions regarding regime consolidation, leadership style, and sources of legitimate authority revolve on the viability of a Castroite strategy for consolidating political power. Such a model, essentially Latin in temperament, "scientific" in inspiration, Leninist in method and effectiveness, ruthless in the pursuit of ends though prudent and tactical in the development of its means, is not necessarily replicable in Nicaragua. There, the charismatic appeal of a single dominant figure is absent, and the collective leadership strategy exhibits greater viability in the post- rather than pre-consolidation stage, which is coming to a close. In contrast, the need for unity creates the perception of monolithic leadership, when in fact faint signs of division and factionalism may often be perceived. Nonetheless, even if the elements of resistance can still deploy their own anti-regime resources, though with substantial difficulty and at high cost, the regime is clearly in a superior position and is unlikely to expand the role of its opponents into top decision-making positions.

Whether the Sandinista commanders can achieve the same success as Castro is debatable. The regime's monopoly of the instruments of coercion minimizes the prospects of effective anti-regime mobilization, but the threat of massive popular resistance is a strong deterrent against the banning of all forms of anti-regime expression and behavior. In addition, contra raids along the Honduran and Costa Rican borders demonstrate that the Sandinista regime is not in control of all of its territory. Armed opposition to the regime is not likely to be disbanded until the government realizes that its political intransigence is too costly and as a consequence moves toward a genuine rapprochement. Still, vestiges of pluralism exist and periodic manifestations of opposition are evident, but both must be taken as signs of the regime's caution and insecurity rather than as "proof" that it is willing to tolerate legitimate criticism indefinitely, or that it seeks to incorporate non-Sandinista sectors into the governing process. In any case, social confrontation, ideological stridency, and statization are evident. The regime may be vulnerable to massive open defiance, widespread noncompliance with its orders and measures, and insurrection, but the absence of institutional means through which legitimate opposition is expressed suggests that such prospects are not welcome by the leadership. Social divisions, popular discontent, foreign meddling, bureaucratic ineptitude, and mismanagement retard the consolidation of an absolutist regime.

The argument here is not intended to mean that Nicaragua's slide toward a "hard" leftist dictatorship is due directly to Havana's infuence, or that Castro is recklessly pushing the Sandinistas to assert total political control once and for all. Complex forces within the leadership as well as the society are at work which have a bearing on the formation and consolidation of an exclusionary coalition. Some of these forces are subject to manipulation, others are able to resist, thus preserving greater autonomy or flexibility. What is being emphasized is that Havana can feel relatively secure and satisfied with a government that challenges the "hegemonic presumption" of the U.S., is inclined to support and promote insurgency beyond its borders, and adds weight and credibility to the radical alignment in regional affairs. If that regime were to enter into a multifaceted relationship with the Soviets, identify in principle and action with Soviet clients in the Nonaligned Movement or at the UN, and preserve its economic and financial linkages to Western countries, that would be optimal. In short, a Nicaraguan regime that is ideologically, politically, and militarily aligned with Cuba and the Soviet bloc without becoming an economic burden on them, does not make intolerable security demands, is on good terms with Venezuela and Mexico, and still adds to the geopolitical worries of the United States, would be desirable from Cuba's perspective.

CUBA AND THE CARIBBEAN

Since 1980, Havana's intrusions have produced mixed results among the micro-states of the Caribbean, most of which retain strong parliamentary institutions and elected governments. In states where radical parties exist, nationalism, indigenous cultural factors, and pragmatic leadership shape a curious ideological outlook with strong dependista and anti-colonialist over-tones. Problems of internal and horizontal integration remain unsolved, and though democracy is the modal political pattern, it "is not always deeply rooted, and an extended period of political stability may be coming to an end" (Lowenthal, 1984:187). On the other hand, U.S. programs such as the Caribbean Basin Initiative (CBI), the demise of Grenada's Marxist dictatorship, and strong pro-U.S. governments in Jamaica, Dominica, Barbados, and the Dominican Republic minimize the political prospects of groups that are still sympathetic to Havana. On the whole Havana's formal ties to members of the Caribbean Community are stable, with emphasis on commercial and economic matters and not on deepening political involvement. Given its limitations and costs, the Cuban model is not as admired as it once was and Cuban political gains have been reversed.

Cuba's relations with Jamaica deteriorated rapidly once the non-socialist Jamaica Labor Party under Seaga came to power in 1980. Seaga had been an outspoken critic of Michael Manley's close ties to Castro and Havana, accusing the latter of massive interference in Jamaican politics. Seaga threw the Cuban ambassador out shortly after he became Prime Minister, severely curtailing the overall Cuban presence in Jamaica. According to Seaga, party-to-party links had been established between the Cuban

Communist Party and Manley's People's National Party (PNP), Cuban intelligence networks thrived in Jamaica, and a process was underway "gearing Jamaican society for a transformation into the Cuban-type model" (Davis, 1981:14). The fact that the largest share of Caribbean Basin Initiative (CBI) funds allocated to any Caribbean nation went to Jamaica ($U.S. 50 million), and that over $U.S. 1 billion in economic aid and loans has been secured through 1984 from Western institutions is evidence that Jamaica is no longer perceived by Washington as "ripe" for leftist subversion and that Seaga's government has learned to play its "Cuba card" in order to extract U.S. and western assistance (Braveboy-Wagner, 1984:173-174).

In the wake of the U.S. invasion of Grenada, several former British colonies, especially in the Eastern Caribbean, continue to view Havana with suspicion, but are now less apprehensive. More than ever before, Barbados remains strongly pro-U.S. and its forces participated in the Grenada invasion, as did Jamaica's. Altogether, Cuba's fortunes in the Eastern Caribbean have plummeted, and Castro's claim that the U.S. made a major political error by invading Grenada is not shared by area governments. In fact, Castro laid the blame for the Bishop's regime collapse on "intoxicated" (U.S. Department of State, 1983a) revolutionaries within the New Jewel Movement itself, whom he angrily denounced as a "Pol Potist" faction. Finally, undisputable evidence of secret military treaties between Grenada and the Soviet Union, Cuba and North Korea leave little doubt that what was repeatedly portrayed as a "genuine, nationalist and populist" regime was in fact rapidly becoming a Soviet-Cuban satellite. Such facts are not likely to be forgotten.

The emergence in Suriname of a radical regime headed by still another "sergeant turned colonel" making predictable anti-Western, anti-colonialist sounds while promoting the theme of "building a new society" once provided new opportunities for Havana. Described by Granma as a "country in Revolution" in 1982 while Suriname's government dismantled the remnants of a colonialist infrastructure in order to promote development, is today a regime undeserving of Cuba's affection. In fact, Col. Bouterse in late 1983 expelled 25 Cuban diplomats and 80 advisers from Suriname because he suddenly saw them as a potential threat to his regime's survival. The Cuban press no longer carries glowing commentaries of the Colonel's heroics, and the latter has embarked on a policy of mending fences with the U.S. and Brazil. Simply put, Cuba's painstaking cultivation of Caribbean radicals have been dealt a major setback and present trends suggest that its future intrusions will be met with resistance. In the face of superior power, the emperor (Castro) was shown to have no clothes.

Havana's close ties to radical states in the Caribbean or South America affected its chances of restoring full ties to Venezuela, strained during most of Herrera Campins' administration due to incidents at the Venezuelan Embassy in Havana, exile politics, and the crisis in Central America. But in the post-Malvinas environment, the prospects of renewing political and diplomatic ties with Cuba appeal to some Venezuelan policy makers, especially now that Acción Democrática is back in power. Scaling down the intense rivalry in which both countries engaged regarding the elections in El Salvador (1982) and the direction of the Nicaraguan revolution through an incremental restoration of bilateral ties produces mutual advantages. So far, officials from Cuba have visited Caracas and vice versa, and each government appears ready to continue the dialogue at fairly high levels. The prospects for renewed ties would be further enhanced if Cuba were to reduce its meddling in Central America and if "an evolution of the

Cuban authorities' attitudes toward greater independence from the Soviet Union" was to emerge (Boersner, 1983:102). Cuba's support of the Contadora process is certainly in line with a potential rapprochement, but at this point the Contadora agenda is far from being fulfilled.

Havana's ability to exploit the Malvinas conflict in 1982 for its own political purposes illustrated how a core element of its global policy--anti-colonialism--can be articulated in a politically satisfactory manner in order to renew ties with a democratic nation. Despite the fact that Havana and Caracas have quite different objectives in Central America and that they remain political and ideological rivals, they both have some mutual interests. If Havana can restore credible ties to Venezuela without markedly reducing its commitments to revolution in Central America, it would have achieved a major gain, enabling Havana to pursue its goals more aggressively and with little concern over how the mobilization of Venezuelan resources might affect its policies.

Attaching greater value to normalization of relations with an important Latin nation than to supporting revolutionary movements is part of Havana's track record. Such was the case in the early to mid-1970s when Havana reduced its isolation, de-escalated its radical rhetoric, sent numerous positive signals to the U.S. and other democratic states, welcomed the prospects of "ideological pluralism" in the Basin, and shelved the idea of "armed struggle." It is entirely possible that similar sets of trade-offs could be worked out between Havana and its nonMarxist rivals in the region, involving Havana's efforts to "leash" the radical left in exchange for a re-legitimation of its role in regional affairs. Initiatives would come from democratic states fearful that guerrilla violence might threaten their stability, and it would presumably entail firm guarantees from Havana not to encourage or support insurgents. On the other hand, the extent to which Havana is able to impose effective restraints on the "hard" left is open to question. Factionalism and personal disputes have divided leftist forces in the past and Havana's ability to control often disunited movements is less than absolute. Havana's leverage on the armed left is considerable, though it falls short of total control; in turn, Castro's views weigh heavily on any political or military calculations made by the left, including how far calls for negotiations should go in Nicaragua or El Salvador. In the final analysis, it is in the interests of the region's democracies and Mexico to demand that Havana exercise its influence on the insurgents in exchange for improving or normalizing relations.

CHOICES AND DILEMMAS

Area governments attempting to influence Havana's behavior confront the absence of effective means to affect Havana's policies as well as the fact that the latter's revolutionary ideology is a compelling factor behind its activism. Coping with Havana's specific instances of intrusion, direct or indirect intervention leaves the revolutionary ideology and its messianistic pretentions unaffected. Political divisions among states in the Basin also weaken efforts to "contain" Havana, especially when key actors perceive U.S. hegemony as a greater threat. In effect, Havana's adversaries are constantly on the defensive, often reaching out to Cuba as a way of distancing themselves from the U.S. and vice versa. For instance, shifts in Panamanian and Colombian policies--the former toward the U.S., the latter in the opposite direction--can be attributed in part to the value attached to relations with

Cuba, especially if core interests or domestic tranquility are affected.

Havana's responses to pressures for moderation depend on its assessment of how greater gains can be achieved, i.e., depending on how its interests are best served, through relaxation or increased activism. At times, Havana's priorities have been accommodation and reintegration; at other instances, vigorous promotion of revolutionary causes and unity. Both have been evident over the past few years as Havana wavers "between supporting armed revolution and negotiated settlements, and between imposing its own leadership and tolerating the idiosyncracies of different guerrilla groups" (Riding, 1983: 643).

Lastly, because constraints limit Havana's freedom of action, one must not underestimate the drive in Havana's foreign policy; ideologically defined, the latter is remorseless in pursuit of its ultimate objectives. As self-confessed Marxist-Leninists, Havana's leaders have a duty to support revolutionary movements, though the struggle and the means through which assistance is rendered take various forms. What is often perceived as a major concession from Havana by its adversaries, for example, a willingness to enter into a dialogue, is in effect an effort to settle on terms that are unachievable through other means. Negotiations are but a tactical device, used in order to secure partial, even limited gains. Seldom are they viewed as final, i.e., producing irreversible outcomes not subject to change through political means.

CONCLUSIONS

Guerrilla wars in Central America, deepening divisions in revolutionary Nicaragua, and greater assertiveness by the U.S. bring into focus how foreign policy considerations affect processes of political change. In the Isthmus's convoluted environment, clashes between the forces of order and those seeking participation and demand satisfaction are often transformed into intense conflicts that lead to absolutist outcomes. Sustained by doctrines justifying struggles of national liberation as proper responses to socio-economic inequity and political exclusion, politicized sectors seek legitimacy through political violence. Armies, traditionally protective of elites' and oligarchies' privileges, refuse to defend the old order, but protecting their own corporate interests through repression and counter-violence generates a spiral of terror precluding the realization of satisfactory political arrangements.

The prospect that breakdowns might lead regimes to contemplate new political alignments means that opportunities for influencing outcomes grow, and intrusive powers, directly or through surrogates, compete for local loyalties. Without subscribing to an East-West model, one can fathom Havana's involvement in the Basin, especially in the guerrilla wars of Central America, and in the attempted consolidation of Nicaragua's Marxist-Leninist regime. As a revolutionary state committed to the destruction of capitalist orders that it considers illegitimate, Cuba can arrogantly deploy political, military, and ideological assets on behalf of its allies and in pursuit of its goals, and do so as a matter of "national right."

At the core, processes of transformation underway in the Isthmus seek either to create viable political communities through genuine democratization, or to impose statist and authoritarian models through regimentation, class warfare, and the de-legitimation of political opposition. Caught between extremes, without centrist movements capable of forging moderate, consensus-type arrangements or shaping national institutions rather than class-dominated ones, sectors that would normally refrain from "going to the barricades" see their <u>other</u> choices disappear. Accordingly, a large part of the problem in Central America "is that actors seeking an opening, those elements aspiring to democratic change, cannot afford to wait, not out of subjectivism or leftist infantilism, but simply because their survival is threatened" (Baloyra, 1982b:90).

In such a context, foreign intrusion can only lead to greater complications, since local forces can claim external support and the sheer number of actors with a stake in the outcome multiplies. On the other hand, the often-expressed lament from the Isthmus about "why don't you simply leave us alone," is neither credible nor realistic. A crossroad for centuries and an area where great power rivalries influence domestic politics, the whole region retains geopolitical significance even if its strategic value has declined. Invariably, politics and crises in the region will attract non-Basin contenders. The fact that Bulgarian advisers are present in Nicaragua, that the Palestine Liberation Organization (PLO) cultivates ties among radical groups, that Israel is making its influence felt, and that Soviet cultural missions travel through the area belie the naivete of purists and noninterventionists alike. In sum, struggles in Central America and throughout the Basin suggest that the regions are far from becoming political communities, that disparities invite instability and disorder, that antagonistic conceptions of how societies are to be organized are a core element in various states' regional policies, and that mechanisms for conflict resolution fail to work if force is believed to produce outcomes that are more politically desirable.

NOTES

1. Defined here as the islands in the Caribbean main, the Central American Isthmus, and the northern tier of South America.

2. Subversion is taken to mean rebellious activity in a country with the distinguishing feature that "it is organized, supported or directed by a foreign power, using for its own purposes disaffected elements in a society. As such, subversion involves a series of essentially clandestine actions undertaken by one state, enlisting some citizens abroad through propaganda, infiltration and terror to overthrow the established regime in their own country" (Holsti, 1983: 256).

Part 4

Directions for Research
on Latin American Foreign Policies
in the 1980s

15
Toward a Theory for the Comparative Analysis of Latin American Foreign Policy

Elizabeth G. Ferris

The articles in this volume illustrate both the strengths and weaknesses of research into Latin American foreign policy behavior. As in-depth case studies, they offer insights into a relatively neglected research area and provide the basis for moving toward development of theories of Latin American foreign policies. In this concluding chapter, we present the outlines of a theoretical approach for the study of Latin American foreign policies. The hallmark of a good theory, as any research methods course illustrates, is that it guides in the formation of research questions and helps us to interpret our results. There has been very little guidance for researchers interested in Latin American foreign policy matters in the past. Research questions have been formulated with a more solid grounding in history than in political science. Researchers into Latin American foreign policy have devoted more efforts to tracing the historical development of unique national experiences than to searching for patterns of regularities within the region's pattern of international relations.

There are two bodies of research literature which are useful in formulating our theoretical approach, each of which brings a different perspective to the subject of Latin American foreign policies. The literature from the field of comparative foreign policy is rich in middle-range theoretical propositions (e.g., the governments of larger nations exhibit more conflict in their foreign policies than the governments of smaller countries); furthermore, it provides an increasing amount of research which empirically tests these theoretical propositions. A large number of these hypotheses are relevant to the case of Latin America; others seem useful theoretically and yet are practically difficult to test given the paucity of data on whole ranges of factors--such as bureaucratic and individual factors--hypothesized to be influential in determining foreign policy actions. In addition to difficulties in testing hypotheses derived from the literature on comparative foreign policy, the literature ignores those cultural factors which set Latin America apart from the rest of the world. A theory of Latin American foreign policy behavior would enable theoretical propositions to be drawn which, in effect, control for common historical and cultural factors. Such a theoretical approach could contribute to our understanding of foreign policy making generally as well as to our understanding of Latin American political processes.

A second body of literature includes two major theoretical approaches which are based on Latin America's unique cultural and historical development. The dependencia theories suggest the paramount importance of economic

factors, particularly external factors, in determining Latin American foreign
policy behavior. A host of case studies and an increasing assortment of cross-
national analyses use this approach in explaining foreign policy actions by
Latin American governments (Kaufman et al., 1975; Fagen, 1977; Cockroft
et al., 1970; Bonilla and Girling, 1973; Bodenheimer, 1971; Bath and Dilmar,
1976; Evans, 1979; Chilcote and Edelstein, 1974). However, dependency
theory was developed principally to explain Latin America's lack of development and not to explain differences between behavior of Latin American
governments. A second theoretical approach currently in vogue among some
Latinamericanists is the authoritarian or corporatist approach which focuses
on the influences of Latin American political culture as a determinant of the
region's political structures and lack of economic development (Pike, 1974;
Malloy, 1977; O'Donnell, 1973, 1978; Morris and Ropp, 1977; Collier, 1979).
Both of these approaches make useful distinctions between Latin America and
the rest of the world, particularly the now-developed nations; yet they are
less useful as tools for differentiating between Latin American governments.
Clearly the foreign policy differences between Cuba and the Dominican
Republic, between Chile and Colombia, or between Mexico and Panama are
greater than analyses of their dependent development would suggest. We
maintain here that dependent development is a real and pervasive influence
on Latin American foreign policy actions and that it affects foreign policy
behavior by setting limits within which foreign policy can be carried out.
Certainly, Latin American nations which depend on the U.S. for a large part
of their investment and other capital will not choose to antagonize the
country that provides these benefits. However, within those limits, the
nations have substantial latitude and a range of foreign policy options which
are available to them. Exploring this range of options is our primary interest.
We are seeking to explain the differences in the foreign policy stances taken
by Latin American nations; while differences in the degree of dependence of
Latin American nations on the U.S. and other European nations may account
for some foreign policy differences, there are still other foreign policy differences which cannot be explained by a dependency model. Similarly, the
authoritarian or corporatist approach establishes a predisposition toward a
certain form of political and social organization, establishing a context
within which foreign policy decisions are made. In sum, while both of these
approaches offer insights into Latin American foreign policy behavior, they
are insufficient to stand by themselves as the basis for a theory of Latin
American foreign policy behavior.

As discussed in the first chapter of this volume, research on foreign
policy can focus on one (or more) of the following four dimensions: causes,
processes, policies, and consequences of foreign policy. While some studies
have tried to relate two or more of these four components--usually by considering the possible causes of foreign policy behavior--there has been no
attempt to link studies from all four components into logically consistent,
theoretically useful approach. An outline for the development of such an
approach, together with suggestions of specific hypotheses derived from the
literature on Latin American politics, are presented here in an effort to
begin the process of filling the vacuum of theoretically based foreign policy
research. As with all initial efforts at theoretical formulation, the suggestions made here are tentative in nature. Hopefully, they will serve as a
starting point for further discussion and other theoretical endeavors.

A theme common to both the literature on comparative foreign policy
and on Latin American politics (particularly the developmentalist and

dependencia schools) is the importance of understanding policy decisions in the context of specific issue-areas. A reformulation of the issue-area concepts serves as a useful organizing tool for the development of theory for the comparative analysis of foreign policy. The proposition that nations exhibit different patterns of internal political processes in response to the different types of international issues on which they interact has a long tradition in comparative foreign policy studies. This proposition was initially derived in large measure from theoretical arguments elaborated in the context of U.S. domestic politics. Lowi's (1964) distinction between arenas of power has been extended to questions of foreign policy (although Lowi himself only briefly mentioned foreign policy). Despite the initial casting of most issue-area research into a domestic political framework, scholars studying foreign policy have persistently returned to the idea that different patterns of behavior can be understood through analysis of the issues on which nation-states interact (Hermann et al., 1973; Keohane and Nye, 1977; Brewer, 1973; O'Leary, 1976; Brecher, 1969; East et al., 1978). Yet, Potter's (1980) survey of the literature on issue-areas shows, while many scholars have pointed to the need for an emphasis on issue-areas, there have been few attempts to generate hypotheses capable of being empirically tested based on such issue-areas.

In the case of studies of Latin American foreign policies, there has been little effort to determine the issues of particular importance in patterns of regional relations and there have been even fewer efforts to develop empirically testable hypotheses based on these areas. Indeed, with the exception of Ferris et al. (1977) and Wittkopf et al.(1974), we know of no efforts to utilize issue-areas in research specifically on Latin American foreign policies. Other studies, focusing on Latin America as one of many regions, have discussed such issues. These studies have generated issue-area categories for nations in general and then applied these categories to Latin American--as well as European and African--governments (Rosenau and Haggard, 1974; East, 1978; Hermann, 1973; Zimmerman, 1973). There has been no attempt to formulate issue-areas for specific application to Latin America.

However, the importance of issue-areas has been implicitly recognized by scholars researching Latin American foreign policies and is manifest in the divisions existing in the field. On the one hand, there are those studying geopolitical components of foreign policy, usually focusing on security and territorial issues, while another group focuses almost exclusively on economic determinants of foreign policies. A third identifiable group considers Latin America in international fora--usually the United Nations--and typically consists of scholars who are not primarily specialists on Latin America, but rather solidly grounded in international relations generally.

There have been countless efforts to develop typologies of issue-areas. James Rosenau's (1966) original specification of issue-areas produced four issue-areas--status, territory, human resources, and non-human resources-- which were obtained by considering two dimensions of the processes by which policies were made, specifically with the tangibility of means and ends. Michael Brecher (1969, 1972) and others classify issues on the basis of their substantive content instead of the process by which decisions are made; they identify the principal issue-areas as military-security, political-diplomatic, economic-developmental, and cultural-status. Hermann's CREON project is based on five substantive "problem-areas"--e.g. physical safety, economic wealth, respect/status, well-being/welfare, enlightenment, and a residual "other" category (Hermann et al., 1973). Keohane and Nye (1977) identify issues as those sets of problems or issues regarded by policy makers as closely interdependent and dealt with on a collective basis. These differing typologies illustrate the different ways in which issue-areas have been conceptualized and used in foreign policy research. The literature on issue-areas further suggests a basic division between those who view issues as substantively differentiated from one another and those who (in the tradition of Ted Lowi) classify issues into areas on the basis of hypothesized differences in decision-making processes. There is also a split in the literature between those who are interested in issue-areas as heuristic devices for providing theoretical insights into foreign policy and those who seek to operationalize indicators and empirically test hypotheses. The theoretical formulation of issue-areas one finds most useful depends on the purpose for which one is using the theory.

As our purpose here is to develop a theoretical approach which will aid in our understanding of Latin American foreign policy behavior and to guide research in the area, the substantive approach would appear to be the most useful.

ISSUE-AREAS IN LATIN AMERICAN FOREIGN POLICY ANALYSIS

In the context of the Latin American political reality, the issues on which nations interact can be grouped into three issue-areas: the military-strategic area (corresponding to traditional conceptions of national security), the economic development area (encompassing components of present-day national security concerns), and a status-diplomatic area. The first issue-area, strategic-military, encompasses those issues related to the physical protection of the nation-state. In addition to national defense and security policies, this would include actions taken to define boundaries, to increase military strength via purchases of military hardware and military training, and to resolve territorial disputes (including water, seabed, and air rights).

The second issue-area, that of economic development, includes those issues related to a government's economic concerns. This would include a nation's search for markets, foreign investments, loans, and debt refinancing; attempts to secure energy and technology from abroad, aid, and regional economic integration. In the Latin American context this issue-area is increasingly viewed as a national security issue. National security was originally re-defined by the Brazilian military to include issues of economic growth and stability in addition to the more traditional view of national security as physical protection of the nation's boundaries. Increasingly too Latin American nations are coming to see economic independence as a paramount national developmental goal. The search for greater national autonomy in those economic decisions which are vital to a nation's security is playing a more important and a more visible role in Latin American foreign policy decisions.

The third issue-area, the status/diplomatic area, encompasses those issues which guide Latin American more-or-less routine interactions with the rest of the world. Foreign policy actions in this issue-area include participation in international and regional organizations; exchange of diplomatic representatives and bilateral agreements with other nations; interactions involving international law, human rights, and refugees; routine agreements on culture and tourism issues; and symbolic statements of regional solidarity or unity. Most issue-area typologies include a military and economic dimension as we have done, but they also include several other issue-areas in place of our single area of status-diplomatic issue-area (e.g., East et al., 1978; Rosenau, 1966; Wittcopf et al., 1974; Zimmerman, 1973). We maintain that further

TABLE 15.1

Issue-Areas in Latin American Foreign Policies

Issue-Areas	Levels	
	Regional Level	Global Level
Military/ strategic	regional ideological alliances, fear of revolutionary spillover, joint security alliances, border disputes and traditional rivalries	depending on the regime's political orientation support for anti-communist groups for communist insurgents, search for military allies, action concerning the 200-mile limit, oil rights, extra-regional military aid and sales
Economic/ developmental	regional integration, aid, cooperation in technologies, transfers, joint planning	policies to obtain new foreign markets, investments, loans and debt refinancing; and resolution of balance-of-payments difficulties from extra-regional powers; actions to increase access to energy and technology; balance of payments
Status/ diplomatic	bilateral and multilateral agreements on cultural, tourism, education, and health issues, participation in regional organizations, formulation of joint registration positions, granting political asylum	participation in international organizations, support for international law, human rights, actions on behalf of refugees

delineations within this group are simply not useful. Cultural and educational exchanges, for example, are primarily used in Latin America as ways of improving relations with other countries and only secondarily as attempts to improve education or culture at home. A further example of the way in which foreign policy interactions on culture or human resource dimensions are more indicative of a status-diplomatic issue-area than of other, more substantive issue-areas is that of human rights. The reaction to Carter's human rights policies in Latin America indicated much less concern with the "integrity of the person" than with questions of sovereignty, intervention, and a desire to have good relations with the U.S.

These three issue-areas thus provide an exhaustive set of mutually exclusive types of issues on which Latin American nations act. In an earlier volume, we drew a basic distinction between foreign policies on the global and regional levels. Together with our three issue areas, these two dimensions produce a table (Table 15.1) which is useful in characterizing foreign policy behavior and in providing for more systematic cross-national comparisons. Examples of foreign policy actions are included in the appropriate cells. Researchers seeking to understand Latin American foreign policy behavior can thus compare a single nation's regional and global foreign policies in a particular issue-area or can compare several nations' actions on an issue-area at a particularl level. In addition, this schema makes it easier to compare very different policies which are intended to meet the same goals. For example, the question of the relationship between foreign policy and economic development goals would lead to quite different responses for Peru and Venezuela and even more differences between Mexico and Brazil.

Our focus on issue-areas also provides for the generation of empirically testable hypotheses. As we indicated earlier, research efforts in the comparative analysis of foreign policy behavior can be classified into four groups: research focusing on causes, processes, policies, and consequences. Using this classification scheme, thirteen hypotheses are developed for each of the three issue-areas and presented in the sections below.

CAUSES OF LATIN AMERICAN FOREIGN POLICY BEHAVIOR

The literature on Latin American politics suggests three principal determinants of Latin American foreign policy--a regime's choice of developmental model, the extent of national economic dependence on the U.S. and perceived territorial threats. These three hypothesized determinants of foreign policy differ from the customary emphasis on national attributes and measures of national capability by those studying comparative foreign policy generally. The first two of our hypothesized causes of foreign policy behavior primarily determine foreign policy behavior in the economic development issue-area while the latter is concerned with the military-strategic dimension. All three of the hypothesized causes of foreign policy actions focus on the interactions between what have traditionally been considered external and domestic determinants of foreign policy. It is argued here that external conditions impinge on foreign policy making through the ways in which they are perceived by decision makers. Thus, some "traditional rivalries" have all but disappeared from national consciousness while others remain in the forefront of public controversy. Similarly the fact that a nation is economically dependent on the U.S.--by some objective indicator--is less important as a determinant of foreign policy behavior than the way in which these officials perceive that dependency limits their policy choices. An analysis of the inter-relationships between external and internal policy determinants is more significant than a more simplistic division of causes into domestic and foreign components.

All Third World governments are seeking economic development. Apart from protection of territory, the drive to develop is hypothesized to be the most powerful influence on Latin American foreign policy behavior. Although all Third World nations seek to increase their development, they have different developmental models as goals; the choice of a developmental model determines the type of foreign policies a Latin American government will pursue.

H_1 Governments seeking economic development in terms of rapid industrialization, development of a manufacturing export capability, and increased economic power will be more likely to emphasize their global over their regional foreign policies. Specifically, they will be more interested in formulating military alliances and obtaining military aid from First World powers; they will aggressively seek markets, aid, and investments from nations outside the region and will be more active in and attach more importance to bilateral relations with global powers than with nations in the region.

Those governments which aspire to First World status--and those in which leaders perceive that this is an attainable option--will emphasize global foreign policies. The developmental focus of these nations is on acquisition of the technology and the domestic economic capability necessary to break into the ranks of the presently developed nations. The aspirants follow policies of global challenge and regional aloofness. They are most likely to support those Third World demands which will enable them to emulate First World economic progress. However, their support of Third World causes is pragmatic; they support those measures which will increase their access to the rewards of the international capitalist system, but they do not support the re-structuring of that system to enable all Third World countries to share in the wealth. The reason for this pragmatism is clear: these nations aspire to the lifestyles and the power of the First World and they think they have a chance at achieving that capability. The aspirants seek to be treated as equals by the First World nations and are sensitive to intentional or unintentional slights. Traditionally, the aspirants have not been supportive of Latin American integration schemes or other attempts to forge unified Latin American bargaining positions.

H_2 Nations pursuing economic development policies based on improving their current status in the international system via increasing and modernizing their export capacity of traditional products will be more likely to emphasize policies of regional cooperation and to display more ambivalence toward extra-regional powers than those nations aspiring to First World status. Specifically, they will seek military equipment from First World governments in smaller quantities than the global aspirants, they will emphasize bilateral ties with nations in the region, and will be more supportive of Third World solidarity movements which are not perceived as threatening to their immediate economic situation.

Nations seeking economic development through increasing exports of traditional products and through improvement of the terms under which these

products are exported will follow different patterns of foreign policy behavior
than those nations aspiring to First World status. While all Latin American
governments seek industrial development and the economic independence
industrialization brings, the chances of most Latin American governments to
achieve this industrial development are slim. Governments of these nations
tend to follow policies of <u>regional cooperation</u> and <u>global ambivalence.</u>
Governments of these nations perceive that they have the most to gain from
regional integration in terms of both accelerating their economic development
and in terms of improving their weak international bargaining position. Yet,
although they are the most enthusiastic supporters of regional integration,
real (i.e., non-rhetorical) support for such schemes is difficult in view of the
real structural constraints they face. Thus, while they support regional integration as a means of overcoming their economic underdevelopment, that
underdevelopment ensures that regional integration schemes--as currently
constituted--will not be able to be successful. In attempts to improve their
relative position vis-à-vis the First World, this group of Latin American
nations adopts policies of support for Third World movements to change the
international economic structure. This group has the most to gain from
re-structuring the international system to allow other nations a chance to
develop economically. At the same time, however, this group has the most
to <u>lose</u> from antagonizing the First World powers, creating a situation of
ambivalent policies in their dealings with the developed countries. Members
of this group include both the most active Latin American supporters of
Third World efforts to re-structure the international system and the most
ardent opponents of such efforts. Support for the United States is strongest
in this group, however, as regimes perceive that they must not antagonize the
U.S.--typically their principal trading partner and frequently a principal
political ally.

> H_3 Nations which are economically dependent on the U.S. or other
> developed countries will seek to satisfy those major powers and will
> thus be unlikely to take an active role in regional organizations or to
> engage in foreign policy behavior which is not in accord with the
> overall interests of the U.S.

A second hypothesized determinant of foreign policy behavior is the
extent to which the nation is dependent on external powers, particularly the
U.S. The <u>dependencia</u> approach has a long tradition in scholarship on Latin
American political processes; certainly the contribution of the <u>dependencia</u>
approach to our understanding of the role of external actors in Latin American politics is tremendous. It is suggested here that perception and evalua-
tion of the dependency relationships in terms of national developmental goals
is a vital part of the dependency-policy conversion process. Many dependency
theorists tend to overlook this process and end up making broad conceptual
"leaps"; thus Weisskopf (1972:11) states:

> Continued economic dependency implies also continued political sub-
> ordination. So long as governments of poor countries must seek short-
> and long-term economic aid from the advanced capitalist countries
> and the international organizations that are primarily funded by those
> same countries (the International Bank for Reconstruction and
> Development, the International Monetary Fund, etc.) their political
> autonomy will be severely restricted.

The literature on dependency is theoretically rich and quite diverse; indeed it is difficult to refer to dependency theory as a single theoretical orientation. Certainly the ideas expressed by Bodenheimer (1971), Frank (1972, 1974), O'Donnell (1974, 1978), and Evans (1979), while building on a general theoretical orientation, differ greatly in both their theoretical and methodological approaches. Nevertheless, certain common assumptions about the effects of economic dependency on foreign policy behavior can be identified. The dependencia theorists suggest that economic dependency inevitably acts as a constraint on policy decisions, that the process is virtually inevitable, and that there is relatively little national variation between dependent nations. By focusing on the external determinants of foreign policy decisions with particular emphasis on the linkages between national decision making and/or elite groups and the international capitalist system, this approach maintains that the potential for meaningful major changes in either the domestic or international contexts is unlikely to be produced by the foreign policy behavior of dependent Latin American nations. For example, dependency theorists argue that regional integration schemes are unlikely to be successful in light of the participant's integration into the existing capitalist system. Rodolfo Stavenhagen (1974:135) asserts that "the principle fruits of integration clearly will be harvested by those Latin American countries which are already more developed and more powerful and what is more, by the very non-Latin American multinational firms which, through regional integration, manage to establish their economic domination even more solidly throughout Latin America."

While the literature on dependency is theoretically rich and practically diverse, it has been over-simplified and reduced by North American scholars who have sought to test empirically the relationship between dependency and development through reliance on easily obtained statistical data instead of the more holistic approach intended by the originators of dependency theory. Thus, given the asymmetrical relationship between Latin American nations and the U.S., the success of Latin American foreign policy depends primarily on how the center nations (particularly the United States) respond and the outcomes are usually, if not inevitably, in accord with North American interests. There have been a number of studies seeking to examine the effects of economic dependency on foreign policy behavior (Kaufman et al., 1975; Richardson, 1979; Ray, 1976; Hollist and Johnson, 1979; Jackson et al., 1977; Caporaso, 1979). However, these studies are controversial in that the original Latin American formulators of dependencia theory maintain that the emphasis on easily quantifiable indicators of economic dependence obscures the real way in which dependency influences Latin American politics. Leaving aside for the time being questions of operationalization and measurement of concepts, the dependency theorists share a basic assumption that foreign policy choices of economically dependent Latin American nations will be limited. As long as a government depends on close relations with a global power for its economic developments, its ability to carry out independent foreign policy positions and particularly to undertake policies in opposition to those of the nation on which it depends will be limited.

H_4 The nature of historical patterns of conflict and cooperation with other nations in the region will influence present-day foreign policies on both the global and regional levels and on all issue-areas of interaction.

A third factor hypothesized to play a major determining role in Latin American foreign policies is the existence and nature of traditional rivalries. This variable is virtually ignored by those seeking to quantify the causes and consequences of foreign policy behavior, and yet any scholar researching patterns of Latin American foreign policy behavior confronts the existence of such traditional--and to outsiders often irrational--rivalries between Latin American nations. Certainly, the importance of such historical disputes is not confined to Latin America; indeed such rivalries are more important in more nations than political scientists like to admit. The existence of historical patterns of regional conflict will largely determine a nation's foreign policies in the military-strategic issue-area and will influence foreign policies in the other two issue-areas as well. These traditional rivalries will be important on both the regional level of relations and--to a lesser extent--on the global level as governments seek regional and global support for their foreign policy positions. This hypothesis has substantial theoretical support from those examining patterns of incremental decision making. Clearly, the best predictions of future foreign policy behavior are based on knowledge of past behavior. We are suggesting more, however, than a prediction that what happened in the past affects later behavior. Rather the pattern of traditional regional rivalries and historical territorial threats affects foreign policies toward third parties and across all issue-areas as well.

PROCESSES OF LATIN AMERICAN FOREIGN POLICY MAKING

A basic underlying reason for analyzing foreign policy in the framework of issue-areas--whether theoretically formulated in terms of substance or process--is the assumption that distinct actors and processes can be identified for each issue-area. The authoritarian or corporatist approach as formulated by authors such as Collier (1979), Malloy (1977), Wiarda (1974), and Schmitter (1974) directs our attention to the processes by which foreign policy decisions are made. This approach suggests that decisions will be made at high levels of government, that policies will be decided pragmatically rather than ideologically, that discussion of alternate strategies will be limited, and that dissenting views will not be expressed or publicized. This theoretical approach, unlike the developmental and dependency frameworks, focuses on the historical and cultural traditions of Latin American nations as explanatory factors for policy decisions. Guillermo O'Donnell's (1974, 1978) synthesis of both the authoritarian and developmental approaches further refines the discussion of the authoritarian nature of Latin American decision making. Basing his analysis on Argentina, he finds that with increasing modernization, there is a rise in the number of groups which are able to formulate demands on the political system. The political system becomes overloaded and is unable to deal with these increased demands. With a breakdown in the political system, authoritarian rule is viewed as the only means of restoring order and directing economic growth. The bureaucracy expands to deal with these problems and becomes an entrenched part of the political process and this entrenched bureaucracy comes to play an important role in the formulation of foreign as well as domestic policies. The actors which play major roles in foreign policy making can be identified and studied.

H5   Military officers will play the dominant role in formulation of policies in the strategic-military issue-areas, técnicos will play the dominant role in the formulation of policies in the economic-development area and diplomats will play the dominant role in the status-diplomatic area.

For each of our three issue-areas we hypothesize that one particular group will play a dominant role in policy making. Obviously (or perhaps not so obviously given the need of civilian governments to placate their military establishments), the military as an institution will play more important roles in foreign policy making under military governments than in civilian governments. However, notwithstanding important differences between the type of regime, military officers will play the dominant role in foreign policy formulation on strategic/military issues, técnicos will play the dominant role in economic development issues, and diplomats will be dominant in status-diplomatic issues. Each of these three groups will play the crucial role of researching specific issues, formulating alternatives, and actually implementing the decisions that are made. While the actual final decision may be made at a higher level--as in the Argentine military junta deciding to pursue a particular strategy on international debt management--the key actors in structuring the debate and in actually implementing the policies will be the three groups mentioned here. In areas where a functional overlap occurs, as in say policies of support for a regional integration scheme which is taking on an active political role, there will also be overlap, and usually a conflict, between the groups involved. Thus we can expect conflicts between técnicos and diplomats among the member governments of the Andean Pact who are increasingly viewing the regional scheme for economic integration as a tool of foreign policy coordination (Ferris, 1981). Similar conflicts between técnicos and military personnel can be observed in efforts in the Rio de la Plata group to arrive at agreements on economic infrastructure questions.

The diplomats, primarily coming out of a legal, historical tradition, have a very different orientation than the técnicos who are generally trained in economics and law. The diplomats, furthermore, tend to be housed in the Foreign Ministry and embassies abroad while técnicos can be found in ministries such as Industry, Trade, Finance, and in national planning institutions. While diplomats and military officers are more influenced by historical patterns of cooperation and conflict and also tend to have a broader vision in terms of seeing the nation's historic destiny, the focus of the técnicos is much more narrow. They tend to formulate policies on the basis of desired outcomes for national developmental policies and to view the nation's international role in terms of its economic stability and prosperity. In recent years as military governments have become more involved in economic policy making--in recognition of its importance to national security--military officers have increasingly been moving toward positions less sharply differentiated from técnicos. Indeed, some might argue that ministries in Argentina and Brazil are largely staffed by military men in technical clothes. Despite the seeming convergence of técnicos and military officers in some nations, the problem of distinguishing between the two actors is primarily a problem of conceptualization and operationalization which can be specified according to the theoretical orientation of the researchers.

H$_6$ Military governments will use issues in the strategic-military area as a way of obtaining legitimacy and popular support for their rule while civilian governments will focus on status-diplomatic issues for the same purposes.

In recognition of the difference between military and civilian governments, we hypothesize a further difference in emphasis on issue-areas. Specifically, military governments will be more likely to emphasize strategic-military issues as a way of gaining legitimacy, while civilian governments will be more likely to use status-diplomatic issues for the same goal of legitimizing their positions with the population. Thus the Argentine and Chilean governments tend to use military threats from one another as a way of creating conditions of national unity and indirectly justifying their continued presence in government, while the Ecuadoran and Peruvian regimes emphasize human rights for the same reasons. Both types of governments will use economic-developmental issues to solidify their positions when they think it is useful to do so.

POLICIES

In developing hypotheses about the policies themselves, the interrelationships between policies in the various issue-areas can be explored.

H_7 Issues in the status-diplomatic issue-area will usually be deemphasized when they conflict with issues in the strategic-military area, or to a lesser extent, the economic development issue. However, in instances where national honor is publicly at stake, compromises are less likely to be made.

For most governments, strategic-military issues are most important in times of perceived immediate threat. When such threats are not present, economic developmental issues are most important. Overall, the status-diplomatic issue-area will always be de-emphasized when it conflicts with strategic areas. For example, the 1980 debate on human rights shows that when governments, such as Argentina, perceive alleged human rights violations to be a matter of national security, they are willing to risk alienating allies and withdrawing from international organizations. At the same time, when national autonomy, sovereignty, or honor is threatened--a status-diplomatic issue--the extent to which other issue-areas will be subordinated to this issue depends on the degree of public knowledge about the issue. Thus, when Carter publicly denounced Brazil for violations of human rights, the Brazilians responded by cancelling a military alliance with the U.S. In other words, when the status-diplomatic issue is public and controversial, it is more likely that there will be compromises made in other issues than when the issues are more obscure.

THE CONSEQUENCES OF FOREIGN POLICY DECISIONS

The consequences of foreign policy decisions are determined by (1) the resource capabilities a nation has for carrying out its foreign policy objectives, (2) the processes through which the foreign policy decisions are made, and (3) the relative success or failure of policies in other issue-areas.

H_8 The more powerful a Latin American government, the more likely that government will have to have an active foreign policy and to be successful in its foreign policy pursuits in all three issue-areas.

Military power will be directly related to governmental success in the
military-strategic issue area while the financial resources available
to the government will largely determine the success of foreign
policies in the economic development area.

There is considerable evidence from the literature on comparative
foreign policy that level of economic development and power are linked with
foreign policy activity (Rummel, 1969; McGowan, 1968, 1969) and success in
foreign policy (Small and Singer, 1970; Fox, 1959; George et al., 1971).
Larger, more militarily and economically powerful nations are more likely to
be successful in pursuing their foreign policy objectives than less powerful
nations simply because they are more likely to be able to influence other
governments and to implement their foreign policy decisions. We argue here
that national power--with its economic, military, political, and geographical
components--is directly related to success in foreign policy pursuits in all
three issue-areas. Furthermore, military power is more closely related to
successful foreign policies in the military-strategic areas while the financial
resources available to a government will largely determine the success of its
economic development   capabilities.

H9   The greater the experience and expertise of policy makers in
all three issue-areas, the more likely they will be to formulate
successful foreign policies. Furthermore, policies in specific issue-
areas will tend to be more successful when formulated by those actors
most familiar with a particular issue--military officers in the military-
strategic area, técnicos in economic development issues and diplomats
in the status-diplomatic.

Considerable research exists on the impact of decision making on
foreign policy outcomes. Most of these studies, however, have been based on
the U.S. example and thus are less applicable to the Latin American case.
Studies have shown, for example, that "the longer the time taken in formulating a policy decision, the more alternatives will be considered and the more
rational will be the process" (McGowan and Shapiro, 1973:191; Haas, 1969)
and that the more conflict between decision-making groups, the more likely
decisions will be made by higher levels and the less likely to be successful.
Furthermore, the literature clearly shows that the greater the expertise and
experience of bureaucratic groups, the greater the chances that foreign policy
will be successful (Brzezinski and Huntington, 1963:384-387; McGowan, 1970:
216; George et al., 1971:231-232; Walters, 1970:168; Gregg and Banks, 1965:
614; McGowan and Shapiro, 1973:69-73). In the case of Latin American
foreign policy making, these two hypotheses indicate that those bureaucrats
with more expertise and experience will be more likely to have successful
foreign policy outcomes than those with relatively little experience and
expertise. (However, in Latin America as elsewhere, the length of time a
bureaucracy has existed is not necessarily commensurate with its expertise
and experience.) In those cases where foreign policies are formulated by
actors not usually responsible for policy-formation in a given issue-area, the
resulting policy will tend to be less successful than when formulated by the
relevant experts. This partially reflects the fact that such decisions are
likely to be more urgent and more quickly approved than the more routine
foreign policy decisions. However, the hypothesized relationship is expected
to exist because actors more experienced in a given area are more likely to

make "good" decisions than less-experienced actors.

H_{10} Foreign policy decisions are more likely to be hastily formulated, less successful, and more violent in the strategic-military issue-
area in times of threat or stress than when immediate threats are not
present.

In addition to these decision-making variables, there is also a whole
field of international relations research showing that in times of crisis or
when a perceived threat is high that a different means of formulating decisions comes into effect. There is less time for a "rational consideration of
alternatives," fewer decision makers are likely to be involved, and normal
procedures are not followed. Studies have shown for example that "the
greater the demands on the decision-making apparatus, the more likely it is
that violent foreign policy will result" (McGowan and Shapiro, 1973:192;
Benjamin and Edinger, 1971:14; Hermann et al., 1973). Thus we would expect
to find more hastily made decisions and perhaps more violent outcomes from
decisions in the strategic-military issue-area when decision-making time is
limited.

H_{11} The more successful a nation is in pursuing its strategic-
military, economic-developmental and status-diplomatic foreign
policy goals on the global level, the less emphasis will be placed on
regional foreign policies.

Foreign policy making is not a static process. Success or failure in
policies formulated in one issue-area will influence the policies formulated
in other issue-areas. In the case of the issue-areas presented here, there is
a relationship between a nation's pursuit of global and regional policies. In
general, successful foreign policies on the global level are correlated with a
de-emphasis on regional foreign policies. The implication running throughout
this study is that regional foreign policies are, for Latin American nations,
less important both in meeting national goals and in terms of the status and
power attached to them than global foreign policies. This is, in part, a function of the dependent nature of Latin American nations on extra-regional
actors, but also is due to the legacy of traditional rivalries and territorial
disputes which have made a genuine sense of shared concerns and goals
difficult to maintain. There are a few--a very few--indications that this
orientation may be changing, particularly in cases such as Venezuela and
Mexico in which regional foreign policies are assuming greater importance.
Cynics, however, might attribute the increased interest in neighboring nations
by Venezuela, Mexico, and Brazil, as less a manifestation of shifting loyalties
than a pragmatic decision that this is an area where these nations can play a
powerful role unavailable to them on the global level.

H_{12} The less successful in meeting its economic-developmental
goals, the more likely a government will use strategic-military or
status-diplomatic issues to get public support for the regime.

In general, we feel that economic-developmental issues are perceived to
be the most important for Latin American governments in terms of meeting
national foreign policy goals. The less successful a government is in meeting
these developmental goals, the more likely there will be public dissatisfaction

with the regime in power and the more likely the government will seek to use foreign policies in one of the other two issue-areas in order to increase public support.

H_{13} The more successful a government is in foreign policies in the economic-developmental and strategic-military issue-areas, the more likely it is to enjoy increased power and respect in the status-diplomatic issue-area.

Finally, success in both the strategic-military and the economic-developmental dimensions will lead to increased power and status in the status-diplomatic issue-area. Those nations perceived as being successful--for whatever reasons--in their developmental and/or military goals will be more likely to have influence in international fora. Conversely, the less successful a nation is in its policies in those two issue-areas, the less likely it is to enjoy power in international organizations. Cuba's position in the Third World movement is perhaps the classic example of this phenomenon. Cuba's Third World leadership position depends largely on its perceived success in developmental and military policies both at home and abroad.

CONCLUSIONS

In this article, we have presented a framework based on three distinct issue-areas for analyzing Latin American foreign policies and have suggested a number of hypotheses based on both the literature of comparative foreign policy and of Latin American political processes which explore the relationships between causes, processes, policies, and consequences of foreign policy decisions. With various degrees of difficulty in conceptualization and operationalization of indicators, the thirteen hypotheses presented here are all suitable for systematic testing. Testing of the hypotheses may be carried out on two levels: through case studies and through more empirically focused cross-national comparisons. Most studies of Latin American foreign policies will probably continue to analyze the foreign policy behavior of one particular nation. Such case studies provide valuable historical and descriptive information, but could also be made more useful through explicit adoption of a theoretical perspective. For example, a number of the case studies presented in this volume provide implicit support for some of our hypotheses. Lincoln's study of Peruvian foreign policy confirms the importance of a regime's developmental model as a determinant of foreign policy behavior. Certainly Pittman's article on Chile and Morales's study of Bolivia underscore the importance of traditional rivalries as determinants of foreign policy making in Latin America. Azicri's analysis of Nicaragua and del Aguila's study of Cuban foreign policy emphasize political components of policy making; and both Ferris and Gordon focus on the interplay of economic and political determinants of foreign policy. Hopefully, future case studies can be made more explicitly theoretical through more focused research questions and more systematic presentation of data. By clearly specifying the dependent and independent variables, as in studies showing the relationship between regime change and foreign policy behavior, case studies can be used as a means of hypothesis testing. However, while case studies--particularly those comparing foreign policies over time--can be made more theoretically useful, they present major problems for theory-development in that they are difficult to replicate and their results are usually not comparable. By focusing on unique national experiences, they make it difficult to determine patterns of behavior.

Empirical cross-national comparisons, on the other hand, suffer from the disadvantages of usually being based on available data (rather than information needed for adequate testing), of being superficial in approach, and of lacking creativity in conceptualization. Nevertheless, we feel that the field is currently in a stage where such efforts can be very useful. Efforts to examine Latin American foreign policy behavior on a systematic basis must be carefully thought out and must take into account the Latin American developmental experience. We are particularly concerned that the dynamics of foreign policy formation be recognized and incorporated into the research design.

One of the major obstacles to the use of more rigorous cross-national comparisons is the lack of systematic indicators and measures for the dependent variable of foreign policy. Traditionally, foreign policy has been analyzed through the use of either individual expert judgments, reliance on secondary indicators of foreign policy decisions (e.g., trade, aid, and investment figures), or through use of available statistics--such as size of diplomatic mission, UN voting patterns--which are usually not of particular relevance to the Latin American experience. By focusing on foreign policy by issue-area and by global and regional levels, more creative indicators of foreign policy behavior can be devised. For example, systematic use of country experts' judgments, sophisticated use of content and/or events analysis of Latin American sources, official political and trade mission visits, and national participation in regional organizations can all be used to specify trends in foreign policy. The systematic use of interviews with foreign policy officials is a rich source of data for understanding perceptual dimensions of foreign policy--a dimension which we see as crucial and yet one that has been ignored too often in studies of foreign policy. Testing of these--and undoubtedly other--hypotheses through the use of both more theoretically oriented case studies and more sophisticated cross-national comparisons would represent a remarkable advance in our understanding of why Latin American nations behave the way they do. Hopefully, this volume has not only provided evidence of the kind of research now being done, but will inspire researchers in their future theoretical endeavors.

References

Agencia Nueva Nicaragua (1982) International Relations: Nonalignment and the Peace Effort--What the Present U.S. Administration Doesn't Want You to Know about Nicaragua. Managua: Agencia Nueva Nicaragua.

Aguayo, Sergio (1983) "Refugiados: otra pieza en el conflicto crucigrama regional." Mimeo. Colegio de México.

Aguilar, Luis E. (1983) "Cuba and the Latin American Communist Parties: Traditional Politics and Guerrilla Warfare," pp. 107-121 in Barry B. Levine [ed.] The New Cuban Presence in the Caribbean. Boulder, CO: Westview Press.

Alexander, Robert J. (1982) Bolivia, Past, Present, and Future of Its Politics. New York: Praeger.

Amaral Gurgel, Jose Alfredo (1978) Seguranca e Democracia. Rio: Livraria José Olympio.

Ameringer, Charles D. (1982) Democracy in Costa Rica. New York: Praeger.

_____ (1979) Don Pepe: A Political Biography of Jose Figueres of Costa Rica. Albuquerque, NM: University of New Mexico Press.

Anderson, Thomas (1971) Matanza: El Salvador's Communist Revolt of 1932. Lincoln, NB: University of Nebraska Press.

Arias Sanchez, Oscar (1976) Quién Gobierna en Costa Rica? San Jose: Editorial Universitaria Centroamerica.

Armstrong, Robert (1983) "El Salvador: why revolution?" pp. 47-56 in Stanford Central American Action Network [ed.] Revolution in Central America. Boulder, CO: Westview Press.

_____ and Janet Shenk (1983) "El Salvador: A revolution brews," pp. 57-65 in Stanford Central America Action Network [ed.] Revolution in Central America. Boulder, CO: Westview Press.

Arnson, Cynthia (1982) El Salvador--A Revolution Confronts the United States. Washington, D.C.: Institute for Policy Studies.

Arraigada, Génaro [ed.] (1976) Seguridad Nacional y Bien Común. Santiago: Talleres Gráficos Corporación.

Astiz, Carlos [ed.] (1969) Latin American International Politics: Ambitions, Capabilities, and the National Interests of Mexico, Brazil, and Argentina. South Bend, IN: University of Notre Dame Press.

Atkins, G. Pope (1977) Latin America in the International Political System. New York: Free Press.

Atlantic Council of the United States (1983) Western Interests and United States Policy Options in the Caribbean Basin. Washington: The Council.

Auburn, F. M. (1982) Antarctic Law and Politics. Bloomington: Indiana University Press.

Axline, Andrew W. (1979) Caribbean Integration: The Politics of Regionalism. New York: Nichols.

_____ (1977) Underdevelopment, Dependence and the Politics of Integration: A Caribbean Application. Ottawa: University of Ottawa.

Azicri, Max (1982) "A Cuban perspective on the Nicaraguan revolution," pp. 345-373 in Thomas W. Walker [ed.] Nicaragua in Revolution. New York: Praeger.

Babaa, Khalid I. and Cecil V. Crabb Jr. (1969) "Nonalignment as a diplomatic ideological credo," pp. 428-439 in Robert L. Pfaltzgraff Jr. [ed.] Politics and the International System. Philadelphia: J. B. Lippincott Co.

Bagley, Bruce (1981) "Mexico in the 1980s: a new regional power." Current History 80, 469 (November): 353-356.

Balcarcel, Jose Luis (1980) "El Sandinismo, ideologia de la revolución Nicaraguense." Nicarahuac (Julio y Agosto): 112-119.

Baloyra, Enrique A. (1982a) El Salvador in Transition. Chapel Hill: University of North Carolina Press.

_____ (1982b) "Fandango y fantasia de la cuestión Centroamericana," pp. 77-93 in Enrique Baloyra and Rafail Lopez [comp.] Iberoamérica en los Años 80. Madrid: Instituto de Cooperación Iberamericana.

Barra, F. de la (1969) El Conflicto Peruano-Ecuatoriano y la Vigorosa Campaña de 1941 en las Fronteras de Zarumilla. Lima: Procer.

Barros, Alexandre de S. C. (1983a) "Guidado com o pragmatismo irresponsaval." Jornal do Brasil (Cuaderno Especial, March 20):3.

_____ (1983b) "Política exterior brasilena y el mito del Barón." Foro Internacional 93, 1 (July-September): 1-20.

Bath, C. Richard and James D. Dilmus (1976) "Dependency analysis of Latin America." Latin American Research Review 11 (Fall): 3-54.

Bell, John Patrick (1971) Crisis in Costa Rica--The 1948 Revolution. Austin: University of Texas Press.

Bendaña, Alejandro (1982) "The foreign policy of the Nicaraguan revolution," pp. 319-327 in Thomas W. Walker [ed.] Nicaragua in Revolution. New York: Praeger.

Bernstein C., Enrique (1977) "Chile y la politica de defensa continental desde la segunda guerra Mundial Hasta el Presente," pp. 203-222 in Walter Sanchez G. and Teresa Pereira L. [eds.] Cincocincuenta Años de Política Exterior Chilena. Santiago: Editorial Universitaria.

Bishop, William W. Jr. (1953) International Law: Cases and Materials. Englewood Cliffs, NJ: Prentice-Hall.

Black, Jan Knippers (1982) "Government and politics," pp. 145-183 in James D. Rudolph [ed.] Nicaragua--A Country Study. Foreign Area Studies. Washington, D.C.: The American University.

Blank, David E. (1982) "Venezuela: politics of oil," pp. 73-101 in Robert Wesson [ed.] U.S. Influence in Latin America in the 1980s. New York: Praeger.

Bodenheimer, Susanne (1971) "Dependency and imperialism: the roots of Latin American underdevelopment." Politics and Society 1 (May): 327-335.

Boersner, Demetrio (1980) "Cuba and Venezuela: liberal and conservative possibilities," pp. 91-105 in Barry B. Levine [ed.] The New Cuban Presence in the Caribbean. Boulder: Westview Press.

Bond, Robert D. (1982) "Venezuelan policy in the Caribbean basin," pp. 187-

2QO in Richard E. Feinberg [ed.] Central America: International Dimensions of the Crisis. New York: Holmes & Meier Publishers.

Bond, Robert D. (1981) "Venezuela, Brazil, and the Amazon basin," pp. 153-164 in Elizabeth G. Ferris and Jennie K. Lincoln [eds.] Latin American Foreign Policies: Global and Regional Dimensions. Boulder: Westview Press.

_____ (1978a) "Venezuela, Brazil, and the Amazon basin." Orbis 20 (Fall): 635-650.

_____ (1978b) "Regionalism in Latin America: prospects for the Latin American Economic System (SELA)." International Organization 32 (Spring): 401-423.

_____ (1977) "Venezuela's role in international affairs," pp. 227-262 in Robert D. Bond [ed.] Contemporary Venezuela. New York: New York University Press.

Bonilla, Frank and Robert Girling [eds.] (1973) Structures of Dependency. East Palo Alto, CA: Pacific Studies Center.

Booth, John A. (1983) Testimony before the U.S. House of Representatives--Committee on Foreign Affairs--Subcommittee on Western Hemisphere Affairs (March 15).

_____ (1982) The End and the Beginning--The Nicaraguan Revolution. Boulder: Westview Press.

Braveboy-Wagner, Jacqueline A. (1984) "The politics of developmentalism: U.S. policy toward Jamaica," pp. 160-179 in H. Michael Erisman [ed.] The Caribbean Challenge, U.S. Policy in a Volatile Region. Boulder: Westview Press.

Brecher, Michael (1972) The Foreign Policy System of Israel. New Haven: Yale University Press.

_____ , Blema Steinberg and Janice Stein (1969) "A framework for research on foreign policy behavior." The Journal of Conflict Resolution 13 (March): 75-101.

_____ (1962) "Neutralism: an analysis." International Journal 17 (Summer): 222-236.

Brown, Lester R. (1984) "Redefining national security," pp. 340-345 in Charles W. Kegley, Jr. and Eugene R. Wittkopf, The Global Agenda. New York: Random House.

Bruner, Helmut (1977) "Después del Fallo Del Beagle: geopolítica versus derecho." El Mercurio. Santiago. September 24, 1977. Reprinted in German, Carrasco: El Laudo Arbitral Del Canal Beagle. Santiago: Editorial Jurídica de Chile. (1978).

Brzezinski, Zbigniew K. (1970) Between Two Ages. New York: Viking Press.

_____ and Samuel P. Huntington (1963) Political Powers: USA/USSR. New York: Viking Press.

Brewer, Thomas L. (1973) "Issue and context variations in foreign policy." The Journal of Conflict Resolution 17 (March): 89-114.

Burke, Melvin, and Eileen Keremitsis (1982) "Bolivia," pp. 221-232 in Jack W. Hopkins [ed.] Latin America and Caribbean Contemporary Record. New York: Holmes & Meier.

Burr, Robert N. (1965) By Reason or Force: Chile and the Balancing of Power in South America, 1830-1895. Berkeley: University of California Press.

Bushnell, David (1975) "Colombia," pp. 401-418 in Harold Eugene Davis and Larman C. Wilson [eds.] Latin American Foreign Policies: An Analysis. Baltimore: Johns Hopkins University Press.

Buzeta, Oscar (1978) Chile Geopolítico: Presente y Futuro. Santiago: CISEC.

Callcott, Wilfrid Hardy (1968) The Western Hemisphere. Austin: University of Texas Press.

Campos, Roberto de Oliveria (1978) "The new international economic order: aspirations and realities," pp. 73-87 in Norman C. Dahl and Jerome B. Wiesner [eds.] World Change and World Security. Cambridge: MIT Press.

Canas Montalva, Ramon (1940) "La Antartica: visionaria apreciación del General O'Higgins." La Verdad, Punta Arenas, Chile. April 1, 1940. Reprinted in Revista Geográfico de Chile "Terra Australis" 14 (1956-57): 19-21.

Canessa Robert, Julio (1979) "Visión geopolítica de la regionalización Chilena." Text of Address, Montevideo, Uruguay, June 8, 1979:23.

Cantori, Louis J. and Steven L. Spiegel (1973) "The international relations of regions," pp. 335-353 in Richard A. Falk and Saul H. Mendlovitz [eds.] Regional Politics and World Order. San Francisco: W. H. Freeman and Co.

Caporaso, James A. (1978) "Dependence, dependency, and power in the global system: a structural and behavioral analysis." International Organization 32 (Winter): 13-44.

Cardier, Jorge Alvarez (1982) La Guerra de las Malvinas: Enseñanzas para Venezuela. Caracas: Editorial Enfoque.

Cardoso, Fernando Henrique (1977) "The consumption of dependency theory in the United States." Latin American Research Review, 12, 3: 7-24.

Carpio Castillo, Ruben (1981) Geopolítica de Venezuela. Caracas: Seix Barral Venezolana.

Carrasco, German (1979) El Laudo Arbitral del Canal Beagle. Santiago: Editorial Juridica de Chile.

Center for Defense Information (1983) "Peru." The Defense Monitor 12, 1: 22.

Chaplin, David (1976) Peruvian Nationalism: A Corporatist Revolution. New Brunswick, NJ: Transaction Books.

Chernick, Sidney (1978) The Commonwealth Caribbean: The Integration Experience. Baltimore, MD: Johns Hopkins University Press.

Cherol, R. L. and J. Nunez de Arco (1983) "Andean multinational enterprises: a new approach to multinational investment in the Andean Group." Journal of Common Market Studies 21 (June): 409-428.

Chiavaneto, Julio J. (1981) Geopolítica, Arma do Fascismo. São Paulo: Global Editora.

Chilcote, Ronald H. and Joel C. Edelstein [eds.] (1974) Latin America: The Struggle with Dependency and Beyond. Cambridge: Schenkman.

Child, Jack (1980a) Conflicts in Latin America: Present and Potential. Unpublished manuscript prepared for the Stockholm International Peace Research Institute.

_____ (1980b) Unequal Alliance: The Inter-American Military System, 1938-1978. Boulder: Westview Press.

_____ (1979) "Geopolitical thinking in Latin America." Latin American Research Review 14, 2: 89-111.

Chile (1977) Controversy Concerning the Beagle Channel Region Award. Bilingual edition. Geneva, October 1977.

_____ (1947) Presidential Declaration of June 23, 1947 (Sovereignty over Maritime areas).

_____ (1906) Decree No. 260, February 27, 1906 (Fabry-De Todo Herrera Concession).

Chile. CONARA (Comisión Nacional de la Reforma Administrative) (1979) "Regionalización: visión tricontinental de Chile." Special Supplement, El Mercurio, Santiago, Chile, January 15, 1979, p. ix.

Chile. Instituto Geográfico Militar (1978) Atlas Escolar de Chile. 3d edition.

Chile. Ministry of Foreign Affairs (1978) History of the Chilean-Bolivian Negotiations 1975-1978. English text, printed in England 1978.

_____ (1975) Note No. 686, December 19, 1975 to Bolivian Ambassador (Chilean basis for negotiations with Bolivia).

_____ (1940) Decreto Supremo No. 1747. November 6, 1940 (Chilean Antarctic Claim).

Chile. Presidencia de la República (1976) "Chile on its way to the future." Presidential address, September 11, 1976. Reprinted, Santiago: Impresora Filadelfia, 1976.

_____ (1975a) "Chile enciende la Llama de la libertad." Presidential address, September 11, 1975. Reprinted, Santiago: Editora Nacional Gabriela Mistral, 1975.

_____ (1975b) Objectivo Nacional del Gobierno de Chile. Presidential order Res. Exenta No. 3102, December 23, 1975. Reprinted, Santiago: Impresora Filadelfia, 1976.

Cleaves, Peter and Martin Scurrah (1976) "State and society relations and bureaucratic behavior in Peru." CICA series paper number 6. Hayward: Department of Public Administration, California State University.

Cochrane, James D. (1978) "Characteristics of contemporary Latin American international relations." Journal of Inter-American Studies and World Affairs 20 (November):455-466.

_____ (1969) "The politics of regional integration: the Central American case." Tulane Studies in Political Science 12. New Orleans, LA: Tulane University.

Cockroft, James and Ross Gandy (1981) "The Mexican volcano." Monthly Review 33 (May): 32-44.

Cockroft, James D., Andre Gunder Frank, and Dale L. Johnson (1972) Dependence and Underdevelopment: Latin America's Political Economy. Garden City, NJ: Anchor.

Cohen Orantes, Isaac (1972) Regional Integration in Central America. Lexington, MA: D. C. Heath.

Collier, David [ed.] (1979) The New Authoritarianism in Latin America. Princeton: Princeton University Press.

Collins, John M. (1973) Grand Strategy: Principles and Practices. Annapolis: Naval Institute Press.

Comblin, Joseph (1980) The Church and National Security. Maryknoll: Orbis Books.

_____ (1978) A Ideologia da Segurança Nacional. Rio: Editorial Civilização Brasileira.

Connell-Smith, Gordon (1982) "The Organization of American States and the Falklands conflict." The World Today (September): 340-347.

_____ (1966) The Inter-American System. New York: Oxford Unviersity Press.

Cope, Orville G. (1975) "Chile," pp. 309-337 in Harold Eugene Davis, Larman Wilson, et al., Latin American Foreign Policies: An Analysis. Baltimore: Johns Hopkins.

Craig, Richard B. (1983) "Domestic implications of illicit Colombian drug production and trafficking." Journal of Inter-American Studies and World Affairs 25 (August): 325-350.

Craig, Richard B. (1981) "Colombian narcotics and United States-Colombian relations." Journal of Inter-American Studies and World Affairs 23 (August): 243-270.

Cuzan, Alfred G. and Richard J. Heggen (1982) "A micro-political explanation of the 1979 Nicaraguan revolution." Latin American Research Review 17, 2: 156-170.

Dallanegra Pedraza, Luis [ed.] (1981) Geopolítica y Relaciones Internacionales. Buenos Aires: Pleamar.

Dam, Kenneth W. (1983) "The larger importance of Grenada." Current Policy No. 526. Washington: U.S. Department of State (November 4): 1-4.

Davis, Harold Eugene, John J. Finan, and F. Taylor Peck (1977) Latin American Diplomatic History, An Introduction. Baton Rouge: Louisiana State University Press.

Davis, Harold and Larman Wilson [eds.] (1975) Latin American Foreign Policies. Baltimore: Johns Hopkins University Press.

Davis, Stephen (1981) "Jamaican politics, economics and culture." Caribbean Review 10, 4 (Fall): 14-18.

De Castro, Therezinha (1982) Atlas-Texto de Geopolítica do Brasil. Río: Capemi Editores.

_____ (1976) Rumo a Antartica. Río: Freitas.

del Muro, Ricardo, David Siller, and Miguel Angel de Velázquez (1982) "Hay en México 213 mil inmigrantes de 81 paises." Unomásuno, 21 de octubre 1982.

Denton, Charles F. (1971) Patterns of Costa Rican Politics. Boston: Allyn and Bacon, Inc.

Dickey, Christopher (1984) "Central America: from quagmire to cauldron?" Foreign Affairs--America and the World 1983 62, 3: 659-694.

_____ (1983) "'Southcom' hub of U.S. Latin role." Washington Post (May 23): A1 and A15.

Dietz, Henry (1980) "The IMF from the bottom up: social impacts of stabilization policies in Lima, Peru." Paper presented at the Latin American Studies Association Meeting, Bloomington, Indiana.

Dishkin, Martin [ed.] (1983) Trouble in Our Backyard--Central America and the United States in the Eighties. New York: Pantheon.

Dominguez, Jorge I. (1978) "Consensus and divergence: the state of the literature on inter-American relations in the 1970s." Latin American Research Review 13, 1: 87-126.

Dos Santos, Theotonio (1970) "The structure of dependency." American Economic Review 60 (May): 231.

Drekonja, Gerhard (1982) El Diferendo entre Colombia y Nicaragua. Bogota: FESCOL y Departamento de Ciencia Política, Universidad de los Andes.

Drekonja-Kornat, Gerhard (1983) "Colombia: learning the foreign policy process." Journal of Inter-American Studies and World Affairs 25 (May): 229-250.

Duncan, W. Raymond (1982) "Moscow, the Caribbean and Central America," pp. 1-30 in Robert Wesson [ed.] Communism in Central America and the Caribbean. Stanford: Hoover Institution.

Durham, William H. (1979) Scarcity and Survival in Central America: Ecological Origins of the Soccer War. Stanford: Stanford University Press.

East, Maurice, Stephen A. Salmore, and Charles F. Hermann [eds.] (1978) Why Nations Act. Beverly Hills: Sage Publications.

Einaudi, Luigi (1973) "Reform from within? Military rule in Peru since 1968." Studies in Comparative International Development 8: 71-87.
_____ and Alfred Stephan (1971) Latin American Institutional Development: Changing Military Perspectives in Peru and Brazil. Santa Monica, CA: Rand Corporation.
Eliseo Da Rosa, J. (1983) "Economics, politics, and hydroelectric power: the Parana River Basin." Latin American Research Review 18, 3: 77-108.
Embassy of the Argentine Republic (1978) Estado Actual de las Differencias Sobre Límites en la Zona Austral. Washington, D.C.
Encina, Francisco A. (1959) La Cuestión de Límites Entre Chile y la Argentina desde la Independencia hasta el Tratado de 1881. Santiago: Nascimento.
Espinosa Morga, Oscar (1969) El Precio de la Paz Chileno-Argentino 1810-1969. 3 vols. Santiago: Nascimento.
Evans, Peter (1979) Dependent Development: The Alliance of Multi-national, State and Local Capital in Brazil. Princeton: Princeton Unviersity Press.
Ewell, Judith (1982) "The development of Venezuelan geopolitical analysis since World War II." Journal of Inter-American Studies and World Affairs 24 (August): 295-320.
Fagen, Richard (1979) "Mexican petroleum and United States national security." International Security (Summer): 39-53.
_____ (1977) "Studying Latin American politics: some implications of a dependencia approach." Latin American Research Review 12, 2: 3-20.
Falcoff, Mark (1981) "The Timmerman case." Commentary 72 (July): 15-23.
Feinberg, Richard E. (1982) Central America: International Dimensions of the Crisis. New York: Holmes and Meier.
_____ (1981) "Central America: no easy answers." Foreign Affairs 59, 5 (Summer): 1121-1146.
Ferguson, Hale H. (1975) "Trends in inter-American relations 1972-mid 1974," pp. 1-24 in Ronald G. Hellman and H. Jon Rosenbaum [eds.] Latin America: The Search for a New International Role. New York: John Wiley and Sons.
Fernandez Larrain, Sergio (1974) O'Higgins. Santiago: Editorial Orbe.
Ferris, Elizabeth G. (1981) "The Andean Pact and the Amazon Treaty: reflections of changing Latin American relations." Journal of Inter-American Studies and World Affairs 23 (May): 147-176.
_____ (1978) "The Andean Pact: a selected bibliography." Latin American Research Review 13 (Fall): 108-124.
_____ and Jennie K. Lincoln [eds.] (1981) Latin American Foreign Policies: Global and Regional Dimensions. Boulder, Westview Press.
Fifer, J. Valerie (1972) Bolivia: Land, Location, and Politics Since 1825. Cambridge: Cambridge University Press.
Fonseca, Carlos (1982) "Ideario político del General Sandino," pp. 169-199 in Carlos Fonseca, Obras Tomo 2. Managua: Editorial Nueva Nicaragua.
Fontaine, Roger W. (1977) The Andean Pact: A Political Analysis. Center for Strategic and International Studies, Georgetown University, The Washington Papers 5, 45. Beverly Hills, CA: Sage.
_____ and James D. Theberge [eds.] (1976) Latin America's New Internationalism. New York: Praeger.
Fox, Annette B. (1959) The Power of Small States: Diplomacy in World War II. Chicago: University of Chicago Press.

Fraga, Jorge Alberto (1979) Introducción a la Geopolitical Antartica. Buenos Aires: Dirección Nacional del Antartico.

Frank, André Gunder (1974) "Dependence is dead, long live dependence and the class struggle: an answer to critics." Latin American Perspectives 1 (Spring): 87-106.

_____ (1972) "The development of underdevelopment," pp. 3-19 in John Cockroft, Dale L. Johnson, and Andrew Gunder Frank [eds.] Dependence and Underdevelopment. New York: Anchor Books.

Freedman, Lawrence (1982) "The war for the Falklands Islands." Foreign Affairs 61, 1 (Fall): 196-210.

French-Davis, Richard (1978) "The Andean Pact: model of economic integration for developing countries," pp. 165-193 in J. Grunwald [ed.] Latin America and World Economy: A Changing International Order. Beverly Hills, CA: Sage.

Frenkel, Roberto and Guillermo O'Donnell (1979) "The 'stabilization programs' of the International Monetary Fund and their internal impacts," in Richard R. Fagen [ed.] Capitalism and the State in U.S.-Latin American Relations. Stanford: Stanford University Press.

Gall, Norman (1976) "Atoms for Brazil, dangers for all." Foreign Policy 26 (Summer): 155-201.

Gamba, Virginia (1982) Malvinas Confidencial. Buenos Aires: Publinter.

Gannon, Francis (1982) "Globalism versus regionalism: U.S. policy and the Organization of American States." Orbis (Spring): 195-221.

García-Amador, F. V., et al. (1978) The Andean Legal Order: A New Community Law. Dobbs Ferry, NY: Oceana.

George, Phillip (1981) "Mexico and its neighbors." The World Today 37, 9 (September): 356-362.

Gereffi, Gary (1983) The Pharmaceutical Industry and Dependency in the Third World. Princeton: Princeton University Press.

Golbery, Do Cuoto e Silva (1967) Geopolítica do Brasil. Rio: Editorial José Olympio.

Golblat, Josef (1983) The Falklands/Malvinas Conflict: A Spur to Arms Buildups. Stockholm: SIPRI.

Gomez, Leonel, et al. (1981) "Struggle in Central America." Foreign Policy 43 (Summer): 70-92.

Gordon, Dennis R. (1979) "The question of the Pacific: current perspectives on a longstanding dispute." World Affairs 141, 4 (Spring): 321-336.

_____ and Margaret M. Munro (1983) "The external dimension of civil insurrection: international organizations and the Nicaraguan revolution." Journal of Inter-American Studies and World Affairs 25 (February): 59-82.

Gorman, Stephen M. (1981) "Peruvian foreign policy since 1975: external political and economic initiatives," pp. 115-129 in Elizabeth G. Ferris and Jennie K. Lincoln [eds.] Latin American Foreign Policies: Global and Regional Perspectives. Boulder: Westview Press.

_____ (1979) "Present threats to peace in South America: the territorial dimensions of conflict." Inter-American Economic Affairs 33 (Summer): 51-71.

_____ (1978) "Corporatism with a human face? The revolutionary ideology of Juan Velasco Alvarado." Inter-American Economic Affairs 32 (Autumn): 25-37.

_____ and Ronald Bruce St. John (1982) "Challenges to Peruvian foreign policy," pp. 179-196 in Stephen M. Gorman [ed.] Post-Revolutionary

Peru. Boulder: Westview Press.
Green, David (1971) The Containment of Latin America. Chicago: Quadrangle Books.
Grabendorff, Wolf (1983) Political Change in Central America. Boulder: Westview Press.
_____ (1982) "Interstate conflict behavior and regional potential for conflict in Latin America." Journal of Inter-American Studies and World Affairs 24 (August):267-294.
_____ (1978) "Review essay: Mexico's foreign policy--indeed a foreign policy?" Journal of Inter-American Studies and World Affairs 20, 1 (February): 85-92.
Green, Rosario (1977) "México: la política exterior del nuevo regimen," pp. 1-12 in Continuidad y cambio en la política exterior de Mexico. México. El Colegio de México.
Gregg, Phillip M. and Arthur S. Banks (1965) "Dimensions of political systems: factor analysis of a cross-polity survey." American Political Science Review 59 (September): 602-614.
Guglialmelli, Juan E. (1979a) Geopolítica del Cono Sur. Buenos Aires: El Cid Editor.
_____ (1979b) "Patagonia." Estrategia 59 (July):5-31.
_____ (1978) El Conflicto del Beagle. Buenos Aires: El Cid Editor.
Haas, Michael (1969) "Communication factors in decision-making." Peace Research Society Papers 13: 65-86.
Hanratty, Dennis M. (1982) "Mexican policy toward Central America and the Caribbean." Paper presented at the annual meeting of the International Studies Association meeting.
Hanreider, Wolfram F. (1971) "Actor objectives and international systems," pp. 108-125 in Wolfram F. Hanreider [ed.] Comparative Foreign Policy. New York: David McKay Co., Inc.
_____ (1967) "Compatibility and consensus: a proposal for the conceptual linkage of external and internal dimensions of foreign policy." American Political Science Review 61 (December): 971-982.
Hellman, Judith Adler (1978) Mexico in Crisis. New York: Holmes & Meier.
Hellman, Ronald G. and H. Jon Rosenbaum [eds.] (1975) Latin America: The Search for a New International Role. Beverly Hills, CA: Sage Publications.
Hermann, Charles F., Maurice A. East, Margaret G. Hermann, Barbara G. Salmore, and Stephen A. Salmore (1973) CREON: A Foreign Events Data Set. Beverly Hills: Sage Professional Papers.
Hernandez, Pablo (1977) Malvinas: Clave Geopolítica. Buenos Aires: Ediciones Castañeda.
Herrera Campins, Luis (1981) "Speech before the 36th session of the United Nations General Assembly." Venezuela Up-to-Date 22 (Summer-Fall): 2-3.
_____ (1981-82) "Speech to the Permanent Council of the OAS." Venezuela Up-to-Date 22 (Winter): 13-14.
Hewlett, Sylvia Ann (1981-1982) "Coping with illegal immigrants." Foreign Affairs 60, 2 (Winter): 355-378.
_____ (1980) The Cruel Dilemmas of Development. New York: Basic Books.
Hirschman, Albert O. (1963) Journeys Toward Progress: Studies of Economic Policy-Making in Latin America. New York: Twentieth Century Fund.
Hoivik, Tord and Aas Solveig (1981) "Demilitarization in Costa Rica: a

farewell to arms." Journal of Peace Research 18, 4: 333-350.

Hojman, David E. (1981) "The Andean Pact: failure of a model of economic integration." Journal of Common Market Studies 20 (December): 139-160.

Holguin Pelaez, Hernando (1971) Proyecciones de un Limite Maritimo entre Colombia y Venezuela. Bogota: Editores y Distribuidores Asociados.

Holland, E. James (1975) "Bolivia," pp. 338-359 in Harold E. Davis and Larman C. Wilson [eds.] Latin American Foreign Policies. Baltimore: Johns Hopkins University Press.

Hollist, W. Ladd and Thomas H. Johnson (1979) "Political consequences of international economic relations: alternative explanations of United States/Latin American noncooperation." Journal of Politics 41 (November): 1125-1155.

Holsti, K. H. (1983) International Politics. Fourth edition. Englewood Cliffs: Prentice-Hall, Inc.

Horowitz, Irving L. (1981) "Introduction," pp. 1-7 in I. L. Horowitz [ed.] Cuban Communism. Fourth edition. New Brunswick: Transaction Books, Inc.

Horowitz, Paul and Holly Sklar (1982) "South Atlantic Triangle." NACLA Report on the Americas 16, 3 (May-June): 2-43.

Iglesias, Enrique V. (1983) "Reflections on the Latin American economy in 1982." CEPAL Review 19 (April): 7-50.

Ihl C., Pablo (1953a) "Delimitación natural entre el Oceano Pacifico y el Atlántico en resguardo nuestro soberanía sobre la Antartica y Navarino." Revista Geográfica de Chile "Terra Australis" 9 (1953): 45-51.

_____ (1953b) "El mar Chileno." Revista Geográfica de Chile "Terra Australis" 10 (1953): 54.

Immerman, Richard H. (1982) The CIA in Guatemala: The Foreign Policy of Intervention. Austin: University of Texas Press.

Inter-American Development Bank (1983) Economic and Social Progress in Latin America. Washington, D.C.: Inter-American Development Bank.

_____ (1981) Economic and Social Progress in Latin America: 1980-1981. Washington: IDB.

_____ (1979) Economic and Social Progress in Latin America. Washington, D.C.: Inter-American Development Bank.

International Institute for Strategic Studies (IISS) (1983) The Military Balance, 1983-1984. London: International Institute for Strategic Studies.

International Monetary Fund (1980) Direction of Trade Annual Yearbook. Washington, D.C.: International Monetary Fund.

_____ (1970) Direction of Trade Annual Yearbook. Washington, D.C.: International Monetary Fund.

_____ (1960) Direction of Trade Annual Yearbook. Washington, D.C.: International Monetary Fund.

International Peace Academy (1984) Maintenance of Peace and Security in the Caribbean and Central America. New York: The Academy.

_____ (1983) Toward Peace and Security in the Caribbean and Central America. New York: The Academy.

Jackson, Steve, Bruce Russett, Duncan Snidal, and David Sylvan (1977) "An assessment of empirical research on dependencia." Latin American Research Review 14, 3: 7-28.

Jaguaribe, Helio (1975) "El Brasil y América Latina." Estudios Internacionales 8, 29 (Buenos Aires: January-March).

Javier Alejo, F. and Hennan Hurtado (1976) El SELA: Un Mecanismo para la Acción. México: Fondo de Cultura Económica.

Jay, Peter (1979) "Regionalism as geopolitics." Foreign Affairs-America in the World 58, 3: 485-513.

Johnson, Kenneth F. (1978) Mexican Democracy: A Critical View. Revised edition. New York: Praeger Publishers.

Johnson, Kenneth F. and Miles W. Williams (1981) Illegal Aliens in the Western Hemisphere: Political and Economic Factors. New York: Praeger.

Jordan, Amos A. and William J. Taylor (1981) American National Security-- Policy and Process. Baltimore: Johns Hopkins University Press.

Jorge, Antonio (1983) "How exportable is the Cuban model?" pp. 211-233 in Barry B. Levine [ed.] The New Cuban Presence in the Caribbean. Boulder: Westview Press.

Karnes, Thomas L. (1976) The Failure of Union: Central America, 1824-1975. Tempe, AZ: University of Arizona Press.

Kaufman, Robert R., Harry I. Chernosky, and Daniel S. Geller (1975) "A preliminary test of the theory of dependency." Comparative Politics 7 (April): 303-330.

Kenworthy, Eldon (1983) "Central America: beyond the credibility trap." World Policy Journal (Fall): 181-200.

Kirkpatrick, Jeane (1981) "U.S. security and Latin America." Commentary 71, 1 (January): 29-40.

_____ (1979) "Dictatorships and double standards." Commentary 68, 5 (November): 34-45.

Kinzer, Stephen and Stephen Schlesinger (1981) Bitter Fruit: The Untold Story of the American Coup in Guatemala. Garden City: NY: Doubleday.

Klare, Michael T. and Cynthia Arnson (1981) Supplying Repression: U.S. Support for Authoritarian Regimes Abroad. Washington: Institute for Policy Studies.

Klein, Herbert W. (1982) Bolivia, The Evolution of a Multi-Ethnic Society. New York: Oxford.

Kline, Harvey F. (1983) Colombia: Portrait of Unity and Diversity. Boulder: Westview Press.

Kline, William R. and E. Delgado (1978) Economic Integration in Central America. Washington: Brookings.

Keohane, Robert O. and Joseph S. Nye (1977) Power and Interdependence. Boston: Little, Brown and Company.

Keohane, Robert O. (1969) "Lilliputian's dilemma: small states in international politics." International Organization 23 (Spring): 291-310.

Laffin, John (1982) Fight for the Falklands. New York: St. Martin's Press.

Leiken, Robert (1981) "Prepared statement." U.S. House of Representatives. Foreign Affairs Committee. Subcommittee on Inter-American Affairs (September 24).

LeoGrande, William (1981) "A splendid little war." International Security 6, 1 (Summer): 27-52.

Lincoln, Jennie K. (1981) "Introduction to Latin American foreign policy: global and regional dimensions," pp. 3-18 in Elizabeth G. Ferris and Jennie K. Lincoln [eds.] Latin American Foreign Policies, Global and Regional Dimensions. Boulder: Westview Press.

Linowitz, Sol M. (1976) The United States and Latin America: Next Steps. New York: Center for Inter-American Relations.

Linowitz, Sol M. (1975) The Americas in a Changing World. New York: Quadrangle.

Littuma, Alfonso (1976) Doctrina de Seguridad Nacional. Caracas: Biblioteca del Ejercito.

Lowenthal, Abraham F. (1984) "The insular Caribbean as a crucial test for U.S. policy," pp. 183-197 in H. Michael Erisman [ed.] The Caribbean Challenge, U.S. Policy in a Volatile Region. Boulder: Westview Press.

_____ (1976) "The United States and Latin America: ending the hegemonic presumption." Foreign Affairs 55, 1 (October): 199-213.

_____ [ed.] (1975) The Peruvian Experiment: Continuity and Change under Military Rule. Princeton: Princeton Unviersity Press.

Lowi, Theodore J. (1964) "American business, public policy, case studies, and political theory." World Politics 16 (July): 677-715.

López Herrman, F. Bolivar (1961) El Ecuador y su Problema Territorial con el Perú. Quito: Industrias Gráficas GYMA.

Luddeman, Margarete K. (1983) "Nuclear power in Latin America." Journal of Inter-American Studies and World Affairs 25 (August): 377-415.

Malloy, James M. (1977) Authoritarianism and Corporatism in Latin America. Pittsburgh: University of Pittsburgh Press.

_____ (1974) "Authoritarianism, corporatism and mobilization in Peru." Review of Politics 36 (January): 52-84.

Manley, Michael (1983) "Grenada in the contest of history, between neo-colonialism and independency." Caribbean Review (Fall): 45-47.

Manning, Bayless (1977) "The Congress, the executive and intermestic affairs: three proposals." Foreign Affairs 55 (January): 306-324.

Mansbach, Richard W., Yale H. Ferguson, and Donald Lampert (1976) The Web of World Politics: Nonstate Actors in the Global System. Englewood Cliffs, NJ: Prentice-Hall.

Marquez, Javier [ed.] (1977) Pensamiento de México en los periódicos. Páginas Editoriales. Mexico: Editoriales Tecnos.

Martz, John D. (1984) "The crisis of Venezuelan democracy." Current History 83 (February): 73-78+.

_____ (1982a) "Ideology and oil: Venezuela in the circum-Caribbean," pp. 122-148 in H. Michael Erisman and John D. Martz [eds.] Colossus Challenged: The Struggle for Caribbean Influence. Boulder: Westview Press.

_____ (1982b) "Multi-power conflict and competition: the circum-Caribbean." Paper presented at the annual meeting of the International Studies Association, Cincinnati.

_____ (1977) "Venezuelan foreign policy toward Latin America," pp. 156-198 in Robert D. Bond [ed.] Contemporary Venezuela. New York: New York University Press.

Martz, Mary Jeanne Reid (1979) "SELA: the Latin American economic system 'ploughing the seas'?" Inter-American Economic Affairs 32 (Spring): 33-64.

_____ (1978) The Central American Soccer War. Athens, OH: Ohio University Center for International Studies.

Marull Bermúdez, Federico (1978) "Chile: geopolítica del Pacifico sur." Geopolítica (Montevideo) 5 (April-August): 27-34.

McClintock, Cynthia (1983) "Sendero Luminoso: Peru's Maoist guerrillas." Problems of Communism 32, 5 (September-October): 19-34.

_____ and Abraham Lowenthal [eds.] (1983) The Peruvian Experiment Reconsidered. Princeton: Princeton University Press.

McGowan, Patrick J. (1970) "Theoretical approaches to the comparative study of foreign policy." Ph.D. dissertation. Evanston, IL: Northwestern University.

_____ (1968) "Africa and nonalignment: a comparative study of foreign policy." International Studies Quarterly 12 (September): 262-295.

_____ and Klaus Peter Gottwald (1975) "Small state foreign policies: a comparative study of participation, conflict, and political and economic dependence in black Africa." International Studies Quarterly 19 (December): 469-500.

_____ and Howard B. Shapiro (1973) The Comparative Study of Foreign Policy. Beverly Hills: Sage Publications.

Meira Mattos, Carlos (1977) A Geopolítica e as Projecoes do Poder. Río: Liv José Olympio.

_____ (1975) Brasil: Geopolítica e Destino. Rio: Biblioteca do Exercito.

Melo Lacaros, Luis (1977) "Trayectoria del Ministerio de Relaciones Exteriores y los problemas en la conducción de la diplomacia Chilena," pp. 107-127 in Walter Sanchez G. and Teresa Pereira L. [eds.] Cientocincuenta Años de Política Exterior Chilena. Santiago: Editorial Universitaria.

Meneses, Emilio (1983) "Política exterior Chilena: una modernización postergada." Estudios Publicos. No. 12 (Santiago, Chile) (Spring): 123-134.

Meneses Ciuffardi, Emilio (1981) "Estructura geopolítica de Chile." Seguridad Nacional. Santiago, Chile, 21 (1981): 51-98.

Miami Report (1983) University of Miami Graduate School of International Studies. Coral Gables.

Milenky, Edward S. (1978) Argentina's Foreign Policies. Boulder: Westview Press.

_____ (1977) "Latin America's multilateral diplomacy: integration, disintegration, and interdependence." International Affairs (Royal Institute of International Affairs) 53 (January): 73-96.

_____ (1975) "Problems, perspectives and modes of analysis: understanding Latin American approaches to world affairs," pp. 93-114 in Ronald G. Hellman and H. Jon Rosenbaum [eds.] Latin America: The Search for a New International Role. Beverly Hills: Sage.

_____ (1973) The Latin American Free Trade Association. New York: Praeger.

Millett, Richard and W. Marvin Will [eds.] (1979) The Restless Caribbean: Changing Patterns of International Relations. New York: Praeger.

Milia, Fernando (1978) La Atlantartida: Un Espacio Geopolítico. Buenos Aires: Pleamar.

Monagas, Aquiles (1975) Testimonio de una Traición a Venezuela: Demanda de Nulidad del Tratado de Límites de 1941 entre Venezuela y Colombia. Caracas: Ediciones Garrido.

Moneta, Carlos J. (1983) Geopolítica y Política del Poder en el Atlántico Sur. Buenos Aires: Pleamar.

_____ (1981) "Antarctica, Latin America and the international system in the 1980s." Journal of Inter-American Studies and World Affairs (February): 29-68.

Montealegre, Flora (1983) "Costa Rica at the Crossroads." Development and Change 14: 277-296.

_____ and Cynthia Arnson (1983) "Background information on Guatemala, human rights, and U.S. military assistance," pp. 294-307 in Stanford

Central America Action Network [ed.] Revolution in Central America. Boulder: Westview Press.

Monteza Tufar, Miguel (1976) El Conflicto Militar del Perú con el Ecuador. Lima: Editorial Arica.

Moon, Bruce E. (1983) "The foreign policy of the dependent states." International Studies Quarterly 27 (September): 315-340.

Morales, Waltraud Queiser (1984) "Bolivia's national revolution thirty years later: success or failure?" Secolas Annals (forthcoming).

_____ (1980) "Bolivia moves toward democracy." Current History (February): 76-79, 86-88.

Morawetz, David (1974) The Andean Group: A Case Study in Economic Integration among Developing Countries. Cambridge, MA: MIT Press.

Morris, James A. and Steve C. Ropp (1977) "Corporatism and dependent development: a Honduran case study." Latin American Research Review 12, 2: 27-68.

Motley, Langhorne A. (1984) "Is peace possible in Central America?" Current Policy No. 539. Washington: U.S. Department of State (January 19): 1-4.

Moxon, Richard W. (1977) "Harmonization of foreign investment laws among developing countries: an interpretation of the Andean Group experience." Journal of Common Market Studies 16 (September): 22-52.

Muller Rojas, Alberto (1983) Las Malvinas: Tragicomedia en Tres Actos. Caracas: Editorial Ateneo.

Muñoz, Heraldo (1981) "The strategic dependency of the centers and the economic importance of the Latin American periphery." Latin American Research Review 17, 2: 3-30.

_____ (1980) "The international relations of the Chilean military government: elements for a systematic analysis." Paper presented at a May 1980 Workshop sponsored by the Latin American Program of the Woodrow Wilson International Center for Scholars. Smithsonian Institution, Washington, D.C.

Mytelka, Lynn K. (1979) Regional Development in a Global Economy: The Multinational Corporation, Technology, and Andean Integration. New Haven, CT: Yale University Press.

Newfarmer, Richard [ed.] (1984) From Gunboat to Diplomacy--New U.S. Policies for Latin America. Baltimore: Johns Hopkins University Press.

Nicaragua. Junta del Gobierno de la Reconstrucción Nacional (JGRN) (1983) Nicaragua's Peace Proposal (July 19).

Nicaragua. Ministerio de Justicia. Centro de Investigaciones Jurídicas y Políticas. (n.d.) Nicaragua y los Derechos Humanos.

Nicaragua. Ministerio del Exterior (1983) Juridical Foundations to Guarantee Peace and Security of the States of Central America. Official Proposal of Nicaragua within the Framework of the Contadora Process. (October 15): 1-41.

_____ (1982) Nicaragua Denuncia: Agresiones que Sufre Desde el Territorio de Honduras (1980-1982).

Nolde, Kenneth (1980) "Arms and security in South America: towards an alternate view." Ph.D. dissertation. Coral Gables: University of Miami Miami.

Nugent, Jeffrey (1974) Economic Integration in Central America: Empirical Investigations. Baltimore: Johns Hopkins University Press.

Nye, Joseph S. (1968) "Patterns and catalysts in regional integration," pp. 333-349 in Joseph S. Nye, Jr. [ed.] International Regionalism. Boston: Little, Brown, & Company.

Odell, J. S. (1980) "Latin American trade negotiations with the United States." International Organization 34 (Spring): 207-228.

O'Donnell, Guillermo (1978) "Reflections on the patterns of change in the bureaucratic authoritarian state." Latin American Research Review 13, 1: 3-38.

_____ (1973) Modernization and Bureaucratic-Authoritarianism: Studies in South American Politics. Berkeley: Institute of International Studies at the University of California.

Ojeda Gómez, Mario (1976) Alcances y límites de la política exterior de México. México: El Colegio de México.

_____ (1974) "Las relaciones de Mexico con el régimen revolucionario cubano," pp. 47-81 in Mexico y America Latina: la nueva política exterior. Mexico: El Colegio de Mexico.

O'Leary, Michael (1976) "The role of issues," pp. 318-325 in James N. Rosenau [ed.] In Search of Global Patterns. New York: The Free Press.

Orrego Vicuña, Francisco [ed.] (1977) Política Oceanica. Santiago: Editorial Universitaria.

_____ (1974) La Participación de Chile en el Sistema Internacional. Santiago: Editora Nacional Gabriela Mistral Ltda.

PACCA (1984) Changing Course--Blueprint for Peace in Central America and the Caribbean. Washington, D.C.: Institute for Policy Studies.

Padron, G. M. (1978) ¿Perderemos También el Golfo de Venezuela? Caracas: Avilarte.

Palacios Saenz, Carlos (1979) La Guerra del 41. Guayaquil: Ediciones Ara.

Palmer, David Scott (1980) Peru: The Authoritarian Tradition. New York: Praeger.

Paragg, Ralph (1980) "Integration and regional development: the case of the Commonwealth Caribbean." Journal of Inter-American Studies and World Affairs 22 (November): 495-500.

Parkinson, F. (1974) Latin America, The Cold War and The World Powers, 1945-1973. Beverly Hills: Sage Publications.

Patch, Richard W. (1960) "Bolivia: U.S. assistance in a revolutionary setting," pp. 108-176 in Richard Adams [ed.] Social Change in Latin America Today. New York: Vintage.

Payne, Anthony J. (1981) "The rise and fall of Caribbean regionalisation." Journal of Common Market Studies 19 (March): 255-280.

Pellicer de Brody (1981) "La seguridad nacional en México." Cuadernos Políticos 27 (Enero-Marzo): 27-34.

_____ (1980) "Veinte años de política exterior mexicana." Foro Internacional (Octubre-Diciembre): 149-160.

Pentland, Charles (1973) International Theory and European Integration. New York: The Free Press.

Perl, Raphael (1983) The Falkland Island Dispute in International Law and Politics. London: Oceana Publications.

Pierre, Andrew J. (1982) The Global Politics of Arms Sales. Princeton: Princeton Unviersity Press.

Pike, Frederick B. (1977) The United States and the Andean Republics, Peru, Bolivia, and Ecuador. Cambridge, MA: Harvard University Press.

_____ and Thomas Stritch [eds.] (1974) The New Corporatism. Notre Dame: University of Notre Dame Press.

Pineiro, Armando Alonso (1974) "El equilíbrio geopolítico Suramericano." Estrategia 30 (September): 4-12.

Pinochet de la Barra, Oscar (1977) "La Antartica Chilena y sus implicancias diplomáticas," pp. 245-263 in Walter Sanchez G. and Teresa Pereira L. [eds.] Cincocincuenta Años de Política Exterior Chilena. Santiago: Editorial Universitaria.
_____ (1976) La Antártida Chilena. Fourth edition. Santiago: Editorial Andrés Bello.
Pinochet Ugarte, Augusto (1977) Geopolítica. Santiago: Andrés Bello.
_____ (1974) Geopolítica. Santiago: Editorial Andrés Bello.
Pittman, Howard T. (1983) "Geopolitical projections from the Southern Cone: implications for future conflict." Paper presented at the 1983 meeting of the Latin American Studies Association, Mexico City, September 29-October 1, 1983.
_____ (1982) "Geopolitical projections from the Southern Cone, implication for future conflict." Paper presented at the annual meeting of the Section on Military Studies of the International Studies Association, Carlisle.
_____ (1981a) "Geopolitics and foreign relations in Argentina, Brazil and Chile," pp. 165-178 in Elizabeth G. Ferris and Jennie K. Lincoln [eds.] Latin American Foreign Policies: Global and Regional Dimensions. Boulder: Westview Press.
_____ (1981b) "Geopolitics in the ABC countries: a comparison." Ph.D. dissertation. Washington: The American University.
Poitras, Guy (1981) "Mexico's foreign policy in an age of interdependence," pp. 103-114 in Elizabeth G. Ferris and Jennie K. Lincoln [eds.] Latin American Foreign Policies: Global and Regional Dimensions. Boulder: Westview Press.
Ponce Caballero, Jaime (1976) Geopolítica Chilena y Mar Boliviano. La Paz: Ponce Caballero.
Potter, William C. (1980) "Issue area and foreign policy analysis." International Organization 34 (Summer): 405-427.
Premo, Daniel L. (1982) "Colombia: cool friendship," pp. 102-119 in Robert Wesson [ed.] U.S. Influence in Latin America in the 1980s. New York: Praeger.
Ptacek, Kerry (1981) The Catholic Church in El Salvador. Washington: The Institute on Religion and Democracy.
Quagliotti de Bellis, Bernardo (1979) Constantes Geopolíticas en Iberoamerica. Montevideo: GEOSUR.
_____ (1976) Geopolitica del Atlantico Sur. Montevideo: Fundación de Cultura Universitaria.
Ramirez, Sergio (1983) "Nicaragua: un modelo propio." Areito IX 34: 7-11.
_____ (1982) We Are a Decided People. Managua: Dirección General de Divulgación y Prensa.
_____ [ed.] (1980) El Pensamiento Vivo de Sandino. La Habana, Cuba: Casa de las Americas.
Redick, John Robert (1981) "The Tlatelolco regime and nonproliferation in Latin America." International Organization 35 (Winter): 103-134.
Richardson, Neil R. and Charles W. Kegley, Jr. (1977) "International economic dependence and political compliance: a longitudinal analysis." Paper presented at the annual meeting of the International Studies Association, St. Louis.
Riding, Alan (1983) "Central American quagmire." Foreign Affairs-America and the World 1982 61, 3: 639-659.
Robinson, D. J. (1971) "Venezuela and Colombia," pp. 179-246 in Harold

Blakemore and Clifford T. Smith [eds.] Latin America: Geographical
Perspectives. London: Methuen & Co.

Rodriguez Zia, Jorge (1978) De Mar a Mar: el Fallo del Beagle. Buenos
Aires. Editorial Moharra.

Roett, Riordan (1975) "The changing nature of Latin American international
relations: geopolitical realities," pp. 95-111 in Commission on United
States-Latin American Relations. The Americas in a Changing World.
New York: Quadrangle.

Rosenau, James N. (1981) The Study of Political Adaptation. London:
Frances Pinter.

_____ (1969) Linkage Politics. New York: Free Press.

_____ (1966) "Pre-theories and theories of foreign policy," pp. 27-92 in
R. Barry Farrell [ed.] Approaches to Comparative and International
Politics. Evanston, IL: Northwestern University Press.

_____ and Gary Hoggard (1974) "Foreign policy behavior in dyadic rela-
tionships: testing pre-theoretical extensions," pp. 117-150 in James N.
Rosenau [ed.] Foreign Policies: Theories, Findings, and Methods. New
York: Wiley and Sons.

Rosenberg, Mark B. (1984) "Nicaragua and Honduras: toward garrison states."
Current History 83, 490 (February):59-62, 87.

Rothenberg, Morris (1982) "Since Reagan: the Soviets and Latin America."
The Washington Quarterly (Spring): 175-179.

Rothstein, Robert L. (1968) Alliances and Small Powers. New York: Columbia University Press.

Rouco, J. Iglesias (1981) "El mapa del papa." La Prensa (Buenos Aires)
January.

Rout, Leslie B. (1971) Which Way Out? An Analysis of the Venezuela-
Guyana Border Dispute. East Lansing: Michigan State University Latin
American Studies Center.

Rummel, R. J. (1969) "Some empirical findings on nations and their behavior." World Politics 21 (January): 226-241.

Sánchez G., Walter (1977) "Las tendencias sobresalientes de la política
exterior Chilena," pp. 374-411 in Walter Sánchez G. and Teresa
Pereira L. [eds.] Cinco cincuenta Años de Politica Exterior Chilena.
Santiago: Editorial Universitaria.

Sanz, Pablo R. (1976) El Espacio Argentino. Buenos Aires: Pleamar.

Schilling, Paulo (1978) El Expansionismo Brazileno. Buenos Aires: El Cid.

Schmitter, Philippe C. (1977) "Intercambio, poder y lealtad en la integración
internacional: nuevas perspectivas de teoría y medición." Integración
Latinoamericana 2 (Enero-Febrero): 5-28.

_____ (1974) "Still the century of corporatism," pp. 93-115 in Fredrich B.
Pike and Thomas Stritch [eds.] The New Corporatism. Notre Dame:
University of Notre Dame Press.

_____ (1972) "Autonomy or dependence as regional integration outcomes:
Central America." Research Series 17. Berkeley, CA: Institute of
International Studies, University of California.

Schoultz, Lars (1983) "Guatemala social change and political conflict," pp.
173-202 in Martin Dishkin [ed.] Trouble in Our Backyard. New York:
Pantheon Books.

Schydlowsky, Daniel and Juan Wicht (1983) "The anatomy of an economic
failure," pp. 94-143 in McClintock and Lowenthal, The Peruvian
Experiment Reconsidered. Princeton: Princeton University Press.

Selcher, Wayne A. (1982) "Recent strategic developments in South America's

Southern Cone." Paper presented at the conference on "Latin American Foreign Policies: Comparative Perspective," Vina del Mar, Chile.

Selcher, Wayne A. (1981) "Brazil in the world: multipolarity as seen by a peripheral ADC middle power," pp. 81-101 in Elizabeth G. Ferris and Jennie K. Lincoln [eds.] Latin American Foreign Policies: Global and Regional Dimensions. Boulder: Westview Press.

Seligson, Mitchell A. and William J. Carroll III (1982) "The Costa Rican role in the Sandinist victory," pp. 331-344 in Thomas W. Walker [ed.] Nicaragua in Revolution. New York: Praeger.

Selser, Gregorio (1983) El Pequeno Ejército Loco--Sandino y la Operación Mexico-Nicaragua. Managua: Editorial Nueva Nicaragua.

_____ (1982) Reagan entre El Salvador y las Malvinas. México: Editorial México-Sur.

Shaw, Royce Q. (1979) Central America: Regional Integration and National Development Policy. Boulder: Westview Press.

Shumavon, Douglas H. (1981) "Bolivia: salida al mar," pp. 179-190 in Elizabeth G. Ferris and Jennie K. Lincoln [eds.] Latin American Foreign Policies: Global and Regional Dimensions. Boulder: Westview Press.

Sigmund, Paul E. (1983) "Reagan's two-track policy in Central America." The New Leader (August 8-22): 3-5.

Small, Melvin and J. D. Singer (1970) "Patterns in international warfare, 1816-1965." Annals of the American Academy of Political and Social Sciences 391 (September): 145-155.

St. John, Ronald Bruce (1977a) "The boundary dispute between Peru and Ecuador." American Journal of International Law 71 (April): 322-330.

_____ (1977b) "Hacia el mar: Bolivia's quest for a Pacific port." Inter-American Economic Affairs 31 (Winter): 41-74.

Stavenhagen, Rodolfo (1974) "The future of Latin America: between under-development and revolution." Latin American Perspectives 1 (Spring): 124-148.

Stepan, Alfred (1978) The State and Society: Peru in Comparative Perspectives. Princeton: Princeton University Press.

Stephen, Hoadley J. (1980) "Small states as aid donors." International Organization 34 (Winter): 212-238.

Sunkel, Osvaldo (1972) "Big business and 'dependencia.'" Foreign Affairs 50 (April): 517-531.

Taran, Patrick A. (1983) "Central American refugees: no haven from war." Refugees and Human Rights Newsletter (Summer): 4-8.

Taylor, William J. [ed.] (1982) The Future of Conflict in the 1980s. Washington: Center for Strategic and International Studies, Georgetown University.

Thorn, Richard S. (1971) "The economic transformation," pp. 157-216 in James M. Malloy and Richard S. Thorn [eds.] Beyond the Revolution, Bolivia Since 1952. Pittsburgh: University of Pittsburgh.

Tomasek, Robert D. (1967) "The Chilean-Bolivian Rio Lauca dispute and the OAS." Journal of Inter-American Studies 9 (July): 351-366.

Toriello Garrido, Guillermo (1983) La agresión imperialista contra dos revoluciones, Guatemala (1944-1955) y Nicaragua (1979), semejanzas y diferencias. Managua: Dirección General de Divulgación y Prensa de la JGRN.

"Trading companies: 10 años de exportação" (1983) Informativo CE-Fundação Centra de Estudos do Comercio Exterior (July):11.

Turner, Frederick C. (1983) "The aftermath of defeat in Argentina."

Current History (February):58-87.

Ungo, Guillermo (1983) "The people's struggle." Foreign Policy 52 (Fall): 50-63.

U.S. Arms Control and Disarmament Agency (1983) World Military Expenditures and Arms Transfers, 1971-1980. Washington, D.C.: Arms Control and Disarmament Agency.

U.S. Department of Defense (1983a) Grenada: October 23 to November 2, 1983. Washington: Government Printing Office.

U.S. Department of State. Bureau of Public Affairs (1983) "Grenada--a preliminary report." (December) Washington, D.C.: U.S. Government Printing Office.

_____ (1983b) "U.S. policy in Central America--refugees." Washington, D.C.: U.S. Government Printing Office.

_____ (1983c) "U.S. policy in Central America, an overview." Washington, D.C.: Government Printing Office.

_____ (1982) Current Policy No. 376. "Cuban support for terrorism and insurgency in the Western Hemisphere." Washington, D.C.: Government Printing Office. (March)

_____ (1981a) Country Reports on Human Rights Practices. Washington, D.C.: U.S. Government Printing Office. (February)

_____ (1981b) "Cuba's renewed support for violence in Latin America." Special Report No. 90. Washington, D.C.: U.S. Government Printing Office.

_____ (1981c) "El Salvador: the search for peace." Washington, D.C.: U.S. Government Printing Office. (September)

_____ (1981d) "Response to stories about special report no. 80." Washington, D.C.: U.S. Government Printing Office. (June)

_____ (1981e) "Strategic situation in Central America and the Caribbean." Current Policy No. 352. Washington, D.C.: U.S. Government Printing Office. (December)

U.S. Library of Congress. Congressional Research Service (1984) "Foreign aid issues in the 98th Congress." Issue Brief Number IB83084.

U.S. National Bipartisan Commission on Central America--Kissinger Commission (1984) Report. Washington: Government Printing Office.

Urquidi, Victor L. et al. (1982) "Latin America and world problems: prospects and alternatives." Journal of Inter-American Studies and World Affairs 24 (February): 3-36.

Valencia Vega, Alipio (1982) Geopolítica en Bolivia. La Paz: Libreria Editorial "Juventud."

Van Klaveren, Alberto (1982) "The analysis of Latin American foreign policies: a critical review." Paper presented at the annual meeting of the International Studies Association, Cincinnati.

Villalobos R., Sergio (1979) El Beagle: Historia de una Controversia. Santiago: Editorial Andrés Bello.

Villanueva, Victor (1980) "Doce años bajo la cruz y la Espada." Paper presented at the Latin American Studies Association meeting, Washington, D.C.

_____ (1972) Nueva Mentalidad Militar en Perú? Lima: Editorial Juan Mejía Baca.

Villegas, Osiris G. (1983) "El processo de mediación en el caso Beagle." Geosur. (Uruguay) IV: 43 (April): 35-40.

Volk, Steven (1981) "Into the Central American maelstrom." NACLA Report on the Americas XV, 6 (November-December): 26-29.

304

Wonder, Edward (1977) "Nuclear commerce and nuclear proliferation: Germany and Brazil." Orbis 21 (Summer): 277-306.

Wood, Bryce (1978) Aggression and History: The Case of Ecuador and Peru. New York: Columbia University Institute of Latin American Studies.

Woodward, Ralph Lee Jr. (1976) Central America--A Nation Divided. New York: Oxford University Press.

World Bank (1983) World Development Report 1983. New York: Oxford University Press.

———— (1982) World Development Report. New York: Oxford University Press.

Wriggins, Howard (1968) "Political outcomes of foreign assistance: influence, involvement or intervention." Journal of International Affairs 22: 217-230.

Zimmerman, William (1973) "Issue area and foreign-policy process: a research note in search of a general theory." American Political Science Review 67 (December): 1204-1212.

NEWSPAPERS AND PERIODICALS CITED

A Defensa Nacional (Brazil)
Barricada (Nicaragua)
Barricada Internacional (Nicaragua)
Boletín Informativo Semanal (Bolivia)
Boletín Semanal (Nicaragua)
Business Week (U.S.)
El Comercio (Peru)
El Mercurio (Chile)
El Observador (Peru)
El Tiempo (Honduras)
El Día (Spain)
Excelsior (Mexico)
Foreign Broadcast Information Service (FBIS) (U.S.)
Geopolítica (Argentina)
Geopolítica (Uruguay)
GEOSUR (Uruguay)
Granma (Cuba)
Granma Resumen Semanal (Cuba)
Honduras Update (U.S.)
Joint Publications Research Service (JPRS) (U.S.)
La Nación (Argentina)
La Nación (Costa Rica)
La Nación International (Costa Rica)
La Prensa (Argentina)
Latin America Political Report (LAPR) (Great Britain)

Latin America Regional Reports (LARR) (Great Britain)
Latin America Weekly Report (LAWR) (Great Britain)
Latinamerica Press (Peru)
Los Angeles Times
Miami Herald (U.S.)
New York Times
Newsweek (U.S.)
Nicarahuac (Nicaragua)
Pensamiento Propio (Nicaragua)
Pittsburgh Press (U.S.)
Presencia (Bolivia)
Revista Geográfica de Chile
Segurança e Desenvolvimiento (Brazil)
Seguridad Nacional (Chile)
Soberania (Bolivia)
The Economist (Great Britain)
The Militant (U.S.)
The Washington Times
Times of the Americas (U.S.)
Unomásuno (Mexico)
Washington Post
Washington Report on the Hemisphere (WRH)
Weekly Compilation of Presidential Documents (U.S.)

Index